To Vân !

Good luck in your
next steps after
Dundee

Peter Cameron

# THE GLOBAL ENERGY TRANSITION

Global energy is on the cusp of change, and it has become almost a truism that energy is in transition. But what does this notion mean exactly? This book explores the working hypothesis that, characteristically, the energy system requires a strategy of the international community of states to deliver sustainable energy to which all have access. This strategy is for establishing rules-based governance of the global energy value-cycle.

The book has four substantive parts that bring together contributions of leadings experts from academia and practice on the law, policy, and economics of energy. Part I, 'The prospects of energy transition', critically discusses the leading forecasts for energy and the strategies that resource-rich countries may adopt.

Part II, 'Rules-based multilateral governance of the energy sector', details the development and sources of rules on energy. Part III, 'Competition and regulation in transboundary energy markets', discusses principal instruments of rules-based governance of energy. Part IV, 'Attracting investments and the challenges of multi-level governance', focuses on the critical governance of the right investments.

This book is a flagship publication of the Centre for Energy, Petroleum and Mineral Law and Policy at the University of Dundee. It launches the Hart series 'Global Energy Law and Policy' and is edited by the series general editors Professors Peter D Cameron and Volker Roeben, and also Dr Xiaoyi Mu.

**Global Energy Law and Policy: Volume 2**

# Global Energy Law and Policy

**Series Editors**
Peter D Cameron
Pieter Bekker
Volker Roeben
Leonie Reins
Crina Baltag

Energy policy and energy law are undergoing rapid global transformation, characterised by the push in favour of decarbonisation. The 2015 Sustainable Development Goals and the 2015 Paris Agreement on international climate action have forged a consensus for a pathway to a universal just transition towards a low-carbon economy for all states and all societies.

This series publishes conceptual work that help academics, legal practitioners and decision-makers to make sense of these transformational changes. The perspective of the series is global. It welcomes contributions on international law, regional law (for example, from the EU, US and ASEAN regions), and the domestic law of all states with emphasis on comparative works that identify horizontal trends, and including transnational law. The series' scope is comprehensive, embracing both public and commercial law on energy in all forms and sources and throughout the energy life-cycle from extraction, production, operation, consumption and waste management/decommissioning. The series is a forum for innovative interdisciplinary work that uses the insights of cognate disciplines to achieve a better understanding of energy law and policy in the 21st century.

**Recent titles in this series:**
*Decarbonisation and the Energy Industry*
edited by Tade Oyewumni, Penelope Crossley, Frédéric Gilles
Sourgens and Kim Talus
*The Law and Governance of Mining and Minerals: A Global Perspective*
by Ana Elizabeth Bastida

# The Global Energy Transition

*Law, Policy and Economics for Energy
in the 21st Century*

Edited by
Peter D Cameron
Xiaoyi Mu
and
Volker Roeben

·HART·
OXFORD · LONDON · NEW YORK · NEW DELHI · SYDNEY

HART PUBLISHING

Bloomsbury Publishing Plc

Kemp House, Chawley Park, Cumnor Hill, Oxford, OX2 9PH, UK

1385 Broadway, New York, NY 10018, USA

29 Earlsfort Terrace, Dublin 2, Ireland

HART PUBLISHING, the Hart/Stag logo, BLOOMSBURY and the Diana logo are
trademarks of Bloomsbury Publishing Plc

First published in Great Britain 2020

A catalogue record for this book is available from the British Library.

Library of Congress Cataloging-in-Publication data

Names: Cameron, Peter D., editor. | Mu, Xiaoyi, editor. | Roeben, Volker, editor.

Title: The global energy transition : law, policy, and economics for energy in the 21st century /
edited by Peter D Cameron, Xiaoyi Mu, and Volker Roeben.

Description: Oxford, UK ; New York, NY Hart Publishing, an imprint of Bloomsbury Publishing, 2020. |
Series: Global energy law and policy ; volume 2 | Includes bibliographical references and index.

Identifiers: LCCN 2020032515 (print) | LCCN 2020032516 (ebook) | ISBN 9781509932481
(hardback) | ISBN 9781509932498 (ePDF) | ISBN 9781509932504 (Epub)

Subjects: LCSH: Energy industries—Law and legislation. | Energy development—Law and
legislation. | Power resources—Law and legislation. | Renewable energy sources—Law and
legislation. | Energy policy—Economic aspects. | Energy industries—Law and legislation—
European Union countries.

Classification: LCC K3981 .G56 2020 (print) | LCC K3981 (ebook) | DDC 333.79094—dc23

LC record available at https://lccn.loc.gov/2020032515

LC ebook record available at https://lccn.loc.gov/2020032516

ISBN:  HB:      978-1-50993-248-1
       ePDF:    978-1-50993-249-8
       ePub:    978-1-50993-250-4

Typeset by Compuscript Ltd, Shannon

To find out more about our authors and books visit www.hartpublishing.co.uk. Here you will find extracts,
author information, details of forthcoming events and the option to sign up for our newsletters.

# CONTENTS

## PART III
## COMPETITION AND REGULATION IN
## TRANSBOUNDARY ENERGY MARKETS

## PART IV
## ATTRACTING INVESTMENTS AND THE CHALLENGES
## OF MULTI-LEVEL GOVERNANCE

# LIST OF CONTRIBUTORS

**Christoph G Benedict**, Legal Director, Pinsent Masons LLP; formerly General Counsel for General Electric Power AG, Germany; Honorary Professor, Swansea University; Lecturer, International Economic Law, Heidelberg University

**Adrian Bradbrook**, Emeritus Professor of Law, Law School, University of Adelaide

**Peter D Cameron**, Professor of International Energy Law, Director of the Centre for Energy, Petroleum and Mineral Law and Policy, University of Dundee

**Penelope Crossley**, Senior Lecturer, The University of Sydney Law School

**James Cust**, Economist, World Bank, and Non-Resident Expert, Payne Institute for Public Policy, Colorado School of Mines

**Dylan Geraets**, Docent, UEF Law School, University of Eastern Finland; Senior Affiliated Researcher, Leuven Centre for Global Governance Studies and Institute for International Law, KU Leuven; Associate, Mayer Brown Europe-Brussels LLP.

**Iñigo del Guayo Castiella**, Professor in Administrative Law, University of Almería

**Jakob Haerting**, PhD Candidate, University of Turku

**Raphael J Heffron**, Jean Monnet Professor in Energy and Sustainability, Centre for Energy, Petroleum and Mineral Law and Policy, University of Dundee

**Patrick Heller**, Advisor, Natural Resource Governance Institute; Senior Visiting Fellow at the Center for Law, Energy & Environment at the University of California, Berkeley

**Martin Jarrett**, Senior Research Fellow, Max Planck Institute for Comparative Public Law and International Law, Heidelberg

**Dilip K Jena**, PhD candidate, Centre for Energy, Petroleum and Mineral Law and Policy, University of Dundee

**Rafael Emmanuel Macatangay**, Lecturer in Energy Economics, Centre for Energy, Petroleum and Mineral Law and Policy, University of Dundee

**David Manley**, Senior Economic Analyst, Natural Resource Governance Institute

**Gökçe Mete,** Research Fellow, Stockhold Environment Institute; formerly Knowledge Centre Principal Coordinator, The Energy Charter Secretariat

**Petra Minnerop**, Associate Professor of International Law, Durham Law School, University of Durham; Visiting Professor, China University of Political Science and Law, Beijing

**Xiaoyi Mu**, Reader in Energy Economics, Centre for Energy, Petroleum and Mineral Law and Policy, University of Dundee

**Kevin Ramnarine**, Independent energy consultant and former Minister of Energy, Trinidad and Tobago

**Leonie Reins**, Assistant Professor, The Tilburg Institute for Law, Technology and Society, Tilburg University

**Volker Roeben**, Professor of Energy Law and Global Regulation, Centre for Energy, Petroleum and Mineral Law and Policy, University of Dundee; Visiting Professor, China University of Political Science and Law, Beijing; Adjunct Professor, University of Turku

**Anita Rønne** (deceased), Associate Professor in Energy Law, Centre for Regulation and Administration, Faculty of Law, University of Copenhagen

**Kim Talus**, James McCulloch Chair in Energy Law, Tulane Law School; founding Director of Tulane Center for Energy Law; Professor of European Economic and Energy Law, UEF Law School, University of Eastern Finland; Professor of Energy Law, University of Helsinki

**Joseph P Tomain**, Wilbert and Helen Ziegler Professor of Law, College of Law, University of Cincinnati

# TABLE OF CASES

# Introduction

PETER D CAMERON, XIAOYI MU AND VOLKER ROEBEN

It has become commonplace to say that energy is in transition. But even if the ultimate goal – a lower carbon global economy – is clear, the pathways to achieving such a transformation are still under construction or even at the design stage. So what does 'energy in transition' really mean?

Certainly, the sources of energy long relied upon by the industrialised economies are changing their roles in the engine of the global economy. Available evidence confirms a transition is taking place. For example, there is a decline in the shares of coal and nuclear energy in the global energy mix when measured by consumption;[1] and the share of oil in energy consumption has remained stationary during the same period. The share of renewable energy in the global energy mix, when measured by consumption, has grown to four per cent in 2018 from one per cent in 2009.[2] So, the energy mix is changing, not least due to the impact of government policies, but also technology. Low-carbon energy technologies are maturing fast, becoming cheaper and growing in market share year-on-year. Even among fossil fuels, a transition is evident. Natural gas is rapidly becoming a globally tradeable commodity due to exports from the shale gas revolution in the US and to advances in liquefied natural gas (LNG) technology. The LNG market size in 2018 tripled from 2000 values.[3] At the same time, the centre of energy consumption in the global economy is shifting, in a dramatic and probably irreversible way, eastwards to Asia and southwards to Africa. In the last 10 years, primary energy consumption in the Asia Pacific region, Africa and the member countries in the Organisation for Economic Co-operation and Development (OECD) has grown at an annual rate of 4.0 per cent, 2.4 per cent and 0.6 per cent respectively, with total energy consumption in Asia Pacific surpassing the total consumption in the OECD countries.[4] The annual growth rate of renewable energy consumption in

---

[1] Based on data from BP Statistical Review 2009, 2019.

[2] Energy Economics: Home (BP global), https://www.bp.com/en/global/corporate/energy-economics/statistical-review-of-world-energy/downloads.html> accessed August 2019.

[3] IGU, IGU World LNG Report 2019 <https://www.igu.org/publication/302341/31> accessed August 2019.

[4] Compounded annual growth rate. Data from BP Statistical Review 2009, 2019.

Asia Pacific is 27 per cent compared to 13 per cent in the OECD countries over the past 10 years.[5]

Among these changing patterns in the global energy economy, some profound, one stands out. There appears to be only a limited transition towards significant change in the global energy consumption mix. There is a change certainly, but not yet a qualitative one. Left to its own devices, the global energy system will continue to evolve, but it is unlikely to transition to a fundamentally different system.

There lies the problem. Most states have signed up to initiatives that seek to change the current energy system to achieve specific social objectives. The 2015 UN Sustainable Development Goals (SDGs) postulate that this system should ensure that all the world's citizens have access to affordable, reliable, sustainable and modern energy by 2030. The Goals also include targets to increase the share of renewables, encourage gains in energy efficiency and to improve infrastructure. As a complement to this, the 2015 Paris Agreement to the UNFCCC adds the objective of holding the global temperature rise to well below 2°C. It seeks to enforce this by giving it the weight of international law. Given that the energy sector accounts for more than 70 per cent of global carbon emissions,[6] action to mitigate the effects of climate change has become action to promote low-carbon energy, and vice versa.

These twin sets of goals from 2015 for energy that meets environmental (climate) and universal socio-economic (access for all) goals are grafted onto an old one. A more traditional balancing of energy policy goals would seek to ensure, ultimately from the perspective of producers and consumers of energy, that the supply of energy is both secure and affordable. The 'energy trilemma' supersedes the 'energy dilemma', and provides both new goals and a new reference. The reference of this energy trilemma is humanity, or put differently, citizens of both developed and developing countries. These are goals of tomorrow that urgently invite us to take a strategic rather than a managerial approach to the diverse elements (and policy goals) of today's global energy economy.

Even a cursory acquaintance with the workings of the world's energy economy shows what an immense challenge this represents. Few, if any, other economic sectors underscore the determination of states to retain control over it: over the mix of energies made up of domestic resources and imports, the rate at which they are used up, the conditions on which foreigners are allowed access to them, and so on. Energy nationalism in diverse forms has been a feature of global economic development over the past century much more than the few examples of multilateral cooperation such as the International Energy Agency or the Organisation of Petroleum Exporting Countries. Apart from the obvious strategic considerations affecting all states through their energy sectors,

---

[5] Based on data from BP Statistical Review 2009, 2019.
[6] https://www.epa.gov/ghgemissions/global-greenhouse-gas-emissions-data. Only agriculture is not related to energy, and some of the industry emissions are not energy-related.

there are many low- and middle-income states that view their energy resources as a ticket to accelerated economic growth, to catch up with the industrialised economies which built their economic success on abundant supplies of coal and access to oil. Indeed, examples of states conceding powers over their national energy economies are few: consent to arbitration by foreign investors through the Energy Charter Treaty is one; consent to common rules in an energy chapter of the European Union treaty by its members is another. The states parties in these examples are many but still regional rather than global in origin. Indirectly, of course, in the fields of environment, taxation and investment, there are more ambitious global initiatives demonstrating cooperation among states. But perceived intrusions into the domestic organisation of a national energy sector remains sensitive.

A paradox it is then. To meet the objectives of the SDGs and the Paris Agreement, and benefit from them, states need to cooperate *strategically* and reorient the familiar energy policy goals (the energy trilemma) around these relatively new goals, which make sense only over a mid- to long-term timeframe. Within this strategy objectives will have to be set that mark the desired state of the energy system of the future within specific timeframes, and then determine the political, legal and economic actions needed to achieve it. Such multilateral cooperation needs to align itself with a bottom-up approach by individual states taking actions that respect their energy endowments, diverse energy mixes and policy preferences, both with respect to energy but also more widely, and any relevant legacy from the past.

This book takes this paradox as its starting point, using *strategy* as a concept to analyse the trajectory of energy law and policy, and the challenges and governance solutions that are only now emerging but will become prominent in the near to medium future. The book has three working hypotheses to this effect.

First, strategy demands analytical devices for comprehending the drivers of energy markets and investment. Forecasting, scenario and modelling techniques provide critical information on prospects and future trends in energy consumption and the relative roles of all primary energy sources (fossil fuels and renewable sources) in the global mix, as well as for individual secondary energy sources (electricity, LNG, and hydrogen) and the situation of fossil resource-endowed states. These prospects set out the context within which strategic political and legal decisions on the speed and intensity of that transition are being made.

The second hypothesis is that a strategy for moving away from a forecast evolution of the energy system creates a need for rules-based cooperative governance of worldwide scope for the energy sector. Such governance in the sense of collectively binding decision-making comprises the setting of goals and targets for the future, the regular assessment of progress toward the agreed goals, and the capacity to take collectively binding readjustment decisions. This cooperative, multilateral governance then depends on the development of law to be effective, certain and rational. It would therefore entail the development of distinct principles and a dedicated body of international law, substantive, procedural and organisational in character, that ideally extends to all states on subjects ranging from trade to investment to the oceans.

Third, the strategy will then focus on dimensions of action. As one such dimension, it will aim to restructure the global value-chain of energy, from generation, through markets connecting producers with consumers, and the underpinning infrastructure for transmission and transport. That will require a set of innovative instruments to design and govern transboundary and ideally integrated energy flows, trade and markets, among which may count competition, regulation and alternatives of transnational commercial self-regulation. The strategy comprises another dimension on (mostly private) investment in energy generation capacity and infrastructure to meet rising demand, and particularly reinvestment in renewable energy production, natural gas as bridge fuel, and new kinds of energy. There arise governance challenges that range from balancing legal certainty for such investment against regulatory flexibility, addressing general security concerns, and creating the right fiscal regime in host states.

The book tests these hypotheses and probes their explanatory power. The book has four substantive Parts: Prospects for an energy transition (I); Rules-based multilateral governance of the energy sector (II); Competition and regulation of transboundary energy markets (III); and Attracting energy investments and the challenges of multi-level governance (IV). On this basis, the final chapter, by the editors, develops a Concept of Global Energy Transition and its Agenda.

The editors are delighted that a group of eminent international experts have contributed to this project, addressing the issues from perspectives shaped by their expertise evident in the three to five chapters which each part comprises.

The book in its theme, structure and circle of authors is a product of the Dundee Energy Forum. The Dundee Energy Forum, held by the CEPMLP and the International Energy Forum, has established itself as the annual venue for exchange and debate between academics, senior representatives of international organisations and the profession on the global energy system. The 2018 Forum brought many of the authors of this book to Dundee. Others came to the Centre on other occasions. The contributions and the intense discussions that they triggered now form the basis of this book. Invaluable editorial assistance in producing the manuscript was provided by Dilip Jena. John Chinda compiled the table of cases. Both are PhD students at the CEPMLP.

# Part I. Prospects for an Energy Transition

Part I lays out the problematique, discussing the analytic tools on the drivers and prospects of global energy that will inform any decision-making.

Chapter 1, **Xiaoyi Mu** and **Dilip K Jena**, 'Comparison of Outlooks and Implications for an Energy Transition', compares the three influential outlooks made by the International Energy Agency, BP and the Energy Information

Administration of the US Department of Energy. It then analyses the techno-economic uncertainties affecting the speed and scope of energy transition with a focus on electric vehicles and increased penetration of renewables in the electric power sector.

Chapter 2, **David Manley**, **Patrick Heller**, and **James Cust**, 'Oil-rich Countries' Responses to Energy Transition: Managing the Decline', highlights the dependence of resource-endowed states on oil, gas and coal; and their perception of diversification to renewable energy as a threat aggravated by the slow liquidation of carbon wealth, poor diversification and inadequate policies, requiring the countries to re-examine their policies and laws strategically depending on the actions of others.

# Part II. Rules-based Multilateral Governance of the Energy Sector

Part II explores to what extent the demand for a rules-based multilateral governance of the energy sector is being met. The chapters cover the principles of energy law, the concept of the international law of energy, and the governance and rule-making mechanism on energy of the Paris Agreement, and models of regulation, leading into the concepts that will be discussed in Part III.

Chapter 3, **Raphael J Heffron, Anita Rønne, Joseph P Tomain, Adrian Bradbrook** and **Kim Talus**, 'A Treatise for Energy Law', expounds the normative parameters of a modern, universal energy law.

Chapter 4, **Volker Roeben** and **Gökçe Mete**, 'What do we Mean when we Talk about International Energy Law?', argues that a meta-norm of sustainable energy directs the development of a body of international law dedicated to energy; that this body of international law has a characteristic, operational regulatory structure; and that potentially all established regimes of international law realign themselves with this meta-norm and support its implementation.

Chapter 5, **Petra Minnerop**, 'The Legal Effect of the "Paris Rulebook" under the Doctrine of Treaty Interpretation', argues that the meeting of the states parties to the Paris Agreement is an institutionalised mechanism on the direction and pace of energy transition. It does so through an iterative procedure that combines international objective-setting of carbon emission reduction with nationally determined action on the energy economy. To this effect, the meetings may also take consent-based legal decisions.

Chapter 6, **Penelope Crossley**, 'How will Energy Market Regulation have to Change in the Era of Energy 4.0?', analyses the impact of the Fourth Industrial Revolution in changing the traditional roles of energy market regulators, market participants and end-consumers. The discussion is of increasing complexity of systems, new changing market technologies and structures, use of big data, introduction of smart contracts, and the changing role played by consumer protection.

# Part III.   Competition and Regulation
# in Transboundary Energy Markets

Part III focuses on the challenges of governing transnational energy and particularly electricity markets, and principal responses to these challenges. There are three chapters, covering the roles of contract, regulation and competition for transnational infrastructure projects, transboundary and ideally integrated markets and the supporting interconnectors.

Chapter 7, **Christoph G Benedict**, 'Between Transnational Private Law and Public International Law: Engineer-driven Self-governance in Transboundary Energy Megaprojects', discusses that large transnational energy projects typically rely upon contract principles reflecting a substantial amount of global regulatory coherence.

Chapter 8, **Rafael Emmanuel Macatangay** and **Volker Roeben**, 'Managing the Threat of Regulatory Capture under the European Energy Union', demonstrates that transboundary energy market regulation is in principle welfare-maximising overall, but at the same time creates a specific risk of regulatory capture: the possibilities of national regulatory agencies furthering national interests rather than collective interests. The chapter devises maxims to mitigate this risk, referencing the recently adopted legislative package Clean Energy for All Europeans.

Chapter 9, **Jakob Haerting**, 'Power over Power: The Global Energy Interconnection and Potential Cyber-threats', discusses critical transnational infrastructure, which usually involves transmission subject to regulation. It specifically analyses the security risk malicious cyber operations pose to global energy interconnection projects, and argues that it takes a concerted, unified, and multilateral effort to minimise the risks.

# Part IV.   Attracting Investments and the
# Challenges of Multi-level Governance

Part IV takes up investment in energy generation and infrastructure. The chapters demonstrate that attracting such investments may raise conflicts between international law and regulatory flexibility at the regional level, and it shows the space for critical decisions on the right investment taken at national level.

Chapter 10, **Martin Jarrett**, 'Implementing the Energy Transition in the Face of Investment Protection Sandards', debates the Energy Charter Treaty taking on new responsibilities other than providing the legal infrastructure for facilitating investments – a new responsibility for the treaty regime is to determine where do the investment losses relating to processes of phasing-out carbon-based energy projects fall most fairly, on investors or states?

Chapter 11, **Leonie Reins** and **Dylan Geraets**, 'The EU FDI Screening Regulation as an Example of the Proliferation of FDI Screening Processes Affecting the Energy Sector,' points out that, worldwide, states are establishing mechanisms to screen foreign direct investments. It critically analyses the potential impact of such screening on desirable investments in the energy sector, referencing the EU's new FDI Screening Regulation.

Chapter 12, **Iñigo del Guayo Castiella**, 'International Arbitration in the Renewable Field: Recent Developments in Spain' discusses the introduction of and exit from financial support for investments in renewable electricity generation as a problem of the multi-level governance of the energy sector. The chapter focuses on the reform experience in Spain, the application of the ECT, and the prescriptions of the new EU Renewables Directive on such policy exit.

Chapter 13, **Philip Daniel, Alan Krupnick, Thornton Matheson, Peter Mullins, Ian Parry** and **Artur Swistak**, 'How Should Shale Gas Extraction be Taxed' analyses taxation as a policy lever in the energy transition. It focuses on shale gas extraction and the countries that have been at the forefront of this revolution in the global energy system.

Chapter 14, **Kevin Ramnarine**, 'Trinidad and Tobago's Oil and Gas Sector in a Changing World (2010–2019)' is a reflective, first-hand case study on the significance of appropriately designed fiscal regimes in host states to attract investment in natural gas.

The book is intended, also, to launch the series *Global Energy Law and Policy*, edited under the auspices of CEPMLP and published by Hart Publishing. It conveys an idea of what the series aims to contribute to the debate, while covering only some of the relevant topics and only from one of many possible perspectives. It is accompanied by the publication of five further volumes in the series:

- Elizabeth Bastida, *The Law and Governance of Mining and Minerals: A Global Perspective*;
- Victoria Nalule, *Land Law and the Extractives Industries: Challenges and Opportunities in Africa*;
- Rahmi Kovar, *Stability and Legitimate Expectations in International Energy Investments*;
- Thomas Muinzer (ed), *Climate Change Legislation and Energy*; and
- Kim Talus et al (ed), *Renewable Energy Law and Policy*.

Each deepens and follows up on one or several themes of the present book.

# PART I

## Prospects for an Energy Transition

# 1

# Comparison of Outlooks and Implications for an Energy Transition

XIAOYI MU AND DILIP K JENA

## I. Abstract

The global economy is experiencing a transition from high-carbon energy resources to low-carbon resources. To shed light on the trajectory of the future energy system, we compare three influential outlooks made by the International Energy Agency (IEA), BP and the Energy Information Administration (EIA) of the US Department of Energy. Ultimately an energy transition is determined by technology and economics, but influenced by government policies. We highlight two technological challenges affecting the speed and scope of renewables penetration in the transportation and electric power sector. Our analysis about the total cost of driving indicates that at the current levels of battery prices and vehicle efficiency, only short-range electric vehicles can be cost-competitive with internal combustion engine vehicles when the crude oil price is above \$64/bbl. By contrast, wind and solar photovoltaics are becoming increasingly cost-competitive with natural gas in electric power generation. Yet the intermittency issue remains a challenge, since it requires a high level of back-up power and a large quantity of ramp-up resources.[1]

## II. Introduction

The global economy is experiencing a transition from high-carbon energy resources to low-carbon resources. To shed light on the trajectory of the future energy system, we compare three influential outlooks made by the International

---

[1] The power-generating (or load-reducing) resources that can increase its generation (or reduce load) at an agreed rate.

Energy Agency (IEA),[2] BP[3] and the Energy Information Administration (EIA)[4] of the US Department of Energy in 2019. Although these outlooks are not necessarily a prediction of what will happen in the future, these have the merit of providing insights on how the global energy system is likely to evolve under different assumptions, and therefore aid our analysis and debate about many important economic, political and legal issues. In addition, we conduct a techno-economic analysis on the potential of replacing conventional gasoline-based internal combustion engine vehicles with battery-powered electric vehicles, and then discuss challenges posed by the increased penetration of renewables in electric power systems.

## III.  Comparison of Global Energy Outlooks

Figure 1.1 compares the shares of primary energy resources in global energy mix in 2040 from various published outlooks. Both the IEA and BP consider a variety of scenarios to explore the effect of policy and technology uncertainties.

- The IEA Current Policies Scenario (CPS) assumes no policy changes from today. In other words, the outcome of 2040 is extrapolated from today's trend.

- The IEA Stated Policies Scenario (SPS) considers policies and targets for carbon reduction announced by governments. The SPS seems to be the reference case of the IEA outlook although not explicitly labelled so.

- The IEA considers a third scenario, the Sustainable Development Scenario (SDS). This scenario assumes the key energy-related elements of the United Nations Sustainable Development agenda, including energy access, air quality and climate objectives, are achieved. As a result, the emissions trajectory is fully in line with meeting the long-term objectives of the Paris Agreement.

Among the three IEA scenarios, the CPS one leads to an additional rise in energy-related $CO_2$ emissions compared to 2018 levels; the SPS also leads to an additional rise in energy-related $CO_2$ emissions although much lower than the CPS one. Only the SDS will lead to a substantial reduction in energy-related $CO_2$ emissions.

BP also considers a range of scenarios, including the 'Evolving Transition' scenario which is their base case; the share of world population consuming less than 100 GJ energy per day, in the 'More Energy' scenario, is assumed to reduce to one-third of its 2018 value in 2040 (its reduction is two-thirds in the 'Evolving Transition' scenario); the 'Less Globalization' scenario in which trade disputes

---

[2] IEA, 'World Energy Outlook 2019' (WEO, 2019), available at www.iea.org/weo2018.
[3] BP plc, 'BP Energy Outlook', available at www.bp.com/en/global/corporate/energy-economics/energy-outlook.html.
[4] US Energy Information Administration (International Energy Outlook, 2019), available at www.eia.gov/outlooks/ieo.

**Figure 1.1** Share of primary energy consumption in 2040

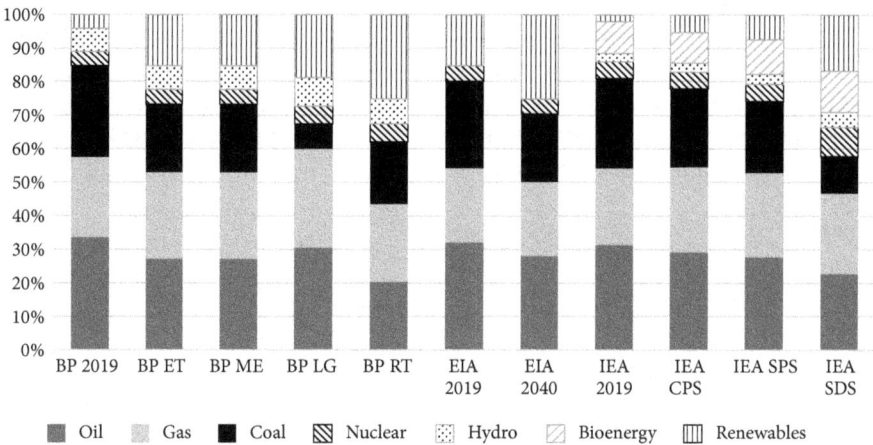

*Notes*: Bioenergy is only separately listed in IEA outlooks; the category 'Renewables' in EIA outlook includes hydroelectric power.

IEA 2019: The shares of primary energy sources in 2018 according to IEA statistics.

IEA CPS: IEA current policy scenario.

IEA SPS: IEA stated policy scenario.

IEA SDS: IEA sustainable development scenario.

BP 2019: The share of primary energy supply in 2018 according to BP statistics.

BT ET: BP evolving transition scenario.

BP RT: BP rapid transition scenario.

*Source*: IEA, 'World Energy Outlook 2019' (WEO, 2019); BP plc, 'BP Energy Outlook'; US Energy Information Administration (International Energy Outlook, 2019).

escalate and have a persistent impact on growth; and the 'Rapid Transition' scenario, which is broadly similar to the IEA's SDS in terms of carbon reduction. Because the shares of primary energy resources in the 'More Energy' and 'Less Globalization' scenarios are quite similar to those of the base case 'Evolving Transition scenario', in this chapter we focus on the 'Evolving Transition' (ET) and 'Rapid Transition' (RT) scenarios.

When we compare the different scenarios from these outlooks, several common features are worth noting.

First, by 2040 the share of oil and gas in global energy demand remains around 50 per cent and the projection is remarkably consistent across various scenarios. Only in the IEA sustainable development scenario and in the BP rapid transition scenario does, the share of oil and gas dips slightly below 50 per cent to 48 per cent and 43 per cent respectively. When compared to 2018, while the share of oil in global energy demand is projected to decrease, from 31 per cent to 28 per cent in IEA's stated policy scenario and from 34 per cent to 27 per cent in BP's 'Evolving Transition' scenario, the total oil demand is expected to continue to grow in both the IEA's stated policy scenario and BT's 'Evolving Transition' scenario. Compared to aforementioned projections, BP projected global oil demand plateaus in the 2030s.[5]

In Figure 1.2, we compare the expected global oil demand relative to 2018 in various scenarios. It shows that the global oil demand is expected to grow in all scenarios but the IEA's SDS and BP's RT. The demand for liquid fuels will continue to be dominated by the transportation sector which accounts for around 55 per cent of total oil consumption.[6]

**Figure 1.2** Global oil demand outlook (relative to 2018)

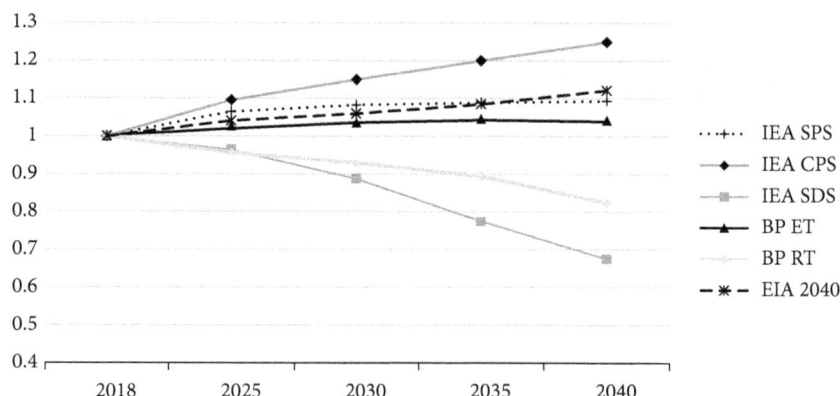

*Note*: Figure 1.2 shows total demand for oil in various scenarios relative to their respective 2018 levels.
*Source*: IEA, 'World Energy Outlook 2019' (WEO, 2019); BP plc, 'BP Energy Outlook'; US Energy Information Administration (International Energy Outlook, 2019).

In all scenarios, the share of natural gas in primary energy demand is expected to expand. In fact, natural gas is the only fossil fuel that expands its share in the global energy mix. It is projected to overtake coal to become the second largest source of global energy by 2040 in all three base case scenarios of the IEA, BP and EIA outlooks. The increased share of natural gas results from both a demand 'pull' led by the electric power and industry sectors, and a 'supply push' led by growing production in US (mainly shale gas) and the Middle East.

Second, renewable energy is the fastest growing source of energy, accounting for around half of the increase in energy, with its share in primary energy increasing from four per cent in 2018 to around 15 per cent by 2040 in BP's base case scenario, and from two per cent to seven per cent in the IEA's stated policy scenario.[7]

---

[5] Here the oil demand includes other liquid fuels such as condensate, gas-to-liquids (GTL) and natural gas liquids (NGL).

[6] In BP's ET scenario, the share of oil within the transportation sector decreased from 94% in 2017 to around 85% by 2040, with the balance coming from electricity, biofuel and natural gas.

[7] The difference in the percentage of renewables between BP and IEA appears to arise from the inclusion of bioenergy. In the IEA stated policy scenario, bioenergy accounts for 10% of the global energy mix in both 2018 and 2040. The BP outlook does not separately list bioenergy while the EIA outlooks even lump hydroelectric power and other renewable sources together.

In both cases, the renewable energy is projected to grow at an annual rate of around six per cent from 2018 to 2040. The share of renewables grows further to 17 per cent in IEA's sustainable development scenario and 25 per cent in BP's 'Rapid Transition' scenario. Much of the renewables growth comes from the electric power sector, with BP projecting renewables to overtake coal as the largest source of energy for the power sector by 2040. The rapid expansion of renewables is at the expense of coal and, to a lesser extent, oil. According to BP, the share of renewables in world energy increases from one per cent to 10 per cent in around 25 years. This is far quicker than any fuel has ever penetrated the energy system in history.

Third, the growth in global energy demand comes primarily from non-OECD countries while the demand in OECD countries is expected to be flat or to enter a modest decline. As a result, the importance of OECD countries in global energy demand shrinks, as shown in Figure 1.3. For example, the share of OECD countries is reduced from 41 per cent in 2018 to 32 per cent in 2040 in both of BP's scenarios, and from 39 per cent to 29–32 per cent in IEA's scenarios. The demand growth is predominantly concentrated in China, India and other Asian countries, where rising prosperity and improving living standards support increasing per capita energy consumption.

**Figure 1.3**  Global demand for primary energy in 2040 (OECD v non-OECD)

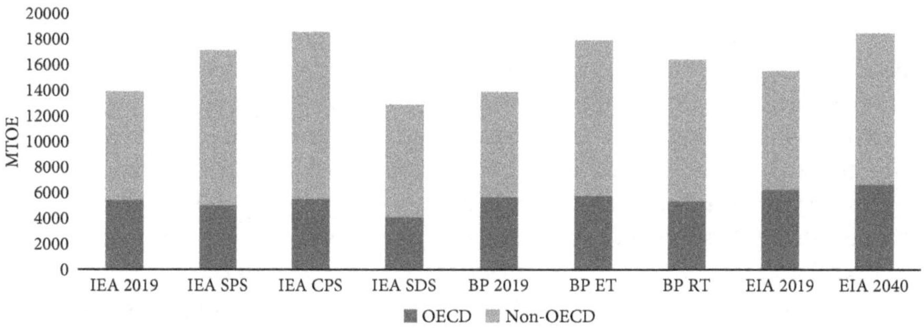

*Note*: Figure 1.3 shows the projected primary energy demand by OECD and non-OECD countries in various outlooks.
*Source*: IEA, 'World Energy Outlook 2019' (WEO, 2019), BP plc, 'BP Energy Outlook', US Energy Information Administration (International Energy Outlook, 2019).

# IV.  A Techno-economic Perspective on Energy Transition in Transportation and Electric Power Generation

There are multitudes of uncertainties surrounding the outcome and assumptions of the outlooks. Ultimately, an energy transition is determined by technology and economics, but influenced by government policies. Here we highlight two technological challenges affecting the speed and scope of renewables penetration in the transportation and electric power sectors.

## A. Replacing Oil Usage in Transportation

While there are several alternative resources that can substitute for fossil fuels in electric power generation, the primary method of replacing oil in the transportation sector is the use of battery powered electric vehicles. However, there are several challenges for the large penetration of electric vehicles. First, how soon can the battery technology break through so that not only the electric vehicles (EV) are cost-competitive to internal combustion engines but also the time needed to charge the batteries is significantly shortened? It may be surprising that the demand for oil is projected to rise in all three base case scenarios of the outlooks as outlined above, given the aggressive government policies to ban the sales of internal combustion engine vehicles in over a dozen of countries.[8] However, if one realises the high energy density and moderate carbon emissions of oil, this shouldn't be all that surprising. When comparing EV with internal combustion engines, it is important to consider both the cost of driving and the convenience of use.

The high energy density of oil products offers great convenience of use and makes oil very difficult to replace with other fuels in the transportation sector. For example, a full tank of gasoline in a 2018 Honda Accord (1.5L, 4 cylinder, automatic, tank size: 14.8 gallon) gives a combined city/highway driving range of 459 miles, which is 50 per cent more than Tesla's long-range models and more than three times the 2019 Hyundai Iconic Electric model.[9] Further, the charging time of EVs is a significant constraint. While it takes a few minutes to refill the fuel tank of a gasoline or diesel vehicle, it takes much longer to fully charge the battery of an EV, even for the most advanced electric vehicles, such as Tesla's.[10]

On the cost of driving, based on some 'back of the envelope' calculations, Covert et al (2016) argue that 'even if oil prices were at $100 per barrel, the price of batteries that store the energy necessary to power these vehicles needs to decrease by a factor of three'.[11] The good news in this regard is that battery

---

[8] Austria, Britain, China, Costa Rica, France, Germany, India, Ireland, Israel, the Netherlands, Norway and Scotland have decided to completely phase out the sale of internal combustion engine (ICE) vehicles between 2020 and 2040: I Burch and J Gilchrist, 'Survey of Global Activity to Phase Out Internal Combustion Engine Vehicles' (A Hancock and G Waaland eds, Center for Climate Protection, September 2018), available at www.climateprotection.org.

[9] The combined city/highway fuel economy for the 2018 Honda Accord is 31 miles per gallon. The driving range of the 2019 Hyundai Iconic Electric is 124 miles: see 'Compare Side-by-Side'(The official government source for fuel economy information), available at www.fueleconomy.gov/feg/Find.do?action=sbs&id=39596&id=40384.

[10] Even with a supercharger, it takes around 20 minutes to charge to 50%, 40 minutes to 80%, and 75 minutes to 100% of Tesla's 85 kWh battery.

[11] T Covert, M Greenstone and CR Knittel, 'Will We Ever Stop Using Fossil Fuels?' (2016) 30 *Journal of Economic Perspectives* 117.

costs have been falling quite rapidly in the past decade or so. According to the Bloomberg battery price survey published in December 2018, the volume-weighted average price of a lithium-ion battery pack is \$176/kWh,[12] almost 50 per cent of the 2015 price level referred to in the Covert et al (2016) study. The negative relationship between unit cost and cumulative production of a technology is commonly referred to as the learning curve. The Bloomberg study calculates a learning rate of around 18 per cent, meaning that for every doubling of cumulative volume, the battery price would reduce by 18 per cent. However, a caveat to the learning curve is that as the cumulative production increases the cost reductions will level off. The US Department of Energy (2014) sets a target of \$125 per kWh battery cost in 2022. At \$125 per kWh battery price, Covert et al (2016) suggests that the oil price would have to rise above \$115 per barrel for EV to be cost-competitive with internal combustion engines. Obviously, the speed of EV penetration depends, to a large extent, on the cost-competitiveness of batteries.

In this paper we update the cost of driving calculations of Covert et al (2016) by considering the latest development in battery cost and other vehicle costs in the US. Following Covert et al (2016), we compare the present value of the cost to a consumer driving an EV with that of driving an internal combustion engine vehicle (ICEV). In each case, we assume the car will be driven 15,000 miles per year for 10 years, and use a discount rate of three per cent. Our non-battery vehicle cost numbers and technical specifications are taken from Lutsey and Nicolas (2019), which is in turn adapted from a detailed cost study of UBS (2017) and adapted to average US vehicles.[13] Table 1.1 presents the breakdown of the non-battery costs for both ICEV and EV where the indirect cost of the ICEV is assumed to be 20 per cent of the direct cost. For the ICEV, we assume fuel efficiency to be 30 miles per gallon, and for EV we consider three versions: the short range (150 miles) EV consumes 0.28 kWh of electric power per mile; the mid-range (200 miles) consumes 0.29 kWh of electric power per mile; and the long-range (250 miles) consumes 0.30 kWh of electric power per mile. The increased electric power per mile for longer-range electric vehicles is due to larger and heavier battery packs. The technical parameters of ICEV and three versions of EV are presented in Table 1.2.[14] Following Lutsey and Nicolas (2019), we also assume a five per cent profit margin and 15 per cent dealer mark-up to arrive at the final price for the vehicle, ie the cost to the consumer, which is within the range of average market prices of the relevant vehicles sold in the US for the 2019 model year.

---

[12] L Goldie-Scot, 'A Behind the Scenes Take on Lithium-Ion Battery Prices' (Bloomberg NEF, 5 March 2019), available at https://about.bnef.com/blog/behind-scenes-take-lithium-ion-battery-prices/?sf99535078=1.

[13] N Lutsey and M Nicholas (2019). 'Update on electric vehicle costs in the United States through 2030', International Council on Clean Transportation working paper 2019-06.

[14] Here we assume the non-battery cost of the EV does not change with battery capacity, which may not be the case.

**Table 1.1** Vehicle non-battery cost breakdown

|  | ICEV | EV |
|---|---|---|
| **EV powertrain[15] excluding battery[a]** |  | $3,449 |
| **Conventional powertrain[b]** | $8,024 | – |
| **Vehicle assembly** | $13,462 | $13,356 |
| **Indirect cost[c]** | $4,297 | $7,850 |

*Notes*
a EV powertrain components include thermal management, power distribution module, inverter/ converter, electric drive module, controller, control module, high voltage cables, on-board charger, charging cord.
b Conventional powertrain includes engine, transmission, exhaust, etc.
c Indirect cost includes depreciation, amortization, research and development, and general administration expenses.

**Table 1.2** Technical specifications of ICEV and EV in the base case

|  | ICEV | EV short range | EV middle range | EV long range |
|---|---|---|---|---|
| **Fuel efficiency (miles/gallon)** | 30 | – | – | – |
| **Electric efficiency (kWh/mile)** | – | 0.28 | 0.29 | 0.30 |
| **Driving range (miles)** | 450 | 150 | 200 | 250 |
| **Battery pack (kWh)** | – | 42 | 58 | 75 |

The operating cost of driving depends primarily on the prices of gasoline and electric power. As our focus is on the sensitivity of battery cost and the cost of operating an EV is relatively low, we consider a fixed electric power price. We use the US average retail price of 10.38 cents per kWh for March 2019 in this analysis. Other costs include vehicle registration, maintenance and insurance. EVs cost less to maintain owing to the simplicity of a battery-electric motor system compared with the frequent maintenance required for the operation of an ICEV.[16] On the other hand, the insurance cost for an EV is higher because they require specialised parts and are serviced by specialist mechanics.[17] In this exercise, the cost of insurance is indexed to the value of the vehicle. Figure 1.4 depicts the total costs (in present values) of owning a car over 10 years, assuming the gasoline price is $2.8 per gallon and battery cost is $150/kWh.[18] The BEV150 (BEV200, BEV250) represents the

---

[15] The mechanism that transfers the power from the engine/batteries to the axle of a car.
[16] J. Brennan and T. Barder, 'Battery Electric Vehicles Vs. Internal Combustion Engine Vehicles: A United States-Based Comprehensive Assessment' (Arthur D Little, 2016), available at www.adlittle. com/bev_icev.
[17] 'Electric Car Insurance' (Pod Point, 7 June 2019), available at https://pod-point.com/guides/driver/ electric-car-insurance.
[18] In this analysis, all price and cost figures are presented in constant dollars.

short-range (middle-range, long-range) battery EVs. Under these assumptions, while the short-range EV is close to be cost-effective with the internal combustion vehicle, the long-range EV is much more expensive (17 per cent higher) than the conventional ICEV even though the driving range of the long-range EV is only 56 per cent of the internal combustion engine vehicle.

**Figure 1.4**  Present value of the cost of car ownership

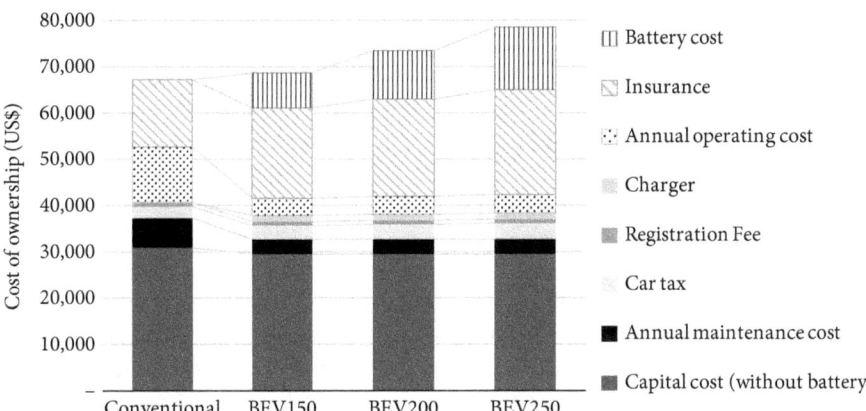

*Note*: Figure 4.4 depicts the total cost of owning a car for 10 years assuming the gasoline price is $2.8 per gallon and battery cost of $150/kWh.

For every level of the battery cost, there is a break-even gasoline price at which a consumer would be indifferent between driving an EV and an ICEV. Since the gasoline price is primarily affected by the price of crude oil, we can find the corresponding crude oil price by estimating a gasoline–crude oil price relationship. Figure 1.5 plots the break-even crude oil price for a range of battery cost assumptions where the crude oil price is estimated by regressing gasoline price on the price of crude oil assuming a log–log relationship.[19] At the current battery pack cost of $175/kWh,[20] the break-even crude oil price is respectively $233/bbl, $161/bbl, and $102/bbl for long-, middle- and short-range EVs. If the battery price is reduced to $125/kWh, the corresponding break-even price for crude oil is $146/bbl, $101/bbl and $64/bbl.[21] In other words, the short-range EV (BEV150) can be cost-competitive when the price of crude oil rises above

[19] In log–log relationship the log values of dependent and independent variable are used for regression analysis.

[20] According to the aforementioned Bloomberg battery price survey, the average EV battery pack cost in 2018 was $176/kWh.

[21] Compared to the CGK (2016) study, the break-even price for the long range (BEV250) EV in our analysis is higher perhaps because we did not 'credit' $1,000 to the EV as CGK (2016).

$64/bbl while the long-range EV (BEV250) can be cost-competitive only if the crude oil price rises above $146/bbl.

Considering the potential for improvement in battery technology, we calculate an alternative scenario where the fuel efficiency of the ICEV is improved to 32 miles per gallon and the EV efficiency is also improved to 0.26, 0.27 and 0.28 kWh of electric power per mile respectively for short-, mid- and long-range cars. We further assume the indirect cost (including research and development, depreciation and amortisation, and general expense, etc) is reduced to 50 per cent of its current level, which will be lower than the ICEV, as a larger number of vehicles will spread the indirect cost. The resulting break-even oil prices for various battery cost levels are plotted in Figure 1.6. In this scenario, at a battery cost of $125/kWh, even the long-range EV (BEV250) can be cost-competitive when the oil price is above $63/bbl.

The analysis above illustrates that while the EVs are not yet cost-competitive, they are on the trajectory to become so, at least for the short- and mid-range EVs (BEV150 and BEV200). Our analysis here is calibrated to US situations. In countries where the price of gasoline is more expensive, EVs could be cost-effective at a lower price of crude oil because the difference in gasoline prices across countries is due mainly to taxes. We also ignored certain features, such as the faster speed of acceleration for EVs, which could have improved consumers' experience and hence demand a premium in price and improve the commercial viability of EVs. On the other hand, battery degradation may require a change of battery over the life cycle of an EV, which would increase the cost of EVs. In summary, with fast-declining battery cost, the total cost of ownership may not present a significant challenge to EV penetration. However, the driving range and the speed of charging remain significant barriers.

**Figure 1.5** Break-even crude oil prices for EV in base case

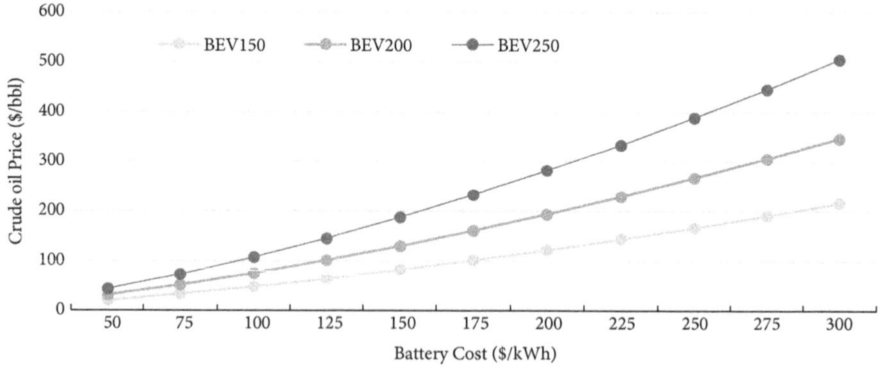

*Note*: Figure 1.5 depicts the break-even crude oil price at different battery cost levels such that the total cost (present value) of owning and driving an EV equals that of driving a gasoline-based internal combustion engine vehicle. It is assumed that the car has 10 years of life and each year can be driven 15,000 miles. BEV150 (BEV200, BEV250) indicates EVs with a driving range of 150 miles (200 miles and 250 miles).

**Figure 1.6** Break-even crude oil prices for EV in Alternative Case

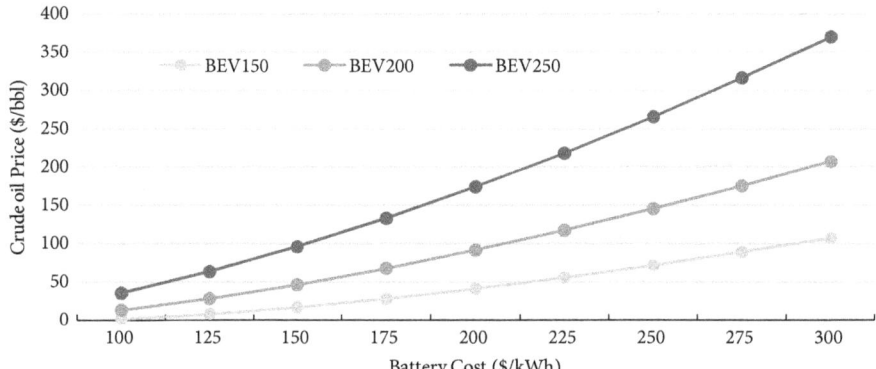

*See Figure 1.5 notes.*

# B. Penetration of Renewables in Electric Power Generation

In the electric power sector, the extent to which renewables can replace natural gas and coal depends on both the levelised cost of energy and the cost of addressing the intermittency problem associated with renewables. The levelised cost of energy (LCOE) is the present discounted value of costs over the life cycle divided by the present discounted value of output, and therefore represents the long-run average cost of the energy associated with a particular technology. There have been significant cost improvements in both solar photovoltaics and wind energy. For example, in its 2018 annual outlook the EIA projected that the capacity-weighted LCOE of onshore wind will be on par with combined cycle turbines (CCGT) by 2022. The LCOE of solar PV has also been reduced, although still 20 per cent or $11/MWh higher than the natural gas-based combined cycle turbines.

The levelised cost of energy is only one dimension in comparing different technologies for electric power generation. Solar and wind power are inevitably intermittent. The increased penetration of these resources in an electric system requires either an increase in back-up power (often supplied by natural gas generators) or an increase in energy storage that isn't typically reflected in the numerator of the basic levelised cost of energy calculation. These costs depend upon a variety of factors, such as the level of renewables penetration, the degree of variation in generation from the renewable resources, and the correlation in generation across renewable resources. These costs are site-specific, but there exist some empirical estimates based on simulation studies. Mills and Wiser (2010) find that a 10 per cent penetration of solar power can add as much as $39 per MWh[22] when

---

[22] A Mills and R Wiser, 'Implications Of Wide-Area Geographic Diversity For Short-Term Variability Of Solar Power' (Lawrence Berkeley National Laboratory (LBNL), Berkeley, CA (USA), 2010), available at www.osti.gov/servlets/purl/986925.

**Figure 1.7** The net energy demand in the California ISO (26 June 2019)

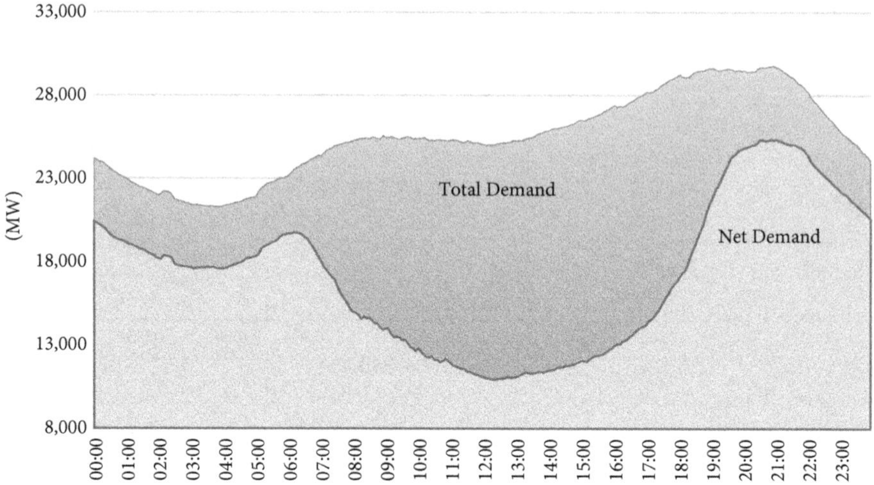

*Date source:* CAISO (www.caiso.com). Figure 1.7 shows the total and net demand of the California ISO by hour (averaged five minutes) on 26 June 2019. The net demand is equal to the total demand minus renewable resources.

the solar is installed in one location, to as little as $3 per MWh when it is installed across 25 different sites in the Midwestern US.

Furthermore, because the generation from solar (and wind) resources in a given area tends to be positively correlated, large-scale penetration of either resource will vastly increase the demand for ramping power and decrease the value of incremental capacity additions. The impact of this net demand for electric power (after netting out the supply of renewable resources) is best illustrated by the so-called Duck Curve in California (as shown in Figure 1.7). The Duck Curve illustrates that as more and more renewables hit the market, the net demand will be lowest during the daytime and prices during those hours will obviously fall, making additional investments in renewables less valuable. Further, from late afternoon to early evening, when solar generation fades and total demand picks up, the net demand dramatically rises, which requires a large amount of generation resources to ramp up in a short period of time. Figure 1.7 shows the total and net demand of electric power in the area covered by the California Independent System Operator on 26 June 2019. Between the hour of 17:00 and 20:00, the system requires over 10,000 MW of ramping resources. To put this in perspective, the capacity of a standard size nuclear power station is 1000 MW. The ramping requirement on that day is the equivalent of bringing 10 nuclear power stations from idle to full capacity. This is challenging to any electric power system operator.

The levelised costs for fossil fuel technologies presented above ignore the external costs of coal and natural gas fired powerplants. However, as Covert et al (2016) have argued, 'the carbon dioxide externality for the typical natural gas plant is $20 per MWh, while the externality for the typical coal plant is $40 per MWh'. While considering these costs would certainly make up the difference in the levelised costs between natural gas and solar power, the additional system costs associated with the intermittency of renewables may balance this out.

# V.  Conclusions

This chapter has compared the energy outlooks made by the IEA, BP and EIA and draws implications for a global energy transition. We argue that energy transition is determined by technology and economics, but is influenced by government policies. Our key findings can be summarised as follows. First, oil and gas are expected to continue to account for around 50 per cent of the total primary energy mix by 2040. While the share of oil in the global energy mix declines somewhat by 2040, the absolute value is expected to continue to grow in all base case scenarios. Natural gas not only expands its share in the global energy mix but is also projected to overtake coal to become the second largest source of global energy by 2040. Second, renewable energy is the fastest-growing source of energy in all scenarios, accounting for about half of the increase in the global energy mix. The rapid expansion of renewables is at the expense of coal, and to a lesser extent, oil. Third, our analysis about the total cost of driving indicates that at the current levels of battery prices and vehicle efficiency, only short-range electric vehicles can be cost-competitive with internal combustion engine vehicles when the crude oil price is above $64/bbl. With further improvements in battery technology and improved economies of scale in reducing indirect cost, long-range EVs are also very likely to become cost-competitive in the future. However, some technological barriers, particularly in terms of charging speed and driving range, remain to be overcome. Fourth, renewables such as wind and solar photovoltaics are becoming increasingly cost-competitive with natural gas in electric power generation. Yet the intermittency issue remains a challenge, and requires a high level of back-up power and a large quantity of ramp-up resources.

# 2

# Oil-rich Countries' Responses to Energy Transition: Managing the Decline

DAVID MANLEY, PATRICK HELLER AND JAMES CUST*

## I. Abstract

Extracting oil and gas is an important source of revenue for many – particularly less developed – countries. For their total wealth to increase, countries must transform their oil and gas wealth into productive assets above ground.

However, while the rise of renewable energy and other low carbon technologies may steer the world away from the worst effects of climate change, for a group of countries low-carbon technologies pose an economic threat to address. In response, this chapter argues that countries must evaluate the transformation of oil and gas into production assets. Their policy response could incorporate a mix of four strategies. First, whether to attempt to increase the pace of production. Second, how to increase the social value the country receives per barrel of oil. Third, whether to divest from carbon-linked assets like national oil companies. Fourth, whether to increase the national savings rate from oil revenue.

Governments must choose their response under significant uncertainty about the timing and extent of a possible transition between energy sources. They may therefore be tempted to continue reinvesting wealth in their oil and gas industries in the hope that prices do not decline. Further, the efficacy of these strategies depends on the future course of oil prices and the specific context of each country.

* This chapter is an evolution of previous work: D Manley, J Cust and G Cecchinato. 'Stranded Nations? The Climate Policy Implications for Fossil Fuel-Rich Developing Countries', OxCarre Policy Paper series (2016) 34; J Cust, G Cecchinato and D Manley, 'Unburnable Wealth of Nations' (2017) 54 *Finance and Development* 46; and J Cust and D Manley, 'The Carbon Wealth of Nations: From Rents to Risks' in G-M Lange, Q Wodon and K Carey (eds), 'The Changing Wealth of Nations 2018: Building a Sustainable Future' (World Bank, 2018).

For many countries, all four strategies will be difficult to follow, particularly the latter three. This chapter suggests that perhaps the easiest strategy is to increase production, contributing further to global carbon emissions, as predicted by the green paradox theory. Further, without effective governance reforms the risk is that this production is hollow – resulting in greater carbon emissions but without a corresponding benefit to the people of these countries.

# II.  Introduction

Over the past 30 years, four-fifths of energy use has come from burning oil, gas and coal.[1] This is bringing humanity ever closer to spending its global 'carbon budget' – the amount of carbon humans can emit to limit the rise in global temperature to below 2°C.[2] A 2015 International Energy Agency study suggested that keeping to this budget required leaving 80 per cent of coal deposits, 50 per cent of oil reserves and 40 per cent of gas reserves in the ground.[3,4]

It appears increasingly unlikely that the world will keep to this budget. But in order to come as close as possible, businesses, governments and societies need to pursue technological innovation, carbon taxes and other mechanisms that facilitate the burning of less fossil fuel. The alternative scenario (in which people continue to burn more fossil fuel than the world can bear) will require planning of a different sort – mitigating the effects of an increasingly chaotic climate, building flood barriers, dealing with crop failures and managing migration.

While humans' efforts to reduce their carbon emissions have so far been disappointing, the prospects for renewable energy at least have risen.[5] This pace is not sufficient to stop climate change, but it might be enough to significantly reduce how much fossil fuels are burned in the future. This would be a remarkable success for the planet, but it poses a question for those societies in which producing fossil fuels is a major part of their economy. If the governments of these countries do not adequately plan for a future in which there is increased use of renewable energy and other low-carbon technologies, they face severe repercussions, including

---

[1] 'Statistics' (Iea.org, 2019), available at www.iea.org/statistics.

[2] Specifically, the amount of carbon humans can emit while having a 50% chance of limiting the rise in global ground temperature to below 2°C by 2100, compared with the estimated average temperature between 1850 to 1900 (Carbontracker.org, 2019), available at www.carbontracker.org/wp-content/uploads/2018/02/Carbon-Budgets_Eplained_02022018.pdf.

[3] International Energy Agency, 'World Energy Outlook 2015' (IEA, 2015).

[4] C McGlade and P Etkins, 'The geological distribution of fossil fuels unused when limiting global warming to 2 degrees' (2015) 527 *Nature* 187.

[5] Measured by actual electricity produced, renewable energy has increased significantly. By production of electricity, the IEA reports that the contribution of total electricity produced in the OECD countries by solar, wind and geothermal rose from 2.5% in 2008 to 9.6% in 2017. International Energy Agency, 'Statistics' (IEA, 2019), available at www.iea.org/statistics.

impoverished government treasuries and strained financial markets.[6,7] These challenges may destabilise the geopolitics in some parts of the world (eg Russia, Middle East) and create further poverty in others (eg West Africa). And these additional challenges in turn make mitigating and adapting to climate change more difficult.

However, the timing and uncertainty of these impacts makes government planning difficult. Even if market prospects for oil and gas shine dimmer than in previous decades, the industry may still make large profits for years to come, and countries rich in oil and gas will not want to miss out on a share of these profits to fund government spending. As is often the case, short-term thinking is likely to dominate policy-making.

Conversely, it is feasible that the growth of renewable energy might affect the returns of some oil and gas investments made in the forthcoming years. The uncertainty of future oil and gas demand weighs heavier for countries that have just started producing oil and gas, or that are planning on doing so in the next few years. Large oil and gas discoveries in countries like Tanzania and Uganda may have to wait many years for companies to develop their projects and to start paying taxes to their governments. Conversely, economies already dominated by oil and gas like Saudi Arabia and Russia face different challenges: whether to substantially increase the savings rate from these revenues and prioritise economic diversification away from oil and gas.[8]

In this chapter we argue:

- Extracting oil and gas is important for many – particularly impoverished – countries.

- While the rise of renewable energy and other low-carbon technologies may steer the world away from the worst effects of climate change, for a group of countries renewables pose an economic threat to address.

- Governments must choose their approach to transforming their country's subsoil oil and gas assets into aboveground productive assets. This choice requires considering whether to:

  ○ increase the pace of exploration and production;
  ○ increase the social value the country receives per barrel of oil;

---

[6] 'Mark Carney warns investors face "huge" climate change losses', *Financial Times*, 29 September 2015; M Carney, 'A Transition in Thinking and Action', International Climate Risk Conference for Supervisors, de Nederlandsche Bank, Amsterdam, 6 April 2018.

[7] Henceforth, as short-hand, we refer to all low-carbon technologies as 'renewable energy'. Other low-carbon technologies potentially include but are not limited to supply side contributions such as nuclear energy, demand side contributions such as electrification of economic activities and digitisation, as well as carbon capture and sequestration. However, we do not comment on the relative merits and feasibility of each technology.

[8] A Malova and F Van Der Ploeg, 'Consequences of Lower Oil Prices and Stranded Assets for Russia's Sustainable Fiscal Stance' (2017) 105 *Energy Policy* 27.

- ○ divest from related assets like national oil companies; and
- ○ increase the national savings rate from oil revenues.
- • The efficacy of these strategies depends on the future course of oil prices and the specific context of each country.

Failing to manage a possible decline in oil and gas may result in the world pumping greater amounts of oil – a tragedy in itself – while having little economic development to show for it. Further, a mismanaged decline may create further social and economic crises in these countries that will make managing the global climate crisis even more difficult.

# III. The Energy Transition Threatens the Carbon-dominated Economic Model of Many Producer Nations

The World Bank measures each country's wealth of oil, gas and coal as the rental value of fossil fuels in a country.[9] In both absolute dollar terms and the share that this wealth has as a proportion of total wealth, much of this carbon wealth is in the Middle East and North Africa. Carbon wealth makes up a substantial share of total natural wealth in other regions too – almost a tenth of all wealth in Sub-Saharan Africa is in fossil fuels. Further, almost all of the wealth in fossil fuels is in the form of oil.

**Table 2.1** Shares of carbon, natural, produced, and human wealth to total wealth in a country, by region and income group (2014)

| | Natural capital (total) (%) | of which: coal (%) | of which: gas (%) | of which: oil (%) | Net foreign assets (%) | Produced capital (%) | Human capital (%) |
|---|---|---|---|---|---|---|---|
| **By region** | | | | | | | |
| East Asia & Pacific | 11 | 1 | 0 | 1 | 1 | 28 | 60 |
| Europe & Central Asia | 5 | 0 | 1 | 2 | 0 | 33 | 62 |
| Latin America & Caribbean | 18 | 0 | 0 | 3 | −2 | 24 | 60 |

*(continued)*

[9] This is the present value of expected revenues, based on reported reserves and recent oil, gas or coal prices, less the costs of extracting each resource. Cust and Manley, 'The Carbon Wealth of Nations' (2018).

**Table 2.1** *(Continued)*

| | Natural capital (total) (%) | of which: coal (%) | of which: gas (%) | of which: oil (%) | Net foreign assets (%) | Produced capital (%) | Human capital (%) |
|---|---|---|---|---|---|---|---|
| Middle East & North Africa | 44 | 0 | 2 | 38 | 6 | 15 | 35 |
| Sub-Saharan Africa | 36 | 1 | 0 | 7 | −1 | 16 | 50 |
| **By income** | | | | | | | |
| Low income | 47 | 0 | 0 | 1 | −2 | 14 | 41 |
| Lower middle income | 27 | 1 | 1 | 4 | −3 | 25 | 51 |
| Upper middle income | 17 | 1 | 0 | 3 | 0 | 25 | 58 |
| High income: non-OECD | 30 | 0 | 3 | 23 | 5 | 22 | 42 |
| High income: OECD | 3 | 0 | 0 | 0 | −1 | 28 | 70 |
| *World* | *9* | *1* | *0* | *3* | *0* | *27* | *64* |

*Note:* Total wealth is the estimated value of natural, produced, human capital in a country plus the value of net foreign assets owned by state and citizens. Produced capital: machinery, buildings, equipment, and residential and non-residential urban land, measured at market prices. Natural capital: energy and minerals, agricultural land, forests and protected areas. Natural capital is measured as the discounted sum of the value of rents generated over the lifetime of the asset. Human capital: the value of skills, experience, and effort by the working population over their lifetimes disaggregated by gender and employment status. Human capital is measured as the discounted value of earnings over a person's lifetime.
*Source:* World Bank, Changing Wealth of Nations.

For many countries, the proceeds from this fossil fuel wealth is concentrated in the hands of governments and their national oil companies.[10] Figure 2.2 shows the 20 governments most dependent on oil and gas revenue for their budgetary revenue.

Further, in almost every non-OECD country with oil reserves, a significant portion of the state's share of oil proceeds is managed by national oil companies (NOCs).[11] These companies also hold a sizable amount of public assets. As of 2017, these companies collectively own more than USD 3.1 trillion of assets and employ millions of people.[12] They are often amongst the largest and seemingly

---

[10] Malova and Van Der Ploeg, 'Consequences of Lower Oil Prices' (2017).

[11] P Heller and D Mihalyi, 'Massive and Misunderstood: Data-Driven Insights into National Oil Companies' (Natural Resource Governance Institute, 2019).

[12] Natural Resource Governance Institute, 'National Oil Company Database' (React Redux Example, 2019), available at www.nationaloilcompanydata.org.

**Figure 2.1**  Fossil fuel rent as a percentage of GDP, by country (2014)

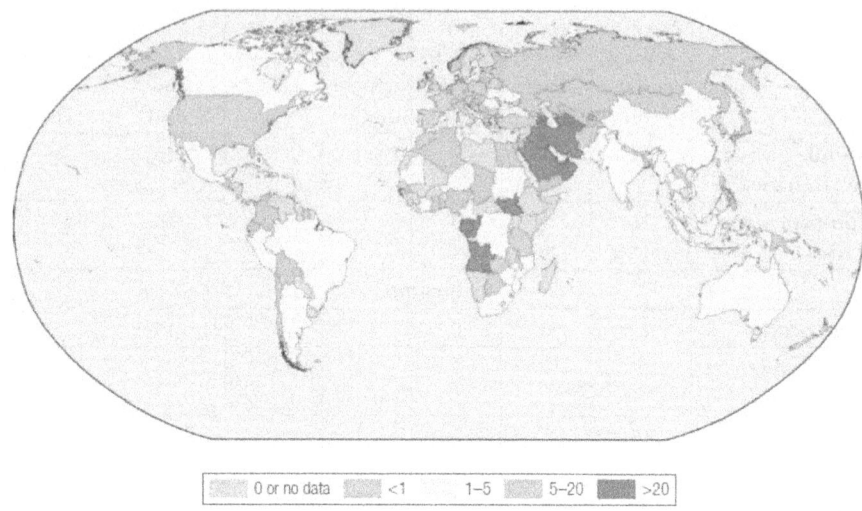

*Source:* Cust and Manley, 'The Carbon Wealth of Nations' (2018).

**Figure 2.2**  Share of government revenue derived from oil, gas and minerals (2010–14)

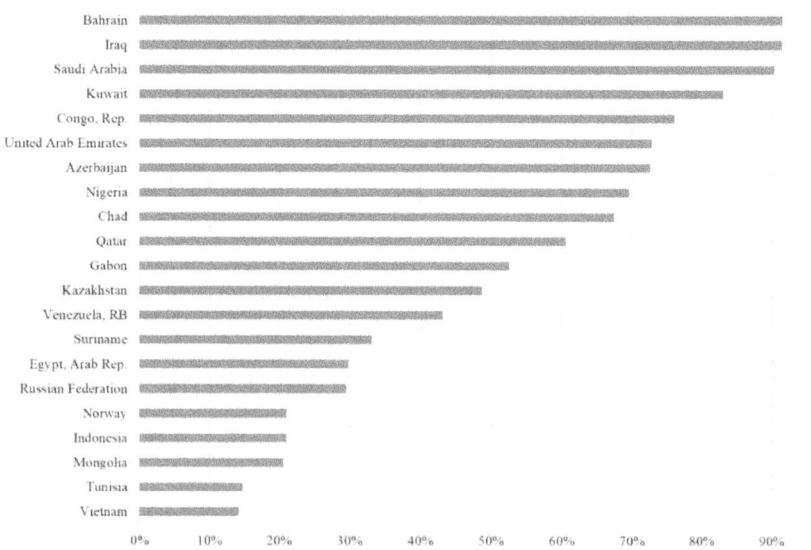

*Source:* International Centre for Tax and Development–United Nations University, Government Revenue Database, available at www.wider.unu.edu/project/government-revenue-dataset.

*Note:* The ratio of resource revenues to total revenues was calculated as the average over the period 2010–14. Several countries are missing data for either fossil fuel wealth or government revenues. The source does not distinguish between oil, gas, coal and other minerals. Comparing against relative production values of each of these countries, in most cases the dominant share of the revenues reported as 'resource revenues' derives from oil and gas.

most successful businesses in their countries – some, such as Malaysia's Petronas and Norway's Equinor, becoming major international oil companies. At the peak of the oil boom in 2013, at least 25 countries were NOC-dependent, meaning that the NOC collected revenues equivalent to 20 per cent or more of total government revenues – see Figure 2.3.[13] Further, Figure 2.5 shows that some NOCs have net asset values that are a significant portion of national wealth, given that for most countries this portion is held by just one company.

**Figure 2.3**  Revenue received by national oil company as a proportion of total government revenue (2013)

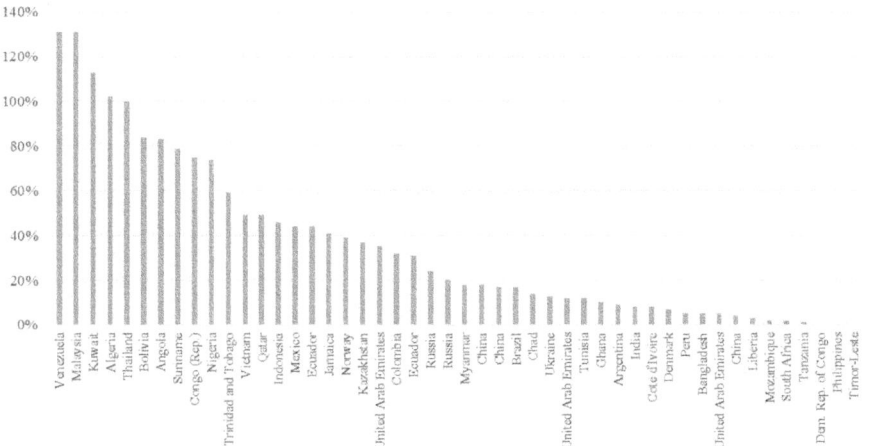

*Source:* National Oil Company Database.

## IV.  The Future Value of Oil and Gas is Uncertain

Given how much of their wealth comes from fossil fuels, some countries are particularly exposed to a fall in oil and gas prices.[14] Future prices are always uncertain, but the rise of low-carbon technologies adds to this uncertainty. It is unwise to forecast oil prices, so instead we can outline what we know – and importantly don't know – about the factors that influence these long-term values.[15]

For the world economy to meet the global carbon budget, a significant proportion of oil and gas assets must not only remain undeveloped, but current extraction rates will also need to fall dramatically.[16] Given this necessary pace, keeping within

---

[13] Heller and Mihalyi, 'Massive and Misunderstood' (2019).

[14] This might arise from a weakening demand for fossil fuels, an accelerated growth in supply of fossil fuels (such as via the 'green paradox' effect) or might arise from a carbon tax driving a wedge between the price paid and the price received.

[15] C Baumeister and L Kilian, 'Forty Years of Oil Price Fluctuations: Why the Price of Oil May Still Surprise Us' (2016) 30 *Journal of Economic Perspectives* 139.

[16] C McGlade and P Ekins, 'Un-Burnable Oil: An Examination of Oil Resource Utilisation in a Decarbonised Energy System' (2014) 64 *Energy Policy* 102.

**Figure 2.4**  Net asset value of national oil companies as proportion of total national wealth (2014)

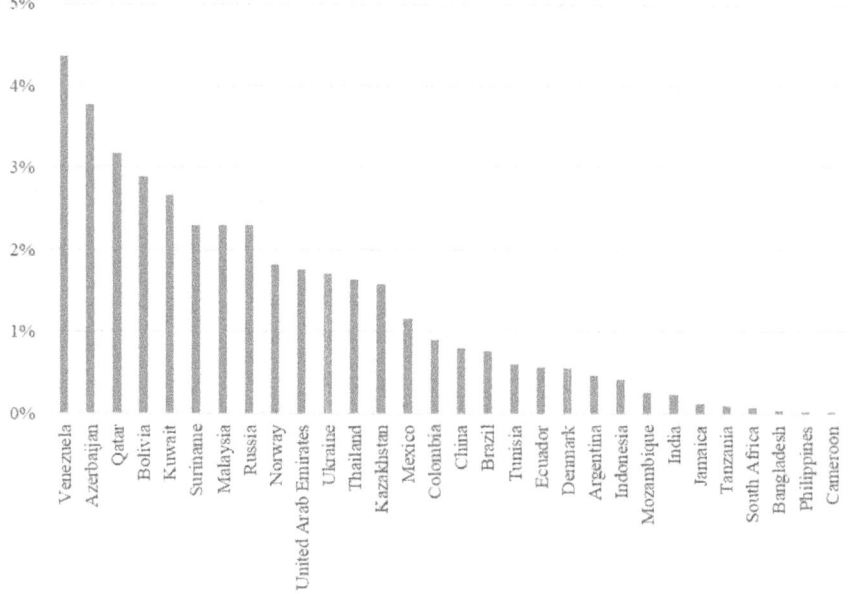

*Source:* National Oil Company Database.

**Figure 2.5**  Crude oil price (2018 prices) – what happens next?

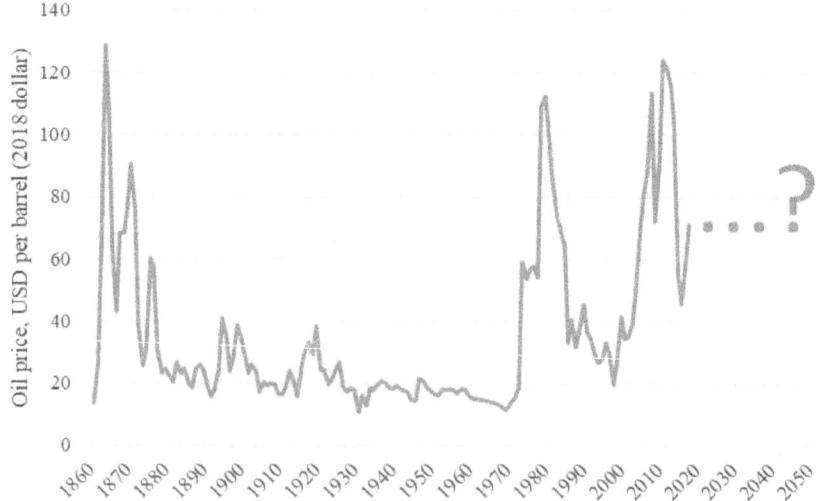

*Source:* BP, Statistical Review of World Energy 2018 (2019).

the carbon budget seems unlikely; but the rise of renewable energy sources and other low-carbon technologies is somewhat independent of carbon policies. The economic incentives to innovate and the so-called 'experience curve' effect exemplified in the manufacture of solar photovoltaic panels and related technology suggest that the renewables industry could continue to grow even in the absence of coherent international policy to achieve global climate goals.[17]

However, the future market share of renewable energy remains uncertain. One way to understand the nature of the next energy transition is to look at previous transitions – for example, from the time when the dominant source of energy for most countries in the world transitioned from coal to oil.[18] Such studies suggest three aspects relevant to the next energy transition.[19] First, past energy transitions have been slow, eg it took over 100 years for oil to replace coal as the dominant source of energy. But present conditions differ from previous transitions – primarily because a large number of governments are imposing or considering policies to promote a fast transition.[20] Second, past transitions did not result in the complete replacement of the old energy source. Third, if renewable energy does take a significant share of the energy market from fossil fuels, both the rise in renewable energy's share and decline in oil and gas prices is unlikely to be smooth. Uncertainty breeds volatility, and particularly in oil and gas markets prices are likely to continue being volatile with years of high prices – even if the long-term trend is downward.

Given the uncertainty around energy markets, considering the future by envisioning scenarios may be useful.[21] For the rest of the chapter, we consider the implications of two scenarios, which probably represent two extreme visions of the future. The first scenario is Business as Usual – the demand for fossil fuels continues as it has done for past decades. Prices are volatile but there is no long-term downward trend. Even with the currently rising share of renewables, this scenario remains plausible. As the global economy grows, the demand for oil and gas can also grow, at least at the rate at which supply can keep pace. The second

---

[17] C Goodall, *The Switch: How solar, storage and new tech means cheap power for all* (Profile Books, 2016).

[18] R Fouquet, 'Historical energy transitions: Speed, prices and system transformation' (2016) 13 *Energy Research & Social Science* 202.

[19] B Fattouh, R Poudineh and R West, *The Rise of Renewables and Energy Transition: What Adaptation Strategy For Oil Companies And Oil-Exporting Countries?* (Oxford Institute for Energy Studies, 2019).

[20] Although governments played important roles in past energy transitions too – for example, the British Government's decision to switch the primary source of power for its navy from coal to oil. However, the next transition benefits from international support and cooperation amongst governments, even if often this support and cooperation is insufficient given the climate crisis.

[21] J Bentham, 'The Scenario Approach to Possible Futures for Oil and Natural Gas' (2014) 64 *Energy Policy* 87; B Benedict 'Benefits of Scenario Planning Applied to Energy Development' (2017) 107 *Energy Procedia* 304.

scenario is the Energy Transition – the demand for fossil fuels falls in the long term as the global economy satisfies an increasing amount of its energy needs from renewable energy rather than fossil fuels. Prices continue to be volatile, but trend downwards.[22]

Shell's Sky scenario could be a model in this case. One of a set of scenarios used by Shell for the company's long-term decision-making, the Sky scenario is Shell's most optimistic scenario, and envisions a global net-zero carbon emissions by 2070. Shell describes this as 'technologically, industrially and economically possible', although not necessarily politically feasible.[23] Similarly, modelling suggests it is technically feasible to reach net-zero carbon emissions by 2050.[24] Further, the UK Government has targeted net-zero carbon economies by 2050. An energy transition by 2050 to 2070 therefore represents a very optimistic yet feasible scenario to consider.

## V.  Strategies for a Managed Decline of Oil and Gas

A terminal fall in oil prices is a threat to oil investors. But, on the whole, investors in international oil companies can reduce their exposure to this risk and share the risk amongst a large number of investors.[25] Conversely, people in oil-dependent countries, by definition, are particularly exposed to the risks of a terminal fall in the oil price. And for them divesting from oil is more difficult.

To divest from oil, and benefit from oil and gas extraction in a sustainable manner, a country must not only extract but transform the subsoil asset into aboveground productive assets – such as human and physical capital.[26] (This process is called the Hartwick Rule.[27]) In practice, this transformation process has proved difficult, with few oil-rich developing countries following the process successfully.[28]

---

[22] For a quantitative assessment of the impact of different price trends on low-income, oil-rich countries, see S Bradley, G Lahn and S Pye, 'Carbon Risk and Resilience: How Energy Transition is Changing the Prospects for Countries with Fossil Fuels' (Chatham House, 2018).

[23] Shell, 'Shell Scenarios Sky: Meeting the goals of the Paris Agreement', available at www.shell.com/energy-and-innovation/the-energy-future/scenarios/shell-scenario-sky.html.

[24] D Bogdanov, J Farfan, K Sadovskaia, A Aghahosseini, M Child, A Gulagi, AS Oyewo, L Barbosa and C Breyer, 'Radical Transformation Pathway towards Sustainable Electricity via Evolutionary Steps' (2019) 10 *Nature Communications* 1.

[25] As of 2016, international oil companies had booked oil and gas reserves sufficient to last 13 years at current production rates; see Manley, Cust and Cecchinato, 'Stranded Nations' (2016).

[26] F Van der Ploeg and A Venables, 'Harnessing Windfall Revenues: Optimal Policies for Resource-Rich Developing Economies' (2011) 121 *The Economic Journal* 1.

[27] J Hartwick, 'Intergenerational Equity and the Investing of Rents from Exhaustible Resources' (1977) 67 *American Economic Review* 972.

[28] A Venables, 'Using Natural Resources for Development: Why Has It Proven So Difficult?' (2016) 30 *Journal of Economic Perspectives* 161.

**Figure 2.6** The asset transformation process

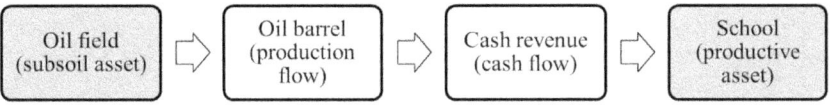

Given the potential terminal decline in oil prices, we consider how a government might manage this process. First, it may seek to 'beat the clock' by increasing the pace of oil production and selling this oil before prices decline. Second, it can seek to increase the *social value* that it generates from oil production via more effective economic policy and stronger governance. Third, it can reorient its approach to public spending and savings, shifting public resources away from risky investments in oil and gas projects and prioritising divestment from the sector. Fourth, it can reduce the amount of oil revenue the country consumes and increase the share of investments that benefits future generations. All of these strategies are difficult to achieve, and there is not clear path given the uncertainty of energy transition. Further, these strategies are not mutually exclusive; a combination of all four to varying degrees is likely suitable for countries.

## A. Beat the Climate Clock – Risk Mitigation or Race to the Bottom?

Some governments could increase production in the hope of benefiting from prices while they remain high. One way to measure this time is the reserves-to-production ratio, which shows how many years it would take for a country to deplete its entire stock of oil if it produced the same amount in the future as it does today.[29] For example, given its immense stock of oil and relatively small production each year, Venezuela would need more than 300 years to deplete its oil wealth. As Figure 2.7 illustrates, based on reserves and production in 2014, there are 29 countries with depletion horizons of more than 30 years, and 20 countries with depletion horizons of more than 50 years. An energy transition as envisioned by our most optimistic scenario described in the previous section would mean the global energy market becoming carbon neutral before some of these countries have depleted their reserves.[30]

Some countries, like Saudi Arabia and some other OPEC countries, often have spare capacity to increase production. If necessary, Saudi Arabia could produce to its capacity and draw down reserves faster.[31] Although the country moderates

---

[29] This measure also assumes no further discoveries.

[30] However, carbon neutrality does not restrict carbon emissions to zero. So limited production from some of these countries might be consistent with these scenarios.

[31] Over the past decade, the OPEC group of countries have had an average spare capacity of 2.3 million barrels of day. Compare this with world oil consumption of 100 barrels per day in 2018.

**Figure 2.7** Oil reserve-to-production for countries with at least 30 years of production remaining

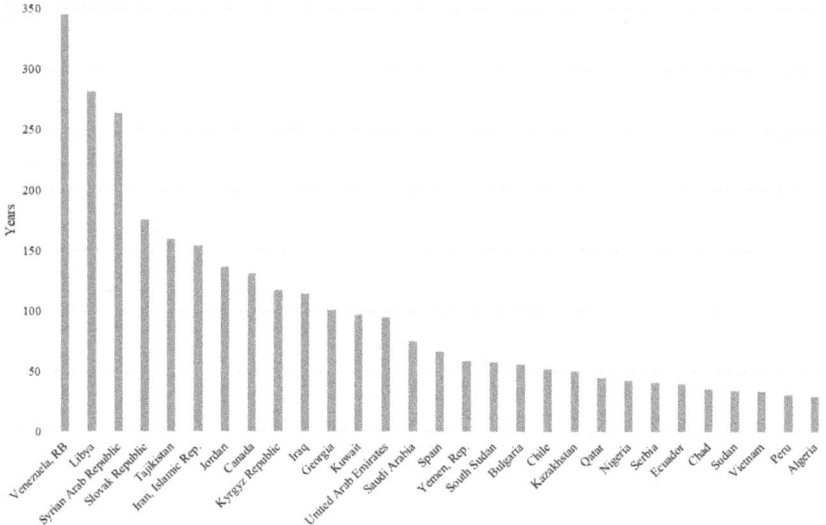

*Source:* Cust and Manley, 'The Carbon Wealth of Nations' (2018).
*Note:* The figures are calculated as reported oil reserves divided by production in 2014. Only countries with depletion horizons of more than 30 years are shown.

this production to try to ensure the price of oil remains high. Other countries do not have this luxury. Instead, their governments can influence how quickly subsoil resources are developed and produced by managing the pace of exploration licensing and by making marginal projects more or less attractive for investors to develop new oil fields.

Governments could focus on increasing the pace by which they license their countries' subsoil for exploration by oil companies. They could do this by increasing the frequency of licensing rounds, increasing the size of oil blocs, or offering incentives to increase investors' expected return, such as reducing taxes or weakening regulations that impose some cost on companies. Improving governance and reducing political risk is also likely to attract more exploration investment to the country.[32] Further, even with speedy licensing, the prospects for actually 'beating the clock' is uncertain.

Once licensed, companies do not automatically start exploring and developing fields, and even once a discovery has been made it can take many years to begin production. Therefore, another element would involve strengthening rules and

US Energy Information Administration, 'Short-term Energy Outlook' (9 July 2019), available at www.eia.gov/outlooks/steo/report/global_oil.php.
[32] J Cust and T Harding, 'Institutions and the location of oil exploration' (2020) 18 *Journal of the European Economic Association* (forthcoming).

incentives for companies to invest in exploring and developing the acreage they control; by shortening time periods allowed for exploration or development; or raising investment requirements attached to licences or contracts. Given the threat from competing renewable energy, oil companies themselves may be willing to accelerate the development of the fields for which they hold a licence. The interests of government and companies may, in principle, be aligned. Otherwise, incentives may be necessary.

Less costly than accelerating the pace of licensing or giving out tax incentives is a stronger approach to choosing the appropriate companies that have the technical and financial capacity to develop fields efficiently. Many licensing rounds include criteria on the technical competency and financial capacity of companies to develop an oil field quickly, efficiently and safely. But poor governance of these procedures can mean the wrong type of company gets the licence.[33]

It is important to understand that, collectively, accelerating production may be a poor strategy for oil producers, and a poor outcome for the climate. This response has been described as the 'green paradox', a situation in which oil producers, in anticipation of a climate policy (such as carbon tax) or dramatic shifts towards more competitive renewable technology, increase production before these changes have set in. The paradox under this scenario is that the anticipation of a climate policy *increases* near-term carbon emissions.[34] Accelerating production therefore risks exacerbating climate change and the related impacts which impose particularly heavy burdens on the people of tropical developing countries, including many that are oil-dependent.

Not only would this extra production contribute to global emissions, acceleration can implicate countries in a 'race to the bottom' in governance standards, which reduces expected benefits and exacerbates governance and environmental challenges. Licensing a larger amount of acreage in a shorter amount of time risks straining oversight capacity and damaging the state's ability to build the institutions required to govern the oil sector effectively. It also risks limiting economic returns, especially if tax incentives reduce the government's fiscal take from the sector. Incentives to develop faster may result in greater impacts on the local environment from weaker regulations, and more dangerous working conditions for employees.

Governments pursuing an accelerated development strategy undertake these risks without any certainty that they will bear strong returns. Investment dollars are finite, and there is a limited effectiveness of fiscal and regulatory incentives to shift private investment to higher-risk, more expensive geological prospects.[35]

---

[33] A Sayne, A Gillies, A Watkins, 'Twelve Red Flags: Corruption Risks in the Award of Extractive Industry Licenses and Contracts' (Natural Resource Governance Institute, 2017).

[34] H Sinn, *The Green Paradox* (MIT Press, 2008).

[35] World Bank, 'Global Investment Competitiveness Report 2017/2018'; and International Monetary Fund 'Options for Low Income Countries' Effective and Efficient Use of Tax Incentives for Investment' (2015).

Further, if a government provides incentives for projects that would have developed quickly in any case, this becomes a cost for the country. Ideally, a government needs to incentivise only the marginal projects – those that would not have developed without the incentive. But practically speaking, identifying these projects is difficult as governments typically don't have sufficient information on the costs of the prospective project.

## B.  Generate More Social Value per Barrel

An alternative to increasing production is to increase the *value* that governments earn from each barrel of oil extracted. Many of the lessons learned about governance of extractive industries – even absent energy transition considerations – apply here.[36] But they may take on a special urgency for oil producers facing growing uncertainties and thus a stronger imperative to make the most out of their extraction. Several steps stand out:

### i.  Taxing Companies

Rather than maximising the number of barrels of oil produced, governments could focus on maximising revenue collected on each barrel. This might involve both increasing the tax burden and ensuring that actual payments reflect the increase tax burden.

### ii.  Prolonging Current Operating Fields

Governments could encourage companies to prolong the operational life of oil fields. This can have a more immediate effect for government revenue than accelerating the development of new fields, as the former have paid off more capital expenditure and so are more likely to be profit-making and tax-paying positions. This might be achieved by incentives for the company or enabling licences to be sold to companies specialised in operating mature fields.

### iii.  Reducing Fossil Fuel Subsidies on Domestic Consumption

Subsidies on consuming oil and gas are common, including in oil- and gas-rich countries.[37] As well as being a strain on government budgets and benefiting the

---

[36] For an encapsulation of best practices for resource governance see Natural Resource Governance Institute, 'Natural Resource Charter – Second Edition' (2014).

[37] D Coady, I Parry, N Le and B Shang, 'Global Fossil Fuel Subsidies Remain Large: An Update Based on Country-Level Estimates'. International Monetary Fund working paper (2019).

rich more than the poor,[38] subsidies reduce the proportion of a country's oil and gas production that it can export. For many governments this reduces the available revenue, as export prices are often higher than domestic prices for the oil or gas. Eliminating these subsidies may therefore release more oil and gas for export. Further, in the longer term, a relatively cheap supply of fossil fuels may have made the economies of fossil fuel-rich countries more carbon intensive, and may limit the competitiveness of renewable energy in these countries.[39]

### iv. Improving Transparency, Accountability and Government Institutions

A potentially least-cost approach could be establishing petroleum laws that promise a reasonable level of stability for investors, as well as establishing open government and strong accountability processes. Such measures also help the country benefit from oil extraction.[40] However, developing government institutions that are effective enough to offer this stability and help the country benefit from oil and gas extraction can take many years. In the past, a slow development of the resource might have been a better approach to develop these institutions.[41] But this may be too slow, given the risks of an energy transition.

## C. Stop Capital Reinjection into the Oil Sector

The two approaches discussed so far emphasise attempts to increase government ability to generate value from subsoil fossil fuels. This third approach represents a more fundamental attempt to divest from fossil fuels by changing the way that a government approaches public spending.

Oil-rich countries face strong incentives to invest large shares of their capital back into the petroleum business, including by establishing and retaining capital in NOCs, and encouraging domestic businesses and workers to participate in the oil and gas industry and its supply chain. This can involve both a country's financial and human capital. For instance, hundreds of young engineering graduates seeking employment in the oil business rather than in manufacturing and service sectors.

---

[38] For instance, the wealthiest 20% in developing countries get a disproportionate 43% of the benefit from fossil fuel subsidies, while the poorest 20% get only 7%. A del Granado, F Javier, D Coady, and R Gillingham, 'The Unequal Benefits of Fuel Subsidies: A Review of Evidence for Developing Countries' (2012) 40 *World Development* 2234.

[39] J Friedrichs and O Inderwildi, 'The carbon curse: Are fuel rich countries doomed to high $CO_2$ intensities?' (2013) 62 *Energy Policy* 1356.

[40] A measure of how transparent and accountable governments are in managing the transformation process is provided by: Natural Resource Governance Institute, 'Resource Governance Index' (2017).

[41] P Stevens, G Lahn and J Kooroshy, 'The Resource Curse Revisited', Chatham House Research Paper (2015).

## i.  NOCs as Vehicles for Public Spending

A common rationale for governments to spend in the oil business is to gain a greater share of the benefits of production. Governments can gain a share of the financial benefits by taxing companies more, but oil- and gas-rich countries often aim to also increase 'national control' over the industry. A second incentive is political power of NOCs. The concentration of national wealth, expertise and political connections can in extreme cases make NOCs a true state within their states. In many oil-dependent countries, NOCs lie at the centre of the structures employed to convert oil and gas assets into revenue.

NOCs control much of the money generated by a country's oil industry. As noted above, huge shares of public revenues pass through the hands of NOCs in a large number of oil-dependent countries. Unless they are subject to strong oversight, NOCs may have little incentive to remit the money to the government treasury (where it could be used to invest outside the industry). In 2013, there were 45 NOCs worldwide that published sufficient information to determine the share of company gross revenues that were transferred to governments via taxes, royalties, dividends and other transfers. The median NOC in this sample transferred only 23 per cent of revenues to government. This number dropped to 17 per cent by 2015, when prices had fallen. NOCs spend most of what they do not transfer to government on operational and capital costs.[42]

The public nature of NOC spending has major implications for how we consider their spending. An NOC that spends a large share (even the majority, in many cases) of its revenues is, essentially, taking public revenue generated by the nation's subsoil assets and reinvesting them right back into the sector – concentrating the country's wealth in the oil sector rather than diversifying. The rules governing how much an NOC must transfer to its government often give significant scope for NOC managers to make spending decisions in line with the company's strategic and growth plans, without in-depth analysis by the NOC or government of the risk-reward opportunity cost of forsaken public investment.

Traditionally, the decision to allow NOCs to spend such large shares of the public revenues they manage has often been justified by a growth mindset. If, over time, an NOC grew into a technically and commercially effective company, it could help the country capture a greater share of the rents from its natural resources and drive the pace of extraction in line with national priorities.[43] The track record of NOCs in achieving these goals has always been mixed. The prospect of terminal decline in oil and gas prices makes waiting for these benefits riskier. A government has to compare the time it will take for an NOC to develop and give back benefits for the country against the prospect of oil and gas prices declining before this happens.

---

[42] Heller and Mihalyi (n 11).

[43] D Victor, D Hults and M Thurber, 'Introduction and Overview' in D Victor, D Hults and M Thurber (eds), *Oil and Governance: State-Owned Enterprises and the World Energy Supply* (Cambridge University Press, 2012).

## ii. Incentives and Weak Oversight to Control National Oil Company Borrowing (Claims on Future Revenue)

Furthermore, NOCs not only hold a substantial share of public wealth and manage government revenue, but have the potential to require additional infusions of public funds if they do not manage the energy transition successfully. Many of the world's NOCs already hold large amounts of debts – effectively claims on future oil and gas revenues, the opposite of bringing forward the benefits described above. For example, Azerbaijan's NOC (SOCAR) held debts worth more than 27 per cent of GDP in 2017.[44] Many others hold debt worth at least 10 per cent of GDP. This is a significant amount, particularly when compared with all other debt their governments hold. Worse, a few of these companies – such as Mexico's Pemex – have negative equity. If their governments were to completely sell off the shares in these companies, the value they would receive from the equity would not be enough to cover the long-term liabilities.

While this capital helps NOCs to invest for future returns, large debt-to-equity positions make some NOCs vulnerable to a fall in oil prices, and an impending bankruptcy may implicate the rest of the country. NOCs are often major employers in their country,[45] and some are strongly linked to the country's financial system. Lenders might be economically important banks or other agents in the country, or even state banks – the government may have tied up even more public capital in its NOC. A government may wish to bail out its NOC rather than have unemployed workers or non-payment of debt create problems with other investors.

This might result in investors considering some state-owned companies to be 'too big to fail'. A number of countries have needed to bail out their NOCs after the fall in prices in 2014 – including Mexico, where as of early 2019 the Government had announced plans for injections of funds of nearly USD four billion.[46] Gradually falling prices could reduce equity values, and, without sufficient controls over NOCs accumulating debt and managing their finances in general, NOCs could respond by borrowing more, making future bail-outs more likely.

In spite of their significance, many NOCs are not subject to strong oversight or scrutiny for their use of public resources. Of the 52 NOCs researched for the 2017 Resource Governance Index – which measures transparency and accountability in oil- and mineral-rich countries worldwide – 62 per cent exhibited 'weak', 'poor' or 'failing' performance on public transparency and institutional checks and balances.[47] Without the possibility for strong scrutiny by citizens and public oversight bodies, there may be a strong disconnect between what the NOC does and the wider interests of the country.

---

[44] National Oil Company Database.

[45] Heller and Mihalyi (n 11).

[46] A Martinez and D Garcia, 'Mexico to Inject $3.9 Billion in Pemex, Seeks to Prevent Credit Downgrade', Reuters (15 February 2019).

[47] 'Resource Governance Index' (2017).

## iii.  *Difficulties in Divesting from an NOC*

As the prospects for energy transition change the calculus on NOC spending and debt, governments may consider reducing or reorienting NOC spending and borrowing, or selling shares of their NOCs on private markets. Such attempts would require overcoming at least two hurdles. First, selling an NOC (or even a share of an NOC) appears difficult for companies that are not transparently governed. Finances must be revealed, and truths about actual reserves and liabilities reckoned with, which tends to be politically challenging. Second, government owners of NOCs must find investors who think there is a profitable enough future in the oil business, and one that is free of government intrusion. If increasing numbers of investors start to expect a terminal decline in oil and gas prices, the asking price for NOC shares will decline.

Given the incentives for NOCs to retain political and economic power, a potentially more feasible approach is to move capital from oil and gas to the renewable sector within the NOC. Some governments are calling on their NOCs to invest in renewable energy sources to help the country's energy transition. But there are reasons to be sceptical of the likely success of such initiatives, not least because NOCs are so entrenched in the fossil fuel business and the politics associated with it; developing expertise in renewable energy may challenge some NOCs.[48]

## D.  Save and Invest Oil Revenues to Diversify Economy

The final state in the transformation process, after getting the oil out of the ground and monetising it, has been transforming this money into other assets that can support economic prosperity. Given a possible terminal decline in oil and gas prices, this final stage of diversifying an economy becomes an even greater imperative for oil-rich countries. In general, this involves saving a high portion of revenues from oil and gas production and investing these revenues either in foreign assets (such as Norway's Government Pension Fund Global) or within their own economies. The latter is particularly suitable for lower-income, capital-scarce countries.

A common way to measure how well countries follow the transformation process is the adjusted net saving rate. It takes into account income generated from the depletion of fossil fuels, the depreciation of all forms of capital in the economy (including damage to natural capital), and investments in physical assets and human capital (measured as the expenditure on education and health). A positive savings rate indicates the country is depleting the subsoil asset, but saving a sufficient share of the cash generated to be accumulating net assets elsewhere in the

---

[48] P Heller and D Manley, 'Fiscal futures: are national oil companies champions or obstacles for energy transition?' (International Budget Partnership, 2019), available at www.internationalbudget.org/2019/05/fiscal-futures-are-national-oil-companies-champions-or-obstacles-for-energy-transition.

**Figure 2.8** National oil company long-term liabilities to total government revenue (average of 2011–2017)

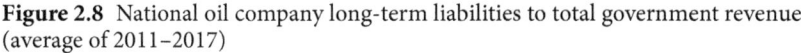

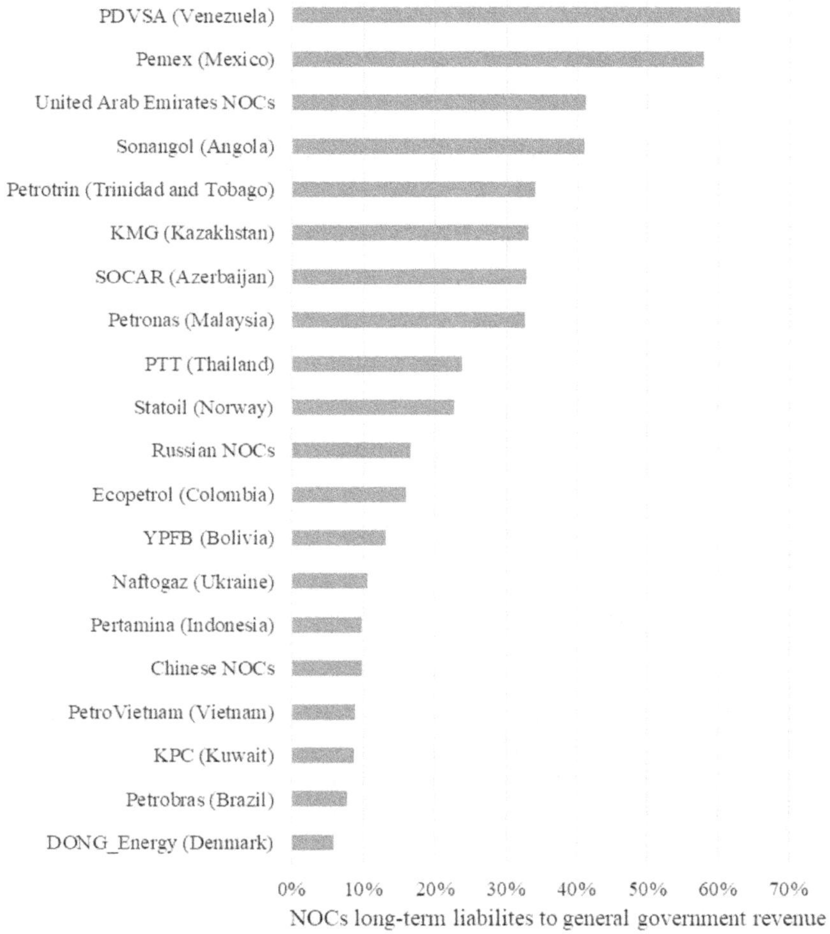

*Source:* National Oil Company Database.

economy. A negative savings rate means the country is selling its non-renewable resources and running down its overall asset base.

So far, the savings rate for many oil-rich countries has been poor.[49] Some of these countries have seen average rates that are negative, meaning that while they have depleted their subsoil resources, they have failed to use the proceeds to accumulate other assets.

---

[49] A Venables, 'Using Natural Resources for Development' (2016); A Warner, 'Natural Resource Booms in the Modern Era: Is the Curse Still Alive?' (International Monetary Fund Working Papers, 2015).

**Figure 2.9**  Adjusted net savings of resource-rich countries

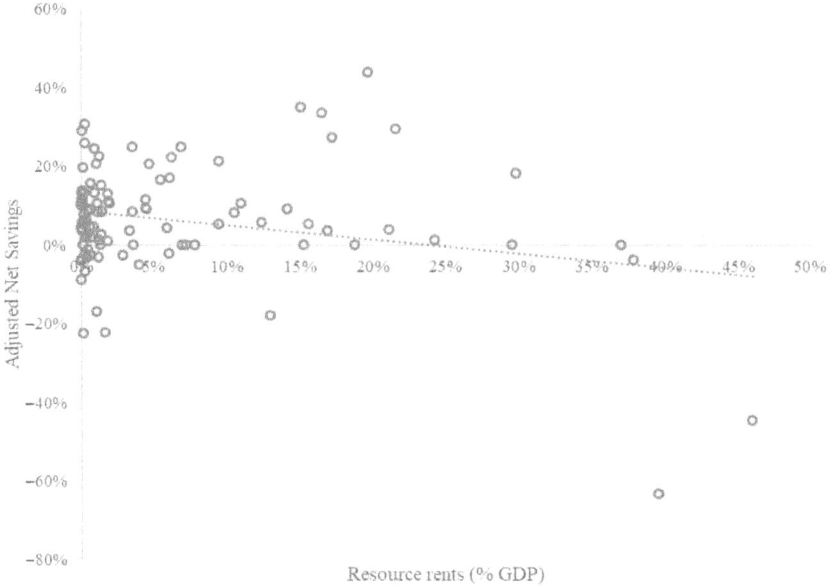

*Source:* Cust and Manley, 'The Carbon Wealth of Nations' (2018).

*Note:* Resource-rich countries (including oil, gas, and minerals), defined as countries having non-renewable resource rents greater than two per cent of GDP averaged over 2004–14.

At a fundamental level, increasing the resilience of economies that are today dependent on fossil fuels requires reversing this trend. But convincing citizens to accept higher savings rates – and therefore less immediate consumption – will challenge many governments. And without well-governed institutions managing the saving and spending of these revenues, the effort may be wasted. Further, these countries will have even less time to develop these institutions.[50]

# VI.  Country Contexts may Determine How Far to Pursue Each Strategy

To complicate matters further, the appropriate mix of strategies may also depend on the specific context in which each country exists. There are at least three factors that are relevant here.[51] And in each case, governments have the potential to change these factors to varying degrees – thus improving their ability to implement a mix of strategies.

---

[50] R Ploeg, 'Fossil Fuel Producers Under Threat' (2016) 32 *Oxford Review of Economic Policy* 206.

[51] A similar line of reasoning and set of factors is described in A Goldthau and K Westphal, 'Why the Global Energy Transition Does Not Mean the End of the Petrostate' (2019) 10 *Global Policy* 189.

## A. Costs of Development and Production

The cost of producing a barrel of oil differs across individual fields, and across countries. For instance, in 2016 extracting a barrel in Saudi Arabia cost on average USD 9, while in the UK the cost was USD 44.[52] Those oil fields with the highest costs are most exposed to a terminal fall in oil and gas prices. Production costs fall as the oil price falls, but usually not as fast.[53] Therefore, a long-term fall in prices implies a faster decline in taxable profits available to producing countries. The smaller the proportion of rents to revenue in a particular country, the faster the corresponding decline. High-cost (low-rent) countries will experience a steeper decline, even if those countries with absolute larger production amounts see a larger absolute decline in revenues.

For high-cost countries, it may therefore be appropriate to bring forward production and benefits, and divest the country's capital from these fields. However, these may also be the assets companies are least willing to operate themselves if they also expect a falling oil price. To encourage faster development and production may require incentives that ultimately reduce benefits for the country.

## B. Economic Dependence

The more dependent a country's economy and its government is on oil production, the greater will be the economic and social consequences from a fall in oil prices. Dependency can be high even if production costs are low, as the sector is generating more income for the country. Bringing forward revenues from oil and investing these elsewhere in the economy may reduce this dependency. But, conversely, the greater the dependency on the oil sector, the more likely that the political power of the oil sector in the country will be strong – so achieving this may be more difficult.

Those countries with dependence on oil, low costs of production and large enough production volumes to influence global prices face a dilemma. As of 2016, Saudi Arabia, the UAE, Iran, Iraq and Kuwait produced about 30 per cent of world production, at an average cost below USD 10 per barrel. These countries, under OPEC, may have the market power to influence the global oil price by increasing production rates, forcing other countries to stop production. However, they also have a 'social cost of production': they rely on high revenues from selling oil to fund their government spending, social welfare payments, and in some cases large

---

Another scenario analysis considers the compositing strategies of IOCs against IOCs, and IOCS and NOCs; see B Caldecott, I Holmes, L Kruitwagen, D Orozco and S Tomlinson, 'Crude Awakening: Making Oil Major Business Models Climate-Compatible' (E3G, 2018).

[52] Combined capital and operating cost: Rystad Energy, 'UCUBE database', available at www.rystad energy.com.

[53] G Toews and A Naumov, 'The Relationship Between Oil Price and Costs in the Oil and Gas Industry', Oxford Centre for the Analysis of Resource Rich Economies Working Paper (2015).

military budgets.[54] In periods of low oil prices, these countries may try to increase production to keep overall revenues high enough to fund government budgets.

## C. Governance Standard

A third factor is the quality of governance in a country.[55] Better governance of the oil sector is likely to lead to more investment overall.[56] Those countries with an established set of institutions and history of extraction may be able to develop their reserves faster, if they wish. And are likely in a better position to manage a process of transforming oil assets into aboveground assets. Emerging producers – and countries still developing these institutions – may not have enough time to effectively manage oil revenues.

# VII.  Conclusions

Previous studies have suggested that following a process of transforming subsoil oil assets into human and physical assets above ground is likely the best path to economic development.[57] This chapter asks how countries might manage this transformation process, given the uncertainty that a potential energy transition creates. To conclude, we outline the rationale, policies, and risks of each part of the transformation process.

| Strategy: Beat the climate clock | |
|---|---|
| *Rationale* | Brings forward extraction of oil reserves to sell before the possible terminal decline in oil prices, so may reduce state-held stranded assets. |
| *Policies* | Accelerate licensing, provide investment incentives, eliminate restrictions on production rates and mandate national oil companies to pump faster. Better governance is also likely to attract investment. |
| *Risks* | Production not only contributes to increased global emissions, but may also be hollow for the country. Country may fail to manage the transformation process and this production is not transformed into lasting benefits. If energy transition is slower than expected, this strategy risks rushing production needlessly. |

---

[54] S Dale and B Fattouh, 'Peak oil demand and long-run prices' (Oxford Institute for Energy Studies, 2018).

[55] See NRGI, 'Resource Governance Index' (n 40) for an approach to measuring the aspects of governance related to oil and gas extraction for the benefit of producer countries.

[56] Cust and Harding, 'Institutions and the Location of Oil Exploration' (2017).

[57] Studies summarised in NRGI, 'Natural Resource Charter' (2014).

| Strategy: Generate more social value per barrel | |
|---|---|
| *Rationale* | Since oil production is typically a means to an end for countries, improving governance and reducing fuel subsidies is likely to be appropriate whatever the pace of energy transition. |
| *Policies* | Increase taxes; prolong currently operating fields; reduce fossil fuel subsidies; improve overall transparency and accountability; and fight corruption. |
| *Risks* | If energy transition is faster than expected, this strategy risks the country not improving governance sufficiently to increase social returns per barrel. While for many countries, improving performance in this area has been difficult. |

| Strategy: Stop capital reinjection back into the oil sector | |
|---|---|
| *Rationale* | Diversifies economy and government tax base, so reduces exposure to a potential fall in oil prices. Avoids potential 'too big to fail' and other debt problems in NOCs. Frees up oil revenues for investment in other sectors. |
| *Policies* | Divest state capital from NOC, strong oversight over NOC retention of oil revenues, investment and borrowing, increased national saving rate and higher government investment in human capital, infrastructure and other means to support growth in non-oil sector. |
| *Risks* | Potentially reduces some upside return that a government can achieve from the oil sector. To the extent the NOC provides net benefits to the country, if energy transition is slower than expected the country may lose from divesting too early. However, in such a context, selling shares in the NOC may be easier, while the country may also enjoy a return from using the proceeds from the NOC sale. |

| Strategy: Save and invest oil revenue to diversify economy | |
|---|---|
| *Rationale* | If a government expects an energy transition to reduce the total value of their country's oil, increasing the rate of national savings is necessary to ensure the economy has alternative assets to generate social benefits. |
| *Policies* | Increase investment in human capital, infrastructure and other assets. If the economy's absorptive capacity is limited, parking revenue in foreign assets may be required before investing within the country. Strengthening budgeting and government spending processes to ensure savings targets are met and government spending is effective. |
| *Risks* | If an energy transition is slower than expected, a higher rate of saving risks unwarranted reduction in consumption spending for people's welfare today. If investment is poorly governed, higher spending on infrastructure and other investments may be poorly executed and wasteful. |

Beating the clock and pumping oil faster out of the ground may be the easiest of the four strategies to follow. But if not backed up by efforts to transform this production into lasting benefits for the country, this may just be hollow production. Worse, the green paradox concept suggests this 'panic and pump' approach would have severe implications for the world's attempts to limit climate change. Further, all four strategies likely require preparation and sufficient time to execute. If governments continue as business as usual and do not recognise the potential threat of energy transition, they may run out of time to develop the policies and institutions they need to manage the possible decline without severe hardship for their citizens.

Whatever approach governments take, the consequences of these strategies may be overshadowed by the challenges many of these countries face as the climate changes. Betting on a Business as Usual scenario may be the right strategy if the global economy fails to sufficiently transition to renewable energy, but this may be a pyrrhic victory in the long term. Similarly, the global community in general should hope that oil-rich governments make the right choices, as the possible resulting financial crises, sovereign defaults and increasing poverty in these countries could become unwanted additional challenges to address while the world seeks to transition away from burning fossil fuels and towards generating renewable energy.

# Rules-based Multilateral
# Governance of the Energy Sector

# 3

# A Treatise for Energy Law

RAPHAEL J HEFFRON, ANITA RØNNE, JOSEPH P
TOMAIN, ADRIAN BRADBROOK AND KIM TALUS**

## Abstract

It is now over twenty years since the seminal paper on energy law as a discipline
was published. The aim of this paper is to review what currently constitutes energy
law after this 20-year hiatus. There are two main ambitions of this paper, which we
hope will have a similar impact on the field. The first is to develop for scholars and
practitioners a view of what constitutes energy law – and to make this accessible
to both law and non-law energy scholars. The second is to advance a set of core
principles that guide energy law, in essence a treatise for energy law. We advocate
for a paradigm-shift in our current understanding of what constitutes energy law.
We advance that it should revolve around this set of guiding principles; however,
we acknowledge that to some degree it is perhaps not a paradigm-shift due to the
current absence of any core principles of energy law. Nevertheless we argue that in
our advancing of a guiding set of principles we set out a new path for the study of
energy law and thus we aim to change what constitutes energy law and challenge
the assumptions of existing researchers as globally society moves towards a transition to low-carbon economies.

## Introduction

A review of what constitutes 'energy law' as a discipline in academic literature
is currently needed with the last such review completed over 20 years ago.[1]

** Corresponding Author: R.J. Heffron r.heffron@qmul.ac.uk. This chapter reproduces a joint article
in honour of Anita Ronne who passed away in late 2018. It was an honour and privilege for all the
authors to work with her on this paper over a two-year process. She was an inspiration. The article is
reproduced with thanks to Oxford University Press and their Journal of World Energy Law & Business:
R.J. Heffron, A. Ronne, A. Bradbrook, J.P. Tomain, and K. Talus, 'A Treatise for Energy Law' (2018) 11
*Journal of World Energy Law & Business* 34–48.
[1] A. Bradbrook, 'Energy Law as an Academic Discipline' (1996) 14 *Journal Energy and Natural
Resources Law* 193–217.

There are many reasons for this both in legal practice and in research. Over the past three decades, largely because of privatization and liberalization of energy markets across the globe, the ongoing "energy transition" (primarily related to climate change considerations), and the internationalization of and changes in energy markets, energy law as a legal discipline has grown and matured.

In practice, energy law has flourished, with energy law and related legal practice becoming one of the major practice areas.[2] Indeed, in considering energy law from a practice perspective, governments have identified the importance of energy and put it high on the political agenda due both to its environmental impact and its economic consequences. There have for example, been government 'Energy Departments' and energy regulators in many countries for a long-time – spurred by the oil crisis of the 1970s for the former and by the liberalization trends in the 1980s and 1990s for the latter. Further, now legal job advertisements in the energy sector have increased both in academia and practice. Private law firms across the globe have created specific energy practice areas focusing on all facets of energy markets, from extraction to production to transportation and end use. As noted elsewhere, *"there are hundreds of different industries, and only a few have, so far, given rise to a particular professional and academic sub-discipline"*, and energy is one where this has happened.[3]

In academia, while a debate of what constitutes energy law has continued for three decades this has only occurred to a very limited extent. The aim of this paper is to return to this debate and update and advance the literature. Although to some degree environmental, climate change and energy law are interrelated, energy law has not evaluated itself and grown theoretically as the other two have. For example, we identify later in this paper how environmental law has developed core principles that have not only been adopted legally into international, European, national and local law, but also outside the legal profession by the business sector and the general public.

The origin and debate of what constitutes energy law is evident in the leading texts on energy law, albeit only mentioned to a limited extent. It is only recently, however, that academics are moving to analyse this in more detail again and advance energy law as an academic field.[4] And it should be remembered that the last paper to do this was Adrian Bradbrook's 1996 seminal paper entitled

---

[2] For example, energy practices can range from 10 to 50% of a firm's revenues in many cases.

[3] K. Talus, *EU Energy Law and Policy: a Critical Account* (Oxford University Press 2013).

[4] There are a number of early texts and papers in this regard, see for example: (1) M.M. Roggenkamp, C. Redgwell, A. Rønne, and I. del Guayo (eds.), *Energy Law in Europe* (Oxford University Press: Oxford) (1st ed, 2001) p. 7, and (3rd ed, 2016) p. 8 and on the concept of EU Energy Law, p. 188; (2) R.J. Heffron and K. Talus, 'The Evolution of Energy Law and Energy Jurisprudence: Insights for Energy Analysts and Researchers' (2016) 19 *Energy Research and Social Science* 1–10; (3) R.J. Heffron and K. Talus, 'The development of energy law in the 21st century: a paradigm shift?' (2016) 9 *Journal of World Energy Law and Business* 189–202; (4) A. Wawryk, 'International Energy Law as an Academic Discipline', in P. Babie and P. Leadbeter (eds), *Law as Change: Engaging with the Life and Scholarship of Adrian Bradbrook* (University of Adelaide Press, 2014) 223–255.

*Energy Law as an Academic Discipline.*[5] In other areas of the law and in energy studies this is completed on a more regular basis. In contrast, energy law has suffered from attempts at splintering it further with some scholars suggesting separate legal areas for oil and gas (*lex petrolia*), and for mining (*lex mineralia*); however, recently Daintith has critiqued extensively the aim of scholars to state there should be such a energy law area as *lex petrolea*[6] and the same can be said for *lex mineralia*.

This paper reviews what currently constitutes energy law after a near 20-year hiatus in doing so (21 years since Bradbrook's paper),[7] and also advances principles that guide energy law. In essence, we advocate for a paradigm shift in our current thinking of energy law; to some degree it should be stated it is not a paradigm shift due to there being no core set of principles of energy law. We argue that in our advancing of guiding principles we set out a new path for the study and practice of energy law and thus we aim to shift what constitutes energy law and assist in challenging and developing current assumptions of existing researchers. This is of vital importance as globally countries are transitioning to low-carbon economies. Further, energy law also has to reach out beyond just the energy law community and appeal to more practitioners, and interdisciplinary energy researchers as well as the public. In this context energy law has been less successful than environmental law where its principles (stated in Table 1 below) have been far more effective and have found their way into legislation at local, national and international levels.

**Table 1**  Principles of Environmental Law

| |
|---|
| • **The principle of a high level of environmental protection** |
| • The polluter-pays principle |
| • The principle of prevention |
| • The precautionary principle |
| • The principle that environmental damage should, as a matter of priority, be remedied at source |
| • The principle of responsibility for transboundary harm |
| • The principle of public participation |
| • The principle of sustainable development |
| • The principle of integration |
| • Inter-generational and intra-generational equity |
| • Access and benefit sharing regarding natural resources |

---

[5] See Bradbrook (note 1).

[6] Terrence Daintith, 'Against '*lex petrolea*'' (2017) 10 *The Journal of World Energy Law & Business* 1–13.

[7] It is now 21 years, but this project was begun in early 2016. See also Bradbrook (note 1) 193–217.

In addition, in considering the energy transition, energy law has to some degree been a forgotten discipline.[8] There are few legal principles of law specific to the energy field and most energy issues have to be resolved by general principles of law established in other contexts (such as contracts, torts or property law). Even where specific laws exist in relation to energy, they are often inadequate and ill-suited to impact upon the energy transition, and even if *"Laws on the book are one thing. Laws implemented and enforced are another."*[9] There are numerous examples where general areas of law rather than energy-related laws have been the decisive factor in legal decision-making. One illustration is the Deepwater Horizon incident in the US in 2010, where the legal solution came from tort law rather than any principles or theories of energy law itself.[10] In the solar access context, where disputes arise over shading of solar collectors by buildings or vegetation on neighbouring properties, similar use had to be made of the tort of private nuisance to provide a remedy for the solar user in cases such as *Prah v Maretti*.[11] The fault lies with both the legislature and the courts. The courts have been slow and reluctant to develop new principles and the legislatures have failed to take appropriate action to support the energy transition. In the future there should surely at the very least be some reference to principles and/or theories of energy law in the resolution of energy-related disputes.[12]

# 1. A Review of What Constitutes Energy Law

In advancing the principles of energy law, the question arises of what energy law is. There is a rather limited academic literature, which discusses this but more recently several key leading texts from 2015 and 2016 have raised this issue. These latter texts and the key literature are discussed in the proceeding paragraphs.

Many of the key texts (literature) in this area since the Bradbrook article twenty years ago ask the question – what is energy law – in some way, but all fall short of advancing a more complete definition, or suggesting a theoretical framework

---

[8] This has been an on-going problem for decades: see A. Bradbrook, 'Energy Law: The Neglected Aspect of Environmental Law' (1993) 19 *Melbourne University Law Review* 1–19.

[9] D.N. Zillman, C. Redgwell, and L. Barrera-Hernandez (eds.), *Beyond the carbon economy: energy law in transition* (Oxford University Press: Oxford, United Kingdom, 2008), 551.

[10] For a discussion of the outcome of liability and in relation to the Deepwater Horizon incident see: R. Heffron, S. Ashley, W. Nuttall, 'The Global Nuclear Liability Regime Post Fukushima Daiichi' (2016) *Progress in Nuclear Energy* 1–10.

[11] (1981) 2 Solar Law Reporter 1013 (Circuit Ct); (1982) 108 Wis 2d 223, 321 NW 2d 182 (Wisconsin Sup Ct). Discussed in (1983) 21 *Duquesne Law Review* 1159. See also A. Bradbrook, *Solar energy and the law* (Law Book Co: Sydney, Australia, 1984).

[12] Contrast this conservatism and inaction with the occasional judicial cry for change. As long ago as 1904, Griffith CJ of the High Court of Australia posed obiter the possibility of a novel easement of access to the sun's rays to protect solar access: *Commonwealth v Registrar of Titles for Victoria* (1918) 24 CLR 348, 354.

or advancing guiding principles. As the following discussion below highlights, scholars[13] have been demonstrating thinking in this direction, but as of yet they have not made the final step towards advancing what constitutes energy law on a more holistic basis. Indeed, the same can be said for practitioners, who have perhaps had more success in contributing to the development of energy law, with contributions ranging from model-contracts[14] to practitioner texts, case law developments and legal issues from day-to-day practice. However, as of yet, energy law has not benefited from a set of principles like environmental or climate change law, which have through these principles engaged more effectively with non-law scholars and practitioners, and also the judiciary and policy-makers.[15]

## Assessing the literature

There are a core set of leading texts on energy law. Many of these debate in the first chapter of the book what is energy law. However, few debate this in depth but there are several in need of highlighting. In considering one of the leading texts in this area, *EU Energy Law*[16] (Roggenkamp et al.) it is evident this is the case. The latter text has a section on 'Energy Law as an Academic Discipline' and it details the definition (according to Bradbrook's seminal definition) and also his eight 'social considerations' and seven 'jurisprudential considerations'. The multi-disciplinarity of energy law is mentioned while an important statement is made that 'Although energy law is gradually developing as an academic discipline in Europe it is still very diverse in its approach'. Both the first and second edition of the book follow each other in this context. (pg. 8, 1st Ed., pg. 10 2nd ed). Importantly the observation is also made that '… developments at EC level may lead to a more common approach to and standardization in this field'. With the third edition stating the same fifteen years later, it adds a view on EU energy law as the evolution of a distinctive legal field and not merely a case of applying general EU law to the energy sector, and concludes that "there is no longer any doubt that a discrete subgenre of EU law has emerged". (pg 188). Another supplement is a statement on the need to consider the boundaries of "European Energy Law" (pg 1234).

In *EU Energy Law and Policy: a Critical Account*, Talus asks the question "Is there such a thing as 'European Energy Law'?" He does not give a comprehensive definition for "energy law" or EU energy law but argues that "The answer one might

---

[13] In particular, Daintith notes the benefit of developing a subject discipline within law; see section 2 in the paper cited note 6.

[14] For example, model contracts have been developed by many organizations, in particular Association for International Petroleum Negotiators (AIPN), the International Bar Association, and the OECD.

[15] For example, the polluter-pays-principle is a great example of this.

[16] M. Roggenkamp, C. Redgwell, A. Rønne, I. del Guayo, *Energy Law in Europe*. (3rd, Oxford University Press, Oxford, 2016).

give to this question depends on the specificity of the particular problems experienced by the energy industries in relation to EU law, the level of interest – public, professional, academic and commercial – in these problems, EU law's response to them, and distinctive, significant features which permit focus on the economic regulation of energy by the EU and in the EU with some degree of insulation from other industries."[17]

It is important in this context to refer to the engagement of other legal scholars with energy law, something that does not take place to the degree energy lawyers could hope for. For example in the *Oxford Handbook of EU Law*, although the editors note "It is a truism that the European Union has grown out of (nearly) all recognition since its birth as the European Coal and Steel Community in the early 1950s)" and in essence acknowledge the importance of managing energy resources. However, the book fails to have any chapter on energy, and consequently fails to account for one division of the Commission – they overlook 1 out of the 12 EU Commissions.[18]

There are other texts that review to a limited extent what energy law is. The IUCN Academy of Environmental Law Research Studies produced a text on Compendium of Sustainable Energy Laws.[19] They call for a broadening of the definition of energy law away from just addressing: 'how to generate electricity, mine coal, extract oil and gas, and distribute energy sources. It needs also to focus on energy efficiency, demand side management, and the sustainable use of energy. Indeed, they call for a 'law of sustainable energy' discipline (Preface X). However, they fail in part to consider the full energy life-cycle, and therefore their approach remains a limited view of energy law. In contrast, Bradbrook and Wahnschaft[20] propose guidelines on sustainable energy production and consumption. They produce a 'non-legally binding statement of principles for a global consensus on sustainable energy production and consumption'. This includes a focus on efficiency in supply and consumption; energy pricing; mitigation of environmental impacts; consumer information and environmental education; policies and strategies for implementation; and international cooperation. (p. 196-201). To a degree this article is an exception to the rest of the literature and this article aims to builds on these authors' efforts.

Makuch and Pereira produce a different edited collection on *Environmental and energy law*.[21] However, it is mainly an environmental text and is to a degree a good example of the failure to appreciate environmental law and energy law as separate disciplines. Another example of a similar omission is McHarg *et al.*

---

[17] Talus (note 3).

[18] A. Arnull, D. Chalmers (eds), *The Oxford Handbook of European Union Law* (Oxford University Press, 2015), Preface.

[19] R.L. Ottinger, N. Robinson, and V. Tafur (eds), *Compendium of Sustainable Energy Law* (Cambridge University Press, 2005).

[20] A. Bradbrook and R. Wahnschaft, *The Law of Energy for Sustainable Development* (CUP, 2005).

[21] K. E. Makuch, R. Pereira, R, *Environmental and energy law* (Oxford, Wiley-Blackwell, 2012).

where again while energy law is mentioned in the title, the focus of the book is on Property Law (though in an energy law context), and the meaning of 'energy law' is not defined.[22] A more advanced approach is the book, *Energy law and the environment*, by Rosemary Lyster and Adrian Bradbrook, where the authors explain the relevance of the environment and environmental law to energy but emphasise the need for energy law, both at national and international levels, to develop its own independent goals and principles to provide for a sustainable energy future.[23]

This article aims to build on the previous literature and the directions many scholars pointed towards in advancing a set of principles for energy law. In the next section these principles are advanced and then in the following section stated in more depth.

## 2. Energy Law's Seven Principles

What prompted this search for Energy Law's guiding principles was a workshop (organized by two of the authors and attended by a third) where we presented and discussed the Evolution of Energy Law.[24] The evolution of energy law is guided by certain influences, one of which is 'energy justice'. Energy justice has its own conceptual basis, which is recognised in several early and now more influential articles. However, energy justice has its own principles and this prompted what would be energy law's guiding principles. Energy justice as a concept and its principles have an interdisciplinary focus.[25] Energy law has to concern itself also with what law is and what it should be and this prompted a need to examine and identify what the guiding principles of energy law should be and the role that law can have in the development of the concept of energy justice.

The prompt to determine guiding principles of a discipline are many. For energy law & climate change scholars the need for guiding principles is clear. It will assist in the understanding of the design and development of a legal field that has been shaped in a piecemeal fashion in response to different geopolitical circumstances and increasing environmental and costs awareness impacting the whole global society. Its related subject, environmental law, has a clear core and guiding

---

[22] McHarg, A, Barton, B, Bradbrook, A and Godden, L (2010) *Property and the law in energy and natural resources* (OUP, 2010).

[23] R. Lyster, A. Bradbrook, *Energy law and the environment* (Sydney, Cambridge University Press, 2006).

[24] The early-movers in this project can be said to be those who attended a workshop organized jointly by Raphael Heffron and Kim Talus entitled 'The Development of the Theory of Energy Law', Helsinki, Finland (November 2015) and commented by Anita Rønne. Two publications have followed this workshop and these have been: (1) *Ibid*, Heffron and Talus. 2016a; (2) Heffron and Talus, 'The development of energy law in the 21st century: a paradigm shift?' (2016) 9 *Journal of World Energy Law and Business* 189–202.

[25] R. Heffron, D. McCauley, 'The concept of energy justice across the disciplines' (2017) 105 *Energy Policy* 658–667.

principles as stated earlier in Table 1. Climate change law, a related sub-discipline where energy contributes the majority share of greenhouse gas emissions (and $CO_2$ emissions), also has its own core set of principles which are stated below in Table 2. These principles are first and foremost reflected in the Framework Convention for Climate Change but further elaborated upon by the International Law Association, Committee on Legal Principles Relating to Climate Change.[26] The core aim of setting out principles is to seek the increased application of human rights on a particular issue, and this is the same whether it be for the environment, the climate or the energy sector.

**Table 2** Principles of Climate Change Law[27]

| |
|---|
| 1.  **Principle of Common but Differentiated Responsibilities** |
| 2.  **The Precautionary Principle** |
| 3.  **Principle of Intra-Generational Equity** |
| 4.  **Principle of Inter-Generational Equity** |
| 5.  **Principle of Developed States to take the Lead and Protecting the most Vulnerable** |
| 6.  **Sustainable Development Concept** |
| 7.  **Principle of Cost-effectiveness** |
| 8.  **Principle of Cooperation and Knowledge Transfer** |
| 9.  **Principle of Accountability and Transparency** |
| 10. **Principle of the Common Concern of Humankind** |

As may be understood several of the climate change principles coincide with the listed principles under environmental law and indeed also principles relating to human rights.

Despite the longer existence of energy law, it lacks such principles. To redress this omission, we propose that there are seven guiding principles that have developed in practice and legislation which are stated below in Table 3 and then explained in more detail in the following text of this section.

---

[26] Conference Resolution 2/2014: Declaration of Legal Principles Relating to Climate Change and conference report for the Washington Conference (2014), Sofia 2012 and the Hague 2010 on Legal Principles Relating To Climate Change.

[27] This set of principles are from *The Oxford Handbook of International Climate Change Law*, see C.P. Carlarne, K.R. Gray, and R.G. Tarasofsky, (eds.), *The Oxford Handbook of International Climate Change Law*. (OUP, 2016). And in terms of the principles see the following chapters within that text: Chapter 1 – International Climate Change Law: Mapping the Field (by the editors); Chapter 8 – Precaution and Climate Change (Wiener, J. B.); Chapter 9 – Principles and Emerging Norms in International Law: Intra- and Inter-generational Equity (Redgwell, C.); Chapter 10 – Common Concern of Humankind (Soltau, F.); and Chapter 11 – Human Rights Principles and Climate Change (Knox, J. H.). The principles are articulated in the Climate Change Convention Art. 3 but also reflected in other articles and in the Kyoto- and Paris Agreements.

**Table 3** The Seven Principles of Energy Law

| |
|---|
| 1. The Principle of National Resource Sovereignty |
| 2. The Principle of Access to Modern Energy Services |
| 3. The Principle of Energy Justice |
| 4. The Principle of Prudent, Rational and Sustainable Use of Natural Resources |
| 5. Principle of the Protection of the Environment, Human Health & Combatting Climate Change |
| 6. Energy Security and Reliability Principle |
| 7. Principle of Resilience |

## 3. The Principles of Energy Law Explained

### I: The Principle of Sovereignty over onshore and offshore energy resources

The principle of permanent sovereignty over natural resources is closely connected with energy resources. The discussion over sovereignty over natural resources, petroleum in particular, emerged after the end of the colonial period.[28] Prior to this, the international oil companies controlled exploration and production of petroleum resources in many of the colonial and post-colonial states and, by default, the government's revenue by regulating production. This placed severe constraints of national sovereignty and the wealth these energy resources could mean for a country.

In the post-World War II era, which was marked by rising nationalism in the post-colonial world, many of the ex-colonial countries started to demand a change. Similarly, governmental interference with energy activities through regulation started to grow. That era is marked by the creation of Organization of the Petroleum Exporting Countries (OPEC) and several important UN Resolutions on the permanent sovereignty over natural resources. The 1962 UN General Assembly resolution recognized the "*inalienable right of all states freely to dispose of their natural wealth and resources in accordance with their national interests*"[29]

---

[28] For example, UNGA Resolution 1803 (XVII) 1962 proclaimed '[t]he right of peoples and nations to permanent sovereignty over their natural wealth and resources'. For an interpretation, see *Texaco Overseas Petroleum Company and California Asiatic Oil Company v. The Government of the Libyan Arab Republic* awards. (The award on the merit, 19 January 1977) available in 53 *ILR* (1979) 389, *Clunet* (1977) 350. For the preliminary award of 27 November 1975, see 53 *ILR* (1979) 389.

[29] For example, UNGA Resolution 1803 (XVII) 1962 proclaimed '[t]he right of peoples and nations to permanent sovereignty over their natural wealth and resources'. For an interpretation, see *Texaco Overseas Petroleum Company and California Asiatic Oil Company v. The Government of the Libyan Arab Republic* awards. (The award on the merit, 19 January 1977) available in 53 *ILR* (1979) 389, *Clunet* (1977) 350. For the preliminary award of 27 November 1975, see 53 *ILR* (1979) 389.

was followed by UN General Assembly Resolution 3281 (XXIX) 1974 providing that:

> "Full permanent sovereignty of every State over its natural resources and all economic activities. In order to safeguard these resources, each State is entitled to exercise effective control over them and their exploitation with means suitable to its own situation, including the right to nationalization or transfer of ownership to its nationals, this right being an expression of the full permanent sovereignty of the State. No State may be subjected to economic, political or any other type of coercion to prevent the free and full exercise of this inalienable right."

Likewise, the principle of national sovereignty was agreed as a specific principle in the Stockholm and Rio Declarations of 1972 and 1992, respectively.[30] Today permanent national sovereignty over resources is recognized under international law and its exercise is established under national constitutions.[31]

The close connection between sovereignty and energy is not only significant for energy or hydrocarbon producing states. Energy supply is also considered a sovereign issue in many of the energy importing and consuming states. The organization and division of competences within the European Union energy law and policy area is an example of this. The "sovereignty exception" under Article 194 (2) of the Treaty on the Functioning of the European Union provides that "[EU energy policy] *measures shall not affect a Member State's right to determine the conditions for exploiting its energy resources, its choice between different energy sources and the general structure of its energy supply* [...]". The rationale of this provision is that member states have decided that these issues are and should remain within the scope of national sovereignty.[32] It is moreover reflected directly in the Directive 94/22/EC on the conditions for granting and using authorizations for the prospection, exploration and production of hydrocarbons, preamble and Art. 2.

## II:  The Principle of Access to Modern Energy Services

It has been belatedly recognised in recent decades that in order for sustainable development to occur in developing nations it is essential that modern energy services are available to the general community. The importance of this issue was first recognised in 1986 in the Report of the World Commission on Environment and Development (the Brundtland Report).[33] The issue gained momentum

---

[30] Declaration of the United Nations Conference on the Human Environment 1972, and Declaration of the United Nations Conference on the Environment and Development 1992, principle 21.

[31] For the upstream energy context and sovereignty, see E. Smith, J. Dzienkowski, O. Anderson, J. Lowe, B. Kramer and J. Weaver, *International Petroleum Transactions* (Colorado: Rocky Mountain Mineral Law Foundation, 2010) or E. Pereira, K. Talus, *Upstream Law and Regulation: A Global Guide* (Globe Law and Business 2017).

[32] For the EU context, see A. Johnston, G. Block, *EU Energy Law* (OUP, 2012) or Talus (note 3).

[33] *Our Common Future*, UN Doc A/42/427 (1987) at 8.

in 2000 in a joint report, *World Energy Assessment: Energy and the Challenge of Sustainability*, prepared by the United Nations Development Programme (UNDP), the United Nations Department of Economic and Social Affairs (UN-DESA), and the World Energy Council. The report called for world action to provide access to energy services for all, and emphasised the strong nexus between energy and poverty. The 2000 Report was strengthened and updated by a further 2004 report prepared by UNDP.[34]

"Energy services" is needed rather than simply "energy" as it is not energy in itself that society requires, as energy has no intrinsic value, but rather the lifestyle changes that modern energy services provide. Energy services result from the combined operation of primary energy sources, energy-related technologies, labour, materials and infrastructure.[35] Traditional energy services provided simply for fire, based on the burning of biomass in the form of wood or dung for cooking and heating, and animals for transport. Modern energy services, by contrast, provide for lighting, cooling, refrigeration, clean cooking and transport.

The increasing recognition of the importance of access to energy services is apparent from a comparison between the UN General Assembly's Millennium Development Goals (MDGs), declared in the 2000 Millennium Declaration,[36] and the Sustainable Development Goals (SDGs), also declared by the General Assembly in *Transforming Our World: The 2030 Agenda for Sustainable Development*.[37] In the former case, the goals make no mention of energy. In contrast, goal 7 of the SDGs is expressly devoted to energy: "*Ensure access to affordable, reliable, sustainable, and modern energy for all*". Each of the SDGs contain a number of targets. Target 7.1 declares: "*By 2030, ensure universal access to affordable, reliable and modern energy services*".

The magnitude of the issue is apparent from the fact that according to the most recent international report on the issue, the 2016 report on the realisation of the SDGs, there are still 40 per cent of people living in developing countries still relying on polluting and unhealthy fuels for cooking or gas supplies. The majority of these people live in Africa and south Asia. At present over 65 per cent of the population of sub-saharan Africa is without electricity.[38]

There is currently active legal debate on four related issues:

- Does a right of access to energy services exist in human rights law?

- If not, what other international law strategies exist to provide for universal access to energy services?

---

[34] United Nations Development Programme, *World Energy Assessment: Overview 2004 Update* (2004).

[35] Id, 25.

[36] GA Res 55/2, UN Doc A/Res 55/2 (2000).

[37] GA Res 70/1, UN Doc A/Res/70/1 (2015).

[38] See: United Nations, Goal 7: Ensure access to affordable, reliable, sustainable and modern energy for all, http://unstats.un.org/sdgs/report/2016/goal-07/ (accessed September 2017).

- What role can domestic law play in promoting and/or guaranteeing universal access to energy services?
- Is there a role for the judiciary to play in this context?[39]

## III: The Principle of Energy Justice

Energy justice is a growing moral, philosophical and ethical movement that developed in the late 20th and early 21st centuries. It has been defined as:

> "[Achieving] a global energy system that fairly disseminates both the benefits and costs of energy services, and one that contributes to more representative and impartial energy decision-making".[40]

This social justice issue looks beyond traditional government and industry concerns regarding energy security, economic development and technology to consider morality in decision-making. It is relevant to both international issues (such as the right of people in developing countries to escape the poverty trap by the provision of universal access to energy services and to avoid environmental damage resulting from exploitation from multinational energy corporations or the disposal of nuclear waste shipped from developed nations), and to domestic issues (such as ensuring the affordability of energy supply for the poor or outlawing the forcible abandonment of homes and villages for the creation of new large-scale hydroelectric projects).

The energy justice movement emerged out of and has the same philosophical background as the more general issues of environmental justice and atmospheric and climate justice. The existing literature divides energy justice into three core themes: distributional justice, procedural justice and recognition justice.[41]

Distributional justice seeks to ensure that it is not always the disadvantaged and poor people who suffer most from the siting of energy projects and that objections to new energy projects are examined thoroughly by governments and judicial planning bodies without undue pressure from developers. The denial of distributional justice has tended to occur in the past in relation to governmental decision concerning, for example, the siting of wind generators, coal plant projects

---

[39] There are numerous academic writings on these issues: see, for example, S. Bruce, 'International Law and Renewable Energy: Facilitating Sustainable Energy for All' (2013) 14 *Melbourne Journal of International Law* 1; T. Kaime, R. Glicksman, "An International Legal Framework for SE4All: Human Rights and Sustainable Development Law Imperatives" (2015) 38 *Fordham International Law Journal* 1405; M. Clemson, 'Human Rights and the Environment: Access to Energy' (2012) 16 *New Zealand Journal of Environmental Law* 39; A. Bradbrook, J. Gardam, 'Placing the Access to Energy Services Within a Human Rights Framework' (2006) 28 *Human Rights Quarterly* 389.

[40] B. K/ Sovacool *et al*, "Energy Decisions Reframed as Justice and Ethical Concerns" (2016) 1 *Nature Energy* 1 at 1; www.nature.com/natureenergy.

[41] These issues are considered in detail in D. McCauley et al, "Advancing Energy Justice: The Triumvirate of Tenets" (2013) 3 *International Energy Law Review* 107.

and nuclear power plants. It is argued that all segments of society should benefit and suffer equally from such decision-making.

Procedural justice involves the equal ability of all social groups to be able to participate in decision-making processes in proposed energy developments. While this protection exists already in international environmental law in the 1998 Aarhus Convention,[42] its application in individual cases can often appear compromised. Thus decisions may be taken without full disclosure of all relevant issues to affected parties, and bias and political pressure from powerful vested interests may be unfairly influential when proposed energy developments are assessed. The unequal distribution of subsidies to different energy sources may also result in inappropriate decision making.

Recognition justice involves a consideration of differing community opinions and perspectives based on such matters as gender, race and cultural background as well as ensuring that certain groups and places are not devalued or disrespected. Modern illustrations of the problem include disrespect to local anti-wind farm groups by vested interests in the renewable energy field and the downplaying, ignoring and devaluing opponents of nuclear energy plants. Recognition justice seeks to ensure a level playing field for all stakeholders in energy development decision-making.[43]

## IV: The Principle of Prudent, Rational and Sustainable Use of Natural Resources

Sustainable use of natural resources is a term referred to in several conventions either directly[44] or by using alternative expressions like "conservation",[45] "sustainable management",[46] "optimal, efficient and rational use" or "reduce and eliminate unsustainable patterns of production and consumption" as stated in the Rio

---

[42] 2161 UNTS 447 (entry into force 31 October 2001).

[43] For recent analyses of the energy justice movement, see the writings of L. Guruswamy in: *Global Energy Justice: Law and Poverty* (West, 2016); and 'The Contours of Energy Justice', in A. Shawkatet al (eds), *International Law and The Global South* (CUP, 2015) 529ff.

[44] The Biodiversity Convention 1992, Art. 2 includes an explicit definition of "sustainable use" as " use ... in a way and at a rate that does not lead to long-term decline of biological diversity. Other examples are the Convention on the Law of the Non-navigational Uses of International Watercourses 1997, Art. 5 uses "optimal and sustainable utilization". Convention on Co-operation for the Protection and Sustainable Use of the River Danube 1994 includes the term in the title and in the text but at the same time refers to "conservation", rational use and sustainable management, preamble, Art. 2, 5, 6. Likewise the UN Fish Stocks Agreement 1995, employs both "sustainable use", "conservation", and "long-term sustainability"; the International Tropical Timber Agreement 1992 Art. 1(e) and (l), "sustainable utilization" but also "management" and "conservation" and the Convention to Combat Desertification and Draught 1994 refers to "sustainable use", "sustainable management", "conservation" and "efficient use', cf. Art. 2, 3, 10(4), 11, 17, 19.

[45] The World Charter for Nature 1982, Principle 3; UNCLOS 1982, preamble & Art. 61 (living resources) and UNFCCC 1992, Art. 4 d).

[46] UNFCCC 1992, Art. 4 d).

Declaration on Environment and Development (1992), Principle 8.[47] Already the Stockholm Declaration (1972),[48] however, included the principle (no. 5) that non-renewable resources of the earth must be employed in such a way as to guard against the danger of their future exhaustion and to ensure that benefits from such employment are shared by all mankind.

The principle of sustainable use is also reflected in the objective of UNFCCC Article 2 to *"allow ecosystems to adapt naturally to climate change, to ensure that food production is not threatened and to enable economic development to proceed in a sustainable manner"* in Article 3.4. *"should promote sustainable development ... protect the climate system against human-induced change"* and more directly under the commitments of all Parties to *"Promote sustainable management, and promote and cooperate in the conservation and enhancement, as appropriate, of sinks and reservoirs ..., including biomass, forests and oceans as well as other terrestrial, coastal and marine ecosystems"*, cf. Article 4.1. (d). To reduce harmful atmospheric emissions sustainable use of energy comes to the very forefront implying promotion of energy efficiency, energy conservation and use of renewable energy as also reflected in the Kyoto Protocol (1997) Art. 2. Likewise, the Paris Agreement (2015) acknowledges the need to promote universal access to sustainable energy in developing countries, as well as the deployment of renewables.

The 17 Sustainable Development Goals adopted by the UN General Assembly in 2015,[49] expanded the range of the Millennium Development Goals from 2000[50] to cover among other issues energy and the use of natural resources directly. A goal to reach is thus *Affordable and Clean Energy* (no. 7). Other additional goals like *Sustainable Cities and Communities* (no. 11), *Responsible Consumption and Production* (no. 12) and *Climate Action* (no. 13) also have direct reference and relevance to the sustainable use of natural resources.

Sustainable use of natural resources is also embedded at the European Union level. Environmental protection requirements must thus be integrated into the definition and implementation of the Union policies and activities, in particular with a view to promoting sustainable development, cf. the Treaty on the Functioning of the European Union (TFEU). Article 11. Moreover, Union policy on the environment shall contribute to pursuit of preserving, protecting and improving among others the prudent and rational utilisation of natural resources, and combating

---

[47] 1992 Rio Declaration on Environment and Development adopted 14 June 1992. See also International Law Association, ILA New Delhi Declaration of Principles of International Law Relating to Sustainable Development, 2 April 2002, which as its first principle lists that "States are under a duty to manage natural resources, including natural resources within their own territory or jurisdiction, in a rational, sustainable and safe way ..", and to the conservation and sustainable use of natural resources ..". Moreover, "States must take into account the needs of future generations in determining the rate of use of natural resources" and have a "duty to avoid wasteful use of natural resources ..".

[48] Declaration of the United Nations Conference on the Human Environment adopted in Stockholm, 16 June 1972.

[49] Resolution A/70/1, *Transforming our world: the 2030 Agenda for Sustainable Development* adopted on 21 October 2015.

[50] Resolution A/55/2, *United Nations Millennium Declaration*, adopted on 18 September 2000.

climate change. The objective of Union policy on energy should promote energy efficiency and energy saving and the development of new and renewable forms of energy, cf. Article 194. A long range of directives have over the years implemented these political goals into binding commitments on all member states on eg. waste, water, renewables, and energy efficiency.

Examples of the EU policy implementation may be found in the Sixth Environment Action Programme[51] where sustainable use and management of resources are referred to as one of the priority areas and called for the preparation of "*a thematic strategy on the sustainable use and management of resources ...*" and in practical terms reducing the environmental impact of resource use.[52] Natural resources are defined as encompassing all raw materials including biomass; water; wind, geothermal, tidal and solar energy. The need to take into account the life-cycle and global perspective when tackling unsustainable use of natural resources is emphasized. Sustainable use of natural resources is also recognised as critical for further economic development and became the core point under one of the seven flagship initiatives within the "Europe 2020 Strategy".[53] This Strategy aims to support the shift towards a resource efficient and low-carbon economy and decouple economic growth from resource and energy use. It stresses how resource efficiency will prevent environmental degradation, biodiversity loss and unsustainable use of resources.[54]

Like the EU also some states have adopted constitutional provisions or acts that require sustainable use of the natural environment and natural resources.

Further, all the mentioned international agreements and resolutions recognize that there are limits on the utilization of land, water and ocean, and natural resources if irreversible damage is to be avoided. Whether international law today imposes upon states a customary obligation of sustainable use of natural resources may be arguable but it is beyond doubts that sustainable use of natural resources are accepted as a global objective and has an increasing recognition internationally in treaty law. As far as shared and common resources are concerned there has been established a clear practice endorsing the existence of a general obligation to ensure conservation and sustainable use of the high seas, the deep sea-bed, the Antarctica and the Moon[55] and that these resources are the common heritage of humankind.

---

[51] Decision No 1600/2002/EC of the European Parliament and of the Council of 22 July 2002 (OJ L 242, 10.9.2002, p. 1).

[52] Cf. Thematic Strategy on the sustainable use of natural resources, COM (2005) 670.

[53] COM (2010) 2020.

[54] See Report "On the Progress of the Thematic Strategy on the Sustainable Use of Natural Resources", SEC (2011) 1068 of 20 September 2011, p. 8 and "A Resource-Efficient Europe", COM (2011) 21 and the "Roadmap for a Resource-Efficient Europe", COM (2011) 571.

[55] See also P. Birnie, A. Boyle, C. Redgwell *International Law & the Environment* (3rd ed, OUP, 2009) 199ff. A Boyle and D Freestone (eds) *National Law and Sustainable Development* (OUP 1999), 9 and 29. The Delhi Declaration, ILA Expresses a Duty of States to Ensure Sustainable Use of Natural Resources, Cf MC Cordonier Segger "Sustainable Development in International Law" in Sustainable Development in International and National Law by HC Bugge and C Voigt, 2008, p. 187.

## V:  The Principle of the Protection of the Environment, Human Health & Combatting Climate Change

Energy and the environment are physically linked in the natural fuel cycle. From exploration and extraction through processing and transportation and then to distribution, consumption, and disposal of the natural resources that are used to produce energy, environmental consequences follow. Consequently, energy law and policy and environmental law and policy cannot be treated as distinct areas of regulation. Most notable, the phenomenon of climate change exacerbates the environmental problems attendant with the energy system – the energy sector being the main contributor of CO2 emissions. These environmental problems include degradation of natural environments and the imposition of risks and fatalities on humans.

Inevitably, there are trade-offs[56] between energy and the environment that must be addressed; and, more importantly, overcome. Historically, the traditional energy narrative focused on economic growth. Cheap, readily available, and reliable energy has been and remains a core input into any sophisticated economy. In addition to accessible energy, today energy and national security, as well as environmental protection, are the central parameters for any contemporary energy policy.[57] All forms of energy have their negative impacts – on the environment, human health, energy security and the economy. The key is always to analyze each energy source for its full life-cycle impacts. However, in comparison one thing stands out: fossil fuels have more clear, more numerous, more severe, and more permanent risks than most of the alternatives. Moreover, getting beyond the carbon economy is not just an environmentalist issue but also survival necessity.

Two significant consequences follow from linking energy and the environment. First, a clean power policy can be designed. Traditional energy policies that relied on cheap and readily available fossil fuels, are no longer consistent with the demands placed on the system. Consequently, renewable resources, low-carbon resources, and energy efficiency are an increasingly important part of the energy mix. Second, and more importantly, contemporary and future energy policy is dramatically affected and linked to climate change. While, it can be argued, easily enough, that a clean energy future is valuable in and of itself; a clean future is also usefully aligned with, and complementary to, addressing the challenges of climate change.

Climate change has structural characteristics such that it has been described as a super wicked problem[58] that now demands a new form of regulation, one linking

---

[56] A. Okun, *Equality and Efficiency: The Big Trade-Off* (1975).

[57] J. P. Tomain, Ending Dirty Energy Policy: Prelude to Climate Change, chs. 3 & 4 (2011).

[58] K. Levin et al., 'Overcoming The Tragedy of Super Wicked: Straining Our Future Selves to Ameliorate Global Climate Change', 45 *Policy Sci* 123 (2012); R. J. Lazarus, 'Super Wicked Problems and Climate Change: Restraining the Present to Liberate the Future', (2009) 94 *Cornell Law Review* 1153.

energy law and policy with environmental law and policy. Regulators can no longer rely on their ability to implement *ex post* regulations that address and fix a problem, such as an oil spill or even a nuclear plant malfunction that has occurred in the past. Instead, forward-thinking *ex-ante* regulations are necessary to reduce carbon emissions in an effort to forestall further climate damage.[59]

Energy regulators must realize that the energy/environmental future presents complex problems which are multidisciplinary, intergenerational, multi-jurisdictional, and imbued with scientific, technological, economic and social uncertainties. Additionally, climate change is a non-linear problem with challenges of its own including: "time is running out" for a solution; no central authority can solve the problem; and by not addressing the problem now, the cost of doing so in the future will only increase.[60] Nevertheless, it is a future we must address today because waiting will be costly. Central to addressing the problem of climate change is to recognize the interrelationships between energy and the environment and the detrimental human consequences that follow from ignoring this linkage.[61]

## VI: Energy Security and Reliability Principle

Energy security is at the heart of any modern energy policy system and is reflected in a large number of national energy laws and regulations. Its significance is connected with the general importance of energy for the society.[62] The concept refers to two distinct but related energy policy objectives. It refers to security of supply, which typically means the continuous availability of energy at a reasonable cost. Most modern energy policies also add the social or environmental costs to this definition.[63] It also refers to security of demand, which means the continuous demand for energy products produced within the country in question. Traditionally this refers to hydrocarbons, but it also includes energy from renewable energy sources like hydropower.

While security of supply is a somewhat universal energy policy objective, its practical application at the level of national law and policy depend on the national specificities.[64] For an energy importing country or region security of supply

---

[59] S. A. Shapiro, J. P. Tomain, *Achieving Democarcy: The Future of Progressive Regulation*, ch. 8 (2014).

[60] Energy Innovation Policy and Technology LLC, *The Costs of Delay: Waiting Until 2020 Could Coast Nearly $400 Billion* (October 2015).

[61] Encyclical Letter of the Supreme Pontiff Francis, On Care for Our Common Home: Laudato Si', 70-91(2015).

[62] Emphasised, for example, in the case law of the Court of Justice of the European Union. See Case 72/83 *Campus Oil v Minister for Industry* [1984] ECR 2727.

[63] For notions of security of supply, see K. Talus, 'Security of Supply – An Increasingly Political Notion', in B. Delvaux, M. Hunt and K. Talus (eds.), *EU energy law and policy issues* (Brussels: Euroconfidentiel 2008).

[64] Various elements of energy security has been discussed in detail in B. Sovacool (ed.), *Handbook of Energy Security* (Routledge 2011).

relates to, among other things, import security. This is sought through import diversification, both in terms of sources of supply and transportation routes, sufficient investment into the import infrastructure, mandatory storage obligations and so-on. It also translates into an interest in alternative energy sources, including unconventional sources of oil and gas as well as renewable energy. For an energy producing country, security of supply objective can be sought through very different measures. In cases where the national demand can be met, at least partially, by national supply, the security of supply policy is not always based on securing sufficient imports but by preventing exports. This can be achieved through a national petroleum supply reservation policies.[65]

## VII:  Principle of Resilience

The energy sector of the economy can be assessed in two parts – transportation and electricity although fossil fuels dominate both systems. The crucial difference between the two, however, is that they each have their own particular physical characteristics. Transportation fuels, for example, can be easily identified and stored. Electricity is fungible and storage only possible short-term at best. More importantly, the electricity system must be in balance at all times as well as readily available.

Regardless of these differences, however, energy for both sectors must be reliably available. Additionally, both systems must be resilient. Because transportation fuels are easily storable and dispersed throughout a country, the transportation system is relatively resilient. Not so for the electricity system. In fact, resilience is now become a major concern to the electricity sector as a result of a series of disruptive weather events that have shut down the delivery of electricity at great economic costs. Consequently, the energy future must pay close attention to the concept of resilience.

In the US, the National Academy of Sciences has defined resilience as "the ability to prepare plan for, store, recover from, and more successfully adapt to adverse events."[66] Super Storm Sandy, Hurricane Katrina, and even a tree branch on a wire have all shut down the delivery of electricity while exposing the vulnerability of the electric system.[67] By way of example, the 2003 East Coast power outage is estimated to cost between $4 and $10 billion.[68] These severe weather events are

---

[65] K. Talus, E. Pereira, 'National Petroleum Supply Reservations: Background and Comparison' (2014) 7 *Journal of World Energy Law and Business* 527–537.

[66] The National Academies Committee on the Increasing Resilience to Hazards and Disasters. Disaster Resilience: A National Imperative (2012).

[67] G. Blake, *The Grid: The Fraying Wires between Americans and Our Energy Future* (2016).

[68] US-Canada Power System Outage Task Force, Final Report on the August 14, 2003 Blackout in the United States and Canada: Causes and Recommendations (April 2004).

occurring with increased frequency and have been attributed to global warming thus reinforcing the necessity of a future energy policy that is cognizant of and responsive to climate change.

In addition to climate change, though, concerns about resilience also involve cyber security threats. US Department of Energy, for example, acknowledges that the electricity system faces imminent danger from cyber-attacks which are, in fact, growing more frequent and sophisticated.[69]

In either the case of a catastrophic weather occurrence or a cyber-attack, electricity system operators must make resilience investments for several reasons including preventing or minimizing damage to avoid or reduce adverse event; providing alternatives to enable the system to continue operations during such an event; and promoting a rapid return to normal operations after disruption. In short, resilience measures relate both to the impact on reliability as well as on the impact of the system to recover more rapidly.

As our energy systems transform, greater attention must be paid to the threats and risks presented by climate change and other disruptions. As we describe throughout the book, both the transportation and electricity systems are moving away from their traditional dependence on fossil fuels to an increased reliance on renewable resources and energy efficiency. Additionally, the production, transportation and consumption of energy are moving away from a traditional reliance on large-scale centralized energy producers and distributors to an increased reliance on distributed energy resources that are smaller in scale and closer to consumers. This transition towards decentralization has a dual impact. On the one hand, competition in the energy sector is increased because of new entrants. On the other hand, as energy becomes more dispersed and available at smaller scales, resilience can be improved because the consequences of a disruptive event can be reduced.

# Conclusions

Since the time of St. Thomas Aquinas and his Treatise of Law, scholars have been attempting to establish guiding principles of law.[70] The aim of this article has been to attempt something similar but for energy law. Indeed, in another Treatise, Jean-Jacques Rousseau's Treatise on Education – *Emile, or On Education* – he was aiming to reform our thinking about education. This is also the aim of our Treatise of Energy Law to reform what constitutes energy law and how scholars and practitioners should interact with it.

---

[69] US Department of Energy, Transforming the Nation's Electricity System: The Second Installment of the Quadrennial Energy Review (January 2017).

[70] And indeed this is what the scholar William Bainbridge was doing in his text (which followed the word by Archibald Brown: W. Bainbridge, A Treatise on the Law of Mines and Minerals (4th edn, 1878) Butterworths: London UK.

Energy law's related areas (or sister subjects) of environmental and climate law have many principles which are outlined in section one and three. These two areas have been defining and developing them for close to several decades now. One of the reasons energy law has not followed environmental and climate change law in having its own principles is because the lack of consensus of what energy law is. It remains an issue in energy law scholarship. Evidence of this is presented in section two. Further, it is notable that this year energy law was accepted as a section in one of the world's oldest annual legal conferences – the Society of Legal Scholars Annual Conference[71] – which was held in Dublin (Ireland) from 5–8 September 2017. It was the 108th time this legal conference has been held and it only now has an energy law section – and it is now recognized alongside the other 27 sub-disciplines of law The first energy law keynote speakers at this event notably, in essence, both presented on the issue of what constitutes energy law scholarship and energy law.[72]

As the definition of energy law scholarship has evolved to some degree since Bradbrook's seminal article in 1986, in more recent scholarship it reads as *"energy law is the regulation of energy related rights and duties of various stakeholders over energy resources over the energy life-cycle".*[73] And this definition and Bradbrook's will no doubt be debated in the literature in years to come. However, for energy law to further develop, and to ensure it takes into account the advance of society, new international agreements such as Paris COP21, new technology and new government policies for transitioning to low-carbon economics, it is time for energy law to have its own set of guiding principles. This article states that there are seven energy law principles and a more detailed description is included in section three.

These principles should act as a guide to policy-makers, academics, lawyers, judges and arbitrators when adjudicating, enforcing, making or formulating documentation, laws, regulations, judgments etc. on energy law. The majority of these in operation to varying degrees already in practice and it is the aim of this paper is to advance these principles as the guiding principles of energy law for both research and practice. These seven principles of energy law can also enable other energy scholars to engage more directly with energy law. And in terms of thinking of the study and the definition of energy law in the future, there is a need for more interdisciplinary engagement. Indeed, both the keynotes as the aforementioned 108th Society of Legal Scholars Energy Law section highlighted the importance of interdisciplinary scholarship as a characteristic of energy law.

---

[71] Society of Legal Scholars Annual Conference – Available at: http://www.slsconference.uk/ (accessed September 2017).

[72] It should be noted that both keynotes were allowed to choose their own titles for their keynote addresses. The two keynote speakers were: Professor Peter D Cameron (Centre for Energy, Petroleum, Mineral Law and Policy, University of Dundee) and Professor Catherine Redgwell (University of Oxford). Professor Raphael Heffron is the first Convener of the Energy Law Section at the Society of Legal Scholars.

[73] P.4, *Ibid*, Heffron, R. J. and Talus. K. 2016a.

Finally, the question arises as to whether in light of societal drivers[74] or changes in eras of energy law[75] is energy law as a discipline modernizing? Indeed, scholars have noted this term 'modern energy law' in the literature to-date[76] and as society moves towards low-carbon economies energy law needs a new treatise based on a core set of principles as advanced in this paper to modernize itself.

[74] Such drivers of energy law are stated as: safety; security; economics; infrastructure; and justice. See: (1) *Ibid*, Heffron and Talus. 2016a; and (2) R.J. Heffron, *Energy Law* (Roundhall, Thomson Reuters: Dublin, Ireland, 2015).

[75] As US authors note, but their 'eras of energy law' are specific to the US whereas Heffron & Talus (2016) provide an international perspective as to the evolution of energy law, see: Eisen, J. *et al*. 2015. (4th Ed.). Energy, Economics and the Environment. MN, US: Foundation Press.

[76] See: (1) D.N. Zillman, 'Evolution of Modern Energy Law: a Personal Retrospective' (2012) 30 *Journal of Energy & Natural Resources Law* 485–496; and (2) R.J. Heffron, 'The Global Future of Energy Law' (2016) 7 *International Energy Law Review* 290–295.

# 4

# What do we Mean when we Talk about International Energy Law?

VOLKER ROEBEN AND GÖKÇE METE

## I. Abstract

This chapter seeks to achieve semantic clarity on international energy law. It proposes that two concepts should be distinguished to this effect. One is the traditional, thinner concept: the international law *on* energy. It is structural-descriptive, and it comprises those general rules of the established branches of international law that also apply to energy. By contrast, the novel, thicker concept, the international law *of* energy, is evaluative. It is hence dependent on norms that define a body of international law dedicated to energy. The chapter argues that a master-norm is sustainable energy to which all have access. In the light of this master-norm, a specific regulatory structure that addresses ultimately the conduct of private parties, businesses and consumers, develops. The mater-norm acts like a magnet, orientating and turning all the established branches of international law into means of implementation. The chapter concludes that international lawyers increasingly mean or ought to mean this international law of energy.

## II. Introduction

In the literature it remains hotly debated whether international energy law exists as a distinct subject matter of public international law, if so, and what it comprises. The starting point is that energy has long been considered to fall primarily within the domain of domestic law. That is reflected in principles such as the permanent sovereignty over natural resources, which reserves disposition to the territorial sovereign over their energy resources. Yet the climate-action-driven transition to a low-carbon economy has cast a novel perspective on the dynamic international law relating to energy in all its forms. At this juncture, the purpose of this chapter is to advance conceptual and semantic clarity about what international lawyers mean when they talk about international energy law. It is hence analytic, rather than normative or legally reconstructive. It proposes a distinction between a 'thin' and a 'thick' concept of international law relating to energy.

The thin, structural concept refers to the bundle of international rules that really belong to other sectors, but touch on aspects of energy. This is arguably what astute observers have in mind when stating that an international energy law does not exist; instead there are general principles of international law that apply to the energy sector.[1] We term this the 'international law *on* energy'.

By contrast, the thick concept is evaluative. It evaluates whether there is a distinct body of international law dedicated to the energy sector. The paper unpacks this thick concept by making three arguments. It argues that access to sustainable and affordable energy for all sits at the heart of this body of international law as a meta-norm; that this meta-norm determines the characteristics of an international regulatory approach to the energy value chain; and that it leads several other established regimes of international law to realign themselves with it. These three arguments are interrelated; they set the boundaries of that distinct body of international law. We term this thick concept 'international law *of* energy'. We claim that international lawyers ought to refer to this international law of energy in order to meaningfully speak about the current and future international regulation of the field of energy.

First, the international law of energy rests on a meta-norm that mandates a transition to a low-carbon global economy to provide all with access to sustainable and affordable energy. The meta-norm was formalised in 2015 by the international community of states in the universally accepted Sustainable Development Goals (SDGs) 7 and 13 of the UN Agenda 2030. SDG 7 relates to ensuring access to clean and affordable for all, and SDG 13 relates to international climate action.[2] To this end, it promotes renewable energy sources, transmission through trans-boundary grids, and efficiency in consumption. Agenda 2030 defines the pathway of future legal concretisation of both SDGs. The 2015 Paris Agreement on climate action[3] provides concretisation through universally binding international law of these

---

[1] C Redgwell, 'International Regulation of Energy Activities' in M Roggenkamp, C Redgwell, A Rønne, I del Guayo (eds), *Energy Law in Europe: National, EU and International Regulation*, 3rd edn (Oxford University Press, 2016) 14; D Azeria, *Treaties on Transit of Energy via Pipelines and Countermeasures* (Cambridge University Press, 2016) (applying the general law of treaties and state responsibility). This chapter does not deny the applicability of general international law; it rather is making the point that the international law of energy is specific and that this specificity determines its relation with other international law.

[2] For more information see 'About The Sustainable Development Goals – United Nations Sustainable Development' (United Nations Sustainable Development, 2019), available at www.un.org/sustainabledevelopment/sustainable-development-goals.

[3] Paris Agreement to the United Nations Framework Convention on Climate Change 2015, Doc FCCC/CP/2015/10/Add.1 ('Paris Agreement'). The Paris Agreement was adopted on 12 December 2015 at the 21st session of the Conference of the Parties to the United Nations Framework Convention on Climate Change held in Paris from 30 November to 13 December 2015 and entered into force 4 November 2016, UNTC No 54113. 185 of 197 Parties to the UNFCCC have ratified the Agreement (August 2019).

SDGs for the energy sector that accounts for more than 70 per cent of worldwide carbon emissions. The formalised meta-norm translates into accountability and parameters and benchmarks for states parties on their energy policies.

Second, this meta-norm now underpins a single approach to legal change in international law. This approach is regulatory. 'Regulatory' is used here in the sense that SDGs 7, 13 and the Paris Agreement formulate goals on the future provision of energy that are to be achieved within a certain timeframe by all states acting individually and jointly. The regulatory change deploys institutionalised rulemaking on energy throughout the value-cycle, from generation, through transportation to consumption (end uses). In so doing, the change tests and, indeed, pushes the boundaries of established doctrines of international law, such as institutional oversight, dynamic treaty development and implementation, the regulation of private conduct, and the concern for social justice and the welfare of people.

Third, the extant international law that relates to energy is marked by plurality. There is some significant energy-specific international law. However, the mass originates in regimes across all sectors of international law, reflecting the horizontal nature of energy. The emergence of the meta-norm has profound consequences for this plural law. Each regime self-aligns with the meta-norm to advance its implementation by using the instruments available under each regime. There is clear evidence of such self-alignment under the 1994 Energy Charter Treaty (ECT)[4] that will be documented extensively throughout this chapter. But the trend comprises most, if not all energy-relevant regimes, such as the law of natural resources, trade law, investment law, environmental law, or the law the sea, albeit to different degrees in each regime as will be demonstrated.

The chapter concludes that it is meaningful to speak about the international law *of* energy grounded in a meta-norm directing the development of a dedicated body of international law for energy. This international law is a means with which the international community of states delivers the transition to a different global energy system, in a universally binding, effective and formally rational manner. In the discourse of international lawyers, this thick concept ought to replace an outdated, thinner concept of an international law *on* energy.

# III. A Universal Meta-norm for Energy

At the heart of the international law of energy is a universally accepted meta-norm. This section first discusses the concept of a meta-norm and argues that it has the capacity to direct choices on the development of international law. It then

---

[4] 2080 UNTS 95. The Energy Charter Treaty (ECT) and its Protocol on Energy Efficiency and Related Environmental Aspects (PEEREA) cover energy investments, trade, freedom of energy transit, energy-efficiency, and resolution of state-to-state or investor-to-state disputes. See 'Home – Energy Charter' (Energycharter.org, 2019), available at https://energycharter.org.

demonstrates the role of the SDGs, and of the Paris Agreement, in jointly shaping a meta-norm for the international law of energy.

## A. The Concept of Meta-norm

The concept of a meta-norm originates in the study of collective action, in particular of social rules for actors in complex governance schemes.[5] In this account, a meta-norm embodies the value judgments that those actors refer to when making choices in developing the scheme, and which explain and justify these choices. A meta-norm hence is not prescriptive (ontological) per se. It may and often will be first formalised in policy documents. For a universal meta-norm, a legitimate formalisation would be in a UN General Assembly resolution reflecting the outcome of a universally attended policy-making conference of states.

Energy is subject to such a complex governance scheme. It is complex on both substantive and organisational grounds. Substantively, this governance scheme means making trade-offs between competing energy-internal goals, expressed in the so-called energy trilemma of sustainability, security of supply and affordability. It also means choosing between energy-internal goals and energy-external values and rationales that underpin all those sectors of international law that also apply to energy, ranging from trade to environmental protection. Organisationally, energy governance is decentralised, ensured by the UN, a range of specialised international organisations, and increasingly actively by regional integration organisations, in particular the European Union, as well as each sovereign state. This governance scheme is based on rules being adopted on the international, the regional and the national level. A single meta-norm directs actors in making policy and legal choices, on each of these levels, with the international level being the focus of this chapter.

## B. SDG 7 and 13 for Energy and the 2030 Agenda

A meta-norm for energy has been now been formalised in the 2030 Agenda of the United Nations that was adopted by the General Assembly in 2015 as the outcome of an inclusive drafting process. It contains the Sustainable Development Goals. SDGs 7[6] and 13[7] in their combination provide this first formalisation of a novel meta-norm for energy. SDG 7 aims to ensure access to affordable, reliable,

---

[5] See J Kooiman and S Jentoft, 'Meta-Governance: Values, norms and principles, and the making of hard choices' (2007) 87 *Public Administration* 818; further J Rosenau and E-O Czempiel, *Governance without Government: Order and Change in World Politics* (Cambridge University Press, 1992).

[6] SDG 7: Ensure access to affordable, reliable, sustainable and modern energy for all (2019); https://sustainabledevelopment.un.org/sdg7.

[7] SDG 13: Take urgent action to combat climate change and its impacts (2019); https://sustainabledevelopment.un.org/sdg13.

sustainable and modern energy for all, and SDG 13 aims for urgent action to combat climate change and its impacts. It covers the entire value chain of energy, from generation through transportation/transmission, to consumption and end use. The SDGs are objectives that are to be achieved over a 15-year period and that progress against them can and will be measured. It hence ensures that there is a determined objective that defines a desirable future state of affairs for global energy that is different from the status quo. These SDGs are set within Agenda 2030. Agenda 2030, a programme of action from 2015, mandates all states, developed and developing, and the international organisations to work towards achieving them. It makes them the meta-norm making critical policy and legal choices.

## C. The Paris Agreement and Energy

The meta-norm for energy is distinct in that SDGs 7 and 13 have been concretised and normatively reinforced through the Paris Agreement. In a framework convention-cum-protocol approach, the UNFCCC lays down basic principles, operationalised by the Kyoto Protocol until 2020, and the Paris Agreement from 2020 onwards. The Paris Agreement now enshrines the binding objective to limit the global temperature rise to well below 2°C above pre-industrial levels, and to pursue efforts to limit the increase to 1.5°C, while delivering universal access to energy. The Paris Agreement also defines a binding procedure for all states parties, combining the bottom-up Nationally Determined Contributions (NDCs) with the top-down Global Stocktake. The rulebook adopted at COP24 in 2018[8] clarifies the procedure, which is economy-wide but has energy as the indispensable core. International climate action hence becomes energy action and vice versa.[9]

Human rights provide additional normativity for the meta-norm. This becomes clearer on the backdrop that traditionally human rights had little to say on energy. The International Covenant on Social, Economic and Cultural Rights (ICSECR)[10] enshrines rights to food and housing among others, which presuppose if not directly guarantee a right to energy in the sense of a right of consumers to access secure, affordable and clean energy. Nevertheless, there has been little guidance on a human right to energy from the CSECR.[11] But human rights are now demanding of states positive measures from a functional perspective. The 2016 report of the Special Rapporteur of the UN Human Rights Council on Human Rights and the Environment has identified this human rights normativity for

---

[8] The Paris Rulebook is discussed in ch 5.

[9] See also 2019 Secretary-General's Climate Action Summit Track #4: Energy Transition, available www.un.org/sustainabledevelopment/wp-content/uploads/2019/05/WP-Energy-Transition.pdf.

[10] International Covenant on Economic, Social and Cultural Rights (ICESCR), entered into force 3 January 1976, 993 UNTS 3.

[11] The Committee on Economic, Social and Cultural Rights (CESCR) is the body of 18 independent experts that carries out the monitoring functions assigned in Part IV of the Covenant to the UN Economic and Social Council.

energy policies,[12] which mandates decarbonisation of energy or, in SDG7 terms, providing access for all to sustainable energy.[13] The positive basis is a human right to a healthy environment where regional instruments provide it.[14] Human rights also underpin specific energy policies of states, such as policies on flaring in the Niger Delta[15] or carbon pricing in the port of Rotterdam.[16] The 2019 report of the Special Rapporteur for Food reinforces, from that perspective, that the SDGs are underpinned by human rights.[17]

This meta-norm of climate action, while delivering universal access to energy, then defines the legal responsibility for energy policy and law-making of all states throughout the energy value cycle, from generation, through transportation/transmission, to consumption. This responsibility is para-prohibitive of certain fossil energy sources and promotional of cleaner alternatives; it favours interconnected global energy markets to balance supply and demand in these alternatives; and it seeks efficiencies. This responsibility translates into a regulatory approach to energy (see section IV). It also directs states to reassess the entire gamut of their international cooperation and to align generic commitments with the meta-norm (see section V).

# IV. The International Regulatory Approach to Energy

This meta-norm generates a single approach to the development of new international law. This approach is for the international regulation of energy throughout

---

[12] Report of the Special Rapporteur on the issue of human rights obligations relating to the enjoyment of a safe, clean, healthy and sustainable environment, UN Doc A/HRC/31/52, available at www.ohchr.org/en/Issues/environment/SRenvironment/Pages/SRenvironmentIndex.aspx.

[13] Para 54: 'In particular, the Special Rapporteur agrees with the suggestion of UNEP that wherever possible States should assess the climate effects of major activities within their jurisdiction, "such as programmatic decisions about fossil fuel development, large fossil fuel-fired power plants, and fuel economy standards"'.

[14] Organization of African Unity (OAU), African Charter on Human and Peoples' Rights ('Banjul Charter'), entered into force 21 October 1984, 1520 UNTS 217.

[15] The Federal Government of Nigeria has taken the initiative to prohibit gas flaring and ensure the utilisation of gas flared within the country by oil and gas companies. The Prevention of Waste and Pollution Regulations 2018 seek to provide legal support to the National Gas Flare Commercialization Program (NGFCP) (a policy to eliminate gas flaring through technically and commercially sustainable gas utilisation projects developed by competent third-party investors invited to participate in a competitive and transparent bid process), and reduce the effect of gas flaring on the environment (a major contributor to global warming). See 'Gas Flaring Charges In Nigeria – Energy and Natural Resources – Nigeria' (Mondaq.com, 2019), available at www.mondaq.com/Nigeria/x/756460/Oil+Gas+Electricity/Gas+Flaring+Charges+In+Nigeria.

[16] In the Netherlands, the Port of Rotterdam has made EUR 5 million available via its Incentive Scheme Climate-Friendly Shipping to fund maritime projects using low- and zero-carbon fuel. Shipping companies, fuel and engine manufacturers and suppliers and shipping service providers operating out of Rotterdam will be able to submit for funding if their project relies on green fuel and carbon reduction options. 'Port Of Rotterdam Launches EUR 5 Million Low-Carbon Fuel Initiative' (Bioenergy International, 2019), available at https://bioenergyinternational.com/storage-logistics/26426.

[17] Interim report of the Special Rapporteur on the right to food, UN doc A/74/164, available at www.ohchr.org/EN/Issues/Food/Pages/Annual.aspx.

its value chain. 'Regulation' is used here in the sense of the definition that Professor Adler has provided.[18] Regulation in this definition aims to achieve public policy goals through legal directives. The international regulation of energy then seeks to achieve the state of affairs indicated by the SDGs/Paris objective for the entire value chain of energy.[19] The design of a dedicated regulatory set-up innovates over traditional international law and pushes its classic doctrinal boundaries, in three characteristic respects. There is an institutionalised architecture to oversee the regulatory change (section A); there is regulation of the conduct of private actors and consumers (section B), and there is concern for a socially just regulation that advances the welfare of all (section C).

## A. An Institutional Architecture to Oversee Regulatory Change

The regulation of energy is based on international oversight and rule-making. Treaty is too static for this purpose. It requires institutionalised procedures of iterative international rule-making. Rules are to be reviewed in regular intervals and progressively strengthened. The starting point is the accountability of states and the corresponding oversight of international organisations.

Accountability is a matter of who is accountable to whom for what. In energy, all states become accountable towards the international community of states as a whole and, through it, humanity. Accountability of all states against SDG 7 and 13 is proceduralised through the High-Level Forum on Sustainable Development (HLPF) under the auspices of the UN Economic and Social Council (ECOSOC) and the General Assembly (GA), which has a central role in the follow-up and review of the 2030 Agenda.[20] The HLPF conducts so-called voluntary national reviews, which are 'voluntary, state-led, undertaken by both developed and developing countries, and shall provide a platform for partnerships, including through the participation of major groups and other relevant stakeholders'.[21] They aim to facilitate the sharing of experiences by governments, including successes, challenges and lessons learned in implementing the 2030 Agenda. They also seek to strengthen policies and mobilise support and partnerships for the SDGs. The review of policies is thematic and cuts across several SDGs, but reviews some

---

[18] M Adler, 'Regulatory Theory' in D Patterson (ed), *A Companion to Philosophy of Law and Legal Theory*, 2nd edn (Blackwell, 2010) 590; The UK Task Force Better Regulation, Principles of Better Regulation (2011) 1; see also JHH Weiler, 'The Geology of International Law – Governance, Democracy and Legitimacy' (2004) 64 *ZaöRV* 550.

[19] The international regulation of tobacco consumption and other lifestyle choices is structurally distinct in that it remains limited to reducing certain (limited) risks from tobacco and alcohol consumption, despite some para-prohibitive traits. See A Alemanno and A Garde (eds), *Regulating Lifestyle Risks* (Cambridge University Press, 2015); further D Byrd and C Cothern, *Introduction to Risk Analysis* (Government Institutes, 2000).

[20] GA resolution 70/299 provides guidance on the follow-up and review of the 2030 Agenda and the SDGs.

[21] 2030 Agenda, para 84.

in depth. Such an in-depth review has taken place for SDG 7 on affordable and clean energy within the 2018 thematic review for transformation towards sustainable and resilient societies. The 2019 theme of inclusiveness and equality reviewed, in depth, SDG 13 on climate action.[22] In 2019, the High-level Political Forum convened twice: first under the auspices of the ECOSOC; and then of the General Assembly, meeting at head of state-level – the first SDG summit since 2015.[23]

This accountability is the basis of international institutionalised oversight. A oversight function of international organisations over mandated legal change has been recognised by the International Court of Justice (ICJ) in its 2019 opinion on the legal consequences of the separation of the Chagos from Mauritius in 1965.[24] Upon granting independence to its former colony Mauritius, the UK had separated off Chagos Island and reorganised it as the British Indian Ocean Territory. The ICJ opined that this was in violation of the then applicable international law of self-determination. The UN Charter enshrines a principle of self-determination for people under colonial domination in Article 1(2) and in Chapter XI on trusteeship.[25] Importantly, in this opinion, the ICJ recognises the role of the UN and particularly the General Assembly (GA) in overseeing the implementation of the principle by the concerned (colonial) states, and to exercise this oversight through appropriate resolutions that concretise the Charter. Hence, only GA resolutions[26] operationally spelled out that the integrity of the former colony had to be respected upon gaining independence. On this account, the opinion points out that that this has become a rule of customary international law. A general point can then be made: an international rule arises from two elements – formalisation by an international organisation; and authorisation. These can occur at different points in time.[27]

This account of institutional oversight elucidates the regulation of energy mandated by the meta-norm. Different from other areas of international law, such as health, there is not a single organisation with centralised oversight responsibility for the field. Instead, oversight is decentralised. Organisations such as the Organization of the Petroleum Exporting Countries (OPEC)[28] and the International

---

[22] Further IISD's Hub, 'Discussion Note Identifies Climate–SDG Synergies Ahead Of SDG 13 Review' (Sdg.iisd.org, 2019), available at https://sdg.iisd.org/news/discussion-note-identifies-climate-sdg-synergies-ahead-of-sdg-13-review.

[23] 47 states presented their Voluntary National Reviews at the 2019 Forum, 40 of them for the first time.

[24] International Court of Justice, Legal Consequences of the Separation of the Chagos Archipelago from Mauritius in 1965, Opinion of 25 February 2019.

[25] UN Charter, entry into force 24 October 1945, 1 UNTS XVI.

[26] GA resolutions 1514 (XV) of 14 December 1960, 2066 (XX) of 16 December 1965, 2232 (XXI) of 20 December 1966 and 2357 (XXII) of 19 December 1967.

[27] For a fuller account see V Roeben, 'Institutions of International Law' (2019) *Max Planck Yearbook of UN Law* 189.

[28] OPEC's objective is to coordinate and unify petroleum policies among members, in order to secure fair and stable prices for petroleum producers; an efficient, economic and regular supply of petroleum to consuming nations; and a fair return on capital to those investing in the industry. See www.opec.org/opec_web/en.

Energy Agency (IEA)[29] have historically organised self-selected groups of states by their antagonistic interests as producers and consumers of energy and particularly fossil fuels, although the International Energy Forum (IEF)[30] is to bring both groups together. On the other hand, the International Renewable Energy Agency (IRENA) demonstrates a universal membership approach at least to renewable energy sources.[31] The Energy Charter Conference brings energy consumers and producers together across the full energy value cycle, under the principles of facilitated trade, cooperation and investment protection in energy. Multilateral and bilateral development finance institutions enable energy transitions and low-carbon energy access.[32]

The Energy Charter Conference can serve as primary reference for dynamic institutionalised oversight over transboundary energy. It operates under the authority of the ECT, which in the 1990s constructed the first international organisational and legal architecture specifically for energy. The ECT aimed at energy market creation. Since its adoption in the 1990s, the ECT provisions have hardly been updated, and primarily for the trade dimension. The SDGs and the Paris Agreement now drive a change agenda. There are three, simultaneous phases of a *modernisation* process of the treaty, which involves infra-treaty and treaty-level rulemaking and implementation of the meta-norm.[33]

The 2015 International Energy Charter forms the first phase of the modernisation process. This non-legally binding instrument was adopted by over 90 signatory states both developing and developed.[34] It represents the current consensus of signatories on international action on energy. It transforms the Energy Charter process from a European initiative to an international one and rejuvenates the text of that earlier political declaration. It now reflects some of the most topical energy challenges of the twenty-first century, in particular the 'trilemma' between energy security, environmental protection and equity. The International Energy Charter strengthens the synergies among energy-related multilateral fora on the need to promote access to modern energy services, energy poverty reduction, clean technology and capacity-building. As a result, several non-Eurasian states have since become parties of the ECT, including Jordan in December 2018 and Yemen

---

[29] The IEA is an autonomous organisation which works to ensure reliable, affordable and clean energy for its 30 member countries and beyond. See www.iea.org.

[30] The International Energy Forum (IEF) aims to foster greater mutual understanding and awareness of common energy interests among its members. See www.ief.org.

[31] The Clean Energy Ministerial is an informal forum of intergovernmental cooperation of certain OECD members on clean energies. It is serviced by the IEA.

[32] The World Bank, International Finance Corporation and the African Development Bank support a range of renewable energy technology options to help state to supply energy to their populations in a manner consistent with 2°C pathways.

[33] I Kustova, 'A treaty à la carte? Some reflections on the modernization of the Energy Charter Process' (2016) 9 *The Journal of World Energy Law & Business* 357.

[34] States that have adopted the International Energy Charter as of May 2019 are from Asia and the far East (including China), the Gulf, South America and Africa. Further information on the International Energy Charter is available at: https://energycharter.org/process/international-energy-charter-2015/overview.

in January 2019.[35] Many African states are in the process of joining the ECT.[36] The second phase of modernisation involves streamlining the principles of the International Energy Charter without changing the treaty, developing a range of infra-treaty instruments.[37] The third phase of the modernisation will aim to revise the provisions of the treaty so that they reflect modern investment standards, the right of host states to regulate, and embrace stronger provisions on sustainable development, including on climate change and the clean energy transition in line with the Paris Agreement.[38]

To this should be added the institutional set-up of international climate law that rests on meetings of parties. Oversight over energy also is the remit of the institutional set-up under the UNFCCC, Kyoto Protocol and Paris Agreement. These treaties establish the Conference of the Parties to the UNFCCC (COP), the Meeting of Parties to the Kyoto Protocol (CMP), and the Meeting of Parties to the Paris Agreement (CMA). The thus organised collectivity of parties oversees the bottom-up determination of energy policy by each party. The COP/CMP/CMA concretises through decisions the general, non-operational provisions of the treaties. The legal status of these decisions typically remains undefined under the constitutive treaties, but they have received increased recognition for the interpretation and application of these treaties.[39] There is also state-internal enforceability before national courts. National courts are strategically using human rights doctrine to incorporate the standards of the Paris Agreement to hold governments to account for their energy policies.[40] The positive basis is the general human rights to life and to a private and family life as guaranteed in the European Convention on Human Rights.[41] In so doing, they have to overcome contrary arguments based on the separation of powers, which, at least in the European context, are limited by the human right to an effective remedy and hence effective judicial review. Such rulemaking on energy by meetings of parties

---

[35] For further information on Jordan and the ECT see 'Jordan is the 51st Contracting Party to the ECT' (IEC, 2019), available at https://energycharter.org/media/news/article/jordan-is-the-51st-contracting-party-to-the-ect/?tx_news_pi1%5Bcontroller%5D=News&tx_news_pi1%5Baction%5D=detail&cHash=333d881595d7cea051a562c0e18c7650.

[36] Burundi, Eswatini and Mauritania are in the ratification stage. Uganda is waiting for the formal invitation to accede to the ECT. Niger, Chad, Gambia, Nigeria and Senegal are amongst the countries preparing accession reports.

[37] See section V C.

[38] See section V B.

[39] UN International Law Commission, Draft conclusions on subsequent agreements and subsequent practice in relation to the interpretation of treaties, Conclusion 11 (IUn Doc A/73/10, para 51).

[40] The Hague Court of Appeal, Civil-law Division Case number: 200.178.245/01 Case/cause list number: C/09/456689/ HA ZA 13-1396, *The State of the Netherlands v Urgenda*, Ruling of 9 October 2018 (Urgenda.nl, 2019), available at www.urgenda.nl/wp-content/uploads/ECLI_NL_GHDHA_2018_2610.pdf, confirmed by the Supreme Court, 20-12-2019, ECLI:NL:HR:2019:2007. See P Minnerop, 'Integrating the 'duty of care' under the European Convention on Human Rights and the science and law of climate change: the decision of the Hague Court of Appeal in the Urgenda case' (2019) 37 *Journal of Energy and Natural Resources Law* 149.

[41] Council of Europe, European Convention for the Protection of Human Rights and Fundamental Freedoms, as amended, 4 November 1950, ETS 5.

also takes place under the Biodiversity Convention for sustainability criteria of biofuels types,[42] or the phase-out of certain fuels in global maritime and air transport,[43] or again in the development of technical standards for transboundary energy markets.

Transparency of national policies is a crucial element of this accountability. Transparency measures in the energy sector focus increasingly on dissemination of best practices in the renewable energy sector, energy transitions and climate mitigation measures including carbon reporting. Mandatory and voluntary carbon reporting policies are becoming widespread. States that have put mandatory GHG reporting into legislation, include the UK, EU Member States, the US, Australia, Japan and South Africa. These reports are published in relevant GHG inventories that exist in many parts of the world.[44] Parties to the Paris Agreement have been negotiating the modalities, procedures and guidelines for the enhanced transparency framework established under the Agreement (Article 13) since its inception in 2016. Transparency under the Agreement aims to reveal the actions taken by its parties to mitigate and adapt to climate change and track the process progress toward implementing and achieving individual nationally determined contributions (NDCs) and to improve the support provided and received by the parties.

The institutionalised regulation of energy hence employs a procedure of international rulemaking, infra treaty, that had become entrenched in state practice,[45] but which is reaffirmed by the intensive use being made of it in this context. This has repercussions for the general doctrine of treaty in international law. Energy regulation contributes to a paradigm slip in the concept of treaty foundational to public international law.[46] Paradigm slips are different from full-scale shifts. But the accumulation indicates a slipping of the static consent-based concept of treaty to one that reflects a dynamic understanding of consent.

## B. The Regulation of Private Conduct

A second defining feature of the international regulatory approach to energy is that it addresses the conduct of non-state actors, corporations and consumers, that is normally only of tangential concern to international law. This has first to

---

[42] 1992 Convention on Biological Diversity, COP 9 Decision IX/1. In-depth review of the programme of work on agricultural biodiversity.

[43] The 2020 Regulations governing sulphur oxide (SOx) emissions from ships are included in Annex VI to the International Convention for the prevention of Pollution from ships (MARPOL Convention). Annex VI sets progressive stricter regulations in order to control emissions from ships, including SOx and nitrous oxides (NOx).

[44] https://ghgprotocol.org/life-cycle-databases.

[45] Further A Boyle and C Chinkin, *The Making of International Law* (Oxford University Press, 2007).

[46] R Bradley Kar and MJ Radin, 'Pseudo-Contract and Shared Meaning Analysis' (2019) 132 *Harvard Law Review* 1135.

do with the fact that this is a field where large, centralised corporations remain dominant, even though energy generation is decentralising as a consequence of the rise of renewables technologies. The role of major energy corporations engaged in upstream extraction,[47] and of utilities in their capacity as carbon majors, remains critical and entails a special responsibility over that of small companies or even individuals.

International regulation of energy seeks not necessarily to prescribe the conduct of these actors, but instead to send signals about priorities and the direction of travel in regulatory change. The UN Global Compact signals to corporations active in the energy sector that they are responsible for upholding international standards.[48] Principles 1, 2, and 7 of the UN Global Compact demand that businesses support and respect, within their spheres of influence, the protection of human rights and that they adopt a precautionary approach in addressing environmental challenges. International organisations have implemented standards and requirements for human rights and environmental protection responsibilities, including the World Bank Group and the International Finance Corporation (IFC). These include the World Bank's Environmental and Social Standards,[49] and the IFC's Performance Standards on Environmental and Social Sustainability (latest version in 2012).[50] In the context of the ongoing modernisation of the ECT. In 2019, the European Commission has proposed that the treaty contribute to the promotion of human rights and international labour standards, including through provisions on transparency and corporate social responsibility/responsible business conduct.[51]

An early example of the influence of such human rights and environmental principles on corporate action in the energy sector relates to the Baku-Tbilisi-Ceyhan (BTC) oil and gas pipeline project, which carries up to a million barrels of oil a day over 1,000 miles across the Caspian region. In 1999, the states of Turkey,

---

[47] This category comprises both commercial companies and Stata-owned enterprises (SOEs). SOEs are not state organs, although under certain circumstances their conduct may be attributable to a state, see PCA Case 2005-04/AA227, *Yukos Universal Limited (Isle of Man) v The Russian Federation*, conducted under the UNCITRAL Arbitration Rules (1976) pursuant to the Energy Charter Treaty, in conjunction with PCA Case No AA 226 (*Hulley Enterprises Limited (Cyprus) v The Russian Federation*) and PCA Case No AA 228 (*Veteran Petroleum Limited (Cyprus) v The Russian Federation*), Final Award 18 July 2014.

[48] Information on the UN Global Compact is available at www.unglobalcompact.org, and the 10 Principles of the UN Global Compact are available at www.unglobalcompact.org/what-is-gc/mission/principles.

[49] See 'Environmental and Social Standards (ESS)' (World Bank, 2019), available at www.worldbank.org/en/projects-operations/environmental-and-social-framework/brief/environmental-and-social-standards.

[50] See 'Performance Standards' (Ifc.org, 2019), available at www.ifc.org/wps/wcm/connect/Topics_Ext_Content/IFC_External_Corporate_Site/Sustainability-At-IFC/Policies-Standards/Performance-Standards. The BTC Joint Statement and Human Rights Undertaking mention World Bank Group Standards.

[51] Commission proposal for a negotiating mandate and annex available at http://trade.ec.europa.eu/doclib/press/index.cfm? Id=2017.

Azerbaijan and Georgia entered into an intergovernmental agreement to develop the BTC Pipeline, and between 1999 and 2002, host government agreements were entered between the states and a consortium of corporate companies, with BP as project operator. BP sought to establish a new benchmark for a major infrastructure project. To this effect, BP incorporated into core project documents a commitment to respect applicable standards articulated in the UN Universal Declaration of Human Rights (UDHR), the Tripartite Declaration of Principles established by the International Labour Organization (ILO), and the Guidelines for Multinational Enterprises promulgated by the Organization for Economic Cooperation and Development (OECD). BP caused Turkey, Azerbaijan and Georgia to enter into a 'Joint Statement',[52] guaranteeing adherence to internationally recognised human rights, labour rights, and environmental standards, including a commitment to the standards espoused in the Voluntary Principles on Security and Human Rights for the extractives industries. The BTC Company also signed a legally binding Human Rights Undertaking,[53] designed to protect the rights of the three host governments to promote and regulate human rights and environmental issues.

The signalling effect of the Paris Agreement and its objectives is reflected in the current oil majors' strategies. A recent voluntary undertaking is Royal Dutch Shell's decision to invest USD 300 million over three years in reforestation projects, including in the Netherlands and Spain.[54] This initiative aims to offset the carbon emissions produced when customers consume the fossil fuels that Shell produces and is creating a programme to allow drivers to support the company's purchase of carbon credits from ecoprojects. This company plans to double the investment in new energy forms to USD 4 billion per year.[55] The effect extends to the level of shareholders using corporate governance instruments to bring about changes in company strategy. At the same time, international finance institutions and pension funds are divesting away from extreme fossil fuels. As an example, the World Bank will end its financial support for oil and gas extraction within the next two years. The Bank already ceased lending for coal-fired power stations in 2010.

Public international bodies reinforce this signal through incentives and voluntary instruments. Signal-based public-private cooperation to scale new clean technologies is being used under the informal Clean Energy Ministerial, for instance, in its initiative to promote hydrogen throughout its value chain.[56] The Energy Charter Secretariat has established an Industry Advisory Panel (IAP)

---

[52] Baku-Tbilisi-Ceyhan Joint Statement, 11 May 2003, available at https://subsites.bp.com/caspian/Joint%20Statement.pdf.

[53] Baku-Tbilisi-Ceyhan Human Rights Undertaking, 22 December 2003 available at https://subsites.bp.com/caspian/Human%20Rights%20Undertaking.pdf.

[54] Shell published its energy transition report in April 2018, available at www.shell.com/energy-and-innovation/the-energy-future/shell-energy-transition-report.html.

[55] 'Shell Invests In Nature As Part Of Broad Drive To Tackle $CO_2$ Emissions', press release (Shell, 2019), available at www.shell.com/media/news-and-media-releases/2019/shell-invests-in-nature-to-tackle-co2-emissions.html.

[56] The Hydrogen Initiative will leverage and benefit from the knowledge, expertise and early investments made by both the private and public sectors. Leading industry stakeholders and collaborative

in 2004 to strengthen the dialogue with the private energy sector in line with international regulatory objectives.[57] The IAP provides policy advice from energy companies, international business associations and financial institutions on energy investment and the functioning of energy markets. In 2001, the Energy Charter Secretariat set up a voluntary Legal Advisory Task Force (LATF) of experts inter alia from private companies and SOEs to assist in drafting Model Agreements on Cross-Border Pipelines and Electricity Lines on the transport of energy materials and products across borders.[58] These Model Agreements standardise the host-government agreements signed typically between states involved in the project and between the project company and host states. The first Model Agreements were published in 2004 and were last updated in 2008.[59] From 2018, the modernisation phase II has focused on adapting the Model Agreements.[60] This modernisation has also involved signal-based regulation of corporate conduct in case of emergencies. In 2004, in response to reoccurring energy transit interruptions and its major implications on energy access, the Energy Secretariat developed an Early-Warning Mechanism. This mechanism is for voluntary acceptance by parties, providing a tool for transparency, exchange of information, consultation, and verification (monitoring).[61] For instance, in July 2016, Ukraine's SOE, Naftogaz, wrote to the European Commission informing about gas pressure irregularities in the main gas transmission system and proposing the use of existing ECT procedures such as the Early Warning Mechanism.[62]

The international law of energy, driven by a meta-norm, goes beyond regulating private operations of incumbents, and it ultimately aims at social welfare maximisation. While this is the aim of regulation in all sectors of the economy, in the sphere of energy it sets public policy objectives that are underpinned by the scientific expertise that the Intergovernmental Panel on Climate Change (IPCC)

---

forums such as the Hydrogen Council will contribute to work undertaken through the initiative. 'Countries launch a new international effort on hydrogen to help achieve global clean energy ambitions', 29 May 2019 (Clean Energy Ministerial, 2019), available at www.cleanenergyministerial.org/news.

[57] For further information on the Energy Charter Secretariat's IAP see https://energycharter.org/who-we-are/industry-advisory-panel.

[58] Dr Mete had served in the LATF of the Energy Charter Secretariat prior to joining the Secretariat full time in February 2019. The knowledge shared here is based on her involvement in the LATF.

[59] See https://energycharter.org/what-we-do/trade-and-transit/model-agreements.

[60] Further information on the update of the Energy Charter Model Agreements on Cross Border Pipelines is available at: https://energycharter.org/media/news/article/technical-subgroup-on-transit-holds-its-secondmeeting/?tx_news_pi1%5Bcontroller%5D=News&tx_news_pi1%5Baction%5D=detail&cHash=0925febe267437c2badb9f6274600820.

[61] 'Energy Charter, Early Warning Mechanism', available at: https://energycharter.org/media/news/article/the-energy-charter-early-warning-mechanism-2014-russia-ukraine-eu-transit-issues/?tx_news_pi1%5Bcontroller%5D=News&tx_news_pi1%5Baction%5D=detail&cHash=3aa4c1424688c6325b0d34a87d5ddaf9.

[62] See https://energycharter.org/media/news/article/naftogaz-proposed-to-use-model-energy-charter-early-warning-mechanismnaftogaz-predlo/?tx_news_pi1%5Bcontroller%5D=News&tx_news_pi1%5Baction%5D=detail&cHash=670d1b49b65bfea5daaf873c69076074.

provides. At the same time, the means of achieving these objectives are subject to the parameter of cost-effectiveness. Cost-effectiveness determines preference for market-based instruments that incentivise private investment in cleaner energy. For instance, the polluter-pays principle that internalises environmental costs was first established in international environmental law and applied to quintessentially environmental problems, such as levels of pollutants in air, land or water. The principles of international environmental law reflect an understanding of 'principle' as a norm of unlimited application.[63] The regulatory approach now extends their application to the specifics of energy, such as the carbon emissions that are the by-products of energy production, transport and consumption.[64]

Regulation of private conduct can be achieved through indirectly effective international rules, obligating states to license or otherwise control private conduct. The classic example is deep seabed mining under the 1982 UN Convention on the Law of the Sea.[65] The Convention directly prescribes states' licensing of operators and indirectly the conduct of the licensed operators in mineral resource exploitation.[66] For energy, such indirect, legal regulation is performed by the EU's Emissions Trading System (ETS) for utilities and similar emissions trading schemes.[67] Under these schemes, states are to license the energy operators and allocate maximum carbon emissions allowances, which can be traded, in order to indirectly steer their conduct. This indirect regulation is being extended throughout the energy value chain to consumption. For instance, the International Civil Aviation Organisation (ICAO) now operates a system of voluntary State Action Plans on climate action by Member States.[68] Further, under the ICAO Assembly Resolution A39-3, international air companies will be accountable for their consumption and will have to offset their carbon emissions.[69]

---

[63] Further N MacCormick, *Institutions of Law* (Oxford University Press, 2007).

[64] That being said, regulation also aims at creating markets and incentives to invest – and in some respect it relates to profit maximisation, or at least reasonable return of the investment.

[65] United Nations Convention on the Law of the Sea, entered into force 16 November 1994, 1833 UNTS 3.

[66] International Tribunal for The Law of The Sea, Reports of Judgments, Advisory Opinions and Orders, Responsibilities and obligations of States sponsoring persons and entities with respect to activities in the Area (Request for Advisory Opinion Submitted to The Seabed Disputes Chamber), List of cases: No 17, Advisory Opinion of 1 February 2011.

[67] The EU emissions trading system (EU ETS) is a cornerstone of the EU's policy to combat climate change and its key tool for reducing greenhouse gas emissions cost-effectively. It is the world's first major carbon market and remains the biggest one. A detailed overview of EU ETS is available at https://ec.europa.eu/clima/policies/ets_en.

[68] 114 ICAO Member States had submitted their State Action Plans by May 2019. Further information on ICAO climate action State Action Plans are available at www.icao.int/environmental-protection/Pages/ClimateChange_ActionPlan.aspx.

[69] Carbon Offsetting and Reduction Scheme for International Aviation (CORSIA), ICAO, Assembly Resolution A39-3: 'Consolidated statement of continuing ICAO policies and practices related to environmental protection – Global Market-based Measure (MBM) scheme' (ICAO, 2019), available at www.icao.int/environmental-protection/documents/resolution_a39_3.pdf.

The meta-norm of the SDGs and Paris objective also promotes reduction of energy consumption, that is energy-efficiency.[70] The Energy Charter Protocol for Energy Efficiency and Related Environmental Aspects[71] is an early example setting international legal principles designed to promote energy-efficiency. The Protocol obligates states to cooperates to implement state-specific policies and to create market conditions to scale up investments in energy-efficiency.

## C. Social Justice, Solidarity and Fairness

Regulation for sustainable and clean energy is disruptive of the status quo. Energy regulation has necessarily distributive and redistributive consequences between and within states. It entails parameters of social justice to steer this regulatory change.[72] Social justice, in this context, has two aspects: solidarity and fairness. International regulation of energy hence pushes another doctrine of international law to slip, ie that states are primarily responsible to serve the needs of their people.

SDG 7 demands that all have access to sustainable and affordable clean energy, and in particular to electricity. Ensuring such access becomes a prerequisite of social justice that applies worldwide. It also underpins a claim of developing fossil resource-endowed states to solidarity in making the required transition. That claim is being honoured through mechanisms such as technology transfer, international research, development support and foreign direct investment, as well as capacity-building programmes, in order to speed up the spread of clean energy technologies in developing countries. For instance, the ECT promotes and supports techno-logical solutions and improving access to clean and affordable energy, promoting regional market integration to secure energy transition, and promoting clean and smart energy technologies.[73] The Paris Agreement envisages technology develop-ment and transfer for both improving resilience to climate change and reducing GHG emissions.[74] It establishes a Technology Mechanism to this effect.[75]

A second aspect of social justice relates to fairness. This concerns the disrup-tive effect of an energy transition on the skilled workforces in many states employed in the extractive industries. The international climate action under the UNFCCC recognises this, as in 2018 the 24th meeting of the Conference of the

---

[70] Energy-efficiency is a cost measure but also a means to change consumer behaviour. Energy-efficiency is about behaviour of individuals and companies, and $CO_2$ reduction and trade initiatives, while the polluter pays principle focuses on regulating behaviour of companies.

[71] More information on the Protocol on Energy Efficiency and Related Environmental Aspects (PEEREA) is available at https://energycharter.org/process/energy-charter-treaty-1994/energy-efficiency-protocol.

[72] M Adler, 'The normative foundation of risk regulation' (2003) 87 *Minnesota Law Review* 1293.

[73] ECT Art 8.

[74] This list of available GHG inventories can be found at http://ghgprotocol.org/life-cycle-databases.

[75] The Technology Mechanism consists of two bodies: the Technology Executive Committee; and the Climate Technology Centre and Network. They work together to enhance climate technology activities. See https://unfccc.int/ttclear/support/technology-mechanism.html.

Parties to the UNFCCC resolved the Silesia Declaration on 'Solidarity and the Just Transition'.[76] The declaration aims to develop measures focused on new skills as well as new infrastructure for the regions concerned.

## V.  From the Plural, International Law on Energy to the International Law of Energy through Realignment with the Meta-norm

Energy is a horizontal matter, cutting across all established branches of international law. The traditional international law on energy is hence marked by the plurality of concerns and objectives that these branches serve. This plurality can be assorted on to two tiers. One is energy-specific international law, and it mostly comprises the multilateral ECT and intergovernmental agreements on supply and infrastructure. Much more voluminous is the second tier comprising international law that is not energy-specific. This extant international law is serving plural objectives and concerns that are non-specific to energy. Its rules may apply to energy falling within its scope *ratione materiae* as much as they do to other objects. Despite the cognitive dominance of the principle of permanent sovereignty over natural (energy) resources, the non-energy specific international law covers several trans-boundary aspects of energy. A good illustration is investment law, the branch of international law developed to ensure legal certainty for foreign direct investments. It applies to all investments, including in upstream and downstream energy. It remains generic, even if a large percentage of all investment arbitration actually concerns energy projects.

As a result of the universal collective action on SDGs 7 and 13 and the Paris Agreement objective, the meta-norm for energy now redefines the relationship with extant international law. There is an impetus for all international law that applies to energy to realign itself with the demands of the new meta-norm. This realignment underpins the conceptual pivot from an international law on energy to the international law of energy.

This section considers this realignment in more depth. Realignment is a not a hierarchical-central affair. Rather, it is an autonomous process within each branch of international law. For present purposes, these branches shall be understood as regimes, capable of autonomous processes of realignment by making use of the procedures and instruments for its development that each regime has developed. In each regime, realignment becomes manifest as a shift from a generic status quo to a novel energy-specific position that absorbs the demands of the meta-norm.

---

[76] https://cop24.gov.pl/fileadmin/user_upload/Solidarity_and_Just_Transition_Silesia_Declaration_2_.pdf. See also European Council Conclusions on the EU strategic agenda, 20/21 June 2019, para 4.

Such realignment is observable in the international law regimes of trade, investment, infrastructure and trans-boundary resource management.

## A. A Realignment of World Trade Law on Energy

Trans-boundary trade in energy is subject to world trade law in goods and services. This trade law is international law on energy in the sense described above. It follows the rationale of comparative advantage that dominates this branch of international law.[77] Energy is, in all its forms, to be considered as a good to which the generic principles and rules of world trade law applies. That is true for commodities such as oil and gas, and also for electricity.[78] It is to be acknowledged that the disciplines of world trade law have not worked too well for energy. This has to do with the fact that direct import tariffs have played a small practical role. Also, the control on national local content rules is weak, and non-discriminatory access to upstream energy is not really the remit of world trade law either. The most important effect of world trade law then may be that is binds tariffs on goods. The current negotiations between the USA and China demonstrate the role of tariffs for the demand of energy, and hence its price.

However, world trade law is realigning itself to implement the meta-norm of a climate action-driven energy transition. This is reflected in the evolving WTO case law on energy that accommodates national support schemes for renewables.[79] More generally, this realignment uses the instrument of regional or bilateral preferential trade agreements. Absorbing the impetus of climate action, these instruments serve to use trade benefits to drive clean energy policies.

Preferential trade agreements with third states are now an essential tool of the EU's commercial policy, which under the Lisbon Treaty also encompasses the exclusive competence for substantive investment protection as well as a shared competence with the Member States for investor-state-dispute settlement. The generic negotiating objective of the EU for its preferential trade agreements is to include a dedicated chapter for trade in energy that provides access to the partners' energy markets and resources, as well as reduced tariffs for clean energy technology.[80] In the latter respect, the EU is following the lead of the Association of Southeast Asian Nations (ASEAN).[81]

---

[77] D Patterson and A Arifalo, *The New Global Trading Order: The Evolving State and the Future of Trade*, (Cambridge University Press, 2008).

[78] V Roeben, *Towards a European Energy Union* (Cambridge University Press, 2018) 72. Also see T Cottier, 'Energy in WTO law and policy' (WTO Publication, 2008) (energy as service); M Desta, 'The GATT/WTO System and International Trade in Petroleum' (2003) 21 *Journal of Energy & Natural Resources Law* 385.

[79] See Roeben (ibid) 75.

[80] For instance, Commission, Transatlantic Trade and Investment Partnership, 'EU TEXTUAL PROPOSAL Energy and Raw Materials', 14 July 2016, available at http://trade.ec.europa.eu/doclib/docs/2016/july/tradoc_154801.pdf.

[81] ASEAN is a regional intergovernmental organisation comprising 10 countries in South-east Asia, which promotes intergovernmental cooperation and facilitates economic, political, security,

Post-Paris Agreement, a new generation of EU preferential trade agreements integrate the demands of the climate action meta-norm. These agreements couple trade preference and the multilateral environmental agreements (MEA) in force for the parties. Compliance with those MEA becomes an obligation under the preferential trade agreement, and non-compliance is subject to dispute settlement under that agreement. The EU–Canada Comprehensive Economic and Trade Agreement (CETA)[82] undertakes this integration through Chapter 24 on trade and environment. Under Article 24.6, a sub-committee of the CETA Joint Committee, the Committee on Trade and Sustainable Development, shall oversee the implementation of this chapter. Hence, there is an institutional mechanism for infra-treaty dynamic integration into the chapter of novel MEA. From 2017, the EU and Canada have been deliberating integrating into the CETA climate action obligations resulting from the Paris Agreement.[83] The CETA Joint Committee has affirmed 'the Parties' commitment to effectively implement the Paris Agreement, as a multilateral agreement within the meaning of Art. 24.4 of CETA'. The committee

> recommends that the Parties cooperate, work together and take joint action relevant to address climate change and promote the mutual supportiveness of trade and climate policies, rules and measures thereby contributing to the purpose and goals of the Paris Agreement and the transition to low greenhouse gas emissions.[84]

The effectiveness and enforceability of integrating such provisions in the trade agreements remain to be tested. The 2017 opinion of the European Court of Justice (ECJ) on the EU–Singapore Free Trade Agreement (FTA)[85] provides an important pointer. The ECJ not only emphasised the direct and immediate effect of sustainability on trade,[86] but also opined that aspects of trade agreements could be suspended if there was a breach of the sustainability chapter. Such a breach would qualify as 'material' within the meaning of the Vienna Convention on the Law of Treaties. The 2019 EU–Japan Economic Partnership Agreement (EPA) is the first with an explicit reference to the Paris Climate Agreement.[87] Under the EPA, Japan

---

military, educational and sociocultural integration among its members and other countries in Asia.

[82] The Comprehensive Economic and Trade Agreement is a free-trade agreement between Canada, the EU and its Member States. The treaty eliminates 98% of the tariffs between Canada and the EU. The negotiations were concluded in August 2014. The agreement was signed on 30 October 2016 and the European Parliament gave its consent on 15 February 2017. CETA entered into force provisionally on 21 September 2017, in accordance with TFEU Art 218(5).

[83] Commission Staff Working Document, Individual reports and info sheets on implementation of EU Free Trade Agreements (SWD(2018) 454) 31 October 2018, 19.

[84] The recommendation of the CETA joint committee on trade, climate action and the Paris Agreement is available at http://trade.ec.europa.eu/doclib/docs/2018/september/tradoc_157415.pdf.

[85] Opinion 2/15 of the Court (Full Court) of 16 May 2017.

[86] Opinion 2/15, para 158: 'Such effects result, first, from the commitment of the Parties, stemming from Article 13.1.3 of the envisaged agreement, on the one hand, not to encourage trade by reducing the levels of social and environmental protection in their respective territories below the standards laid down by international commitments and, on the other, not to apply those standards in a protectionist manner ...'.

[87] Art 16.4(4) of EPA reads: 'The Parties reaffirm their commitments to effectively implement the UNFCCC and the Paris Agreement, done at Paris on 12 December 2015 by the Conference of the

and the EU, 'strive to facilitate' trade in renewable energy and other low-carbon solutions to combat climate change.[88] It remains to be seen whether membership of the Paris Agreement, that is the ratification or the non-exit from that treaty, is made a condition by the EU for it to conclude a preferential trade agreement. The negotiations with the USA may prove a test case.[89]

Other economic and trading blocs employ preferential trade agreements in a similar fashion. The 2018 reformed Trans-Pacific Partnership, the Comprehensive and Progressive Agreement for Trans-Pacific Partnership (CPATPP),[90] has about two-thirds of its provisions identical to the TPP draft at the time the USA was in the negotiating process. The energy-relevant Chapter 17 on state-owned enterprises (SOEs) is unchanged, requiring signatories to share information about SOEs with each other, with the intent of engaging with the issue of state intervention in markets. Chapter 22 on the environment is also preserved. TPP provisions that were priorities of the US were suspended or modified from the CPTPP, including the provision for companies to sue governments on strict regulations over oil and gas developments. The 2018 US–Mexico–Canada Agreement (USMCA), which is a renegotiation of the North American Free Trade Agreement (NAFTA), actually enhances energy trade.[91] The investor–state dispute resolution provision adds protection for oil and gas, infrastructure and clean energy generation; there is support for deepening cross-border ties in the energy sector and also a new chapter on anti-corruption and a separate standalone chapter on the environment.

# B. Realignment of International Law on Energy Investment

Trans-boundary investment in energy is subject to the international law on investment protection and investor-state-dispute settlement (ISDS). Apart from the ECT, this international law is laid down in a web of bilateral treaties. Upstream energy,

---

Parties to the UNFCCC at its 21st session. The Parties shall cooperate to promote the positive contribution of trade to the transition to low greenhouse gas emissions and climate-resilient development. The Parties commit to working together to take actions to address climate change towards achieving the ultimate objective of the UNFCCC and the purpose of the Paris Agreement'.

[88] Art 16.5(c) of EPA reads: '[The Parties] shall strive to facilitate trade and investment in goods and services of particular relevance to climate change mitigation, such as those related to sustainable renewable energy and energy efficient goods and services, in a manner consistent with this Agreement'.

[89] European Parliament, Draft motion for a resolution on the recommendations for opening of trade negotiations between the EU and the US (2019/2537(RSP)).

[90] Comprehensive and Progressive Agreement for Trans-Pacific Partnership, Santiago, 8 March 2018. On 30 December 2018, the agreement entered into force between Australia, Canada, Japan, Mexico, New Zealand and Singapore, and on 14 January 2019 for Vietnam. Summaries of the CPATPP provisions are available at https://international.gc.ca/trade-commerce/trade-agreements-accords-commerciaux/agr-acc/cptpp-ptpgp/chapter_summaries-sommaires_chapitres.aspx?lang=eng#20.

[91] Agreement between the United States of America, the United Mexican States and Canada, signed 30 November 2018, not yet in force; text available at https://ustr.gov/trade-agreements/free-trade-agreements/united-states-mexico-canada-agreement/agreement-between. The agreement has different titles.

whether non-renewable or renewable, is generally considered an investment to which the generic protective rules pre- and post-admission of any investment apply. The general rationale of legal stability of this international law hence also covers energy.[92]

However, a realignment of international investment law with the meta-norm of sustainable energy is under way, providing an energy-specific focus.[93] Investment law moves from stability for investors (and compensation in the event of changes) to a rationale of flexibility and proportionality, in which a regulatory measure that meets a legitimate objective and constitutes suitable and necessary means of implementation is lawful and does not entail a duty to compensate investors. Aligned with the meta-norm, international investment law permits states to have a flexible regulatory policy on energy-related matters. This flexibility permits host states to introduce but also to exit support policies for clean energy investments.

This realignment is well reflected in the new generation EU preferential trade agreements.[94] These carve out a regulatory space for the host state of the investment. There is a list of legitimate public policy concerns that includes climate related action. The agreements also provide that a change in the law or support policy exit per se do not violate the legitimate expectations of investors.

This same alignment is manifest in the ECT context, which is the only multilateral investment protection regime that applies specifically to energy. It is today the most litigated investment agreement in the world, with a total of more than 120 notified disputes. As originally conceived, this regime served to apply the general rationale of legal certainty to trans-boundary mainly upstream energy investments. It promotes foreign investment in the energy sector in its over 50 contracting parties in Part III of the Treaty, and protects investments made against the most important political risks, such as discrimination, expropriation and nationalisation, breach of individual investment contracts, damages due to war and similar events, and unjustified restrictions on the transfer of funds. The dispute settlement provisions of the Treaty, covering both state-to-state arbitration and investor-state dispute settlement, reinforce these investor rights. As there has been a surge of renewable energy investments across its constituency, the majority of the case law in recent years, particularly involving Southern Europe, have evolved around finding the right balance between a state's right to regulate to meet evolving circumstances and the protection of an investor's immutable economic rights.[95] The Southern European host states concerned had phased out subsidies for renewables, and this triggered investment disputes under the ECT. Many of

---

[92] P Cameron, 'Stabilization and the impact of changing patterns of energy investment' (2017) 10 *The Journal of World Energy Law & Business* 389.

[93] Speculative DW Rivkin, SJ Lamb, NK Leslie, 'The future of investor-state dispute settlement in the energy sector: engaging with climate change, human rights and the rule of law' (2015) 8 *Journal of World Energy Law & Business* 130.

[94] See the Singapore and the Japan FTAs discussed above.

[95] See also ch 11 and ch 14.

these cases are ongoing but the outcome of some of these cases are presenting a division among arbitral tribunals over this equilibrium between the need for a stable and predictable investment framework and the right of states to regulate. The general reason for inconsistent outcomes is that especially in the case of Spain, the cases relate to different incentives introduced at different times.[96] In some cases concerning Italy, in addition to the incentives provided by regulation, there were express assurances provided by the states that no amendments would occur and this had a significant role on tribunals' decisions.[97]

The uneven outcome of ECT renewable energy arbitral awards calls for a realignment of the investment law regime. Sustainable energy goals push towards the right of states for policy entry *and exit* on the support that renewable technology required at least initially, but which becomes less important as grid parity is being reached and which support can then de devoted to newer clean technologies. The European Commission has noted in May 2019 that the ECT rules on investment protection are no longer sustainable or adequate for the current challenges.[98] The Commission recommends that the modernisation of the ECT should aim at a high level of investment protection with provisions affording legal certainty for investors and investments of Parties in each other's market.

Treaty texts can be rigid, and changing them requires consensus, which is not always easy to reach when a challenging balance is being sought. The Energy Charter Secretariat has hence produced soft-regulation to modernise the Treaty investment regime, short of treaty change. As part of its *modernisation phase II*, in 2014, the Secretariat established a Conflict Resolution Centre,[99] which provides assistance with mediation and conciliation; neutral, independent legal advice; and assistance in dispute resolution. In 2017, a Guide on Investment Mediation, which aims to promote amicable dispute settlement in investor-state disputes, was published. The Energy Charter Secretariat also has an Investment Facilitation Toolbox focused on removing barriers to establishment of energy investments. The Handbook on General Provisions Applicable to Investment Agreements in the Energy Sector[100] collates different policies and clauses available when negotiating

[96] *Charanne BV, Construction Investments SARL v Spain*, SCC Arbitration No 062/2012 ('*Charanne*'); *Eiser Infrastructure Limited and Energia Solar Luxembourg Sarl v Spain*, ICSID Case No ARB/13/36 ('*Eiser*').

[97] *Jürgen Wirtgen, Stefan Wirtgen, Gisela Wirtgen, JSW Solar (zwei) GmbH & Co KG v The Czech Republic* ('*Wirtgen*') PCA Case No 2014-03; *Blusun SA, Jean-Pierre Lecorcier and Michael Stein v Italy*, ICSID Case No ARB/14/3 ('*Blusun*'); and *Charanne*.

[98] See the Commission proposal for a negotiating mandate and annex at http://trade.ec.europa.eu/doclib/press/index.cfm?id=2017.

[99] In 2014 the Energy Charter Conference mandated the Secretariat to the assist with good offices, mediation and conciliation, as well as to provide neutral, independent legal advice and assistance in dispute resolution and participate in pre-trial proceedings between Contracting Parties before they revert to the mechanisms contained in ECT Art 27 or Annex D.

[100] https://energycharter.org/fileadmin/DocumentsMedia/Other_Publications/20171116-new Handbook.pdf.

an investment agreement. The Energy Investment Risk Assessment (EIRA)[101] publication assists governments improve investment conditions for foreign investors in the energy sector, increasingly focusing on renewable energy investments.

There is, of course, a limit to what can be achieved with soft law instruments. In November 2017, the Energy Charter Conference launched a discussion on the potential modernisation of the treaty text.[102] In 2018, the topics for modernisation were approved.[103] Around a third of the provisions to be revised concern investment promotion and protection in the energy sector in line with the SDGs and Paris Agreement. The Contracting Parties to the ECT are renegotiating new policy options for topics, among others, of pre-investment, definition of 'economic activity in the energy sector', definition of investment and of investor, right to regulate, definition of the Fair and Equitable Treatment (FET) and Most-Favoured Nation (MFN) clauses, definition of indirect expropriation, compensation for losses, as well as the novel concepts of transparency, sustainable development and corporate social responsibility. If a consensus can be reached in due time, this will present a fundamental milestone in the realignment of international investment protection. This quasi-universal realignment under the ECT is likely to entail a realignment of the international investment law of energy beyond that treaty. The start of the negotiations to modernise the Energy Charter Treaty will ultimately be decided by the Energy Charter Conference. Indeed, on 15 July 2019 the European Council adopted two negotiation directives for the modernisation of the ECT which aim to focus on ensuring that climate change and clean energy transition goals are reflected in the modernised ECT.[104] The Energy Charter Conference as the decision-making body approved policy options for the ECT modernisation in October 2019.[105]

## C. Realignment of International Law on Energy Infrastructure

All trans-boundary trade and delivery of energy is infrastructure-bound. This is the case for fossil sources – pipelines for oil and gas, ports and facilities for liquified natural gas (LNG) – as well as for electricity generated from renewables and transmitted through cables. This infrastructure is subject to a plurality of international law. The law of the sea applies to marine infrastructure. A host

---

[101] https://energycharter.org/what-we-do/investment/energy-investment-risk-assessment-eira.

[102] Commission proposal for a negotiating mandate and annex, available at http://trade.ec.europa.eu/doclib/press/index.cfm?id=2017.

[103] A full list of approved topics for the modernisation is available at https://energycharter.org/media/news/article/approved-topics-for-the-modernisation-of-the-energy-charter-treaty.

[104] K Rettig, 'Council adopts negotiation directives for modernisation of Energy Charter Treaty on 15 July 2019', press release, available at: www.consilium.europa.eu/en/press/press-releases/2019/07/15/council-adopts-negotiation-directives-for-modernisation-of-energy-charter-treaty.

[105] See Conference Decision CCDEC201908.

of Intergovernmental Agreements (IGA) between the participating states govern both marine and terrestrial infrastructure projects, these supplemented by contracts with the private, transnational consortia that actually build the project.

The emergence of the meta-norm of sustainable energy has had consequences for this international law. For instance, the meta-norm provides impetus to develop dedicated international law for the LNG infrastructure, given that gas is bridge fuel in the energy transition. In the restarted trade agreement negotiations between the US and the EU, this underpins the EU's readiness to import LNG through an expanded reliquefaction infrastructure.[106] Between the EU and the US, and between the EU and Japan, dedicated bilateral bodies have been set up to this effect.[107] The Energy Charter Secretariat has established an LNG taskforce to work on bolt-on, flexible model clauses, as part of the *modernisation phase II* process.

In the electricity sector, new challenges and concepts of regulation are emerging as trans-boundary grid networks become more widespread.[108] Their operation requires regulatory systems to foster transnational network interconnections and unrestrained power transit under international law. The EU single electricity market regulation currently provides the most elaborate framework for transmission of electricity across borders.[109] There is a rapid expansion of infrastructure projects in new demand centres in Africa, Caucasus, Central Asia and South-east Asia. The emergence of power pools and super grids presents a new opportunity for international law of energy to develop. At the international level, the WTO/GATT and ECT provisions offer an umbrella framework, and UNCLOS becomes relevant when considering undersea cables. The revised draft Energy Charter Model Agreements for Cross-Border Pipelines and Electricity Line Agreements contain new provisions[110] referring to the Paris Agreement and transparency initiatives and confirms that gas pipelines are to be climate friendlier. It proposes incorporation of climate change and human rights clauses, and foresees new

---

[106] 'Joint US–EU Statement following President Juncker's visit to the White House', Washington, 25 July 2018, available at http://europa.eu/rapid/press-release_STATEMENT-18-4687_en.htm'; also 'Liquefied Natural Gas (LNG) imports from the U.S. continue to rise, up by 181%', 8 March 2019 available at: https://ec.europa.eu/energy/en/news/eu-us-joint-statement-liquefied-natural-gas-lng-imports-us-continue-rise-181-0.

[107] 'Memorandum of Cooperation between the European Commission, on behalf of the European Union, and the Ministry of Economy, Trade and Industry of Japan on Promoting and Establishing a Liquid, Flexible and Transparent Global Liquefied Natural Gas Market in the context of enhancing the EU – Japan cooperation on secure and sustainable energy' (11 June 2017), available at: https://ec.europa.eu/energy/sites/ener/files/documents/japanmoc2017_energy.pdf.

[108] RM Plaza, 'Transnational power transmission and international law' (2013) *International Review of Law* 8, available at www.qscience.com/doi/pdf/10.5339/irl.2013.8.

[109] The recast Electricity Directive 2019/944 and Regulation 2019/943, parts of the so-called Clean Energy Package for all Europeans proposed by the Commission in November 2017, were adopted in May 2019. They can be considered as a fourth electricity market package. The Directive sets harmonised rules for a regional market. The Regulation inter alia enables the development of technical codes for trans-boundary electricity infrastructure.

[110] The 2008 Model Agreements are available at https://energycharter.org/what-we-do/trade-and-transit/model-agreements.

methods for effective exchange of information and establishment of responsive technical standards.

However, greater integration of national power systems seems only viable under technically based, dedicated rules at the regional level. In the EU, these are produced through the European Network of Transmission System Operators for Electricity (ENTSO-E) and the Agency for Cooperation of Energy Regulators (ACER).[111] Other regional frameworks are realigning with the more established EU regulatory regimes to meet climate change goals. This regime for regional system operability and infrastructure networks with or without storage solutions – in the absence of an international authority/legal framework – is the most evolved regional framework and is becoming an international best practice and influencing regulatory evolution elsewhere. Conceptually, this EU law could be considered to form international law of energy by way of an institutional dissemination.

This realignment extends to disposing of the generation infrastructure of the past, the so-called decommissioning aspects of oil platforms. There is lack of international law because the initial understanding was that all installations would simply be removed in total. In Europe, the majority of offshore oil and gas installations are located in the North Sea and the Protection of the Marine Environment of the North-East Atlantic (OSPAR) Decision 98/3[112] requires full removal of most offshore installations from the marine environment at the end of their useful life. It also encourages reuse and recycling of these installations. However, reports of possible damage to new marine life have initiated discussion of alternative methods of decommissioning, driving the development of specific international rules.[113] The 1989 International Maritime Organisation (IMO) Guidelines and Standards for the Removal of Offshore Installations and Structures on the Continental Shelf and in the Exclusive Economic Zone allowed structures to be left in place on a case-by-case basis. The guidelines also refer to the possibility of 'new use or other reasonable justification' for in situ disposal. This initiated discussion on possible conversion of obsolete oil or gas platforms into a dedicated artificial reef. Rigs-to-Reefs (RTR) is the practice of converting decommissioned offshore oil and petroleum rigs into artificial reefs.[114] The adoption by the EU of the so-called Clean Energy Package of legislation is driving industry using carbon-capture and storage technology (CCS). It is now considered that the most cost-effective and

---

[111] Many Latin American states, particularly Brazil and India, are looking to copy–paste EU law for transmission. In the immediate neighbourhood of the EU, Balkan states (most of whom are EU candidates) and Ukraine are already implementing the EU energy laws despite not being EU Member States. Georgia recently joined the Energy Community Treaty for this purpose.

[112] OSPAR Decision 98/3 on the Disposal of Disused Offshore Installations, OSPAR Commission, List of Decisions, Recommendations and Other Agreements Applicable within the Framework of the OSPAR Convention – Update 2018.

[113] A Scarborough Bull and MS Love, 'Worldwide oil and gas platform decommissioning: A review of practices and reefing options' (2019) 168 *Ocean & Coastal Management* 274.

[114] US Bureau of Safety and Environmental Enforcement's definition of rigs-to-reef is available at www.bsee.gov/what-we-do/environmental-focuses/rigs-to-reefs.

environmentally friendly way of treating old rig infrastructure would be not to remove it all, but rather repurpose it as part of a new CCS network.[115] In December 2018, the UK regulator, the Oil and Gas Authority, awarded its first $CO_2$ appraisal and storage licence.[116]

## D. Realignment of International Law on Trans-boundary Energy Resources

Many natural energy resources, both fossil and renewable, are transboundary. These fall under plural branches of international law, ranging from the law of the sea[117] to transboundary watercourses. Realigning itself with the meta-norm of sustainable energy, the international law on international watercourses is developing an energy-specific governance aspect.[118]

Under the law of the sea, the *Timor-Leste v Australia* conciliation of 2016 charts the path to the governance of marine energy resources that straddle jurisdictional line or are in disputed waters.[119] Conciliation is a dispute settlement mechanism that has long lain dormant when compared to binding arbitration and adjudication. Under the 1982 UN Convention on the Law of the Sea, it applies, mandatorily, for maritime delimitation disputes where one of the parties has opted out of binding third-party dispute settlement. Conciliation then could simply emulate delimitation by the drawing of a line pursuant to the principles of equidistance-cum-relevant circumstances. It would follow a rationale of legal certainty for all marine resources, living and non-living. However, in *Timor-Leste v Australia*, the conciliation commission engaged in structured dialogue with the parties that led to a classic maritime boundary treaty in the Timor Sea *and* to the creation of a special regime for the joint development of the Greater Sunrise Field. The implication is that conciliation, whether mandatory or voluntary, permits the negotiation

---

[115] Circular Economy Scotland, 'Circular Economy Scotland', available at www.green-alliance.org.uk/circular-economy-scotland.php.

[116] Three of the largest ports in Europe – Rotterdam, Antwerp and Ghent – are to be used to capture and bury 10 million tonnes of $CO_2$ emissions under the North Sea in what will be the biggest project of its kind in the world. The ports, which account for one-third of the total greenhouse gas emissions from the Benelux region, are to be used to pipe the gas into a porous reservoir of sandstone about 3km below the seabed.

[117] C Sim, 'Investment disputes arising out of areas of unsettled boundaries: Ghana/Côte d'Ivoire' (2018) 11 *Journal of World Energy Law & Business* 1.

[118] For instance, for the Volta Basin, 'Convention on the status of the Volta River and the Establishment of Volta Basin Authority', 19 January 2007, available at https://iea.uoregon.edu/treaty-text/2007-voltabasinauthorityentxt; implementing the UN Convention on the Law of Non-Navigable Uses of International Watercourses, entered into force 17 August 2014, UNTS.

[119] PCA Case No 2016-10, In the Matter of the Maritime Boundary between Timor-Leste and Australia (The Democratic Republic of Timor-Leste – and – The Commonwealth of Australia), Report and Recommendations of the Compulsory Conciliation Commission between Timor-Leste and Australia on the Timor Sea, 9 May 2018; N Bans, 'Settling the maritime boundaries between Timor-Leste and Australia in the Timor Sea' (2018) 11 *Journal of World Energy Law & Business* 387.

of regimes enabling the socially optimal exploitation of a trans-boundary energy resource, by an agency making decisions on energy projects based on merit-order and to reduce externalities, including their carbon emissions.[120]

# VI.  Conclusions

International law has rapidly moved beyond the principle of permanent sovereignty. This chapter clarifies how international lawyers now ought to think about international law relating to energy. It suggests substituting a thicker, evaluative concept – the international law of energy – for a thinner international law on energy. The international law of energy is centred on the specific meta-norm that has evolved since 2015 by force of SDG 7 and 13 and the Paris Agreement objective, and formalises the transition to a global energy system that provides sustainable and affordable energy for all. The meta-norm creates the impetus for a change in the regulatory approaches and international rules on the global energy value cycle (for instance, the modernisation of the ECT), *and* for a realignment of the extant, plural international law that also apply on energy. The meta-norm determines the boundaries of what does and what does not belong to the international law of energy. It is so substantive and influential that it continuously evolves and challenges other branches of international law that apply to energy, by creating this realignment that draws these energy-related issues from other branches to its very own branch as it evolves – like a magnet it brings them all to a whole under international law of energy. This results in the emergence of energy-specific principles, such as clean energy support, technology transfer and a right to regulate. The conclusion is that the international law of energy is a distinct subject matter of public international law – and lawyers can talk about this international law of energy.

It is important for international lawyers to understand this newly defined concept, inter alia, for assessing cases, investment decisions, new rules when negotiating treaties, when granting new licences for cross-border projects and when signing new trade agreements. It has a specific impact on regulated energy-related trade, investment and business activity as well as on social justice and welfare. It carves out its own sphere, though interrelated with other branches of international law, and it should be interpreted as such.

Analysts will consider the relation of this international law of energy with the rest of international law. The international law of energy remains an integral part of public international law, yet it innovates and contributes to models that may be emulated elsewhere. Some examples have been touched upon in this chapter.

---

[120] Further, V Roeben and R Macatangay, 'Conciliation for marine transboundary energy resources. A law and economics approach' in K Zhou, S Wu & Q Ye (eds), *The 21st Century Maritime Silk Road: Challenges and Opportunities for Asia and Europe* (Routledge, 2019) 179.

These include the slip in the treaty paradigm, spontaneous order for trans-boundary social welfare maximisation, the management of policy exit by states, and corporate responsibility.

Through it, the international community of states delivers strategic change on an existential challenge for all its members. This political community receives the indispensable instrument to bring about a transformation of the global energy system that is universally binding, and hence effective, and that complies with the formal rationality of law. In turn, the international law of energy is an empirical verification of the international community of states as an actor.

# 5

## The Legal Effect of the Paris Rulebook under the Doctrine of Treaty Interpretation

PETRA MINNEROP*

## I. Abstract

This chapter examines the legal effect of the so-called Paris Rulebook under the doctrine of treaty interpretation. The Paris Rulebook is a composition of decisions and annexes, adopted by the 'Conference of Parties serving as the Meeting of the Parties under the Paris Agreement' (CMA) in Katowice in 2018. These further decisions play a significant role for the implementation of the 2015 Paris Agreement, which in itself does not explain in sufficient detail how parties intend to achieve the ambitious goal of holding the increase in the global average temperature to well below 2°C above pre-industrial levels, and more ambitiously, to 1.5°C. The role of the Paris Rulebook is much greater if it can be shown that it has a decisive legal effect in accordance with general international law. This legal effect that the Paris Rulebook has for the implementation of the Paris Agreement is looked at from the perspective of a conceptual analysis of Article 31 of the 1969 Vienna Convention on the Law of Treaties (VCLT) in this chapter. The International Law Commission (ILC) of the United Nations has adopted draft conclusions to establish the legal effect of subsequent agreements of parties for the interpretation of treaties, based on Articles 31 and 32 of the VCLT. These draft conclusions offer analytical tools derived from state practice and international jurisprudence. The interpretative effect of subsequent agreement of parties on key parts of the Paris Agreement will thus be examined with criteria already recognised in international law and a legal effect on parties' nationally determined contributions (NDCs), their accounting for and reporting of greenhouse gas (GHG) emissions, and the

* Dr Petra Minnerop, Associate Professor of International Law, University of Durham Law School; Visiting Professor, China University of Politics and Law, Beijing. I thank Daniel Bodansky, Jean d'Asprémont, Nilüfer Oral, Justice Brian Preston, Colin Reid, Volker Roeben and Don Smith for their thoughtful comments in the development of this chapter. The usual disclaimer applies.

operation of the Paris Agreement's oversight mechanism such as the so called 'global stocktake' and the compliance procedure can be identified.

## II. Introduction

The Paris Rulebook comprises decisions and annexes, including, in many parts, highly technical and detailed provisions. It was adopted by the 'Conference of Parties serving as the Meeting of the Parties under the Paris Agreement' (CMA) to provide guidance for implementing the Paris Agreement, to improve clarity, transparency and understanding of parties' NDCs and to devise procedures for the global stocktake and the compliance mechanism. The Paris Agreement and the accompanying decisions with which the Paris Agreement was adopted in 2015[1] require the CMA to adopt these further implementing decisions, albeit without explaining whether they will create a new legal source of their own, fall under the remit of the doctrine of treaty interpretation, or represent politically relevant statements which are not intended to produce any legal effect.

This chapter contends that the Paris Rulebook forms part of a norm-interpretation process under the authority of the CMA.[2] The framework proposed here for the analysis of the legal character of these decisions is thus derived from *treaty interpretation* in accordance with the VCLT.[3]

The ILC[4] finalised its 'Draft conclusions on subsequent agreement and subsequent practice in relation to the interpretation of treaties' ('draft conclusions') in 2018.[5] These draft conclusions aim at explaining the role that parties' subsequent agreements and subsequent practice play as authentic means of treaty interpretation.[6] Despite their significance as criteria rooted in general international

---

[1] Decision 1/CP.21 FCCC/CP/2015/10/Add.1. It should be noted that the legal effect of decisions adopted with the treaty and of those adopted after the conclusion of a treaty must be distinguished in the process of treaty interpretation. Agreements established at the time of the conclusion of the treaty are part of the context to be used in ascertaining the ordinary meaning of the terms used. Conversely, subsequent agreements are 'to be taken into account, together with the context', RK Gardiner, *Treaty Interpretation*, 2nd edn (Oxford University Press, 2015) 228.

[2] International law can be understood as a system of norm-generation, norm-interpretation and norm-recognition; see further A D'Amato, 'International Law as an Autopoietic System' in V Roeben and R Wolfrum (eds), *Developments of International Law in Treaty Making* (Springer, 2005) 335, 338.

[3] Vienna Convention on the Law of Treaties (concluded 23 May 1969, entered into force 27 January 1980) 1155 UNTS 331. For a discussion of the Paris Rulebook's balance between prescriptiveness, bindingness and differentiation see L Rajamani and D Bodansky, 'The Paris Rulebook: Balancing International Prescriptiveness with National Discretion' (2019) 68 *International and Comparative Law Quarterly* 1023, 1027.

[4] Established by the General Assembly, in 1947, under Art 13(1)(a) of the Charter of the United Nations (adopted 26 June 1945, entered into force 24 October 1945) 1 UNTS 16.

[5] Adopted by the International Law Commission at its seventieth session, in 2018, and submitted to the General Assembly as a part of the Commission's report covering the work of that session (A/73/10, para 51). Yearbook of the International Law Commission, 2018, vol II, Part Two.

[6] Commentary to draft conclusion 1 para 1. The term 'authentic' is used here in line with draft conclusion 3, where subsequent agreements and subsequent practice are referred to as authentic means

law for the identification of parties' statements regarding the interpretation of a treaty, these draft conclusions have not yet been applied as analytical instruments to subsequent decisions adopted by a parties' conference.

This chapter thus uses treaty interpretation tools derived from *general* international law to advance our understanding in a *specific* area of international law. It shows that consensual treaty interpretation is one of the CMA's key functions under the Paris Agreement. After explaining the methodological perspective from which the argument is developed (section III), the criteria for qualifying the *interpretative* effect of a decision which embodies the common understanding of parties in relation to the treaty's content after its conclusion are examined (section IV). This part will discuss the criteria identified by the ILC for authoritative treaty interpretation by parties. Section V applies the draft conclusions to key parts of the Paris Rulebook. The concluding remarks summarise the findings and the additional questions that arise *en route* – paving the way for future research and debate (section VI).

# III. The Perspective: CMA Decision-making under the Doctrine of Treaty Interpretation

The Paris Agreement is a treaty and the VCLT is applicable to it. This includes the 'rules' on treaty interpretation in Articles 31 and 32 VCLT.[7] The Paris Agreement uses the CMA as the governance mechanism of climate action under the agreement, in addition to the Conference of Parties (COP) under the UN Framework Convention on Climate Change (UNFCCC) and the '... Conference of Parties serving as the Meeting of the Parties to the Kyoto Protocol' (CMP).[8] This role requires

---

of interpretation. The ILC explains in its commentary that 'by describing subsequent agreements and subsequent practice under article 31, paragraph 3 (a) and (b), as "authentic" means of interpretation, the Commission recognizes that the common will of the parties, which underlies the treaty, possesses a specific authority regarding the identification of the meaning of the treaty, even after the conclusion of the treaty. The 1969 Vienna Convention thereby accords the parties to a treaty a role that may be uncommon for the interpretation of legal instruments in some domestic legal systems' (commentary to draft conclusion 3 para 3).

[7] Following Gardiner, the term 'rule' is understood in the following as reference to the progressive encirclement of the meaning of a term through applying the interpretative elements, Gardiner, *Treaty Interpretation* (2015) 39; see also RK Gardiner, 'Characteristics of the Vienna Convention Rules on Treaty Interpretation' in MJ Bowman and D Kritsiotis, *Conceptual and contextual perspectives on the modern law of treaties* (Cambridge University Press, 2018) 335; for intertemporal problems and their solution under static and evolutive interpretation see C Djefall, 'An Interpreter's Guide to Static and Evolutive Interpretations: Solving Intertemporal Problems According to the VCLT' in G Abi-Saab, K Keith, G Marceau and C Marquet (eds), *Evolutionary Interpretation and International Law* (Hart, 2019) 21.

[8] The institution 'meeting or conference of Parties' is a stand-alone concept in international law. Organisationally, it can be described as a hybrid between a diplomatic conference and a permanent plenary body of an international organisation; see further J Brunnée, 'COPing with Consent: Law-making Under Multilateral Environmental Agreements' (2002) 15 *Leiden Journal of International Law* 1, 16. The Whaling Commission is an example of a body of an international organisation with

the CMA to adopt decisions and guidance for the implementation of the Paris Agreement, and the CMA has adopted some of these decisions during its first session.[9]

Law-making and the related interpretative processes of the law must serve 'the need of the actual community' of which they are part, to fulfil law's social function,[10] and they must defend the 'universal virtue of the law as law', through the mode of their generation.[11] In contemporary international law, multiple modes of law-creation exist and the identification of what constitutes law under the doctrine of sources is the consequential, often ambiguous, process.[12] Legal effects in the international legal order, as in others, can also be effectuated by interpretation, under the doctrine of interpretation.[13] The doctrine of interpretation is not always uniformly understood in international legal theory and different modes of interpretation exist.

Interpretation can be defined as giving effect to the expressed intention of the parties[14] or as an attempt to justify a particular interpretation given to a norm, thus either stressing the cognitive or the creative aspect of the interpretative process.[15] Given the subject matter of this chapter and its purpose to analyse these

---

relatively far-reaching competences, see Arts III, V of the International Convention for the Regulation of Whaling (signed 2 December 1946, entered into force 10 November 1948) 161 UNTS 72; V Röben, 'Conference (Meeting) of States Parties' in R Wolfrum (ed) *Max Planck Encyclopedia of Public International Law* (Oxford University Press, 2008-), available at www.mpepil.com.

[9] The 'Paris Rulebook' is still partially incomplete; J Lin and A Zahar, 'Introduction to the Special Issue on the Paris Rulebook' (2019) 9 *Climate Law* 1.

[10] M Reisman, *General Course on Public International Law* 106 (Hague Academy of International Law, 2012) 134, 167; E Bjorge, 'The Convergence of the methods of treaty interpretation: Different regimes, different methods of interpretation?' in M Andenas and E Bjorge (eds), *A Farewell to Fragmentation. Reassertion and Convergence in International Law* (Cambridge University Press, 2015) 486; P Allott, 'The Concept of International Law' (1999) 10 *European Journal of International Law* 31, 32.

[11] Raz explains that rule of law principles 'are not about the content of the law, but about its mode of generation and application: they require that legal decisions and rules be anchored in stable general legal doctrines', J Raz, 'The Law's Own Virtue' (2019) 39 *Oxford Journal of Legal Studies* 1, 2.

[12] Reisman calls it the 'professional task of international lawyers', which 'would be simpler if the lawmaking system were unitary, or at least, more organized', Reisman, *General Course* (n 10) 167; see further A Peters, 'The Rise and Decline of the International Rule of Law and the Job of Scholars' in H Krieger, G Nolte and A Zimmermann (eds), *The International Rule of Law: Rise or Decline?* (Oxford University Press, 2019) 56; this has always been a concern of international legal scholars – see the discussion in A Cassese and JH Weiler, *Change and Stability in International Law-Making* (De Gruyter, 1988).

[13] Gardiner (n 1) 26; G Ulfstein, 'Evolutive interpretation in the light of other international instruments' in A van Aaken and I Motoc (eds), *The European Convention on Human Rights and General International Law* (Oxford University Press, 2018) 83, 85; J d'Aspremont, 'The International Court of Justice, the Whales, and the Blurring of the Lines between Sources and Interpretation' (2017) 27 *European Journal of International Law* 1027, 1028.

[14] A McNair, *The Law of Treaties* (Clarendon Press, 1961) 365; O Dörr, 'Article 31. General rule of interpretation' in O Dörr and K Schmalenbach (eds), *Vienna Convention on the Law of Treaties* (Springer, 2012) 521, 522.

[15] See J Kammerhofer, Taking the Rule of Interpretation Seriously, but Not Literally? A Theoretical Reconstruction of Orthodox Dogma (2017) 86 *Nordic Journal of International Law* 125, 127; M Fitzmaurice and P Merkouris, 'Canons of Treaty Interpretation: Selected Case Studies from the World Trade Organization and the North American Free Trade Agreement' in M Fitzmaurice, O Elias

CMA decisions, norm-interpretation is perceived here as a dominantly cognitive process to identify the (potentially, but not necessarily, pre-existing) meaning of a treaty rule that has now been articulated more clearly by the CMA in the Paris Rulebook.[16] Treaty negotiation is, as Philipp Allott puts it, 'a process for finding a third thing which neither party wants but both parties can accept',[17] and the CMA is seen here as authentic interpreter for explaining the 'thing' that parties can accept for the implementation of the Paris Agreement. This authentic interpretation harks back to state consent as the ultimate source of international law.[18]

However, the CMA is not an international organisation under a so-called lawmaking treaty, where the treaty confers the competence to set legally binding rules to the organisation it creates.[19] In the absence of such organisational framework, decision-making competences are often assigned to conferences or meetings of parties;[20] they thus remain in the parties' own realm. This is especially the case in multilateral environmental treaties, with the UNFCCC, the Kyoto Protocol and now the Paris Agreement representing illustrative examples. This allows contracting parties *themselves* to clarify authoritatively the content and develop the treaty through strategic decisions. These decisions carry the potential for a dynamic interpretation of the treaty to ensure that it fulfils its objectives, and the Paris Agreement is not the only or the first treaty to adopt this approach.[21]

and P Merkouris (eds), *Treaty Interpretation and the Vienna Convention on the Law of Treaties: 30 Years on* (Martinus Nijhoff, 2010) 153, 154.

[16] In that sense, for this article, the VCLT constitutes the 'only game in town'; see further T W Wälde, 'Interpreting Investment Treaties: Experiences and Examples' in C Binder, U Kriebaum, A Reinisch and S Wittich (eds), *International Investment Law for the 21st Century: Essays in Honour of Christoph Schreuer* (Oxford University Press, 2009) 724, 725; M Herdegen, 'Interpretation in International Law' in R Wolfrum (ed), *Max Planck Encylcopedia of Public International Law*, available at https://opil. ouplaw.com. Defining obligations will have a consequential effect for climate litigation; see for the role of the Paris Agreement in courts, B Preston, 'The Impact of the Paris Agreement on Climate Change Litigation and Law', judicial speech held at the Dundee Climate Conference 'Elements of a "European", "International", "Global" Climate Consensus after Paris?' available at http://www.lec.justice.nsw.gov.au/ Pages/publications/speeches_papers.aspx. For an excellent discussion of the Paris Agreement's role in litigation see J Peel and J Lin, 'Transnational Climate Litigation: the Contribution of the Global South' (2019) 113 *American Journal of International Law* 679.

[17] P Allott, 'The Concept of International Law' (1999) 10 *European Journal of International Law* 31, 43.

[18] For a discussion of the role of consent see N Krisch, 'The Decay of Consent: International Law in an Age of Global Public Goods' (2014) 108 *American Journal of International Law* 1, with a discussion related to the UNFCCC at 18.

[19] Examples are the United Nations, the World Health Organisation, the World Trade Organisation and the International Maritime Organisation; see further J Klabbers, *An introduction to International Organisations Law*, 3rd edn (Cambridge University Press, 2015) 24. Draft conclusion 12 concerns the constituent instruments of international organisations and thus covers decisions adopted within such institutionalised framework. These are specifically addressed in Art 5 VCLT, which states that the VCLT is applicable to the constituent instrument and any treaty adopted within an international organisation.

[20] See G Handl, 'International "Lawmaking" by Conferences of Parties and Other Politically Mandated Bodies' in Wolfrum and Roeben, *Developments of International Law* (2005) 127.

[21] Parties' conferences often adopt highly technical decisions on treaty implementation, which nevertheless have far-reaching consequences, for example when revising standards and adopting new ones.

Consequently, the law-quality of the Paris Agreement and its provisions has attracted much debate and Daniel Bodansky pointed out that a legally binding obligation – that is, under the doctrine of legal sources – can be created by the CMA under certain conditions. It either requires that the CMA adopts guidelines in mandatory language, based on a treaty provision that already lays down a legal obligation for each Party – for example Article 4(2) Paris Agreement – or based on a treaty provision that authorises the CMA to adopt a binding decision, thereby creating a new legal obligation; for instance, based on Article 4(8) or 4(13).[22]

The doctrine of interpretation does not conflict with this reading but complements it with a different perspective. It analyses the legal effect of the Paris Rulebook based on norm-interpretative criteria designated to find the underlying meaning of the treaty in parties' own articulations. Thus, if the Paris Agreement authorises the CMA to adopt a legally binding decision and thereby impose a new legal obligation on parties, the interpretative effect of this decision does not diverge from its effect under the doctrine of sources. However, viewing CMA decisions from the perspective of norm-interpretation allows us to identify their legal relevance in the absence of a conferred competence for norm-creation and in cases where a clear legal obligation as the only option for implementation does not emerge. Of greatest interest for this chapter is the finding of the ILC that decisions of parties' meetings or conferences can be legally binding, and while

Under the Montreal Protocol on Substances that Deplete the Ozone Layer (adopted 16 September 1987, entered into force 1 January 1989) 1522 UNTS 3, adjustments to the ozone depleting potentials of controlled substances can be enacted by a two-thirds majority, and the decisions are binding without the requirement of further consent of states and without offering an opt-out procedure (Art 2(9)(c) and (d)). The Kigali amendment was adopted in 2016 during the 28th Meeting of the Parties to the Montreal Protocol and its goal is to achieve over 80% reduction in HFC consumption by 2047, see C.N.872.2016.TREATIES-XXVII.2.f; other examples are the less often mentioned Convention on International Trade in Endangered Species Convention on International Trade in Endangered Species of Wild Fauna and Flora, 3 March 1973, 993 UNTS 243 (entered into force 1 July 1975) and the Basel Convention on the Control of Transboundary Movements on Hazardous Waste Basel Convention on the Control of Transboundary Movements on Hazardous Wastes and their Disposal, 22 March 1989, UN Doc UNEP/WG.190/4, reprinted in 28 LLM 652 (1989) (entered into force 5 May 1992), amendments to annexes II, VIII and IX addressing plastic waste, BC-14.12, adopted during the 14th Meeting of the Conference of the Parties to the Basel Convention, 29 April to 10 May 2019. See for a discussion also FL Morrison, 'Changing Approaches to Environmental Law' in R Wolfrum and FL Morrison (eds), *International, Regional and National Environmental Law* (Kluwer, 2000) 801, 809.

[22] I am grateful to Daniel Bodansky for stressing this point when reviewing this chapter; see also D Bodansky, 'The Legal Character of the Paris Agreement' (2016) 25 *Review of European Comparative & International Environmental Law* 148; D Bodansky, 'The Paris Climate Change Agreement: A new hope?' (2016) 110 *American Journal of International Law* 288; applied to the Paris Rulebook, L Rajamani and D Bodansky, 'The Paris Rulebook' (2019) 1027; for a discussion of the legal character of the Paris Agreement more generally see R Falkner, 'The Paris Agreement and the new logic of international climate politics' (2016) 92 *International Affairs* 1107; D Klein, MP Carazo, M Doelle, J Bulmer and A Higham (eds), *The Paris Agreement on Climate Change. Commentary and Analysis* (Oxford University Press, 2017); M Gervasi, 'Rilievi critici sull'Accordo di Parigi. Le sue potenzialità e il suo ruolo nell'evoluzione dell'azione internazionale di contrasto al cambiamento climatico' (2016) 71 *La Communità Internazionale* 21; A Huszár, 'Preliminary Legal Issues in the Historic Paris Climate Agreement' (2016) *Hungarian Yearbook of International Law and European Law* 195; L Rajamani, 'Ambition and Differentiation in the 2015 Paris Agreement: Interpretative Possibilities and Underlying Politics' (2016) 65 *ICLQ* 493; L Rajamani, 'The 2015 Paris Agreement: Interplay between Hard, Soft and Non- Obligations' (2016) 28 *Journal of Environmental Law* 337.

the competence-conferring provision in the treaty has an *indicative* function of such legal bindingness, 'it cannot simply be said that because the treaty does not accord the Conference of States Parties a competence to take legally binding decisions, their decisions are necessarily legally irrelevant and constitute only political commitments'.[23] Consequently, these decisions can be legally relevant in the absence of a conferred competence to adopt a decision. An explicit authorisation to adopt a specific guidance can be seen as an important factor in determining the legal effect of a decision, because it was already anticipated by parties when they concluded the treaty; however, such an authorisation is neither a necessary nor a sufficient condition for identifying the legal effect of the adopted decision. This perspective does not ignore that the CMA may create new norms under the doctrine of sources pursuant to a specific treaty provision or that mandatory language used in a treaty provision may well denote a legal obligation for parties which the CMA can decide to refine further. Rather, norm-interpretation through decision-making is viewed here as a *sui generis* method for concretising the content of an international treaty, and not as a 'minus' to the mode of norm-creation. This change of perspective allows us to take a different look at the provisions in the Paris Agreement and in Decision 1/CP.21, which request the CMA to adopt further decisions. Instead of focusing on the entitlement that this entails for the CMA to potentially develop legal obligations, these requests can also be seen as representing parties' understanding that the CMA has the crucial function (and potentially the duty) to *interpret* the treaty so that parties are then in a position to implement the treaty accordingly. Thus, the expectation expressed in a treaty provision that further decisions are necessary and will be adopted strengthens the legal effect that they will have as interpretative tools under the Paris Agreement.

The starting point in the following section is Article 31 VCLT in conjunction with the 2018 ILC draft conclusions on subsequent agreements and subsequent practice in relation to the interpretation of treaties. The section then explores this interpretative framework which the draft conclusions articulate, with a view of applying it to some crucial parts of the Paris Rulebook (section V).

# IV. The ILC Draft Conclusions – A Framework for Analysis of CMA Decisions

## A. The Mandate of the ILC to Develop Criteria for Identifying Norm-interpreting Decisions of a Parties' Conference

The ILC originally included the topic 'Treaties in time' into its programme of work.[24] However, the format of the work on this topic and its title was changed in

---

[23] Commentary to draft conclusion 11 para 26; *Whaling in the Antarctic (Australia v Japan: New Zealand intervening)* [2014] ICJ Rep 226, 257 [83].

[24] UN A/RES/63/123 para 6.

2012 to 'Subsequent agreements and subsequent practice in relation to the interpretation of treaties'.[25]

They relate to Article 31(3)(a) and (b) VCLT, which makes such agreements and practice contextual means of interpretation. They also relate to Article 32, which makes them subsidiary means of interpretation. These draft conclusions have not yet been applied to establish the legal effect of a decision of a parties' conference in scholarly debate. This is surprising, because they form a specific and authoritative set of secondary rules on treaty interpretation,[26] in conjunction with the primary rules enshrined in the VCLT.[27]

The draft conclusions are specific because they address the function of subsequent decisions adopted by parties' conferences which clarify the substance of a treaty. They are authoritative due to the mandate, the function and the procedure through which the ILC generates its findings.[28] The ILC was established by the General Assembly in 1947 pursuant to Article 13(1)(a) of the UN Charter to 'initiate studies and make recommendations for the purpose of ... encouraging the progressive development of international law and its codification'. These draft conclusions have been welcomed by the UN General Assembly as part of the ILC's 'continuing contribution to the codification and progressive development of international law'.[29]

The carefully formulated draft conclusions are based on a thorough analysis of state practice and the jurisprudence of international and domestic courts, who have acknowledged that Articles 31 and 32 VCLT reflect customary international law.[30] The International Court of Justice (ICJ) has confirmed that even recommendatory decisions of a conference of parties can constitute subsequent agreement between parties regarding the interpretation of the treaty in the sense of the VCLT.[31] Much depends on whether these resolutions are supported by all state parties,[32] while the form is not decisive to

---

[25] See http://legal.un.org/ilc/guide/1_11.shtml.

[26] G Nolte, 'The International Law Commission and Community Interests' in G Nolte and E Benvenisti (eds), *Community Interests Across International Law* (Oxford University Press, 2018) 103.

[27] The Vienna Conference on the Law of Treaties was held in 1968 and 1969 and the Convention was adopted on 23 May 1969, 1155 UNTS 311; see also the Report of the International Law Commission on the work of its eighteenths session, *Yearbook of the International Law Commission* 1966, Vol II, 177 paras 36, 37.

[28] See for an example of the use of ILC conclusions as evidence of customary international law *Jurisdictional Immunities of the State (Germany v. Italy: Greece intervening)* [2012] ICJ Rep 99, 123 [55], [58], [64].

[29] A/RES/73/202 of 3 January 2019 paras 1 and 2.

[30] A/RES/73/10, 18 para 4; for the application of Art 32 VCLT in international investment law see MM Mbengue, 'Rule of Interpretation (Article 32 of the Vienna Convention on the Law of Treaties)' (2016) 31 *ICSID Review - Foreign Investment Law Journal* 388.

[31] *Whaling in the Antarctic (Australia v Japan: New Zealand intervening)* [2014] ICJ Rep 226, 248 [46]: 'These recommendations, which take the form of resolutions, are not binding. However, when they are adopted by consensus or by a unanimous vote, they may be relevant for the interpretation of the Convention or its Schedule'.

[32] ibid 257 [83]; see for an intriguing discussion of the oscillations between the doctrine of sources and the doctrine of interpretation created by the ICJ, d'Aspremont, *Whales* (n 13) 1035.

identify an agreement.[33] The draft conclusions in turn will assist the actual interpretative process performed by courts under Articles 31 and 32 VCLT, identifying the agreement of parties relating to the dynamic interpretation of a treaty after its conclusion.

## B. Criteria for Identifying the Interpretative Effect of a CMA Decision

Draft conclusion 2 'situates subsequent agreements and subsequent practice as a means of treaty interpretation within the framework of the rules on the interpretation of treaties set forth in Articles 31 and 32 of the 1969 Vienna Convention'.[34] The VCLT and the work of the ILC leading to the adoption of the 'treaty on treaties' distinguishes several means to establish the meaning of a treaty provision. Draft conclusion 2(5) draws on the 1966 commentary of the ILC to Article 31 VCLT and emphasises that the process of interpretation remains 'a single combined operation'.[35] Before the means of interpretation can be applied in this unified interpretative process, the 'precise relevance' of different means of interpretation must be identified, and to achieve 'proper interpretation' they have to been given 'appropriate weight in relation to each other'.[36]

The ILC categorises subsequent agreements or subsequent practice under Article 31(3)(a) and (b) as 'authentic' means of interpretation, because they form an expression of the common will of the parties themselves, 'which underlies the treaty' and thus possesses a 'specific authority regarding the identification of the meaning of the treaty'.[37] These understandings of parties will be reached after the conclusion of a treaty and be related to the interpretation of the treaty or the application of its provisions.[38]

Draft conclusion 9 provides some guidance for the evaluation of the appropriate weight of subsequent agreements and subsequent practice in this process of treaty interpretation. The provision states: 'The weight of a subsequent agreement or subsequent practice as a means of interpretation under Art. 31, paragraph 3, depends, inter alia, on its clarity and specificity'.

The examples given in the commentary to this provision by the ILC explicate that in the presence of a specific and clear understanding between parties on a treaty provision, which can emerge from subsequent negotiations, this understanding will overrule the practice of one of the states that might point to a

---

[33] Gardiner (n 1) 248–50 points out that a less formal agreement increases the significance of subsequent practice confirming the agreement or understanding.

[34] Commentary to draft conclusion 2 para 1.

[35] ibid para 11; *ILC Yearbook 1966*, vol II, document A/6309/Rev 1, 209–20 para 8.

[36] Commentary to draft conclusion 2 para 13.

[37] Commentary to draft conclusion 3 para 11.

[38] Draft conclusion 4 para 1.

different interpretation of the same provision.[39] The ILC refers again to the criteria of 'clarity' and 'specificity' in its commentary to draft conclusion 11, the conclusion that is explicitly concerned with 'Decisions adopted within the framework of a Conference of States Parties'. The commentary explains that the specific character of a decision of a parties' conference 'must always be carefully identified' when scrutinising its legal significance. For that purpose, the decision's 'specificity and the clarity of the terms chosen' in the light of the decision as a whole need to be taken into account.[40]

The relevance of the criteria 'clarity and the specificity' of the parties' decision is thus twofold. It matters for the *weight* given to the decision in the context of treaty interpretation under Article 31 VCLT, and it is relevant for identifying its *legal* value.

Such a subsequent agreement that satisfies the criteria of clarity and specificity may result in 'narrowing, widening, or otherwise determining the range of possible interpretation, including any scope for the exercise of discretion which the treaty accords to the parties'[41] and it may determine whether or not a term of the treaty is capable of evolving over time.[42] An agreement under Article 31(3)(a) and (b) VCLT stipulates that a 'common understanding' exists between parties regarding the interpretation of the treaty, and parties must be aware of it and accept it.[43] It is not necessary that such an agreement is legally binding for it to be taken into account as a means of interpretation.[44]

Against the background of these general rules, draft conclusion 11 addresses the particular forum of action for parties, constituted by a conference or meeting of parties.

The provision reads:

1. A Conference of States Parties, under these draft conclusions, is a meeting of parties to a treaty for the purpose of reviewing or implementing the treaty, except where they act as members of an international organisation.

2. The legal effect of a decision adopted within the framework of a Conference of States Parties depends primarily on the treaty and any applicable rules of procedure. Depending on the circumstances, such a decision may embody, explicitly or implicitly, a subsequent agreement under Art. 31, paragraph 3 (a), or give rise to subsequent practice under Art. 31, paragraph 3 (b), or to subsequent practice under Art.32. Decisions adopted within the framework of a Conference of States Parties often provide a non-exclusive range of practical options for implementing the treaty.

---

[39] The Commentary refers to a decision of the ICSID Tribunal in *Plama Consortium Limited v Republic of Bulgaria*, ICSID Case No ARB/03/24, Decision on Jurisdiction, 8 February 2005 (2005) 20 *ICSID Review – Foreign Investment Law Journal* 262, 323–24 para 195.

[40] Commentary to draft conclusion 11 para 23.

[41] Draft conclusion 7 para 1.

[42] Draft conclusion 8.

[43] Draft conclusion 10 para 1.

[44] Draft conclusion 10.

3. A decision adopted within the framework of a Conference of States Parties embodies a subsequent agreement or subsequent practice under Art. 31, paragraph 3, in so far as it expresses agreement in substance between the parties regarding the interpretation of a treaty, regardless of the form and the procedure by which the decision was adopted, including adoption by consensus.

Paragraph 1 defines the scope of application. The commentary divides 'Conferences of States Parties' into two main categories. The first comprises conferences that act as organs of an international organisation. Examples are the meetings of the parties to the World Trade Organisation or the Organisation for the Prohibition of Chemical Weapons. The second category includes conferences which are convened under a treaty, where the 'treaty simply provides, or allows, for more or less periodic meetings of the parties for their review and implementation'.[45] Only the latter category of so-called review conferences are within the scope of application of conclusion 11.[46]

The commentary mentions conferences of parties under international environmental treaties as examples of review conferences, referring explicitly to the COP under the UNFCCC and the CMP under the Kyoto Protocol. The CMA under the Paris Agreement as a further meeting of the parties is in that respect no exception to its relatives under the climate regime; it is in a similar vein established to adopt rules for the implementation of the Paris Agreement and to periodically meet to review the progress of parties.

According to paragraph 2 of draft conclusion 11, the legal effect of a decision primarily depends on the treaty and the rules of procedure. Consequently, the treaty rules including the procedural provisions for the adoption of parties' decisions govern the legal character and these 'powers of conference of States Parties can be contained in general clauses or in specific provisions'.[47]

The rules of procedure for the adoption of decisions of the CMA are the same as those applicable to the COP under the UNFCCC. According to Article 16(5) Paris Agreement, the 'rules of procedure of the Conference of Parties and the financial procedures under the Convention shall be applied *mutatis mutandis*' under the Agreement.[48] The CMA can adopt different rules on the basis of consensus. In Katowice, the COP decided to continue to apply the draft rules of procedure in

---

[45] Commentary to draft conclusion 11 para 2.

[46] To illustrate the differentiation between the two categories further, the commentary mentions the International Whaling Commission under the International Convention for the Regulation of Whaling as a borderline case between the two categories; commentary to draft conclusion 11 para 3, note 456. Draft conclusion 12 concerns the constituent instruments of international organisations and thus covers the first category of decision adopted within such institutionalised framework. These are specifically addressed in Art 5 VCLT, which states that the VCLT is applicable to the constituent instrument and any treaty adopted within an international organisation.

[47] Commentary to draft conclusion 11 para 6.

[48] FCCC/CP1996/2 of 22 May 1996.

their current form,[49] with the exception of draft rule 42 on majority voting,[50] and agreed to continue consideration of the matter at COP25.[51] This excludes for the time being the option of majority voting for the COP under the UNFCCC and – *mutatis mutandis* – for the CMA under the Paris Agreement.

While draft conclusion 11(2) sentence 1 concerns the primarily applicable rule to establish the legal effect of the decision, the second sentence clarifies the relation of the decision to the treaty. Two different routes for the decisions to become relevant in the process of treaty interpretation exist in accordance with the draft conclusion and based on the wording of Article 31(3) VCLT. A decision can embody (explicitly or implicitly) a subsequent agreement under Article 31(3)(a), or it can give rise to subsequent practice under Article 31(3)(b) or under Article 32.[52]

The first route is for a decision to 'embody' an agreement. This requires that two elements are present: that an agreement can be identified, and that the agreement concerns the substance of a treaty provision.

As to the first element, an agreement can be identified if parties explicitly interpret the underlying treaty by 'defining, specifying or otherwise elaborating on the meaning and scope of the provisions'.[53] The VCLT in Article 31(3)(a) does not stipulate a certain form in which this subsequent agreement must be expressed; it could thus be a resolution adopted at a meeting of the parties, or even a decision included in the records of a parties' meeting.[54] The ILC stresses that the decision as a whole must be considered to determine the legal character, and 'its object and purpose, and the way in which it is applied, need to be taken into account'.[55] This is particularly important since parties may not always intend that a decision has legal significance.[56] The third sentence of draft conclusion 11(2) addresses this in stating that, often, parties' decisions provide a range of practical options for implementing the treaty in a non-exhaustive list.[57] However, the ILC concludes that this can still constitute subsequent agreement, because it does not exclude that parties have thereby implicitly agreed 'that the stated options would, as such, be compatible with the Convention'.[58]

---

[49] Partly due to the heavy workload related to the Paris Agreement work programme, ibid para 5.

[50] FCCC/CP/2018/10, II B para 4; for the two alternatives on majority voting see FCCC/CP/1996/2, alternatives A and B to rule 42.

[51] FCCC/CP/2018/10, II B para 6.

[52] The difference between these two provisions is that subsequent practice under Art 32 constitutes supplementary means of interpretation, to which 'recourse may be had' to clarify the interpretation given to a term in the treaty in accordance with Art 31. By contrast, Art 31(3) prescribes a legal obligation ('shall') to take into account, 'together with the context', the subsequent agreement or the practice which establishes the subsequent agreement.

[53] Commentary to draft conclusion 11 para 11.

[54] ibid para 12.

[55] ibid para 23.

[56] ibid.

[57] ibid para 24.

[58] ibid para 25.

The finding of an agreement of parties is most clearly supported if the decision was adopted by unanimous voting.[59] Conversely, adoption by consensus is not sufficient for an agreement under Article 31(3)(a) or (b). It is important to note in this context that consensus is different from unanimous adoption. In international law, consensus is commonly understood as absence of any formal objection.[60] If a decision is adopted by consensus but does not reflect an agreement among all the parties, it may be a form of 'other subsequent practice' under Article 32 VCLT.[61]

More important than the form or procedure 'by which the decision is reached' is that an agreement *in substance* is embodied in the decision.[62] It follows that the second essential element is that the agreement relates to the *substance* of a treaty provision. The decision must reflect a common understanding of a treaty provision and its interpretation, in order to be taken into account as means of interpretation under Article 31(3)(a) VCLT. This point is affirmed in draft conclusion 11(3), which stresses that the embodiment of a subsequent agreement is congruent with the agreement in substance ('in so far as'). The substance is most clearly defined if parties use clear and specific terms combined with mandatory language, without allowing for parties' discretion to interpret the treaty norm differently. Thus, the interpretative effect extends as far as the *substance* is clear. Conversely, if there is room to interpret the treaty provision differently, either because the language is recommendatory or ambiguous, the substance does not entail an agreement that there is only 'the one' interpretation, this ultimately limits the legal effect of interpretation.

To summarise, for a CMA decision to form part of the interpretative toolbox under Article 31(3)(a) of the VCLT, the decision must *embody an agreement in substance* of all parties.

The second route to establish subsequent agreement is subsequent practice under Article 31(3)(b), where the practice establishes the agreement; or under Article 32 (where it would only be a supplementary means of interpretation). In case a decision does not embody an agreement in substance, it could still give rise to subsequent practice. However, at the time of writing, little is known as to how parties will implement the Paris Rulebook in practice. Consequently, the following concentrates on the first route of finding subsequent agreement embodied in the adopted decisions.

Before turning to that question in more detail, in the light of the discussed criteria of the ILC on treaty interpretation, the following section differentiates

---

[59] As explained above, the rules of procedure for the CMA in their current form prescribe unanimous adoption of the decisions.

[60] R Wolfrum and J Pichon, 'Consensus' in *Max Planck Encyclopedia of Public International Law*, available at www.mpepil.com, para 1; see for instance the UN Convention on the Law of the Sea (concluded 10 December 1982, entered into force 16 November 1994, 168 Parties) 1833 UNTS 1, Art 161(8)(e).

[61] Commentary to draft conclusion 11 para 35.

[62] ibid para 28.

between two types of CMA decisions: external and internal decisions. The former concretise parties' obligations, whereas the latter operationalise the treaty's mechanisms.

## C. External and Internal CMA Decisions

According to the draft conclusions, a meeting of parties can adopt a decision with a legal effect under the treaty, even without any competence-conferring provision in the treaty. Given that the Paris Agreement in many instances even requests the CMA to adopt further guidance to operationalise its provisions, not the authority of the CMA to adopt a decision,[63] but the fact that parties already foresaw the necessity of further decisions to interpret the treaty is at the centre of the following section. Two different types of decisions can be distinguished: external decisions addressed at the parties; and internal decisions affecting the operation of the treaty mechanisms, such as the global stocktake. The Paris Agreement requests the CMA to adopt both types of decisions, using a varying degree of strength in its requesting terminology; three different categories can be found accordingly.

The first category consists of external decisions where parties are expected to fulfil their obligations in accordance with 'any relevant decisions' of the CMA,[64] or 'upon a decision' of the CMA,[65] or 'in accordance with guidance adopted' by the CMA,[66] or 'methodologies accepted by the IPCC and agreed upon' by the CMA.[67]

A second category of provisions requires that the CMA adopts external decisions within a specific timeframe, ie at the first session, such as the CMA 'shall consider common time frames' for NDCs at its first session',[68] or it 'shall adopt rules, modalities and procedures for the mechanism referred to in paragraph 4 of this Article at its first session',[69] parties shall provide information in accordance with 'modalities, procedures and guidelines to be adopted' by the CMA,[70] or simply 'adopted' by the CMA at its first session, such as in relation to the compliance committee.[71] The use of the verbs 'consider' and 'adopt' is used decisively to differentiate between the obligations that arise. In some instances, the CMA must do both. For example, the CMA must, at its first session, 'consider and adopt a decision' on institutional arrangements for capacity-building.[72]

---

[63] Which is not limited according to the ILC; see n 23.
[64] See Art 4(8); 4(9).
[65] Art 19(1).
[66] This wording is used in Art 4(11), (13); Art 6(2); Art 6(4).
[67] Art 13(7)(a).
[68] Art 4(10).
[69] Art 6(7), Art 7(3); Art 13(13).
[70] Art 9(7).
[71] Art 15(3).
[72] Art 11(5).

The third category concerns the internal decisions where the CMA is requested to fulfil certain functions under the Agreement to operationalise treaty-internal mechanisms, eg the CMA

> shall ensure that a share of the proceeds from activities under the mechanism referred to in paragraph 4 of this Article is used to cover administrative expenses as well as to assist developing country parties that are particularly vulnerable to the adverse effects of climate change to meet the costs of adaptation.[73]

The Warsaw International Mechanism for Loss and Damage under Article 8 Paris Agreement, associated with climate change impacts, 'shall be subject to the authority and guidance' of the CMA.[74] The CMA is required ('shall') to take periodically stock of the implementation of the Agreement.[75] The CMA could change the schedule of this stocktaking, which is set to begin in 2023 and to take place every five years thereafter, 'unless otherwise decided' by the CMA.[76] The CMA has the competence to change the rules of procedure under the Convention, which shall be applied unless the CMA 'may' decide otherwise by consensus.[77]

The different language used in these three categories of provisions implies that the strength of the expectation that the CMA can provide the respective subsequent agreement varies. This is of particular importance for the interpretative effect of external decisions addressed at parties. If the Paris Agreement uses mandatory language and defines a point in time, a strong request exists for the CMA to adopt the respective decision at that point in time, because parties foresaw that this future decision would be crucial for the implementation of the treaty. A decision adopted on that basis complies with the understanding that parties had when concluding the treaty, and this influences the interpretative effect of the decision. Conversely, a failure to adopt a decision that was expected at a certain point in time would result in the (so far under-explored) perplexing effect that the CMA is in breach of the Paris Agreement or not acting in line with a request made in decision 1/CP.21, unless one could argue that this lack of action could be qualified as a (new) subsequent agreement of parties or as subsequent practice amending the treaty.[78] In this chapter, however, the focus rests not on the consequences of

---

[73] Art 6(6).
[74] Art 8(2).
[75] Art 14(1).
[76] Art 14(2).
[77] Art 16(5).
[78] See Gardiner (n 1) 250. A significant omission in the Paris Rulebook is the set of modalities, rules and procedures that would regulate the market mechanisms under Art 6(4). The relevant provision in Art 6(7) Paris Agreement uses mandatory language in conferring the mandate to the CMA to adopt these MPGs at its first session. However, decision 8/CMA.1 (adopted during this first session) merely notes that parties could not reach consensus on the draft decision proposed by the President. The matter will again be considered at the second session of the CMA in December 2019. Decision 8/CMA.1 paras 2 and 3. Similarly, Art 4(10) Paris Agreement obliged the CMA to consider common timeframes at its first session. The CMA welcomed in Katowice the progress made in the consideration of common timeframes and took note of the rich exchange of views and options expressed by parties. Decision 6/CMA.1. There are currently four different options discussed for the common timeframes

a failure to adopt a decision, but on how such a request placed upon the CMA influences the interpretative effect of the decision that is adopted.

# V. The Legal Character of the Paris Rulebook

The previous section explored criteria to establish the legal effect of the Paris Rulebook. It has concluded that under the doctrine of treaty interpretation, the Paris Rulebook represents an authentic means of interpreting the Paris Agreement.

The present section evaluates parts of the Paris Rulebook to identify specific agreement in substance for key provisions of the Paris Agreement. In particular, it elaborates on the legal effect of external CMA decisions which are intended to clarify the broad terms of existing legal obligations of parties, ie the five-yearly communications of NDCs, the domestic accounting for greenhouse gas emissions and the reporting requirements under the new transparency framework. This is followed by a brief overview of mechanisms such as the global stocktake and the compliance procedure, where the CMA has a certain operational role and has adopted internal decisions. In each case, the essential elements of the relevant CMA decision are set out briefly followed by an analysis of whether and to what extent they embody the agreement of the parties.

## A. NDCs and Further Guidance Relating to Mitigation under the Paris Agreement

To meet the long-term temperature goal of the Paris Agreement, 'each Party' is obliged under Article 4(2) to 'prepare, communicate and maintain successive nationally determined contributions that it intends to achieve'. Article 4(8) provides further that in communicating their NDCs, 'all Parties shall provide the information necessary for clarity, transparency and understanding in accordance with Decision 1/CP.21 and any relevant CMA decision',[79] in the following text also referred to as 'ICTU'. Decision 1/CP.21 requested the Ad Hoc Working Group on the Paris Agreement (APA)[80] to develop three separate sets of

---

which could be five, 10 or even more years; see https://unfccc.int/sites/default/files/resource/SBI49. DT_.i5.1.pdf. Both examples demonstrate that the approach of leaving crucial questions concerning the implementation of the Paris Agreement to the devices of parties' ability to find subsequent agreement, may pose a risk to the successful implementation of some of its provisions.

[79] The wording in this provision does not *require* the CMA to adopt any additional decision on information necessary for clarity, transparency and understanding.

[80] With the adoption of the Paris Agreement, Decision 1/CP.21 established also the APA to prepare for the entry into force of the Paris Agreement, 1/CP.21 para 7, FCCC/CP/2015/10/Add.1.

guidance: one on features of NDCs;[81] a second on information to be provided to facilitate clarity, transparency and understanding;[82] and a third on accounting.[83]

The Paris Agreement itself does not specify what exactly is expected from parties; for example, which elements form part of a NDC, and how clarity is to be achieved. The key characteristic of NDCs is that they are nationally determined, and consequently, parties' submissions reflect a variety of approaches. For example, while the EU sets itself a quantified reduction target of an at least 40 per cent domestic reduction in GHG emissions by 2030 compared to 1990,[84] the US covers the period until 2025 and stresses that it 'intends to achieve an economy-wide target of reducing its greenhouse gas emissions by 26–28 per cent below its 2005 level'.[85] China submits that based on its national circumstances, it aims at achieving 'the peaking of carbon dioxide emissions around 2030 and making best efforts to peak early'.[86] India intends to reduce the emissions intensity of its GDP by 33–35% by 2030 from 2005.[87] The diversity thus concerns the way in which parties frame their targets, including the base year, the point of reference of the planned reduction, the strength of the intention to achieve the target and also the detailed implementation plan that forms part of some but not all NDCs.[88]

Most parties to the UNFCCC submitted so-called 'intended nationally determined contributions' (INDCs) to demonstrate their plans for post-2020 climate action.[89] Following up on these initial pledges, Article 4(2) of the Paris Agreement

---

[81] ibid para 26.

[82] ibid para 28.

[83] ibid para 31.

[84] www4.unfccc.int/sites/ndcstaging/PublishedDocuments/European%20Union%20First/LV-03-06-EU%20INDC.pdf.

[85] www4.unfccc.int/sites/ndcstaging/PublishedDocuments/United%20States%20of%20America%20First/U.S.A.%20First%20NDC%20Submission.pdf.

[86] www4.unfccc.int/sites/ndcstaging/PublishedDocuments/China%20First/China%27s%20First%20NDC%20Submission.pdf.

[87] www4.unfccc.int/sites/ndcstaging/PublishedDocuments/India%20First/INDIA%20INDC%20TO%20UNFCCC.pdf.

[88] For instance, the EU defines the target for the EU and its Member States as a 'binding target of an at least 40% domestic reduction in greenhouse gas emissions by 2030 compared to 1990' and submits quantifiable information on six greenhouse gases (out of seven that are controlled under the Paris Agreement). The EU uses the global warming potential (GWP) of gases on a 100-year timescale in accordance with the IPCC's 4th AR and the methodologies for estimating emissions in accordance with the IPCC guidelines 2006 and the IPCC 2013 Kyoto Protocol (KP) supplement; the US 'intends to achieve an economy-wide target of reducing its greenhouse gas emissions by 26–28 percent below its 2005 level in 2025 and to make best efforts to reduce its emissions by 28%', and it only intends to use the metrics of the 4th AR and will consider future updates to GWP values from the IPCC. Switzerland commits to reduce its GHG emissions by 50% by 2030 compared to 1990 levels, and 'supports internationally agreed rules for accounting and reporting of GHG emissions. As they are yet to be agreed, Switzerland's INDC is based on its own criteria, which are not further explained. For the inventory, the IPCC 2006 guidelines and the IPCC 2013 KP supplement are used. The interim registry of all NDCs can be found at www4.unfccc.int/sites/NDCStaging/Pages/All.aspx.

[89] By 4 April 2016, 189 Parties (96% of all parties to the UNFCCC) had submitted their INDCs; see https://unfccc.int/process/the-paris-agreement/nationally-determined-contributions/synthesis-report-on-the-aggregate-effect-of-intended-nationally-determined-contributions. The synthesis

also requires that each party participates in a five-yearly updating of its NDC with a view of increasing ambition each time.[90] Given the divergence of present NDC submissions, the guidance set forth in the Paris Rulebook is of particular significance for second and future NDC submissions.

It is important to note that the guidance on features of NDCs was not adopted in Katowice. The CMA noted that features of NDCs are outlined in the relevant provisions of the Paris Agreement and decided to continue consideration of further guidance on features at its sevenths session (2024).[91] However, the ICTU guidance on information to be provided[92] and on accounting[93] were adopted by the CMA in Katowice.[94] Both sets of guidance will be addressed in turn in the following.

## B. Guidance on Information to Facilitate Clarity, Transparency and Understanding of NDCs

The ICTU guidance is set out in annex I to decision 4/CMA.1. It elaborates on the Paris decision 1/CP.21, which states that parties may include the following information for clarity of their NDCs:

> [A]s appropriate, inter alia, quantifiable information on the reference point (including, as appropriate, a base year), time frames and/or periods for implementation, scope and coverage, planning processes, assumptions and methodological approaches including those for estimating and accounting for anthropogenic greenhouse gas emissions and, as appropriate, removals, and how the Party considers that its nationally determined contribution is fair and ambitious, in the light of its national circumstances,

---

report based on the INDCs reveals that there is a clear need for parties to receive further guidance on the content of NDCs. The report stresses that 'while the structure and content of the communicated INDCs vary, most (90 per cent and above) Parties explicitly addressed the information elements listed in decision 1/CP.21', Aggregate effect of the intended nationally determined contributions: an update, 2 May 2016, FCCC/CP/2016/2 para 8. The latest Climate action and support trends report of the UNFCCC Secretariat concludes that GHG emission levels are increasing and were 31.2% above the 1990 level in 2016, thus not in line with keeping global warming well below 2°C or even 1.5°C. UNFCCC Secretariat, Climate action and support trends (2019) 2, available at https://unfccc.int/sites/default/files/resource/Climate_Action_Support_Trends_2019.pdf.

[90] 186 parties have submitted their first NDCs and two parties have submitted their second NDCs; a few parties updated their NDCs; the interim registry (which is in place until the final version is established) can be accessed at https://www4.unfccc.int/sites/ndcstaging/Pages/Home.aspx. All NDCs will be maintained by the secretariat in a public registry (an interim public registry already exists); once this is finalised and the Subsidiary Body for Implementation developed, modalities and procedures for the operation and use of the public registry as introduced by Art 4(12) of the Paris Agreement, 1/CP.21 para 29.

[91] Decision 4/CMA.1 paras 19, 20.

[92] Decision 4/CMA.1 annex I.

[93] Decision 4/CMA.1 annex II.

[94] Decision 5/CMA.1 and the annex. Please note that there is a further public registry which is maintained by the secretariat, for the adaptation communication in accordance with Art 7(12); see Decision 10/CMA.1 and the annex, FCCC/PA/CMA/2018/3/Add.1.

and how it contributes towards achieving the objective of the Convention as set out in its Art. 2.[95]

The ICTU guidance adopted in Katowice reiterates this section. Crucially, it adds some more detailed elements to the exemplary list, as will be detailed in the following section.

## i. The Substance

Decision 4/CMA.1 uses mandatory language when requiring parties to provide the information necessary for clarity, transparency and understanding contained in annex I. However, this is coupled with a limiting notion, as the information in the annex only needs to be provided 'as applicable'.[96] The decision further exempts the first NDCs; parties are only strongly encouraged to provide the relevant information.[97]

The annex begins with a list of quantifiable information. This includes information on the reference point and must identify reference years, base years, reference periods or other starting points.[98] Further, quantifiable information on the reference indicators for comparison with the base year must be included[99] and only least developed country parties[100] (LDCs) and small island developing states[101] (SIDS) are exempt from the requirement to submit quantifiable information – they have to provide 'other relevant' information.[102] The guidance requests that the target is identified relative to the reference indicator and that the target is expressed numerically (for example, a percentage or the amount of reduction); no exception is made for this information in favour of any groups of parties. Information is required on the source of data quantifying reference points and on the circumstances under which the party may update the indicators.

Parties are requested to include timeframes and/or periods for implementation, with start and end dates, and they have to do this 'consistent with any further relevant decision' adopted by the CMA.[103] This stresses that parties will continue

---

[95] Decision 1/CP.21 para 27.

[96] Decision 4/CMA.1 para 7 reads: 'Decides that, in communicating their second and subsequent nationally determined contributions, Parties shall provide the information necessary for clarity, transparency and understanding contained in annex I as applicable to their nationally determined contributions, and strongly encourages Parties to provide this information in relation to their first nationally determined contribution, including when communicating or updating it by 2020.'

[97] ibid.

[98] Decision 4/CMA.1 annex I para 1(a).

[99] ibid para 1(b).

[100] There are currently 49 countries identified as belonging to this group, based on three criteria: low income; weak human assets; and high economic vulnerability. Of these countries, 33 are in Africa, 10 in Asia, one in the Caribbean and five in the Pacific. See further 'Least Developed Countries under the UNFCCC', available at https://unfccc.int/resource/docs/publications/ldc_brochure2009.pdf.

[101] There are currently 40 parties to the UNFCCC that fall into this category; 11 of these are also listed as least developed countries. See the UNFCCC report: https://unfccc.int/resource/docs/publications/cc_sids.pdf.

[102] Decision 4/CMA.1 annex I para 1(c).

[103] ibid paras 2(a) and (b).

to review timeframes and periods for implementation, and that relevant decisions will express the then current agreement of parties. The information must include a general description of the target (which could be a single-year target or a multi-year target), sectors, gases, categories and pools.[104] When describing the target, consistency with the IPCC guidelines is requested but limited through the addition 'as applicable'.[105] Parties have to provide information how they considered paragraph 31(c) and (d) of decision 1/CP.21, which refers to the strong recommendation ('Parties strive') to include all categories of anthropogenic emissions or removals and the legal obligation ('shall') to provide an explanation of why any categories are excluded.[106]

As a new point, the ICTU guidance includes mitigation co-benefits resulting from adaptation actions.[107] Thus, while information on adaptation generally remains optional, in so far as mitigation co-benefits are achieved, information must be provided. The guidance covers a prescription of specific details to be submitted in relation to planning processes that the party undertook to prepare its NDC, such as implementation plans, institutional arrangements, national circumstances, best practices, and other contextual aspirations and priorities acknowledged when joining the Paris Agreement.[108] Parties must also explain how the preparation of its subsequent NDC has been informed by the outcomes of the global stocktake.[109] Parties with a NDC that consists of adaptation action and/or economic diversification plans resulting in mitigation co-benefits are required to submit information on how the party has considered the economic and social consequences of response measures.[110] Furthermore, information must be provided on specific projects and implementation plans that contribute to mitigation co-benefits.[111]

## ii. The Agreement

The CMA is expressly required in accordance with Article 4(8) Paris Agreement and Decision 1/CP.21 para 28, to adopt this external decision on providing information on NDC clarity, transparency and understanding. Parties agreed in Paris that they had to further interpret the terms 'clarity, transparency and understanding'. Decision 4/CMA.1 in para 6 recalls this provision and decision 1/CP.21, and the CMA decided to adopt the annex with the above outlined level of detail. This embodies the agreement of parties concerning the interpretation of Article 4(8) Paris Agreement. Decision 4/CMA.1 is a 'relevant decision' as envisaged by

---

[104] ibid paras 3(a) and (b).
[105] ibid para 3(b).
[106] ibid para 3(c).
[107] ibid para 3(d).
[108] ibid para 4(a).
[109] ibid para 4(c).
[110] ibid para 4(d)(i).
[111] ibid para 4(d)(ii).

Article 4(8) and it sets forth guidance for the implementation, using recommendatory language for communicating the first NDC and mandatory language for communicating second and subsequent NDCs.

This is coupled with a general limitation concerning the application of the annex, through the phrase 'as applicable' in the decision. While this combination of mandatory or recommendatory language and a further discretionary phrase may be difficult to reconcile under the doctrine of sources, the doctrine of interpretation can determine the legal relevance of the decision and the annex as a nuanced form of agreement. To determine the legal relevance, the rule laid down in draft conclusion 11 para 3 is crucial. The decision can only embody subsequent agreement of parties 'in so far as' it expresses agreement in substance. Parties have articulated in clear and specific terms their understanding that for second and subsequent NDCs the guidance is the benchmark for lawful implementation of Article 4(8) Paris Agreement; deviation under the term 'as applicable' is not excluded, but may warrant justification. Conversely, for the current first NDCs, parties are only strongly encouraged to apply the guidance.[112] While parties agree that using the guidance is the preferred option for the first NDC, they acknowledge that this may be challenging for some parties. Nevertheless, the interpretative effect of this decision in its entirety, given the precision of the terms and the degree of detail provided in the annex, is that there is an agreement on parties' preference concerning the first NDCs, and even more so for the second and subsequent NDCs. The difference in the language used supports the finding that the agreement in substance includes a gradual increase in the legal effect of the ICTU guidance. The objective of progressively achieving compliance with it to lawfully implement the Paris Agreement is the common will of parties which underlies the treaty, and any reasoning that the ICTU guidance is not – or not fully – applicable will be increasingly difficult to justify for second and subsequent NDCs.

## C.  Guidance on Accounting

Accounting refers to the domestic procedure to be followed when a party assesses the achievement of its mitigation target. Article 4(13) of the Paris Agreement obliges parties to account for NDCs, without further clarifying the methodologies applicable to the procedure.

### i.  *The Substance*

Decision 1/CP.21 requires that parties use the methodologies and metrics as assessed by the IPCC, to ensure consistency, including baselines, between the NDC's communication and its implementation, that parties include all categories

---

[112] Decision 4/CMA.1 para 7.

of anthropogenic emissions or removals and, once they have done so, continue to include it in their NDCs, and to explain why any categories of anthropogenic emissions or removals are excluded.[113] Decision 1/CP.21 para 31 also requested the APA to elaborate, drawing from established approaches under the UNFCCC, guidance for accounting. This guidance was adopted unanimously by parties in Katowice and is now included in annex II of Decision 4/CMA.1.[114]

Decision 4/CMA.1 sets forth the cornerstones of the accounting procedure. The CMA decided that parties shall avoid double counting and that they shall account for their NDCs in biennial transparency reports, 'including through a structured summary'.[115]

The application of the more detailed accounting guidance in annex II is mandatory for the second and any subsequent NDC, while it remains a recommendation for parties' first NDCs.[116]

Decision 18/CMA.1 (concerning the enhanced transparency framework) clarifies that the biennial transparency report must ('shall') be submitted at the latest by 31 December 2024.[117] The mechanism used here is similar to the one discussed above, the CMA uses mandatory language, on the basis of a specific competence conferred to it, to create a specific prescription for parties' accounting procedure. However, the agreement in substance is less clear when compared with the guidance on ICTU. The accounting guidance allows for considerable discretion for parties in choosing methodologies.

Annex II specifies that accounting for anthropogenic emissions and removals in parties' NDCs must, as a general rule, be in accordance with methodologies and common metrics assessed by the IPCC and pursuant to decision 18/CMA.1 on the transparency framework.[118] While this seeks to ensure that all parties will deliver comparable accounting information, a couple of exceptions raise doubts relating to the consistency that can be expected.

Parties can continue to use methodologies other than those assessed by the IPCC, but if they do so, they must provide information on their own methodology.[119] This exception primarily concerns LDCs and SIDS, but is not explicitly limited to these.[120] Further, if parties decide to draw on existing methods

---

[113] 1/CP.21 paras 31(a)–(d).
[114] FCCC/PA/CMA/2018/3/Add.1 annex II.
[115] Decision 4/CMA.1 paras 13, 15 and 17.
[116] 1/CP.21 para 32; 4/CMA.1 para 14.
[117] Decision 18/CMA.1 para 3.
[118] Decision 18/CMA.1 annex II para 1(a).
[119] Decision 4/CMA.1 annex II para 1(b).
[120] ibid annex II para 1(b) provides: 'Parties whose nationally determined contribution cannot be accounted for using methodologies covered by the IPCC guidelines provide information on their own methodology used, including nationally determined contributions pursuant to Article 4 paragraph 6, of the Paris Agreement, if applicable;' Art 4(6) Paris Agreement states that LDCs and SIDS may 'prepare and communicate strategies, plans and actions for low greenhouse gas emissions development reflecting their special circumstances.'

and guidance established under the UNFCCC or the Kyoto Protocol, they can to do so 'as appropriate'.[121]

Consistency is to be maintained, including on baselines, between communication and implementation of NDCs.[122] GHG emission data and estimation methodologies used for accounting should be consistent with GHG inventories; this is a strong recommendation ('should') and a further limitation is added through the phrase 'if applicable'.[123]

The annex reiterates that parties should strive to include all categories of anthropogenic emissions or removals in their NDCs,[124] and once they have included it, continue to do so. An explanation must be provided as to why any categories of emissions or removals are excluded.[125]

## ii. The Agreement

The CMA adopted the guidance in line with the requirement to find this further agreement of parties after the conclusion of the treaty to facilitate implementation of Article 4(13) Paris Agreement. In contrast to the adoption of the NDCs guidance discussed above, Decision 4/CMA.1 uses mandatory language but refrains from coupling this with limiting terms such as 'as appropriate' and 'if applicable'. However, these terms are then to be found in the annex II that details the accounting requirements. As a result, the accounting guidance does not resolve two main problems. First, methodological consistency remains a recommendation, albeit a strong one. Second, and closely related, the annex does not address accounting differences that occur when parties use different methodologies than those supported by the IPCC. This points towards an underlying conflict instead of an agreement of parties. While applying the accounting guidance is a legal obligation in accordance with the mandatory wording of the CMA decision for the second and subsequent NDCs, the guidance in annex II includes some leeway for parties through the addition of phrases such as 'if applicable' and 'as appropriate'. Thus, one could question whether parties found an agreement in substance to concretise their obligation to account for NDCs. Again, the rule of draft conclusion 11 para 3 helps to identify the interpretative effect of the agreement. The agreement on accounting includes the preferred option for the implementation, which is aligned with IPCC methodologies, but it does not exclude different options or clearly determine when these are applicable. However, parties that apply a different methodology will have to provide information on their own methodology. Thus, while the mandatory language of the decision entails that it has weight as a means of interpretation, the substance of the agreement is reduced. It is not clear from

---

[121] ibid annex II para 1 (c).
[122] ibid para 2.
[123] ibid para 2(b).
[124] ibid para 3.
[125] ibid para 4.

annex II under which conditions parties can opt to apply different methodologies. Accordingly, the legal effect of the decision as a means of interpretation is lessened, it can only go as far as parties have agreed that the stated guidance based on IPCC methodologies constitutes a lawful means – and the preferred one – for implementing Article 4(13) Paris Agreement. While being limited in substance, the accounting guidance nevertheless constitutes an interpretative tool under Article 31(3)(a) VCLT that further concretises the legal obligation on accounting. Subsequent practice in accordance with Article 31(3)(b) may establish the subsequent agreement concerning the question when and which other methodologies are acceptable.

## D. Enhanced Transparency Framework

The enhanced transparency framework in Article 13 Paris Agreement aims at providing a clear understanding of climate action and at tracking progress towards achieving parties' NDCs. This is to inform the global stocktake and to provide clarity on the support provided and received by parties in the context of climate change actions.[126]

### i. *The Substance*

One of the major achievements in Katowice was the adoption of the modalities, procedures and guidelines (MPGs) under which parties will be reporting from 2024 onwards. Future reporting requirements include the biennial submission of a transparency report, which consists of the GHG national inventory report and the information to track progress. Submitting these two parts represents a legal obligation ('shall'), and parties shall fulfil this obligation in accordance with the MPGs; this includes reporting on functions related to inventory planning and other national circumstances and institutional arrangements.[127] Providing the information on impacts and adaptation under Article 7 Paris Agreement remains a strong recommendation.[128] The GHG inventory report includes a national inventory document and the common reporting tables.[129]

Article 13(7) Paris Agreement requires parties to provide the national GHG inventory report 'regularly' and for it to be 'prepared using good practice methodologies accepted by the IPCC', providing information 'necessary to track progress in implementing and achieving its NDC'. Article 13(13) requires the CMA at its first session to adopt 'common modalities, procedures and guidelines, as appropriate, for the transparency of action and support'. The Agreement does not specify

---

[126] Decision 18/CMA.1 annex paras 1, 2.
[127] ibid paras 17, 18, 19.
[128] ibid paras 10(a)–(c).
[129] ibid para 38.

the term 'regularly'. Decision 1/CP.21 para 90 defines it as 'no less frequently than on a biennial basis' and 'only the LDCs and SIDS are allowed to submit the information at their own discretion'.[130] Decision 18/CMA.1 confirms that parties are obliged ('shall') to submit their first *biennial* transparency report and national inventory report by 31 December 2024.[131]

The MPGs for reporting in the annex are structured into eight parts (I-VIII), each of them divided into several sub-parts with detailed provisions. The following text will concentrate on the clarification of the flexibility approach (part I subpart C), the methodologies and metrics and reporting guidance (part II subparts C and D respectively) and the description of a party's NDC and the information necessary to track progress made in implementing the Agreement (part III subparts B and C respectively). These provisions determine in more detail how the transparency framework will operate, in the context with the other provisions of the MPGs which explain the purpose, the guiding principles and thus more generally the context for the transparency framework. However, the discussion at the end of this section concerning the legal effect of the more closely examined rules of the MPGs can be transferred to other parts of the MPGs in so far as they follow a similar relevant distinction between mandatory and recommendatory language; this will be detailed below.

Decision 18/CMA.1 reiterates the flexibility approach for LDCs and SIDS to which reference was made already in Decision 1/CP.21.[132] The introduction in part I subpart C of the MPGs clarifies that this flexibility is self-determined. However, there are requirements to be fulfilled for the party invoking flexibility. The party shall indicate the provision to which flexibility is applied and explain the reasons. The technical expert review teams will not review the party's determination ('shall not') or indeed whether in their view the party possesses the capacity to implement that specific provision without flexibility. Accordingly, while the MPGs require parties claiming flexibility to explain their reasons, these will not undergo expert review.

Part II subpart C sets out that 'each Party shall use the 2006 IPCC guidelines and any subsequent version or refinement of the IPCC guidelines agreed upon' by the CMA.[133] Parties are encouraged to use the 2013 Supplement to the 2006 IPCC Guidelines for National Greenhouse Gas Inventories on Wetlands.[134] Parties may use nationally appropriate methodologies, if these 'better reflect its national circumstances and are consistent with the IPCC guidelines'.[135] In the context of ensuring consistency between different reporting years, the MPGs include the recommendation that each party uses the same method and a consistent

---

[130] 1/CP.21 para 90.

[131] Decision 18/CMA.1 para 3.

[132] ibid para 4.

[133] Decision 18/CMA.1 annex para 20. A refinement was included in 2019; see https://www.ipcc.ch/report/2019-refinement-to-the-2006-ipcc-guidelines-for-national-greenhouse-gas-inventories.

[134] Available at www.ipcc-nggip.iges.or.jp/public/wetlands.

[135] Decision 18/CMA.1 annex para 22.

approach.[136] Recalculations shall be performed in accordance with IPCC guide-lines to avoid changes that only occur as a result of different methods across the time series of reporting.[137]

Part II subpart D confirms that the metrics which parties must use ('shall') are those from the IPCC AR5 or any later assessment report as agreed upon by the CMA.[138] For supplementary information on aggregate emissions and removals of GHGs, parties may use other metrics in addition, and in that case, provide infor-mation on the volumes of the metrics.[139]

Part III subpart B addresses the description of an NDC under Article 4 of the Paris Agreement.[140] The description of the NDC as provided by each party will provide the benchmark against which progress will be tracked. More detailed descriptors are set out in subpart B, using mandatory language but also compris-ing the addition 'if applicable'. Subpart C sets forth the obligation for each party to identify its own indicators that were selected to track progress towards implement-ing and achieving its NDCs.[141] The MPGs make proposals for possible indicators which parties can choose, if applicable.[142]

## ii. The Agreement

The MPGs set forth detailed and clear provisions on the enhanced transparency framework, and the agreement in substance is particularly strong where it is phrased in mandatory terms. In those instances, the agreement entails that in the imple-mentation of the treaty provision, the relevant provision of the MPG represents the common understanding of parties and that this further decision was already anticipated when the Paris Agreement was concluded (Article 13(13)). However, the argument that this is the only interpretation of the provisions is considerably weakened in the light of those provisions of the MPGs that use limiting phrases such as 'if applicable' or 'as appropriate'. In line with draft conclusion 11 para 3, the decision and the annexed MPGs qualify as a subsequent agreement only in so far as they express an agreement in substance. The agreed substance is constrained if leeway is given and different implementing options are not excluded. This lessens the legal effect of the MPGs. However, while parties can apply different method-ologies if they better reflect their national circumstances, a legal obligation exists that parties that choose to do so will justify their choice when diverging from the agreed preference of applying methodologies approved by the IPCC. Future prac-tice may also clarify the agreement in accordance with Article 31(3)(b) VCLT.

---

[136] ibid para 26.
[137] ibid para 28.
[138] ibid para 37.
[139] ibid para 25.
[140] ibid para 64.
[141] ibid para 65.
[142] ibid para 66.

## E. Global Stocktake

The CMA has a new oversight function to 'assess the collective progress towards achieving the purpose of this Agreement and its long-term goals (referred to as the "global stocktake")' under Article 14(1) of the Paris Agreement, with the first date set for 2023.[143] This is prepared by the so-called Talanoa Dialogue,[144] a facilitative process which started in 2018 to take stock of the collective efforts of parties in achieving the long-term goal of Article 4(1) and to inform the preparation of NDCs under Article 4(8).[145] Decision 1/CP.21 requested the APA to develop modalities[146] and identify sources of input[147] and to report to the COP, 'with a view to the Conference of the Parties making a recommendation to the Conference of the Parties serving as the meeting of the parties to the Paris Agreement for consideration and adopting at its first session'.[148]

### i. The Substance

The CMA adopted in Katowice further modalities of this process with an internal decision.[149] It confirmed, in line with Article 14(1), that 'equity and the best available science will be considered in a Party driven and cross-cutting manner'.[150] The CMA also decided 'that the global stocktake will consist of the following components',[151] establishing a list that makes reference to information collection and preparation, technical assessment, focusing on taking stock of the implementation of the Paris Agreement, as well as opportunities for enhanced action and support to achieve its purpose and goals; consideration of outputs, focusing on discussing the implications of the findings of the technical assessment with a view to achieving the outcome of the global stocktake and informing parties in updating and enhancing, in a nationally determined manner, their actions and support. The decision contains further details on the technical assessment and the process in which the outputs will be considered.

The CMA further lists 'sources of input',[152] and according to these, the global stocktake will consider 'information at a collective level' on the mitigation efforts undertaken by parties, including the information referred to in Articles 13(7)(a)

---

[143] Decision 1/CP.24 welcomes the 2018 stocktake on pre-2020 implementation and ambition; another stocktake will take place at the 25th session, FCCC/CP/2018/Add.1.

[144] See also the Talanoa platform, available at https://unfccc.int/process-and-meetings/the-paris-agreement/the-paris-agreement/2018-talanoa-dialogue-platform.

[145] Established with Decision 1/CP.21 para 20, FCCC/CP/2015/10/Add.1; see also Decision 1/CP.24 paras 30–37, FCCC/CP/2018/10/Add.1.

[146] 1/CP.21 para 101, FCCC/CP/2015/10/Add.1.

[147] ibid para 99.

[148] ibid.

[149] Decision 19/CMA.1, FCCC/PA/CMA/2018/3/Add.2.

[150] ibid para 2.

[151] ibid para 3.

[152] ibid paras 35–38.

and 4(7), (15), (19) Paris Agreement; the overall effect of parties' NDCs and overall progress made by parties towards the implementation of their NDCs, including adaptation efforts, support, experience and priorities, and finance flows. Sources for input are reports and communications from parties, the latest reports of the IPCC, reports to the subsidiary bodies and the synthesis report by the UNFCCC Secretariat.

### ii. The Agreement

With these modalities, the CMA instils a system into the global stocktake in accordance with its operational function under Article 14. The modalities prescribe how the CMA will operate the mechanism in the future. Thus, these modalities create no legally binding obligations for individual parties but, rather, they define the intended mechanism, on the basis of parties' common understanding of the treaty provision on the global stocktake. These MPGs are legally relevant as specific definition of the envisaged procedure, its input, purpose and outcome, as already anticipated by the COP when adopting the Paris Agreement. They are specific and clear and constitute an agreement of parties in substance concerning the oversight procedure that was created in Paris.

## F. Compliance

### i. The Substance

Article 15 of the Paris Agreement creates the agreement's 'mechanism to facilitate implementation and promote compliance'. This mechanism shall be 'expert based' and 'facilitative in its nature and function in a manner that is transparent, non-adversarial and non-punitive'. The description supports the finding that parties across the developed–developing country divide did not intend to give the compliance procedure a shape similar to the Kyoto Protocol's mechanism, where non-compliance could be sanctioned with exclusion from participation in the Protocol's market mechanisms.[153]

Article 15(3) prescribes that the committee 'shall operate under the modalities and procedures adopted' by the CMA at its first session. Decision 1/CP.21 para 102 gives some further details on the composition of the committee. The COP decided that the committee 'shall' consist of 12 members with recognised competence in 'relevant scientific, technical and socioeconomic or legal fields', elected by the CMA on the 'basis of equitable geographical representation.[154]

---

[153] L Rajamani, 'Ambition and Differentiation in the 2015 Paris Agreement: Interpretative Possibilities and Underlying Politics' (2016) 65 *International & Comparative Law Quarterly* 493, 505.

[154] With two members each from the five regional groups of the UN, and one member each from SIDS and the LDC, taking into account gender balance.

Decision 1/CP.21 requested the APA to develop modalities and procedures for the operation of the compliance committee.[155] These modalities and procedures were adopted as part of the Paris Rulebook. They flesh out the compliance procedure and represent the agreement of the CMA as to the purpose, principles, functions and scope of the compliance mechanism. In particular, the modalities and procedures detail the institutional arrangements and lay down rules on the initiation of the compliance procedure. In a similar vein as the modalities for the global stocktake, the modalities and procedures for the compliance mechanism bind the CMA in the future application of the compliance procedure.

They clarify that 'nothing in the work of the committee may change the legal character of the provisions of the Paris Agreement'. This confirms that a hierarchy exists between the Paris Agreement and the modalities and procedures, the latter elaborate the process which parties intended with Article 15 of the Paris Agreement. The section on 'measures and outputs' of the Committee makes specific reference to the 'legal nature' of the relevant provisions of the Paris Agreement. The committee 'shall be informed by the legal nature of the relevant provisions of the Paris Agreement' in finding the appropriate measures.[156] This reference indicates that the legal nature of the Agreement's provisions varies and that these different legal values will be taken into account when reviewing parties' compliance.

The compliance mechanism is bifurcated, it can address individual compliance[157] and systemic issues where individual compliance 'shall not be addressed'.[158]

In addressing individual compliance, the committee will initiate the consideration of issues in cases where a party has not:

'(i)  Communicated or maintained a nationally determined contribution under Article 4 of the Paris Agreement, based on the most up-to-date status of communication in the public registry referred to in Article 4, paragraph 12, of the Paris Agreement;
(ii)  Submitted a mandatory report or communication of information under Article 13, paragraphs 7 and 9, or Article 9, paragraph 7, of the Paris Agreement;
(iii)  Participated in the facilitative, multilateral consideration of progress, based on information provided by the secretariat;
(iv)  Submitted a mandatory communication of information under Article 9, paragraph 5, of the Paris Agreement; ...'[159]

While this could spark the idea that the committee will examine the information provided by a party as part of the communication of its NDC, the modalities make

---

[155] In accordance with 1/CP.21 para 103.
[156] Decision 20/CMA.1 annex on Modalities and procedures for the effective operation of the committee referred to in Art 15(2) of the Paris Agreement, para 28.
[157] ibid.
[158] ibid para 34.
[159] ibid para 22(a).

clear that this is not the case. The 'consideration of the issues … will not address the content of the contributions, communications, information and reports'.[160]

The measures which the committee can take 'shall' be appropriate. These 'may' include a dialogue with the party to identify challenges, assist the party, make recommendations to the party, recommend the development of an action plan and assist the party if requested. The committee is obliged to report to the CMA annually.[161]

The consideration of systemic issues involves challenges to implementation and compliance faced by a number of parties. The committee may identify these issues and bring them to the attention of the CMA.[162]

### ii. The Agreement

The mandatory language used in the internal decision that adopts the annex binds the future compliance committee. Article 15(3) Paris Agreement requires the CMA to adopt the modalities and procedures at the first session and these are legally binding on the committee ('shall operate under'). In adopting the modalities and procedures, the CMA has created a concrete form of the Paris Agreement's compliance mechanism. The CMA has thus expressed the common understanding on Article 15 and further elaborated its substance. This constitutes a subsequent agreement of parties for the future operation of the compliance mechanism, in a similar fashion as discussed above for the global stocktake. The fact that the content of the NDC communication will be exempt from consideration during the examination of cases where a party has not fulfilled the requirements of communicating or maintaining its NDC, or failed to participate in the facilitative, multilateral consideration of progress, manifests the non-punitive and facilitative character of the compliance mechanism as envisaged in Article 15(2) Paris Agreement.

# VI.  Conclusions

The Paris Agreement represents a complex multilateral treaty regime, where parties expressed the expectation in the treaty itself and in the accompanying decision 1/CP.21 that successful treaty implementation would largely depend on the CMA's articulation of subsequent agreement. This makes the Paris Agreement an evolving instrument with definitive but also yet to be formed normative content.[163] The common understanding of parties that holding the increase in the global

---

[160] ibid para 23.
[161] ibid paras 30, 36.
[162] ibid 32.
[163] Cf *Whaling in the Antarctic (Australia v Japan: New Zealand intervening)* [2014] ICJ Rep 226, 247 [45].

average temperature to well below 2°C and pursuing efforts to limit the temperature increase to 1.5°C would significantly reduce the risks and impact of climate change, is coupled with an ongoing work programme of the CMA to develop and express parties' subsequent agreement to flesh out the agreement's framework.

This chapter has demonstrated that the Paris Rulebook is a result of this 'fleshing out' exercise and that it has a distinct legal effect under the doctrine of treaty interpretation. This legal effect makes the Paris Rulebook crucial for lawful treaty implementation; it goes beyond a statement of politically desirable options. This adds a further perspective to the discussion of the role of parties' conferences and meetings in the literature so far, where it has been discussed that parties' conferences or meetings function as international legislatures more generally,[164] leading to 'legislative law-making' next to 'contractual law-making'.[165] It has been argued that these decisions produce 'soft law',[166] or that they have a merely operational impact.[167] Conversely, this chapter has proposed to analyse the legal character of CMA decisions under the doctrine of interpretation in accordance with Article 31(3) VCLT, using the ILC draft conclusions as analytical tools. It has then exemplified for some decisions of the Rulebook that they have a legal effect under the Paris Agreement and, in so doing, developed a transferable argument that can be applied to other parts of the Rulebook and to future CMA decisions.

Under the doctrine of interpretation, the legal effect of a decision can be viewed through a lens that makes nuances in the articulated agreement of parties identifiable and the underlying treaty provision can thus be interpreted accordingly. Much depends in this interpretative process on the wording that is used. The doctrine of sources and the doctrine of interpretation would both find a legal obligation if mandatory language is used in a treaty provision and in the CMA decision that follows, provided that no further discretion is given to parties. However, the doctrine of interpretation goes beyond this because it can carve out a significant

---

[164] J Brunnée, 'Reweaving the Fabric of International Law? Patterns of Consent in Environmental Framework Agreements' in R Wolfrum and V Röben (eds), *Developments of International Law* (2005) 101, 109; T Meyer, 'From Contract to Legislation: The Logic of Modern International Law making' (2014) 14 *Chicago Journal of International Law* 559, 563; A Steinbach, 'The trend towards non-consensualism in public international law: a (behavioural) law and economics perspective' (2016) 27 *European Journal of International Law* 463, 658.

[165] Meyer (ibid) 571.

[166] The category of 'soft law' has been criticised frequently; see for instance L Blutman, 'In the trap of a legal metaphor: international soft law' (2010) 59 *International & Comparative Law Quarterly* 605, 609; J Ellis, 'Shades of grey: soft law and the validity of public international law' (2012) 25 *Leiden Journal of International Law* 313, 314; V Röben, 'Institutional Developments under Modern International Environmental Agreements' (2000) 4 *Max Planck Yearbook of United Nations Law* 363, 371; P Weil, 'Towards Relative Normativity in International Law?' (1983) 77 *American Journal of International Law* 413, 422. However, 'soft law' might well guide the interpretation of law. The International Court of Justice emphasised the need to take new standards and norms into consideration, with a view of to 'reconcile economic development with protection of the environment' as 'aptly expressed in the concept of sustainable development' *Gabčíkovo-Nagymaros Project (Hungary/Slovakia)* [1997] ICJ Rep 7, 77–78 [140].

[167] D French and L Rajamani, 'Climate Change and International Environmental Law: Musings on a Journey to Somewhere' (2013) 25 *Journal of Economic Literature* 437, 444.

interpretative effect of a decision even in the absence of mandatory language, or if parties still have a margin of discretion. In these cases, an agreement can nevertheless be found; however, its *substance* may be limited. Consequently, a nuanced legal effect for the implementation of the treaty provision can be identified where the doctrine of sources would not be able to see it. It is for this type of decisions that the approach proposed here unfolds the most significant effect.

The extent of the legal effect of a decision for the respective treaty provision thus depends on the question whether parties agreed on much or less substance. Furthermore, the common understanding that the decision articulates only goes as far as the agreement in substance is clear and specific. In particular, recommendatory language and limiting phrases such as 'as appropriate' or 'as applicable' indicate that the agreement only entails a strong preference for the agreed options for implementation, but does not amount to a clear legal obligation because it does not fully exclude other options. Such a decision still constitutes subsequent agreement that parties 'shall take into account' in accordance with Article 31(3)(a) VCLT when implementing the treaty provision. However, the legal effect is lessened if the agreed substance is constraint through the language used in the decision or the annex.

On that basis, three main categories in which the Paris Rulebook has a legal effect for the Paris Agreement can be summarised. The first two categories comprise the external decisions of the CMA, while the internal decisions fall into the third category.

The first category concerns a decision which more narrowly defines an existing legal obligation or creates a new one under the remit of an existing one (for instance, accounting; see below). The second category includes decisions that still have a legal effect through interpretation of the underlying treaty provision, but the substance of the agreement is limited so that a strongly preferred option but not necessary a clear legal obligation can be identified. The third category includes internal decisions that bind the CMA or the compliance committee that will be created.

In the first category, a legally binding obligation for parties emerges if CMA decisions are adopted using mandatory language, coupled with an annex that includes clear and specific elements without allowing other options at parties' discretion. For example, Article 4(13) Paris Agreement obliges parties to account for their NDCs. The accounting guidance states that parties drawing on existing methods and guidance established under the Convention 'as appropriate' are legally obliged ('shall') to provide information as to how they have done so.[168] With this obligation, the CMA created a new rule with 'ought' character. This constitutes an authentic means of consensual interpretation and as such, has to be taken into account in the interpretation of the treaty provision under which the CMA has adopted the annex, as subsequent agreement of parties which embodies a legal obligation in a concrete form.

---

[168] 4/CMA.1 annex II para 1(c).

The second category of legally relevant decisions comprises decisions coupling mandatory language in a decision with limiting terms such as 'as appropriate' in the decision or the annex itself, or a decision using recommendatory language. An example for the former is the obligation to apply the guidance on information to facilitate clarity, transparency and understanding to second and subsequent NDCs. The decision uses mandatory language in combination with terminology that indicates that parties' still have some discretion ('as applicable'). Parties explicitly agreed on lawful options for the implementation; however, this does not amount to a legal obligation foreclosing parties' discretion. Such a decision still has considerable weight as a means of treaty interpretation, especially when using clear and specific terms for the lawful options. It constitutes subsequent agreement under Article 31(3)(a) VCLT in so far as there is agreement in substance (the lawful options). Given that the common understanding is not as far-reaching as to exclude other options, the legal effect of this decision under the Paris Agreement remains limited in that respect.

Similar, but slightly different, is a decision that is phrased in recommendatory language, as for example in relation to applying the guidance on ICTU to the first round of NDCs. This decision embodies an agreement in substance, albeit one that anticipates that parties may not yet be able to fully apply the guidance, or not all of them. Nevertheless, for the interpretation of Article 4(8) Paris Agreement, this recommendation has to be taken into account as a tool of treaty interpretation in accordance with Article 31(3)(a) VCLT, especially if it is phrased in clear and specific terms explaining the substance (here annex I of Decision 4/CMA.1). While the use of non-binding language weakens the legal effect, the fact that Article 4(8) Paris Agreement anticipated further relevant decisions – such as in the Paris Rulebook – supports the finding that a clear preference for implementation in line with the formulated ICTU guidance exists. On that basis, such an expectation expresses the agreement that at least those parties that are in a position to do so, including those who already have quantified absolute emission reduction targets as annex I countries,[169] are posited to comply with the ICTU guidance provided. This also implies that there is a standard against which non-compliance with the requirements on ICTU guidance will have to be at least explained, if not justified. Consequently, for their first NDCs, parties are given more leeway, but discretion is considerably reduced for second and subsequent NDCs of all parties.

Parties have thus also agreed to *progressively* limit the discretion they have to individually determine the shape and form of their NDC submissions. This progression in the applicable standard defines the existing obligation under the Paris Agreement. The agreement includes an upwards-moving target towards applying an increasingly tighter standard for NDCs submissions.

---

[169] Annex I countries are parties to the UNFCCC that are included in annex I, 1771 UNTS 107. These are industrialised countries that were members of the OECD in 1992, and countries with economies in transition (the EIT parties), including the Russian Federation, the Baltic States, and several central and eastern European states.

The third category of decisions comprises the internal decisions, where the CMA has lined the mechanisms under the Paris Agreement, such as the global stocktake and the compliance procedure. These decisions do not impose new obligations on parties or define existing ones. They evolve around and concretise the role of the CMA to facilitate international cooperation and to supervise the implementation of the Paris Agreement, to ensure that parties' efforts suffice for meeting the agreed temperature goal.

In all three categories, the CMA fulfils a distinctive norm-interpretative function in the post-Paris climate change regime. Generally, if the relevant treaty provision authorises the CMA to adopt a decision, this stresses that parties anticipated when concluding the Paris Agreement that further guidance on interpretation would be necessary for lawful implementation. This strengthens the legal effect in all three categories, but it might have the strongest influence for the interpretation of decisions in the second category.

Given that the Paris Agreement in some instances requests the CMA to adopt decisions, in some cases at a specific point in time, questions for further research arise. These concern the consequences that the failure to adopt a required decision has. Is the CMA under an outcome duty to adopt decisions, and if subsequent agreement cannot be found, is the CMA in breach of the agreement? How does that differ from a situation where only a previous decision of the COP articulates the request? Overall, does this affect the legitimacy of the treaty from the national perspective, where democratic institutions may have approved the treaty in anticipation of future decision-making; and from the international perspective, where a lack of decision-making or the failure to transmit a clear authority signal risk achieving the global temperature goal of the Paris Agreement? Finally, how can the participation of national parliaments be secured in this governance-based approach to international law-making, given that the CMA could adopt a decision with legal effect in the absence of an explicit authority assigned to it under the treaty?[170]

These questions define some aspects that deserve further research and discussion. The Paris Agreement has legitimately been celebrated as a political, diplomatic and legal success, yet its effectiveness in halting the global temperature increase will depend on the ability of the CMA to fully incorporate the scientific evidence behind the agreed temperature goal and to transmit a clear authority signal when elaborating and expressing the common understanding that underlies the treaty.

---

[170] See also P Minnerop, 'Taking the Paris Agreement Forward: Continuous Strategic Decision-making on Climate Action by the Meeting of the Parties' (2017) 21 *Max Planck Yearbook of United Nations Law* 124.

# 6

## How will Energy Market Regulation have to Change in the Era of Energy 4.0?

PENELOPE CROSSLEY

## I. Abstract

With the mass introduction of cyber-physical systems and digitisation of the energy market, there is a fundamental transformation currently underway in the energy sector globally. This chapter analyses the impact of the Fourth Industrial Revolution on the electricity market and considers how Energy 4.0 is changing the traditional roles of energy market regulators, market participants and end-consumers. It finds that the increasing complexity of systems, changing market technologies and structures, use of big data, introduction of smart contracts, and the changing role played by consumer protection, are all posing new risks that regulators will need to address. In particular, this chapter argues that the existing market regulation is acting as a market barrier to innovative new market entrants, and that this is hampering the development of the market, along with investment and competition. Rather, a paradigm shift in the approaches used to regulate the electricity market is required, with a greater emphasis on ensuring system security and reliability, privacy and data protection, and consumer protection. Importantly, the existing approaches to amending market regulation are currently operating too slowly to affect the necessary changes and do not provide a sufficient whole of system approach. In future, a more coordinated approach that supports the optimal use of technology and supports flexibility within the market will be needed to ensure the continued development of competitively functioning energy markets in the era of Energy 4.0.

## II. Introduction

With the mass introduction of cyber-physical systems and digitisation of the energy market, there is a fundamental transformation currently underway in the energy sector globally. This chapter will analyse the impact of the Fourth Industrial Revolution on the electricity market[1] and consider how Energy 4.0 is changing the traditional roles of energy market regulators, market participants and end-consumers. In particular, it will examine how the increasing complexity of systems, changing market technologies and structures, use of big data, introduction of smart contracts and blockchain, and the changing role played by consumer protection, are all posing new risks that regulators will need to address. The chapter will consider the role energy regulators should play in the era of Energy 4.0, as well as asking what ought to be the priorities for regulating in an era of rapid technological developments. A case study of the creation of the Distributed Energy Resources Register within the Australian National Electricity Market will be used to exemplify this discussion. The chapter will conclude with a discussion of the areas that still need to be addressed to ensure the continued development of competitively functioning energy markets.

# III.  Background to the Fourth Industrial Revolution (Industry 4.0)

In the modern era, there have been three periods of significant industrial revolution:[2]

- The First Industrial Revolution (1765–1840): This revolution, which involved the wide scale mechanisation of production, was prompted by the invention of the steam engine.

- The Second Industrial Revolution (1870–1914): This revolution involved technological developments such as the combustion engine and automobile, as well as new organisational modes of production such as Ford's assembly line. These developments were made possible by the adoption of coal-fired electrical generation, the creation of transmission and distribution networks and resulting electrification of society, and the development of the oil industry.

- The Third Industrial Revolution (Post War Period–1982): This revolution saw the rise of consumer and industrial electronics, and the invention of new technologies such as transistor radios, computers and mobile telecommunications. The Third Industrial Revolution also saw the increased deployment of programmable logic controllers, automation and robotics within the industrial sector. This revolution was made possible by the sheer scale and number

---

[1] While Energy 4.0 is also affecting the hydrocarbons and transportation and heating sectors, this chapter focuses on the area within the energy sector where there is likely to be the largest impact, electricity market design.

[2] T Philbeck and N Davis, 'The Fourth Industrial Revolution' (2019) 72 *Journal of International Affairs* 17, 19–20.

of modern base load electricity generation facilities that were fuelled by fossil fuels, nuclear energy or hydropower.

As shown above, each of these industrial revolutions has been made possible by changes in the sources of energy and technologies utilised within the energy sector. Each industrial revolution precipitated significant transformations within the energy sector, which then formed the basis of the next industrial revolution.

The emergence of a Fourth Industrial Revolution or Industry 4.0 (sometimes also referred to as 'Industrie 4.0') was first noted in the early 2010s. The term 'Industry 4.0' originated in Germany, with its first widespread use recorded at the Hanover Fair in 2011.[3] The World Economic Forum subsequently adopted the concept, with its 2016 WEF meeting in Davos addressing the theme of Mastering the Fourth Industrial Revolution.[4] Industry 4.0 relates to the widespread introduction of cyber-physical systems, that is, 'systems composed of physical entities controlled or monitored by computer-based algorithms'.[5] An alternative definition from the German Federal Ministry for Economic Affairs and Energy is that 'In the industrial context, the term "Industry 4.0" refers to the link between the digital world of the Internet and conventional processes and services in manufacturing'.[6] The use of the term reflects the idea that globally, industry is currently undergoing a process of digitisation and automation and that this, coupled with the rise of more smart technologies, has triggered the beginning of the Fourth Industrial Revolution.

The advent of the Fourth Industrial Revolution has not only impacted the industrial sector but has already had, and continues to have, a profound effect on the energy sector.

# IV. The Transformation of the Energy Sector

Energy 4.0 represents a paradigm shift within the energy sector. Previously, energy markets globally relied on large-scale generation fuelled by fossil fuels, nuclear energy or hydropower transmitted to end-consumers through the traditional model of transmission and distribution networks. The focus of the energy market

---

[3] B Lydon, 'The 4th Industrial Revolution, Industry 4.0, Unfolding at Hannover Messe 2014' (Automation, 19 February 2014), available at www.automation.com/automation-news/article/the-4th-industrial-revolution-industry-40-unfolding-at-hannover-messe-2014.

[4] 'World Economic Forum, Mastering the Fourth Industrial Revolution', Global Agenda: World Economic Forum Annual Meeting 2016, Davos-Klosters, Switzerland (20–23 January 2016) (2019), available at www3.weforum.org/docs/WEF_AM16_Report.pdf.

[5] M Lang, 'From Industry 4.0 to Energy 4.0: Future Business Models and Legal Relations' *Digitalisierung in der Energiewirtschaft* XX. Jahrestagung Insitut für Berg- und Energierecht Bochum (17 March 2016), 14.

[6] Federal Ministry for Economic Affairs and Energy (Germany), 'Autonomics for Industry 4.0' (March 2015), available at www.digitale-technologien.de/DT/Redaktion/EN/Downloads/Publikation/autonomik-brochure.pdf?__blob=publicationFile&v=4, 5.

regulators was very much on managing supply rather than demand, with their attention often directed to what a fair market rate of return was for the infrastructure investments that formed part of each market participant's regulated asset base (RAB).[7] The outcome of this process was that in many jurisdictions market participants were incentivised to 'gold-plate' their investments in the RAB, often leading to over-investment in generation and network infrastructure assets.[8] This operated to the detriment of all consumers within the market who ended up paying more for their electricity, which may be at least partially attributed to the absence of targeted pricing mechanisms.[9] End-consumers historically also had very limited data about how the energy they used was generated and their individual energy consumption. The absence of cost-reflective pricing in many markets also meant that poor market signals were sent to consumers about the optimal times for them to consume their electricity.[10] The combination of these factors led to the development of inefficient energy markets, which failed to provide reliable, sustainable and least-cost energy for end-consumers.[11]

A number of new developments over the past 10 years within the energy sector are now challenging the status quo. The most obvious of these developments within the Australian context is the large-scale deployment of renewable energy both onto the grid and also, increasingly, to the edge of grid or off-grid.[12] This has created more variability or intermittency within the national energy supply, which makes balancing the system and providing ancillary services more complex.[13] As a result of this, we are now seeing the increased deployment of utility-scale storage devices and pumped hydro storage, as well as residential-scale integrated systems of PV solar, inverters and energy storage.[14] In addition, due to steadily rising electricity prices, which are now some of the most expensive

---

[7] N Tan, 'How are Electricity Prices Set in Australia?' (Reserve Bank of Australia, 4 February 2011), available at www.rba.gov.au/information/foi/disclosure-log/pdf/101115.pdf.

[8] P Lasker, 'Power prices: Australia has a gold-plated electricity grid that consumers can't afford' (Australian Broadcasting Corporation, 19 July 2017); 'We Have A Gold-Plated Electricity Grid Consumers Can't Afford' (ABC News, 2019), available at www.abc.net.au/news/2017-07-18/australian-gold-plated-power-grid/8721566. In economics, this is referred to as the Averch-Johnson effect, see H Averch and LL Johnson, 'Behavior of the Firm Under Regulatory Constraint' (1962) 52 *American Economic Review* 1052.

[9] Lasker (ibid).

[10] See, eg, Australian Energy Market Commission, 'Distribution Network Pricing Arrangements', available at www.aemc.gov.au/rule-changes/distribution-network-pricing-arrangements.

[11] Productivity Commission, 'Australian Government, Inquiry Report into Electricity Network Regulation', (26 June 2013), available at www.pc.gov.au/inquiries/completed/electricity/report; see Overview and recommendations.

[12] Australian Energy Regulator, 'State of the Energy Market 2017' (30 May 2017) 9, available at www.aer.gov.au/system/files/AER%20State%20of%20the%20energy%20market%202017%20-%20A4.pdf.

[13] Australian Energy Market Operator, 'Energy Supply Outlook for Eastern and South-Eastern Australia (Updating the Energy Adequacy Assessment Projection, and Gas and Electricity Statements of Opportunities)' (June 2017) 23, available at www.aemo.com.au/-/>.media/Files/Electricity/NEM/Planning_and_Forecasting/NEM_ESOO/2017/2017-Energy-Supply-Outlook.pdf.

[14] Clean Energy Council, Energy Storage, 'Energy Storage' (2019), available at www.cleanenergy-council.org.au/resources/technologies/energy-storage.

in the world, increasing numbers of the 2.2 million households with photovoltaic solar already installed on their rooftops are now beginning to retrofit energy storage systems.[15] These changes have led to more decentralised networks, greater distributed generation and more customers/developers seeking exemptions under the National Electricity Law to enable the creation of embedded generation and networks.[16] This in turn has created opportunities for new business models, such as peer-to-peer energy trading (sometimes aggregated by customer preference or demand), which are now being developed and trialled.[17] At the same time, a number of sectors, which have traditionally been fuelled by fossil fuels, are being electrified, such as motor vehicles and heating/cooling systems. All of this additional complexity has led to the introduction of highly information technology-intensive business models within every aspect of the electricity market: generation, transmission, distribution, storage, consumption, trading, retail, system balancing and ancillary services are all heavily reliant on the use of integrated 'smart technologies'. These developments are all changing the patterns of demand, generation and consumption.

# V.  Energy 4.0

It is within this context that Energy 4.0 has emerged. Just as with the changes in the industrial sector, Energy 4.0 promises to further transform the energy sector.[18] Digitisation and cyber-physical systems are being introduced en masse within the sector, providing the energy sector with a level of computational intelligence that is capable of performing high-level analytics on big data.[19] These systems can act autonomously, engage in machine learning, and communicate and interact intelligently over the Internet with people and other machines.[20] This has created a wealth of information not just on the operations of the market participants, but also down to the individual consumer level. This information can be utilised to generate knowledge-intensive smart services, create new tailored products

---

[15] ibid.

[16] Australian Energy Market Commission, 'Review of regulatory arrangements for embedded networks, Information sheet for the Final Report' (28 November 2017), available at www.aemc.gov. au/sites/default/files/content/5b1f101b-f2fb-40c1-9a36-07add0c5a19e/Embedded-networks-review-RPR0006-information-sheet-final-report.pdf.

[17] See eg, A Roy, A Bruce and I MacGill, 'The Potential Value of Peer-to-Peer Energy Trading in the Australian National Electricity Market', Asia Pacific Solar Research Conference (2016).

[18] See eg, T Nagasawa, C Pillay, G Beier, K Fritzsche, F Pougel, T Takama, K The and I Bobashev, 'Accelerating clean energy through Industry 4.0 – Manufacturing the next revolution' (United Nations Industrial Development Organisation, August 2017), available www.unido.org/sites/default/files/ 2017-08/REPORT_Accelerating_clean_energy_through_Industry_4.0.Final_0.pdf.

[19] International Energy Agency, 'Digitalization and Energy' (2017), available at www.iea.org/ publications/freepublications/publication/DigitalizationandEnergy3.pdf.

[20] ibid.

optimised for individual commercial and residential consumers and enable new prosumer models to be developed.

In this environment, some first movers, often in the form of 'neo-retailers', are already seeking to use digital innovations such as blockchain technologies, digital ledgers, distributed energy resource management, cloud computing and smart contracts.[21] Proponents of these technologies argue that their use will enable consumers to shift from short- to medium-term power contracts to 'transaction-based' contracts.[22] Transactive energy is said to lead to 'efficient and adaptive market pricing, improved system reliability and flexibility, a pathway for technological innovation, the data needed to develop additional direct and derivative markets'[23] and to 'improve the balance of risk and reward for asset owners'.[24] Indeed, the International Energy Agency has stated that:

> [T]hese changes will provide consumers with increased choice and possibly also strengthen competition within the sector, both domestically and internationally. By 2040, 1 billion households and 11 billion smart appliances could actively participate in interconnected electricity systems.[25]

Research from Accenture supports the IEA's claim that consumers are seeking increased choice, with 69 per cent of consumers surveyed indicating that they were interested in having more options to buy local or differentiated energy products.[26]

The transformation of the energy sector offers potentially huge rewards for market participants, with USD 718 billion invested in the electricity sector worldwide in 2016 alone.[27] However, the sheer volume of data being collected and analysed by these cyber-physical systems will also increase complexity within the sector and pose new risks for consumers and market participants that regulators will need to address.

## A. The New Risks Posed by Energy 4.0

While Energy 4.0 offers new opportunities for market participants and consumers, it also poses a number of risks that are unlikely to be adequately addressed

---

[21] ibid.

[22] Power Ledger Pty Ltd, White Paper, Version 8 (2018), available at https://powerledger.io/media/Power-Ledger-Whitepaper-v8.pdf, 13.

[23] Exergy Energy, Exergy Business White Paper, (10 February 2018), available at https://exergy.energy/wp-content/uploads/2018/02/Exergy-BIZWhitepaper-v9.pdf.

[24] ibid 8.

[25] IEA, 'Digitalization and Energy' (2017) 23.

[26] Accenture, 'The New Energy Consumer: Trends Shaping the Energy Ecosystem Consumers, The Value of Sharing: Collective Energy Consumption' (2016) 2, available at www.accenture.com/t00010101T000000Z__w__/pt-pt/_acnmedia/PDF-25/Accenture-New-Energy-Consumer-Sharing-Info.pdf.

[27] International Energy Agency, 'World Energy Investment 2017, Executive Summary' 3, available at https://webstore.iea.org/download/summary/225?fileName=English-WEI-2017-ES.pdf.

through the existing electricity market design and regulations. These relate to four key areas:

- the risks associated with the use of big data;
- the risks associated with the increasing complexity of the systems and the resultant impact on electricity market design;
- the risks these new technologies pose to existing models of consumer protection used within the energy sector; and
- the risks associated with the breach of smart contracts.

Each of these risks will be addressed in turn, before considering what this may mean for energy market regulators.

## B. Big Data

In 2017, IBM stated that approximately 90 per cent of the data in the world today had been created in the previous two years.[28] The scale of the changes associated with the introduction of Energy 4.0 is completely inconceivable to many people including, arguably, regulators, market participants and end-consumers. As seen by the rapid rise of companies such as Google and Facebook, while digitisation may encourage innovation and the development of new products, there is also a potential for the owners of big data to use it to establish market power.[29] As the amount of data that market incumbents have access to grows alongside the shift to mass digitisation and adoption of more smart technologies, this runs the risk of creating an ever-increasing barrier to entry for new market entrants. Instead of encouraging competition, this could lead to greater concentration within the energy market as only companies of sufficient scale will have both the data required to optimise their products to consumer needs and be able to afford to take the risks associated with commercialising new technologies and getting them to market.

With the growth of big data, problems of information asymmetries are likely to become more prevalent as companies collect increasing amounts of data on their customers both at an individual and aggregate level. This also creates a challenge for regulators who are then reliant on receiving information about the latest technological developments from the market participants who conduct the research and development. This makes them susceptible to regulatory capture.

Other concerns associated with the use of big data relate to how the data will be stored, who will be able to access the data and the issues associated with the

---

[28] IBM, '10 Key Marketing Trends for 2017 and Ideas for Exceeding Customer Expectations' (2019) 3, available at www-01.ibm.com/common/ssi/cgi-bin/ssialias?htmlfid=WRL12345USEN.
[29] Australian Competition and Consumer Commission, 'ACCC commences inquiry into digital platforms' (4 December 2017), available at www.accc.gov.au/media-release/accc-commences-inquiry-into-digital-platforms.

portability of data. The most prominent of these concerns currently in the public consciousness arguably relate to privacy and cyber-security. Key questions for consumers here are:

- Will consumers be able to stipulate that their data only be used for the specific purpose for which it was initially obtained?
- Who will determine when it is in a consumer's best interests to have their personal information used or disclosed to a third party or for an alternative purpose?
- Will consumers be able to access their own usage data?
- How will the data be protected and how and where will it be stored?
- If a market participant such as an electricity retailer becomes defunct or a consumer wishes to switch retailer or services provider, can their data be ported over to a different retailer? How easy will it be to switch between different retailers/service providers?

These issues have proven difficult in other sectors. For example, there have been cases in the electric/hybrid vehicle market where consumers have been unable to access their own data to see if their system was meeting the stipulated performance standard. This was raised as an issue in the context of electric vehicles in the Nissan LEAF class actions.[30] In that case, consumers alleged that they were not advised of the applicable performance standard prior to purchasing the vehicle and then were unable to access their own data to see if their car battery was meeting the standard or not. A number of consumers took to installing a non-Nissan endorsed app using the USB portal in their cars as a means of recording and storing their battery performance data in order to able to collect the data for themselves. The data they collected showed that their car batteries were failing to meet the performance standards promised when they purchased their vehicles, leading to the class action for damages. This case led Nissan to amend the warranty on their electric and hybrid vehicles to state that the use of any non-Nissan app would void their warranty.[31] Thus the only way Nissan LEAF customers can now legitimately access their data is if Nissan chooses to provide it to them. This case highlights that it is imperative that consumers have the right to access their own data to ensure that they are using the best products and services for their needs and can test that those products and services are living up to the performance claims made by the retailer/supplier. With the mass digitisation of the energy sector, consumer data access rights for all of products and services provided within the energy market will become increasingly important for commercial and residential scale consumers.

---

[30] *Humberto Daniel Klee and David Walla, individually, and on behalf of a class of similarly situated individuals v Nissan North America, Inc* (CD Cal, No. 2:12-cv-08238-BRO-PJW, 10 November 2013).

[31] F Svarcas, 'Turning a new LEAF: A privacy analysis of carwings and electric vehicle data collection and transmission' (2012) 29 *Santa Clara Computer & High Technology Law Journal* 165.

Digitisation is eroding the traditional geographic market boundaries that used to exist in the energy markets, with the growth of foreign market participants and internet-based retailers and service providers.[32] This means that some market participants may have a very limited physical presence in some of the energy markets in which they operate. As a consequence, the big data associated with all aspects of the electricity market also gives rise to an important jurisdictional issue. The storage of big data is highly energy-intensive and thus it is often cheaper for companies operating in developed countries with very high electricity costs such as Australia to store their data in data centres based overseas in countries such as China, Vietnam, the Philippines, India and Russia. Foreign market participants may also prefer to store their data offshore in their 'home' jurisdiction so that they can take advantage of scale. Different countries have differing privacy standards and cyber security standards, so it is important that any data held meets at least the national standards applicable to the end consumer. Further, there also needs to be a regulator who is willing to enforce compliance with the applicable laws, as well as adequate penalties available for a breach of these standards. For market participants with a limited physical presence within the country in which they are selling energy services, the regulator will need to ensure that the market participants retain sufficient assets or security within the jurisdiction to be able to meet a judgment or other penalty imposed against them for a breach of the applicable laws or their contracts.

## C. The Increasing Complexity of Systems and Changing Market Structure

As the design and operation of national energy markets changes and becomes more complex as a result of mass digitisation and automation, a number of challenges are emerging. The same digital technologies which promise to transform the energy sector and help it overcome key challenges such as 'intermittency, aging grids, balancing distribution connected generation, managing consumer self-generation and coping with increasing system complexity'[33] may also exclude vulnerable consumers from the market. These digital systems often have costs associated with them that get passed on to the end-consumer and there may not be subsidies available to low-income households. Increasing digitisation may exclude these consumers from being able to participate equally within the market or fully realise the benefits of Energy 4.0. For example, low-income households often do

---

[32] OECD, 'Going Digital: Making the Transformation Work for Growth and Well-Being, Report for the Meeting of the OECD Council at Ministerial Level, Paris' (7–8 June 2017) 10, available at www.oecd.org/mcm/documents/C-MIN-2017-4%20EN.pdf.

[33] Bloomberg New Energy Finance, 'Digitalization of Energy Systems, Market for Digitalization in Energy Sector to Grow to $64BN by 2025', available at https://about.bnef.com/blog/market-digitalization-energy-sector-grow-64bn-2025.

not have photovoltaic solar cells on their rooftops, which would reduce their electricity costs over the longer term, due to the problem of their high initial capital cost.[34] Low-income households also do not normally have smart meters, which may enable them to better manage the cost of their electricity consumption. At the same time, more and more middle and upper income households within Australia are moving to self-generation and storage as a means of avoiding or offsetting their network distribution costs.[35] Given that network distribution costs make up 48 per cent of the average household electricity bill in Australia, this has led to concerns that low-income households who cannot afford to invest in these technologies will have to increasingly bear a greater burden of these costs in order to maintain the network infrastructure.[36]

Importantly, this issue not only affects low-income households, but also affects renters. In the case of rental properties, this is due to the issue of split incentives; that is, the landlords who bear the cost of installing solar do not receive the financial benefit, which instead goes to their tenants, and as a result, landlords are rarely willing to bear the cost of installing solar.[37] This is a significant issue within the Australian context, which has both the highest market penetration of residential solar per capita in the world and some of the highest residential property prices, meaning that a large portion of the population rent.[38] Resolving this issue and ensuring that costs are fairly allocated between those who can access and afford these technologies and those that cannot may require a fundamental redesign of the basis upon which consumers are charged for network costs. To date, network costs have been charged on a usage basis. This has prompted debate about whether grid-connected consumers who have solar and/or storage installed should be charged a higher grid connection fee to reflect the fact that they benefit from having the *capacity* to use the grid at peak periods, even if they actually use it less frequently than non-solar households.[39]

A further issue arises about the level of understanding required on the part of regulators, market participants and consumers to enable them to effectively and efficiently participate in the market. We have already witnessed in the information technology sector that consumers fail to even read, let alone understand, their

---

[34] Australian Bureau of Statistics, 6523.0 – Household Income and Wealth, Australia, 2015–16, Case Study – Solar Power in Australian Homes (13 September 2017).

[35] ibid.

[36] Australian Competition and Consumer Commission, 'Retail Electricity Pricing Inquiry: Preliminary Report' (16 October 2017) 6, available at www.accc.gov.au/system/files/Retail%20 Electricity%20Inquiry%20-%20Preliminary%20report%20-%2013%20November%202017.pdf.

[37] Bloomberg New Energy Finance, 'Digitalization of Energy Systems' (n 33).

[38] M Janda, 'Home ownership rates continue to plunge, housing stress widespread: Census' (27 June 2017), available at www.abc.net.au/news/2017-06-27/home-ownership-rates-continue-to-plunge-census/8654534.

[39] G Parkinson, 'Networks propose compulsory fees for all – to stop grid defections' (Renew Economy, 5 August 2015); Giles Parkinson, 'Networks Propose Compulsory Fees For All – To Stop Grid Defections' (Renew Economy, 2019), available at https://reneweconomy.com.au/networks-propose-compulsory-fees-for-all-to-stop-grid-defections-28523.

relationship agreements with suppliers due to the complexity.[40] This prompts the question: how can we ensure that market participants understand both the operation of the energy markets within Energy 4.0, and the associated contracts that they are asked to enter into, at a level that guarantees that their participation in the energy market occurs on the basis of informed consent?

## D. Consumer Protection

In addition to the consumer issues addressed immediately above, Energy 4.0 also poses new risks for consumers. The new market models, such as blockchain, smart contracts and digital ledgers, which are now being introduced, frequently cite regulation as the biggest risk to investors considering whether to invest in their businesses.[41] As a result, many of the companies promoting these new technologies advocate for market deregulation.[42] However, given that electricity supply is an essential service, questions must be asked about how consumers will be protected in such an environment. What will happen if a contract is breached? What does this mean for the consumer who is dependent on their electricity supply for life support?

The growing dependence on new technologies, often manufactured overseas, also raises issues about liability for product and system failure. For example, is the provision of fully automated services to efficiently manage the optimal use of smart technologies within a commercial or residential property considered a 'product' for the purposes of product liability laws, and thus capable of having 'defects'?[43] How do you protect a consumer when the overseas manufacturer has no physical presence within the jurisdiction but the consumer also does not have the legal right to pursue a claim against them in the country of manufacture? Further issues relate to the lack of availability of insurance products to protect consumers who are adopting these new technologies. This issue is especially relevant to consumers who have had to apply for permission from their distribution company to install PV solar on their grid-connected property, as it is often a condition of their connection that they agree to bear the liability for any and all of the consequential losses that may arise from their use of that technology.[44]

---

[40] P Harrison, 'Consumers don't understand smartphone contracts' (The Conversation, 3 October 2016), available at http://theconversation.com/consumers-dont-understand-smartphone-contracts-66267.

[41] Power Ledger Pty Ltd, White Paper, Version 8 (2018) 13, available at https://powerledger.io/media/Power-Ledger-Whitepaper-v8>.pdf. Also Exergy Energy, Exergy Business Whitepaper (10 February 2018), available at https://exergy.energy/wp-content/uploads/2018/02/Exergy-BIZWhitepaper-v9 pdf.

[42] ibid.

[43] E Hilgendorf and U Seidel, 'Legal challenges facing digital value chains – structured solution paths for SMEs, (April 2016), available at www.digitale-technologien.de/DT/Redaktion/EN/Downloads/Publikation/autonomik-study-legal-challenges.pdf?__blob=publicationFile&v=4, 14.

[44] See eg, the AusNet Services Embedded Generator (EG) Connection Agreement up to 30kVA.

## E.  Smart Contracts

Smart contracts are a set of 'computer protocols that facilitate, verify, or enforce the performance of a contract'.[45] In many senses, smart contracts are similar to a self-executing embedded derivative contract whereby the date of supply, quantity of electricity, number of renewable energy certificates provided, or the price are varied. One of the neo-retailers, Power Ledger, explains their use of smart contracts as follows:

> With a smart contract, the money is deposited into escrow, on the blockchain for receipt of a transfer of a token (e.g. a digital certificate verifying the generation of renewable energy), which is instantaneously transferred into a counterparty's control once conditions are met.[46]

The use of smart contracts, with the resulting change from payment being made after provision of the service to payment being made automatically based on the satisfaction of specific conditions in an algorithm/or computer protocol, shifts the balance further away from the consumer. On the one hand, it removes the ability of the consumer to withhold payment in the event that they are not satisfied with the service provided, but on the other hand, provided the conditions within the computer algorithm are set appropriately, the use of smart contracts should also remove much of the performance risk.

Of greater concern that the growing adoption of cyber-physical systems, artificial intelligence and machine learning may lead to computers varying the terms and the conditions of contracts autonomously rather than just inputting the data for the embedded derivative. If this happens and fundamentally changes the nature of the underlying commodity or subject matter, or any of the key terms, this will trigger legal issues as there cannot be said to be a true meeting of the minds or intention to create legal relations between a computer and a human counterparty. This is because the computer does not have the status of a 'legal person', and it is a fundamental principle of law that a person should not be held liable for breach of a contract which they have not agreed to.[47] A further concern is that the introduction of smart contracts means that even large commercial consumers are significantly less likely to be able to negotiate the terms and conditions of the contract. These changes will be beneficial to large-market participants who hold the balance of power in conventional contract negotiations and will be able to stipulate that their contracts must be accepted as a whole or the counterparty must walk away. This approach may improve the efficiency of contracting

---

[45] Power Ledger Pty Ltd, White Paper (2018) 8–9.

[46] P Lasker, Power prices (2019). In economics, this is referred to as the 'Averch-Johnson' effect, see H Averch and LL Johnson, 'Behavior of the Firm Under Regulatory Constraint' (1962) 52 *American Economic Review* 1052.

[47] For a greater discussion of this point, see NR Fulbright, 'Can smart contracts be legally binding contracts?' White Paper, available at www.nortonrosefulbright.com/files/r3-and-norton-rose-fulbright-white-paper-full-report-144581.pdf.

within the sector and will almost certainly reduce the legal costs incurred, but at what cost? Is it in the interests of consumers to lose what little is left of their negotiating power within the energy sector? The new technological developments associated with Industry 4.0 and Energy 4.0 could also force a rethink of the essential principles of contract law as they apply in the energy sector. These issues need to be carefully considered before wide scale adoption of these new technologies occurs.

# VI.  What does this Mean for Regulators in the Era of Energy 4.0?

Significant regulatory reforms are going to be required to meet the needs of market participants and consumers in the era of Energy 4.0. Originally, many of the digital technologies that the energy sector is seeking to adopt were conceived of as 'state-remote networks, i.e. networks entirely self-governed on the basis of consensus amongst their users'.[48] However, if there is wide-scale adoption of these technologies, such as is beginning to occur, a new approach to regulation will inevitably be required. Regulation will be needed to ensure that we realise the benefits from increasing digitisation such as increased flexibility, more efficient market optimisation, intelligent grids and more interconnected assets, while avoiding privacy breaches, cyberattacks and vulnerabilities though greater intermittency.

Our existing energy market regulation, which was designed in the latter part of the twentieth century to meet the needs of conventional electricity supply generated from fossil fuels, has not kept pace with the technological developments occurring within the energy sector and the resultant transformation of the energy market. Unless energy market regulation becomes more responsive to the transformation currently taking place, there is a risk that the existing regulation could act as a barrier to entry for new market participants. This could prevent the adoption and commercialisation of new technologies and more innovative business models to the detriment of market competition. However, amending the existing market regulations to remove impediments to new market entrants is not an easy process, as many of the regulations which now act in an anti-competitive manner had a legitimate objective when originally introduced.[49] For example, given all of the new market entrants, regulators have to consider how to create incentives that are structured to optimise outcomes for the system as a whole rather than focusing on what is included within the RAB for the market incumbents.

---

[48] P Paech, 'The Governance of Blockchain Financial Networks' (2017) 80 *Modern Law Review* 1073, 1076.

[49] Directorate for Financial and Enterprise Affairs Competition Committee, OECD, Hearing on Disruptive Innovation (16–18 June 2015) 7, available at www.oecd.org/officialdocuments/publicdispla ydocumentpdf/?cote=DAF/COMP(2015)3&docLanguage=En.

This may mean acknowledging that the unbundling the historically vertically integrated energy market to enhance competition actually impairs the ability of new technologies with multiple functions to compete. This is because technologies such as energy storage possess a number of functions such as generation, transmission support and ancillary services, each of which provides value to the market.[50] However, in the current market structure, storage can only receive financial benefit from one function, as otherwise it is deemed to be a vertically integrated asset in breach of the electricity market rules.[51] This makes financing the deployment of energy storage more difficult and means that it cannot fairly compete with other incumbent technologies providing these services.[52]

The introduction of these new technologies will require fundamental revisions to electricity market designs. At the same time, it is also important that the regulation does not become too responsive, altering with every potential development currently being proposed or in the research phase, as this would create too much regulatory uncertainty. The frequent policy shifts associated with overly responsive regulation could make investing in the sector too risky, driving up the compliance costs for existing investments and hampering market developments.

The role of the regulator in the era of Energy 4.0 is critical. Energy market regulators are being asked to support the development of new technologies, without having to 'pick winners' and increase innovation and investment, all while ensuring competition in existing and emerging markets. Equally, at the same time as the market is becoming more complex, and the tasks of ensuring system stability, reliability and creating resiliency are becoming more difficult,[53] regulators are also being required to create consumer and industry acceptance and encourage confidence in the new technologies and the market. This means that regulators are forced to try and balance system operation requirements and their role in preventing and responding to emergencies, with their roles in encouraging investment, innovation and competition, addressing safety and ensuring consumer protection.

Some of the biggest changes to the role of regulators in Energy 4.0 will relate to their roles in managing access to data and protecting privacy. Traditionally, when the products and services offered within the market were limited, and the data generated by the energy market was less granular and could not be easily reduced to an individual level, this role was relatively straightforward. However, in the era of Energy 4.0, regulators will be expected to deal with a broader array of market participants, as opposed to the traditional generators, transmission companies, distribution companies and retailers. This may include more companies providing energy services such as the coordination and management of the smart devices,

---

[50] PJ Crossley, 'Defining the Greatest Legal and Policy Obstacle to "Energy Storage"' (2013) 4 *Renewable Energy Law and Policy Review* 268, 271–74.

[51] ibid.

[52] ibid.

[53] Australian Energy Regulator, 'State of the Energy Market 2017' (2017).

solar and storage within a property, or companies aggregating residential house-holds with specific characteristics to enable peer-to-peer energy trading or the development of decentralised or distributed networks. The product offered by these service providers is based on the analysis of huge volumes of individual and aggregated customer data to provide optimal outcomes for them, thus rapidly increasing the complexity of the market.

An obvious role for regulators and rulemakers, given the increasing complexity of the market and limited knowledge of the market held by the average consumer, is to take steps to ensure that consumer data and privacy is adequately protected. A further role for regulators, given the lack of comparability of current offers, may be giving consumers assistance in comparing market offers either by providing free comparison sites or by mandating the provision of information suitable for providing a cost comparison. This assistance in the price comparison process will become even more important as the range of tariff offers available through differ-ent sales channels expands. All of this needs to be achieved while we ask regulators to recognise the commercial value of this data and not necessarily require that businesses hand over proprietary information that they have collected which they can monetise or utilise to support new market developments. This is not an easy balance for regulators to achieve. As the variety of new products and services and number of market participants expands, it will become harder for regulators to provide effective oversight and to ensure compliance with the National Electricity Law and National Electricity Rules.

In addition to the obvious data protection and privacy issues, regulators will also have to grapple with a larger consumer protection role. For example, the intro-duction of more standardised smart contracts will allow more information to be provided to consumers on their rights and responsibilities under them. However, they also shift all the negotiating power to the market participant rather than shar-ing some of that power with the end consumer. While the benefits of this could outweigh the costs for residential consumers, the costs for larger commercial consumers or aggregated collections of residential consumers could be consider-able. Regulators will also have to consider how they protect vulnerable consumers. Should consumers who are unable to purchase access to the new Energy 4.0 technologies be given subsidised or free access? How do the fixed network costs get allocated? Can this be done without creating implicit subsidies where some users are charged differential shares of fixed costs? These are not easy issues for regulators.

In order to address the issues that regulators will face due to the transformation of the energy market in the era of Energy 4.0, regulators will need to be more agile and communicate more openly with a broader array of other regulators and stake-holders. Long-term solutions will require whole-of-system planning. For example, the introduction of electric vehicles will require discussions with urban plan-ners and local authorities to forecast the location of population centres to better plan for future energy demands, grid reinforcements and new generation, infra-structure agencies to identify charging station locations on major roads and car manufacturers to identify new technologies such as rapid battery chargers that will impact on market requirements. Long-term planning and coordinated action will increase predictability and certainty and, additionally, remove some of the political risk that is currently present within the sector, as sudden changes in the sector should become less likely. This will create a more positive investment environment by creating the right signals and framework to allow the competitive market to address system needs and minimise the actions required by the market operator.

## VII.  How Well Placed are the Institutions of the National Electricity Market to Provide this? A Case Study of the Distributed Energy Resources Register

One of the new technologies that has been introduced into the Australian energy market as part of Energy 4.0 is battery storage. Even though the introduction of battery storage was identified as a priority area for the creation of Australian Standards as early as 2012, regulators have been slow to respond to the introduction of this technology with the first Standards not released until December 2017.[54] In the Energy White Paper, which was released in 2015 to set the policy direction of the Australian Energy Market, battery storage barely rated a mention.[55]

Once it became apparent that battery storage technology was increasingly becoming cost-competitive in the Australian market, even in the absence of subsidies, due to rapidly rising electricity prices, market participants began to agitate for regulations. In particular, since 2015 there have been repeated calls for a National Energy Storage Register.[56] The Register was considered necessary because the Australian Energy Market Operator did not know how many storage systems had been installed or where they were located, which made system planning and forecasting difficult.[57] Other issues that a Register would help to address include safety concerns relating to the risk posed to first responders in fire emergency situations, and consumer protection concerns about the serious risk posed by faulty battery systems and the need to be able to conduct effective product recalls.[58]

---

[54] M Bloch, International Battery Storage Standard Adopted in Australia (18 December 2017) (Solar Quotes Blog, 2019), available at www.solarquotes.com.au/blog/battery-standard-australia-mb0369.

[55] Department of Industry and Science (Cth), Government of Australia, 2015 Energy White Paper, available at https://industry.gov.au/EnergyWhitePaperApril2015/index.html.

[56] See eg, PJ Crossley, 'Is it time to establish a National Register for Stationary Energy Storage?' (2016) 34 *Energy News* 18; Clean Energy Council, 'Battery Tracking Report', Discussion Paper issued to the COAG Energy Council (January 2016).

[57] Australian Energy Market Commission, 'Consultation Paper on the Register of Distributed Energy Resources' (6 March 2018), available at www.aemc.gov.au/sites/default/files/2018-06/Consultation%20paper.pdf.

[58] See eg, PJ Crossley, 'Submission on the Energy Storage Registration Consultation Paper', Council of Australian Governments Energy Council, Energy Market Transformation (September 2016).

Following a series of documents published in early 2016 in support of such a register by the Clean Energy Council and others,[59] the issue was then raised in mid-2016 at the Council of Australian Governments' Energy Council.[60] Key stakeholders then participated in a stakeholder meeting in September 2016 and made submissions in response to a public consultation document in October 2016.[61] Following the review of these submissions by the Energy Market Transformation Team and the Senior Council of Officials, the creation of the National Energy Storage Register received in-principle support at the COAG Energy Council meeting held on 14 December 2016.[62] The Register was then subjected to a cost–benefit analysis process from March 2017, with the subsequent report being endorsed by the COAG Energy Council in July 2017.[63] On 5 October 2017, the COAG Energy Council submitted a rule change request to the Australian Energy Market Commission for the creation of a far broader Distributed Energy Resources Register.[64] This rule change was subject to further stakeholder consultation and submissions until 17 April 2018.[65] Following consideration of the submissions received, the then AEMC released a draft rule change to implement the Register. This was subject to a further consultation process before the rule change was finalised on 13 September 2018. Questions about the implementation of the Final Rule and the technical operation of the Register are now subject to consultations being carried out by the Australian Energy Market Operator.

This means that despite this rule change not being all that controversial, the earliest this rule change – which has had strong support from the industry, market institutions and consumer advocates – will be introduced is July 2019. In the meantime, battery storage systems continue to be installed and the efficacy of the Register diminishes as the Register will not seek to retrospectively collect data for systems installed prior to its introduction.[66] This process highlights how the pace of energy market transformation is far outstripping the ability of regulators to address the emerging challenges created by the introduction of new technologies, products and services.

# VIII. Conclusions

In the era of Energy 4.0, consumer needs for energy are changing, and this means that energy will also need to be generated and delivered differently. This transformation of the energy market, with the introduction of more complex systems,

---

[59] Clean Energy Council, 'Battery Tracking Report' (2016).
[60] Australian Energy Market Commission, 'Consultation Paper' (2018) 3.
[61] ibid.
[62] ibid 4.
[63] ibid 6.
[64] ibid 1.
[65] ibid.
[66] ibid.

big data, smart contracts and growing concerns around access to data, privacy and consumer protection will require a paradigm shift in the approaches used to regulate the electricity market. Existing market regulation, introduced in the late twentieth century before the advent of widespread renewable generation and the introduction of new technologies, is arguably no longer fit for purpose. This regulation is now actively preventing new market entrants from realising the full value proposition of their technologies and hampering innovation, investment and competition. New regulation, with a greater emphasis on ensuring system security and reliability, privacy and data protection and consumer protection, is required. Importantly, the existing approaches to amending market regulation are currently operating too slowly to affect the necessary changes and do not provide a sufficient whole of system approach. In future, a more coordinated approach that supports the optimal use of technology and supports flexibility within the market will be needed to ensure the efficient introduction of Energy 4.0.

## PART III

# Competition and Regulation in Transboundary Energy Markets

# 7

# Between Transnational Private Law and Public International Law: Engineer-driven Self-governance in Transboundary Energy Megaprojects

CHRISTOPH G BENEDICT

## I. Abstract

This chapter examines the interplay of transnational private law and public international law in the legal framework for transboundary energy megaprojects (TEMs). It describes the evolution of engineer-driven transnational regimes of contract law and procedural law which allow the actors in TEMs to govern a given project in a way that follows engineering rationality. It shows how, within these regimes, norms are created and decisions and interpretations of norms are made possible that follow engineering rationality. It then shows how these norms, decisions and interpretations, even if conflicting with mandatory national rules, are enforced within and between states with the help of treaties under public international law.

## II. Introduction

Engineer-driven self-governance has lately been extensively debated in the context of 'cyberspace governance',[1] especially the growing role of the Internet Corporation

[1] V Röben, 'International Internet Governance' (1999) 42 *German Yearbook of International Law* 400; J von Bernstorff, 'The Structural Limitations of Network Governance – ICANN as a Case in Point' in C Joerges, I-J Sand and G Teubner (eds) *Transnational Governance and Constitutionalism* ((Hart Publishing, 2004) 257; CT Marsden, *Internet co-regulation: European law, regulatory governance and legitimacy in cyberspace* (Cambridge University Press, 2011); R Radu, *Negotiating internet governance* (Oxford University Press, 2019); L DeNardis, *The global war for internet governance* (Yale University Press, 2014); E Brousseau, *Governance, regulations, and powers on the internet* (Cambridge University Press, 2012).

for Assigned Names and Numbers (ICANN)[2] and the considerable power of many software engineering firms active in cyberspace.[3]

This chapter looks at engineer-driven self-governance in an 'old economy' context. Transboundary construction projects have been executed and regulated by engineers for more than 150 years. We are thus looking at a mature system. There is a well-developed body of legal norms that govern the relationships between the private actors, states and national legal systems. The private actors are usually human beings (or the legal entities created by them) acting in real life on construction projects moving many tons of earth, steel and concrete, not algorithms or servers shaping virtual realities.

The chapter finds that in this context of more traditional economic activity, self-governance is well-established, has brought about an astonishing degree of regulatory convergence, was successful in overcoming issues created by inflexible national legal traditions and has enjoyed the consistent support of over 140 sovereign states for many decades without being called into question in any fundamental way.

## A.  TEMs: Definition

Megaprojects may generally be defined as projects that are very expensive and attract a large amount of public attention because of substantial impacts on communities and budgets.[4] Transboundary energy megaprojects (TEMs) are defined for the purposes of this chapter as planned activities to build or maintain physical energy infrastructure on a scale which necessitates the cooperation of actors from different states over a timespan of more than two years[5] and which are very expensive, all the while attracting a large amount of public attention. They are 'transboundary' in the sense that they are usually built by or together with contractors or consortia of contractors from states other than that of the project site, often using technology licensed from companies located in yet other third states.

The construction of the solar thermal power station at Ouarzazate in Morocco cost roughly EUR 3.5 billion, that of the Three Gorges hydropower dam in China roughly EUR 28 billion. Investment in offshore wind power in the EU in 2018

---

[2] S DelBianco and B Cox, 'ICANN internet governance: is it working?' (2008) 21 *Pacific McGeorge Global Business & Development Law Journal* 27; A Rachovitsa, 'International law and the global public interest: ICANN's independent objector as a mechanism of responsive global governance' in J Summers and A Gough (eds), *Non-state actors and international obligations: creation, evolution and enforcement* (Brill, 2018) 342.

[3] D Tambini and M Moore, *Digital dominance: the power of Google, Amazon, Facebook and Apple* (Oxford University Press, 2018); JT Rosch, *Intel, Apple, Google, Microsoft, and Facebook: observations on antitrust and the high-tech sector* (US Federal Trade Commission, 2010).

[4] B Flyvbjerg. *The Oxford Handbook of Megaproject Management* (Oxford University Press, 2017).

[5] Although this is no hard and fast rule, the time span of two years is inspired by the ICSID decision on Jurisdiction of 16 June 2006 in *Jan de Nul / Dredging International v Egypt* ARB/04/13 [93]–[96], where an engagement of two years was held to be sufficient to constitute an 'investment'.

totalled EUR 10.3 billion,[6] mostly for new offshore wind parks, each of which may cost up to EUR 2 billion to construct. All these are examples of TEMs. While the threshold for 'very expensive' is often set around EUR 1 million, projects like the world's largest tidal power station, Sihwa Lake Tidal Power Station in South Korea, which cost roughly EUR 200 million to build, might also be regarded as an energy megaproject, when the local purchasing power of the 313.5 billion Korean won it cost is taken into account.[7]

## B. TEMs: Features and Challenges

Regulation and disputes surrounding transboundary projects offer consider-able factual and legal complexity.[8] Disruptive project events, cost overruns and ensuing litigation or arbitration are not uncommon for TEMs. For example, the construction for the Finnish Nuclear Power Station Olkiluoto was planned to cost EUR 2 billion, but is now estimated at EUR 8.5 billion[9] so that international arbi-tration between the parties on responsibility for the cost overrun took place, which resulted in an agreement in 2018.

Disputes in the field of TEMs almost always involve quite complex facts. A whole host of individual items and quite an array of diverse technical issues are of common occurrence. More often than not, sets and subsets of technical facts are interdependent or even interchangeable. As a rule, they are difficult to estab-lish and sometimes the very question of how to establish them may be in dispute. Usually, though not necessarily, the bigger a project, the more technically complex it is.

Just as the technical complexity of a project may generate particularly entan-gled issues, so may the complexity to organise and manage the number of different actors contributing to the execution of a given project, as their respective spheres of action and responsibility are interdependent in practice. Of course, participants should take great care in trying to define and delineate such spheres contractu-ally. However, they fight an unequal battle against the sheer multitude of possible interactions and interfaces. Even where they succeed on paper, the reality of a construction site is stark. If a problem in fact occurs on site, the actors' factual contribution to its causation is quite often unclear and usually remains unclear for longer than the project execution can wait.

Legal reasoning being dependent on the factual findings, the factual complex-ity in technical and organisational terms obliges the lawyer involved in such

---

[6] 'Wind Energy in Europe in 2018, Trends and Statistics' (Wind Europe, 2018) 23. Investment in 2019 was the second largest amount of capacity financed in a year (Wind Europe, 2019, 23).

[7] HS Lee, 'Ocean renewable energy: Tidal power in the Yellow Sea' (2011) 17 *Journal of International Development and Cooperation* 29, 37: 313.5 billion Korean won, which at the time of the end construc-tion in 2010 equalled EUR 206.7 million.

[8] J Jenkins and S Stebbings, *International Construction Arbitration Law* (Kluwer, 2006) 7; M Lembcke (ed), *Handbuch Baukonfliktmanagement* (Werner, 2013) 11.

[9] 'Suomenkin uusi ydinvoimala maksaa 8,5 miljardia euroa', *Helsingin Sanomat*, 13 December 2012.

disputes to deal with multiple alternative factual bases, and thus with alternative, sometimes contradictory legal reasonings. Moreover, big projects with multiple actors entail a multitude of contractual parties and contractual documents. They should be – in principle, but in practice are not necessarily – in tune with each other. Overlapping spheres of contractual responsibility, incongruent or conflicting documents, unclear hierarchies and conflicts between legal systems may add another layer of analytical challenge.

Furthermore, TEM disputes are particularly prone to amplification through interface miscommunication. The Bible takes a big construction project, the Tower of Babel, to illustrate discord brought about by misunderstandings. Indeed, language issues play an often underestimated role. Usually in big transboundary projects, the actors are coming from different regions or nations and bring along diverse cultural backgrounds and thus different understandings of contractual clauses, which may lie undetected until a problem arises. Legal regimes and languages of contractual documents may differ, and jurisdictional questions, often addressed incoherently by contractual stipulations, may create additional confusion. Another language barrier is persistent even between fellow nationals: engineers and lawyers need quite some experience and training to get to understand each other. Many a dispute has been aggravated by engineers and lawyers working together thinking they understand each other, while they effectively did not.

## C. TEMs: Criticism and Support

Legal, social, environmental, safety or financial aspects of megaprojects in general,[10] and of TEMs more particularly,[11] have been the subject of debate. Scholars' criticism has targeted at, eg, hydropower dams,[12] nuclear power plants[13] and offshore wind parks.[14] In those debates, TEMs are often viewed as intrusive,

---

[10] B Flyvbjerg, N Bruzelius and W Rothengatter, *Megaprojects and Risk* (Cambridge University Press, 2003); B v Wendland, 'The Responsible Public Investor and Public Mega-Projects' (2017) 16 *European State Aid Law Quarterly* 276; W Rothengatter, *Risk management for megaprojects* (Oxford University Press, 2017); K Wegrich (ed), *The governance of infrastructure* (Oxford University Press, 2017).

[11] BK Sovacool and CJ Cooper, *The governance of energy megaprojects: politics, hubris and energy security* (Edgar Elgar, 2013).

[12] W Shapiro, 'China's Three Gorges Dam' (1997) *Colorado Journal of International Environmental Law & Policy* 146; DDA Schaefer, 'The analysis of the anticipated effects on the environment, comparing opinions concerning the central versus local government's views on the three gorges project in China as well as U.S. views on it from 1992–2006' (2009) 7 *Loyola University Chicago International Law Review* 31.

[13] K Ishibashi, 'The Fukushima Daiichi Nuclear Power Plant accident – a provisional analysis and survey of the Government's international & domestic response' (2011) 17 *Asian Yearbook of International Law* 149, and 18 *Asian Yearbook of International Law* (2012) 88; L Tichy, 'The Czech discourse on the completion of the Temelín Nuclear Power Plant' (2012) 21 *International issues & Slovak foreign policy affairs* 21.

[14] MH Nordquist, JN Moore and A Chircop (eds), *The regulation of continental shelf development – rethinking international standards* (Nijhoff, 2013); R Tscherning, 'The European offshore supergrid

external elements that threaten the balance of ecosystems, and/or the health and safety of persons.

While it is true that some TEMs have threatened or indeed have had such external effects which may need to be the subject of current or future governmental regulation under national law, EU law and/or public international law, this chapter looks at engineer-driven self-governance enabling the successful completion of TEMs and how the creation of transnational contractual and procedural law and the application of public international law treaties support TEMs. Such support appears to be based on an assumption that TEMs, even though sometimes challenging for budgets, politics and/or the environment are generally planned and built to enhance the welfare of societies, eg the security of energy supply and/ or the transition towards more sustainable energy production.

The paper will look at the non-governmental actors who organise this support and at the bodies of transnational contract law[15] they have created for transboundary construction contracts. It will go on to show how other non-governmental actors have independently created a body of transnational procedural rules to create a system of private dispute resolution, which may be used to decide disputes on those (and other) contracts. As a next step, it will show how yet other governmental and intergovernmental actors have created and implemented treaties under public international law which organise the public enforcement within and by states of the decisions made in private dispute resolution on private law contracts. As a final step, we will look at two instances showing how, in practice, a conflict between differing rules and interpretations valid within the private transnational system on the one hand and within national legal systems on the other hand are decided in favour of the transnational system.

# III. Self-governance by Non-governmental Organisations

Of course, transboundary projects are subject to many applicable laws and other governmental regulations. International contract law and the law on the settlement of disputes in the field of infrastructure projects generally is a vast subject matter.[16] Still, the day-to-day world of TEMs is a world dominated not by law nor lawyers, but by engineers. Engineers from many nationalities have cooperated over decades for large projects worldwide. It is engineers who build skyscrapers of

---

and the expansion of offshore wind energy in Germany, Ireland and the United Kingdom' (2011) 20 *European Energy and Environmental Law Review* 76.

[15] PHF Bekker, R Dolzer and M Waibel, *Making transnational law work in the global economy* (Cambridge University Press, 2010); M Reimann, JC Hathaway, TL Dickinson, JH Samuels, *Transnational Law, Cases and Materials* (West, 2013).

[16] See eg Jenkins and Stebbings, *International Construction Arbitration Law* (2006); L Klee, *International Construction Contract Law* (XE Publishing, 2015).

more than 100 floors, bridges that span deep valleys or wide bays, who construct artificial waterways that link up oceans and TEMs that can provide energy for millions.

## A. Non-governmental Engineers' Organisations

For more than 150 years, engineers have created non-governmental organisations at the national and international level, among the most venerable being the British Institution of Civil Engineers (ICE), established in London in 1818,[17] and the American Institute of Architects (AIA), founded in 1857 in New York. Some of these national associations have inspired the formation of associations at the international and European level, the most important being the International Federation of Consulting Engineers (Fédération Internationale des Ingénieurs – Conseils (FIDIC)) in Geneva, a private association of Swiss law organised under the laws of the Swiss Canton of Geneva, founded in 1913.[18] At the European Level, the European Engineering Industries Organisation ORGALIME was founded as a non-profit association of Belgian Law in 1973 in Brussels.

## B. The Creation of Transnational Contract Law through Model Forms

Such non-governmental organisations have over time developed, refined and successfully distributed bodies of transnational private law, mostly through the creation of model form construction contracts which can be (and often are) chosen by parties to a construction project as the basis for their contract negotiations.[19] The degree of regulatory convergence in the sector of transboundary construction which has been attained in this way is considerable. As John Uff has put it, 'contract forms have proliferated to the point that a substantial amount of construction work is now carried on under ad hoc forms, based on standard or traditional drafts'.[20] The British ICE[21] or MF/1 contract forms have taken great influence on

---

[17] H Ferguson and M Chrimes, *The civil engineers: the story of the Institution of Civil Engineers and the people who made it* (ICE Publishing, 2011).

[18] R Widegren, *Consulting Engineers 1913–1988: FIDIC over 75 years* (International Federation of Consulting Engineers, 1988).

[19] Many other private non-governmental organisations play a significant role in the defining technical standards. The American Society of Mechanical Engineers (ASME), the Deutsche Institut für Normung (DIN) and other recognised bodies of private law set technical standards, largely without government involvement, which are internationally recognised and are included by parties to IEMPs into the description of contract scope. Since this chapter is mainly interested in institutions creating transnational contract law and international organisations supporting its enforcement, we shall not go further into these institutions which are mainly concerned with technical standards.

[20] J Uff, *Construction Law*, 8th edn (Sweet & Maxwell, 2002) 308.

[21] S Wearne, *Civil engineering contracts: An introduction to construction contracts and the ICE model form of contract* (Thomas Telford, 1989).

the construction contracts in Britain and abroad.[22] In a similar fashion, the FIDIC contracts[23] and the Orgalime model forms[24] have set standards for international construction projects.

Evidently, the contracts, once negotiated, still need to be based on and construed under a national legal system. The regulation density of the model forms, however, is so high, that they factually constitute largely autonomous regulatory frameworks that address the vast majority of legal questions that may possibly arise in a given project.

Although the different model forms vary from each other to a certain degree, there is large convergence on many topics. By comparison, domestic legal systems applicable to works contracts vary to a significantly higher degree. Also, many of them are not readily available in English. Even where good translations exist, they are still translations of a text rooted in a foreign national legal system, while the model forms satisfy highest standards of drafting on an international level. Those organisations have thus created a body of model form contracts which, taken together, quite successfully regulate an important sector of the national and international economy. In that way they have significantly reduced the practical importance of the works contract provisions foreseen by the different local national laws.

## C. The Privatisation of Dispute Resolution through Institutional Arbitration and DRBs

Such material convergence goes hand in hand with the privatisation of dispute resolution. It is difficult today to find a substantial transboundary construction contract that would not contain an arbitration clause. Also, special forms of speedy dispute resolution have evolved, namely the so-called dispute resolution boards (DRB) or dispute adjudication boards (DAB), which are created for the duration of a given project to quickly resolve disputes as soon as they emerge.[25]

Just as there is a number of well-respected organisations that create model form contracts, there is a number of renowned arbitral institutions which help to set up dispute resolution procedures; among the most prominent are the International

---

[22] For a detailed analysis, see J Uff, *Construction Law*, 12th ed (Wiley, 2017) ch 11.

[23] NG Bunni, *The FIDIC forms of contract*, 3rd edn (Wiley, 2013); A Hewitt, *The FIDIC contracts* (Wiley, 2014); W Godwin, *International construction contracts: a handbook with commentary on the FIDIC design-build forms* (Wiley-Blackwell, 2013); R Knutson, *FIDIC: an analysis of international construction contracts* (Kluwer Law International, 2005); MD Robinson, *An employer's and engineer's guide to the FIDIC conditions of contract* (Wiley, 2011).

[24] A Harris, *Orgalime general conditions S 2000: guide on their use and interpretation* (Orgalime, 2000); U Contman, *Commentary on Orgalime SI14* (2014); N Henchie, The Orgalime Turnkey Contract for Industrial Works – an alternative to FIDIS's Silver Book? (2004) 21 *International Construction Law Review* 67.

[25] For more details on DRB/DAB procedure, see C Chem, *Dispute Boards: practice and procedure*, 2nd edn (Wiley, 2011); Jenkins and Stebbings (n 8) 105.

Chamber of Commerce (ICC) in Paris, the London Court of International Arbitration (LCIA), the China International Economic and Trade Arbitration Commission (CIETAC), the Singapore International Arbitration Centre (SIAC) and the Kuala Lumpur Regional Centre for Arbitration (KLRCA).[26]

## D. Drivers and Success Factors

It appears noteworthy that the parties to TEM contracts are in no way bound to adopt these model forms for their contracts. They have, however, become common, global industry practice and a worldwide trade usage. A main driver for this development may perhaps be seen in the acceptance by engineers of rules made by engineer-driven organisations. Also, while national laws on works contracts may differ significantly and are not always available in a language accessible to all, the model forms are familiar, well known and available in many languages. Also, in a TEM, the contractor, the subcontractors, the client who orders the project and the lenders who finance the TEM may (and routinely do) come from different jurisdictions, so that choosing the national law of one party may be perceived as conferring an unfair advantage upon that party. Internationally established model contract forms offer a welcome solution of perceived neutrality.

With regard to the procedural side of the matter, the same is true: although there is no legal provision that would force the parties to adopt an arbitration clause or institute a dispute board, they have become an accepted trade usage. Confidentiality, finality, expertise, speediness and cost-efficiency are advantages commonly attributed to arbitration.[27] Especially for project execution, where a day of delay may cost millions, the aspect of speediness has even been further enhanced by the DRBs and DABs mentioned above. Arbitration is also perceived to be neutral and procedurally flexible, while court systems may be viewed as beholden to national legal tradition and strict procedural codes.

In the context of a TEM, however, there is one feature that recommends arbitration even more than in some other contexts. Most disputes surrounding TEMs are extremely technical or commercial in their nature. The possibility to choose an arbitrator who is not a lawyer, but somebody with necessary language expertise or an engineer or quantity surveyor or other specialist figures prominently among the reasons for the preference of arbitration in transboundary engineering.[28] Some of the most respected arbitrators are not lawyers by training, but engineers or financial experts.

---

[26] For detailed analysis of the arbitration rules and practice of these and other institutions, see RA Schütze (ed), *Institutional Arbitration*, 2nd edn (CH Beck, 2019).

[27] G Born, *International Commercial Arbitration* (Wolters Kluwer, 2009) 71.

[28] Jenkins and Stebbings (n 8) 146.

# IV. The Enforcement by Means of Public International Law

Enforcement of such contract-related awards is enabled by public international law, which provides two main means that are universally available.

## A. Enforcement of International Commercial Arbitration Awards through the New York System

For the enforcement of arbitral awards, parties may rely on the New York Convention on the Recognition and Enforcement of Foreign Arbitral Awards of 10 June 1958.[29] This treaty system counts among the most successful regimes in public international law both by number of ratifications and density of everyday application.[30] Over 140 states have ratified the convention. In fact, it is so successful that transboundary projects do not usually appear in state courts. Although national legal systems have courts which take care of all kinds of works contracts, even specialised courts like the Technology and Construction Court in London, an analysis of jurisdiction of those courts however shows that large transboundary construction projects do rarely figure, as compared to their occurrence in commercial arbitration.

A prominent feature of this treaty regime is enshrined in Article V of the New York Convention, which allows only a very limited amount of grounds for review of a foreign arbitral award by the national court, which is called upon to recognise and enforce said award. Those grounds are limited, roughly stated, to lack of a valid arbitration agreement, lack of arbitrability, blatant disregard for rules of due process and violations of the *ordre public*.[31] In other words, there is no way for the enforcing court to 'correct' an award which relies on a 'false' interpretation of law ('false' meaning here 'different from the interpretation prevalent in state courts'), unless such interpretation qualifies for one of the aforementioned categories (prohibition of a *'revision au fond'*/no review of the merits).[32] Thus, the vast majority of enforcement proceedings for arbitration awards is successful.[33] Commentators speak openly of a 'pro-arbitration bias'.[34] It is important to

---

[29] R Wolff, *New York Convention – Commentary* (Oxford University Press, 2012); H Kronke, *Recognition and Enforcement of foreign arbitral awards a global commentary on the New York Convention* (Kluwer, 2010).

[30] Over 140 states have ratified the convention.

[31] A Maurer, *The public policy exception under the New York Convention* (Juris, 2012).

[32] V Chantebout, *Le principe de non révision au fond des sentences arbitrales* (Theses, 2007).

[33] According to the New York Convention web site (Newyorkconvention.org). An analysis of more than 1,400 court decisions reported in the *ICCA Yearbook Commercial Arbitration* shows that enforcement of an arbitral award is granted in almost 90% of the cases.

[34] Wolff, *New York Convention* (2012) Art V, margin note 5; Born, *International Commercial Arbitration* (2009) 2702; see also 2711: 'Developed international arbitration regimes adopt an avowedly

understand that this relative autonomy of the arbitration system from interpretations given in court systems is not an accident but a defining feature of private dispute resolution. Finality and speediness being among the main advantages of private dispute resolution, much of its purpose would be defeated if all legal reasonings and findings in awards could be challenged in court.

## B. A Special Case: Enforcement through Treaty Arbitration Instituted by Bilateral Investment Agreements (BITs) or International Investment Agreements (IIAs)

For a small number of cases, another dispute resolution mechanism of public international law is available in addition to the traditional transnational commercial arbitration system: the settlement of disputes under mechanisms of international investment law, sometimes referred to as 'investor–state dispute settlement' (ISDS).[35] These disputes can be brought before an arbitral tribunal administered by the International Center for the Settlement of Investment disputes (ICSID) or, depending of the BIT or IIA establishing jurisdiction, by other arbitral institutions.

A TEM or its financing usually qualifies as an 'investment' in the sense of Article 25 of the ICSID convention.[36] Enforcement of ICSID awards is regulated in the ICSID Convention itself (Article 54), but the review of awards by national courts is limited in Articles 52 and 53 to very exceptional cases of blatant illegality,[37] in a manner not unlike Article V of the New York Convention.

Although there is restricted transparency for want of full publication of awards, it appears safe to assume that of the largely 350 investor–state dispute settlement cases which have until today been settled by ICSID, more than a third were centered around an 'investment' that in fact had to do with an transboundary construction project. Some of the most prominent cases of investment arbitration were centered around regulatory influences on an energy project (most notably the case involving the Moorburg power plant in Hamburg[38] and the cases on subsidies for wind power in Spain[39]).

---

"pro-enforcement" approach […] these regimes impose a presumptive obligation on national courts to recognize international arbitration awards'.

[35] R Dolzer and C Schreuer, *Principles of International Investment Law*, 2nd edn (Oxford University Press, 2012) 222ff.

[36] ibid 60.

[37] ibid 224.

[38] M Krajewski, 'Umweltschutz und internationales Investitionsschutzrecht am Beispiel der Vattenfall-Klagen und des Transatlantischen Handels- und Investitionsabkommens (TTIP)' (2014) 25 *Zeitschrift für Umweltrecht* 396.

[39] AM López-Rodríguez and P Navarro, 'Investment arbitration and EU law in the aftermath of renewable energy cuts in Spain' (2016) 25 *European Energy and Environmental Law Review* 2. Further, in this volume, chapter 12.

Treaty arbitration has come under criticism lately[40] and been declared by the ECJ[41] to contravene the autonomy of EU law insofar as agreed between EU Member States. There is a growing perception that treaty arbitration may have developed differently than its inventors foresaw[42] and that it may have certain limits in settings where public entities who have not signed an arbitration clause are 'forced' into arbitration by a treaty that their states signed. Perspicuously, this point has already been made over 20 years ago by a leading practitioner of commercial arbitration.[43] Future developments in this field point in the direction of decreasing the privatisation of dispute resolution, either by creating public international dispute resolution bodies[44] or limiting the scope and means of investment arbitration.[45] It remains to be seen if and how far this rollback will (a) hamper the efficiency of the treaty arbitration system, and/or (b) have repercussions upon the commercial arbitration system in general and more specifically for TEMs, which are the subject of this paper. So far the commercial arbitration system remains largely untouched by the debate and is alive and growing.

# V.  Conflicts between Self-governance and Governmental Regulation

In some instances, the self-governance of transboundary construction projects may cause friction with mandatory norms of national laws or their interpretation. The chapter will now examine two cases where the results of engineer-driven self-regulation in transboundary construction projects differ from results which would be found if mandatory norms of certain national laws or their interpretation by state courts applied.

## A.  Penalties

Model form contracts on TEMs (and also many of the contracts not based on a model form) will routinely foresee penalties or liquidated damages for delay

---

[40] M Waibel, A Kaushai, K-HL Chung, C Balchin (eds), *The Backlash against Investment Arbitration – Perceptions and Reality* (Kluwer, 2010); SW Schill (ed), *International Investment law and Comparative Public Law* (Oxford University Press, 2010).

[41] ECJ, Case C-284/16, *Achmea*, Judgment of 6 March 2018.

[42] S Taylor, *The rise of investor-state arbitration: politics, law, and unintended consequences* (Oxford University Press, 2018).

[43] J Paulsson, 'Arbitration without privity' (1995) 10 *ICSID Review* 232.

[44] S Heppner, 'A critical appraisal of the investment court system proposed by the European Commission' (2017) 72 *Dispute Resolution Journal* 93; M Bungenberg and A Reinisch, *From bilateral arbitral tribunals and investment courts to a multilateral investment court: options regarding the institutionalisation of investor-state dispute settlement* (Springer, 2018).

[45] S Borzu, *International Investment Law and Arbitration: History, modern practice and future prospects* (Brill, 2018).

and sometimes also for certain performance criteria or availability of the project sold.[46] Certain legal systems, including the US and UK legal systems, distinguish between (enforceable) 'liquidated damages' and (unenforceable) 'penalties'.[47] This may pose difficulties for construction projects, as the question of whether a given clause foreseeing payment of a given amount under certain circumstances qualifies as one or the other may not be answered without consulting extensive case law.[48] The answer may depend on whether the sum stipulated may be considered 'an extravagant and unconscionable in amount in comparison with the greatest loss which could conceivably be proved to have followed from the breach',[49] whether 'the same amount is payable upon the breach of several undertakings of varying importance';[50] whether the amount is payable 'regardless of the seriousness or triviality of the breach in question',[51] whether the sum is 'liable to fluctuate according to extraneous circumstances',[52] to name just a few considerations, none of which is conclusive in and of itself. It is evident that such criteria may not be easily handled by an engineer or other legal layman – at times not even by a lawyer.

This prohibition on penalties has historical reasons, which date back to the medieval legal practice of 'penal bonds'.[53] It was common at the time to secure loans with a promise to pay a high penalty in case the loan was not paid back in time, no matter whether the creditor indeed suffered any loss.[54] As the practice and its abuse spread, it was declared void by equity courts. Although the practice was later completely abolished by statute, the principle that penalties are unenforceable has stayed on until today.[55]

For both parties involved in a TEM, however, the institution of penalties with a fixed cap (and without too many thoughts whether this may be in tune with a potential or actual amount of proven damage) may be highly desirable. They relieve the party that suffers the delay or shortcoming from the need to prove causation and quantum of damages. For the party that is in delay or is responsible for the shortcoming, they present a calculable, capped amount of damages, which can be taken into account when calculating the project risks and which may be insured. Penalties have therefore become a worldwide trade usage well-established for TEMs for many decades.

---

[46] P Le Goff, *Die Vertragsstrafe in internationalen Verträgen zur Errichtung von Industrieanlagen* (Tenea, 2005).

[47] HG Beale (ed), *Chitty on Contracts*, 33rd edn (Sweet & Maxwell, 2018) 26–109.

[48] ibid.

[49] *Clydebank Engineering and Shipbuilding Co Ltd v Don Jose Ramos Yzquierdo y Castaneda* [1905] AC 6, 7.

[50] *Lord Elphinstone v Monkland Iron & Coal co Ltd* (1886) 11 App Cas 332, 342.

[51] *Lombard North Central plc v Butterworth* [1987] QB 527.

[52] *Public Works Commissioner v Hills* [1906] AC 368, 376.

[53] Le Goff, *Die Vertragsstrafe* (2005) 29ff (UK) and 36ff (US).

[54] PDV Marsh, *Comparative Contract Law* (Gower, 1994) 19.

[55] S Ferris, 'Liquidated damages recovery under the Restatement (Second) of contracts' (1982) *Cornell Law Review* 862.

The creation of model forms with an independent enforcement mechanism allows the parties to a TEM to agree on penalties and enforce them even in countries and in cases where they might otherwise be forbidden by law. The enforcement of penalties has been found by courts not to violate the *ordre public*.[56]

# B. Overall Limitations of Liability

Internationally recognised model forms for construction contracts will, as a rule, foresee a possibility to limit the overall liability of the contractor. It is often acknowledged among project engineers that the contractor, ie the seller of the respective project, carries the risk of the technology they bring to the project, but not the risk of the project as a whole. The owner of the project derives the benefits from the project, so, as a rule, they have to carry the overarching project risks.[57]

Some national legal systems, especially in civil law countries, make it difficult for parties to a TEM to limit the overall liability of the contract. Some have even been criticised to form a 'dangerous trap' for construction projects for this very reason.[58] For example, for projects located in Germany, the German Unfair Contract Terms Act applies. This statute all but prohibits general limitations of liability on the part of the contractor. On its face, the German unfair contract terms legislation would not apply to contracts which have been individually negotiated between commercial entities.[59] However, the established case law of the German Supreme Court has elevated the threshold for individual negotiations to a point where individual negotiations are almost impossible. In the case law of the Supreme Court, individual negotiations presuppose that the party introducing a contract term into negotiation is prepared to let go[60] of this term insofar as its contractual concept deviates from the contractual concept codified by statute and openly declares such readiness.[61] The problem is that limitations of liability are an established trade usage in the field of transboundary energy engineering, so they are not seriously debated by either party.[62] As a recognised trade usage, they are

---

[56] OLG Celle, *Die deutsche Rechtsprechung auf dem Gebiete des Internationalen Privatrechts*, 205, No 188, 518.

[57] If, for example, the material of the turbine blade of a wind turbine rotor is deficient due to shortcomings in the materials used by the contractor who builds the rotor, the contractor will carry the risk to make good that defect, but (depending on market circumstances) not usually the risk of disruption to the wind power production that ensues, while he is repairing the blade. There may be contracts under which the contractor bears part of this risk, but usually for a premium and/or against participation the benefits of this undisrupted power production.

[58] J Zons, 'The German Law on Standard Terms and Conditions – a dangerous trap for building and engineering contracts' (2012) 7 *Construction Law International* 7.

[59] Section 305(1), third sentence BGB.

[60] Bundesgerichtshof (2017) 70 *Neue Juristische Wochenschrift* 2346; Bundesgerichtshof (2018) 71 *Neue Juristische Wochenschrift* 2950.

[61] Bundesgerichtshof (1977) 50 *Neue Juristische Wochenschrift* 624.

[62] L Leuschner, 'AGB-Recht für Verträge zwischen Unternehmen – unter besonderer Berücksichtigung von Haftungsbeschränkungen', Abschlussbericht vom 30.9.2014, 288.

implicitly accepted. Even if they were debated between the parties, they would still be unenforceable, unless they were effectively changed.[63]

This has the practical effect that overall limitations of liability, even though internationally recognised trade usage and even though they are accepted by both parties, may become unenforceable under German law, just because they do not conform to the liability concept of the legislator and are not seriously debated nor changed in every negotiation. Critics have pleaded to reform the statute to correct this case law,[64] but so far to no avail. The German Ministry of Justice has commissioned an expert report on the issue,[65] which has confirmed the problem, but no steps have so far been taken to overcome the issue.

German parties to energy megaprojects located in Germany cannot opt out of this dilemma by choosing a different legal system. EU rules on the conflict of laws foresee that, in such a case, German mandatory provisions such as this de facto prohibition on the overall limitation of liability may not be derogated from.[66] A German court will thus in all likelihood declare the limitation of liability in the model form contract invalid even if the parties chose to subject their contract to a different legal system, for example Swiss Law.

However, German courts, in practice, rarely get to make a ruling on such cases. They are routinely assigned to the exclusive jurisdiction of arbitration tribunals. Of course, arbitration tribunals are also be bound by the German and EU law applicable to the contract; however, they are not formally bound by the interpretation given to the unfair contract terms act by the German Supreme Court. As arbitration tribunals tend to give much more deference to the will of the parties, it is hardly surprising that empirical research has shown that, in arbitration, policy considerations considered paramount and mandatory by the national legislator are often be given less weight in comparison to the will of the parties and limitations of liability enforced more often than in courts in comparable cases.[67]

It appears noteworthy that an interpretation of the unfair contract terms legislation, which would be in clear violation of the established case law of the German Supreme Court by an arbitration tribunal, would still be enforceable in Germany. The prohibition to review the merits (no '*revision au fond*') of an arbitration award would shield this 'misinterpretation' from a setting-aside or non-enforcement by a national court,[68] as long as that court does not regard this as a violation of public policy. So far, no cases have transpired where a court would have held an award

---

[63] C Grüneberg in *Palandt, BGB* (79th edn, 2019), section 305, margin note 19: 'he who constantly declares his willingness to negotiate a term, but never changes it, may not invoke that the term was individually negotiated' (translation by the author).

[64] H Bubrowski (2012) 62 *Anwaltsblatt* 980; KP Berger (2010) 63 *Neue Juristische Wochenschrift* 465.

[65] R Leuschner, *AGB-Recht für Verträge zwischen Unternehmen* (Beck, 2014).

[66] Art 3(3) of Regulation (EC) Nr 593/2008 Regulation (EC) No 593/2008 of the European Parliament and of the Council of 17 June 2008 on the law applicable to contractual obligations (Rome I), OJ L 177/6.

[67] Leuschner (n 62) 148.

[68] S Kröll and P Kraft, in K-H Böckstiegel, S Kröll and P Nacimiento (eds), *Arbitration in Germany. The Model Law in Practice*, 2nd edn (Beck, 2014) § 1059 ZPO, margin note 43.

upholding an overall limitation of liability to be contrary to the *ordre public*, nor does it appear likely that this will happen anytime soon.

# VI. Conclusions

This chapter has examined the non-governmental actors who organise engineer-driven self-governance to support transboundary energy megaprojects and looked at the bodies of transnational contract law they have created for transboundary construction contracts. It has also described the creation of a body of transnational procedural rules forming a system of private dispute resolution for these (and other) contracts. Drivers and success factors for this kind of substantive and procedural self-governance partly reside in the efficiency of the system itself to its users. Moreover, treaties under public international law help by organising the public enforcement within and by states of the decisions made in private dispute resolution on private law contracts. The prohibition of a review of the merits ('*révision au fond*') of an arbitration ruling by state courts effectively shields those decisions from scrutiny in all but extreme cases. Conflicts between differing rules and interpretations valid within the private transnational system on the one hand, and within national legal systems on the other hand, are therefore routinely decided in favour of the transnational system.

In this way public international law instruments, which support the enforcement of transnational norms created by engineer driven self-governance, routinely achieve what the legislative and adjudicative systems of some states have proven unable or unwilling to do, namely provide a comparatively safe legal framework for the trade usages common to TEMs worldwide.

Arguably, there is, as with many governance issues, a legitimacy debate attached to this form of self-governance as a given norm of transnational law created by self-governance may seem to carry less democratic weight than an act of parliament or the judgment of a court of law. It should not be forgotten, however, that the treaties allowing enforcement of transnational arbitration decisions have been ratified by national legislators in democratic procedures. The leeway given to transnational arbitration tribunals to find differently from state courts and have their awards regularly enforced nonetheless was thus instituted willingly by the national sovereigns.

The example of construction law shows that a considerable degree of regulatory convergence at the international level may emerge through self-governance, non-binding model forms and voluntary arbitration. The decision of over 140 national legislators to embrace this approach and grant it recognition and enforcement by ratifying the New York Convention and staying within the system over decades shows how governments can successfully commit to use public international law to support such transnational law developments.

# 8

## Managing the Threat of Regulatory Capture under the European Energy Union

RAFAEL EMMANUEL MACATANGAY AND VOLKER ROEBEN***

## I. Abstract

Operation or expansion decisions in the energy industry naturally have multiple dimensions across commerce, governance, and community, with additional layers of complexity in a transboundary setting. Under the European Energy Union, the EU has legislated to regulate the European energy industry in pursuit of the collective public interest. However, if the design or implementation of these legal instruments is potentially in the grip of regulatory capture – broadly defined as the sly substitution of public for private interests – the efficiency or equity of transboundary outcomes could be harmed. Our approach, relying on the analytical tools of law and economics, is to investigate the propensities for inefficiency or inequity arising from regulatory capture specifically in transboundary energy industries. Our objective in this chapter is to build a framework for managing the risk of regulatory capture in the context of the European electric power industry. We conduct a reflection on the dangers of regulatory capture in a cross-border context in the electric power industry. We then establish maxims for mitigating the peril of regulatory capture that relate to procedure: promotion of shared meaning of overall welfare maximisation in the regulatory process; indifference of the parties, given their respective claims, if each was in its adversary's role; and the use of cost–benefit analysis as a basis for transboundary compensation. We then test these maxims against the recently adopted legislative package Clean Energy for all Europeans pertaining to the cross-border regulation of the European energy market.

*** For helpful discussions, we are grateful to participants of an interdisciplinary workshop 'Towards the European Energy Union, in Search of Principles' held on 5 June 2018 at CEPMLP.

## II. Introduction

Under the European Energy Union (EEU), the strategy for an energy market without internal frontiers throughout the EU, the EU legislates to protect and promote the European public interest in the setting of an energy industry that crosses the borders of currently 28 Member States.[1] Effective transboundary regulation is desirable, but if the design or implementation of legal instruments on the European energy industry is imprudently in the grip of regulatory capture, used here in the sense of the sly substitution of public for private interests, then the efficiency or equity of outcomes is likely harmed. There is a risk that imprudent regulation leads to the wasteful or unfair distribution of gains or burdens over time or across locations. For example, it could distort the investment signals for electric power generation and/or transmission, unduly altering the appropriate scale, location, timing, or technology of capacity additions, in one EU Member State or across interconnected EU Member States. Left to fester, such seemingly small distortions may unjustifiably cause benefits to be denied or delayed or costs to be imposed or advanced, a painful outcome for economically struggling regions in the EU, but barely noticeable for affluent ones.

How, then, to alleviate an exposure to regulatory capture under the Energy Union? Our objective in this paper is to build a framework for managing the risks of regulatory capture in the context of the European energy industry. Our approach, drawing on the teachings of law and economics, is to investigate, at a high level of abstraction, the propensities for inefficiency or inequity arising from regulatory capture in transboundary energy industries. We show that the features of the electric power industry in the EU or other transboundary contexts have profound implications for the risks of regulatory capture, and we identify these risks as cultural and distributional. We then explicate maxims to counter such effects. We finally test these maxims against potential distortions in operation or expansion decisions in the electric power industry in the EU, with reference to the legislative package Clean Energy for all Europeans, adopted in June 2019.

Our foundational idea is that the concept of efficient, effective and equitable regulation in a transboundary setting has to be affirmed as a meaningful exchange amongst adversarial parties to the proceeding. Regulation is a process-bound mechanism of discovering information, in much the same way that the market tends to be characterised as a process. Our main contribution, then, is to show that the analytical tools of law and economics yield three maxims for mitigating the peril of regulatory capture in transboundary energy industries. The three maxims are: the promotion of shared meaning in the regulatory process; the indifference of the parties given their respective claims, if each was in its adversary's role; and the use of cost–benefit analysis as a basis for transboundary compensation, where

---

[1] See V Roeben, *Towards a European Energy Union: European Energy Strategy in International Law* (Cambridge University Press, 2018).

regulation necessarily produces winners and losers across the participating states, or provision of non-arbitrary justification in the absence of a cost–benefit analysis.

This chapter proceeds as follows. Section III is foundational, expounding generally on the rationale for economic regulation and the possibility of compensation. Section IV explains regulation as process. Section V discusses the risks of regulatory capture in transboundary settings. Section VI establishes our three maxims for controlling the risk of regulatory capture in transboundary energy industries. Section VII examines the nuances of the EU electric power industry from a transboundary perspective. Section VIII introduces the EU clean energy package and the reformed ACER, and Section IX tests the three maxims against the package, with emphasis on the vulnerability to regulatory capture in the EU electric power industry.

# III. The Rationality of Transboundary Regulation

This section lays the groundwork on transboundary energy market regulation. It starts with expounding the overall rationality of such regulation and the possibility of compensation.

Transboundary regulation serves the core purpose of regulatory policy, from a functionalist perspective, to promote social welfare.[2] Defined as the sum of consumer surplus and producer surplus, social welfare is maximised under perfect competition.[3] At the social welfare maximum, all gains from trade are captured, and the allocation is Pareto efficient. Any mismatches, perhaps due to bad luck, between the valuation for and the possession of a good are resolved, and a Pareto improvement (ie some trade making two players better off without harming anyone else) is not possible. An allocation, accordingly, is Pareto optimal if there is no waste.[4] By contrast, away from the social welfare maximum, further gains from trade are yet to be captured, and the allocation is Pareto inefficient (ie a Pareto improvement is possible).[5] Pareto optimality, however, is not concerned with distributional issues. A policy increasing social welfare may not be Pareto optimal if there are both winners and losers,[6] and most policies, in fact, produce both winners and losers.[7]

---

[2] See C Sunstein, 'Cost-Benefit Analysis and Arbitrariness Review' (2017) 41 *Harvard Environmental Law Review* 1.

[3] See H Varian, *Intermediate Microeconomics (A Modern Approach)*, 9th edn (WW Norton & Company, Inc, 2014).

[4] See A Mas-Colell, M Whinston and J Green, *Microeconomic Theory* (Oxford University Press, 1995).

[5] Varian, *Intermediate Microeconomics* (2014) 15.

[6] See R Cooter and T Ulen, *Law and Economics*, 6th edn (Berkeley Law Books, 2016).

[7] See J Coleman, 'The Normative Basis of Economic Analysis: A Critical Review of Richard Posner's The Economics of Justice' (1982) 34 *Stanford Law Review* 1105.

An alternative viewpoint is to consider a potential Pareto improvement, generally known as Kaldor–Hicks efficiency, under which the winners, having gained more than the losers have lost, can compensate the losers and still have leftover surplus for themselves. The difference hence is that the winners *could* have compensated the losers under Kaldor–Hicks efficiency, but actually have compensated them under Pareto efficiency thus satisfying the Pareto criterion that no one is harmed'.[8] The distinction between actual (under Pareto efficiency) and possible (under Kaldor–Hicks efficiency) compensation is a function of practicality. How to realise a move from possible to actual compensation? There is much disagreement over the goals of redistribution,[9] and here we do not aspire to resolve the matter definitively. Yet if Pareto efficiency is not satisfied (in the aftermath, for example, of a free trade policy), governments rarely plan for winners to subsidise losers.[10] In the absence of such subsidisation, value judgements involving inter-personal comparisons have to be made. Under an inter-personal comparison criterion of equal weights for gains and losses, a free trade policy should be implemented if the gains to domestic consumers surpass the losses to domestic producers.

The concept of possible compensation under Kaldor–Hicks efficiency is at the heart of cost–benefit analysis.[11] In cost–benefit analysis, accounting for both private and social costs and benefits, a project is undertaken if benefits exceed costs, implying that winners could compensate losers, but seldom specifying details on how to do so. Apparently, a policy or project, as long as it enhances social welfare, tends to be carried out, whether or not a workable plan for moving from possible to actual compensation has actually been developed.

# IV.  Regulation as Process

Typically, as part of the liberalisation or restructuring of the electric power industry, the regulatory framework provides for both the introduction of competition in the wholesale and retail segments, and the continuation of natural monopoly regulation in the transmission and distribution segments.[12] The objective is not only to

---

[8] Of course, a policy bringing Pareto efficiency necessarily increases social welfare, and indeed 'the economic analysis of law should rely upon the Pareto standard whenever practical; see R Cooter, 'Liberty, Efficiency, and Law' (1987) 50 *Law and Contemporary Problems* 141, 163.

[9] Cooter and Ulen, *Law and Economics* (2016) 7–8.

[10] Under a freetrade policy ending a ban on imports, the gain of domestic consumers may exceed the loss of domestic producers. See J Perloff, *Microeconomics*, 3rd edn (Pearson Addison Wesley, 2004).

[11] Cooter and Ulen (n 6) 42.

[12] See P Joskow, 'Lessons Learned from Electricity Market Liberalization' (2008) *The Energy Journal* Special Issue: The Future of Electricity (Papers in Honor of David Newbery). In a market with a price-taking seller (or price-taking sellers), there is perfect competition, social welfare is maximised, and price is at marginal cost (ie first-best pricing). See O Shy, *Industrial Organization Theory and Applications* (MIT Press, 1995). In a natural monopoly market, the cost function is subadditive at the relevant output (ie the production of the good or service, or all combinations of outputs, by a single firm minimises cost), and price is at average cost or at marginal cost subject to a breakeven

foster robust rivalry in competitive segments in which price-setting is accomplished through markets, but also to encourage efficiency in natural monopoly segments in which price-setting or firm behaviour is controlled through regulation.[13]

Resource planning, especially the coordination of capacity additions, is a vital and complex activity in utilities (vertically integrated or otherwise) and restructured electric power markets.[14] The decision-making process for the joint optimisation of generation and transmission investments is exceedingly difficult due largely to uncertainty across multiple dimensions (eg scale, location, timing or technology)[15] involving various governance arrangements.[16] In the case of restructured electric power markets in the US, transmission providers have to participate in a regional process in order to produce a regional transmission plan, and neighbouring planning regions, including regional transmission organisations (RTOs) or independent system operators (ISOs), are required not only to share information on future needs or possible solutions, but also to identify and jointly assess inter-regional solutions.[17] There is, therefore, a strong need for more sophisticated regulatory processes than those for vertical integration.

How to attain a suitable level of regulatory sophistication? Electric utility regulation involves a quasi-judicial procedure to provide due process for all parties to the proceeding (ie utility, customers, investors, etc).[18] There is a regulatory compact recognising a set of mutual obligations, rights and benefits, in effect, a relational contract between utilities and their customers. The utility is granted an exclusive service franchise or territory, but is obliged to serve all customers in the territory, submits itself to regulation, is asked to supply service efficiently, has the right to recover prudently incurred costs, and has an opportunity to earn a return at its market-determined cost of debt and equity capital. Regulation, in essence,

---

constraint (ie second-best pricing). See W Viscusi, J Harrington and J Vernon, *Economics of Regulation and Antitrust* (MIT Press, 2005).

[13] See F Wolak, 'Regulating Competition in Wholesale Electricity Supply' in N Rose (ed), *Economic Regulation and Its Reform: What Have We Learned?* (University of Chicago Press, 2014) ch 4.

[14] See MIT, 'The Future of the Electric Grid' (2011), available at http://energy.mit.edu/wp-content/uploads/2011/12/MITEI-The-Future-of-the-Electric-Grid.pdf. Although two-thirds of electricity load in the US is served through regional transmission organisations, major areas, such as the West (excluding California) or the Southeast, continue to operate under 'traditional' market structures. See FERC, *Energy Primer (A Handbook of Energy Market Basics)* (US Federal Energy Regulatory Commission, 2015). Of course, even in restructured electric power markets, utilities performing transmission or distribution functions are regulated as monopolies.

[15] See also S Hagspiel, C Jägemann, D Lindenberger, T Brown, S Cherevatskiy and E Tröster, 'Cost-optimal power system extension under flow-based market coupling' (2014) 66 *Energy* 654.

[16] For example, in the case of electric utilities within one state of the USA, a state public utility commission (PUC) reviews or authorises requests for the cost recovery of new power generation plants, the acquisition of rights-of-way for the construction of transmission or distribution lines and related facilities, or the design of rates billed to electricity consumers. Further R Campbell, 'Electricity Markets – Recent Issues in Market Structure and Energy Trading', Congressional Research Service, 7-5700, R43093 (2016).

[17] See M Willrich, *Modernizing America's Electricity Infrastructure* (MIT Press, 2017).

[18] See K McDermott, 'Cost of Service Regulation in the Investor-owned Electric Utility Industry: A History of Adaptation' (Edison Electric Institute, 2012).

works as an administrative replacement for the market in order to determine if customer rates are just and reasonable, rather than arbitrary or capricious.

A sophisticated regulatory process provides a trusted broker-dealer service. Regulation can be seen as a venue for bargaining.[19] In the absence of information asymmetries or transaction costs (ie costless bargaining), parties in the regulatory proceeding would exhaust all the gains from trade and thus reach an efficient allocation (as the Coase Theorem suggests). Regulation, in such a situation, would first maximise total surplus and then pursue a redistribution, but would not result in inefficiency.

There is a relationship between efficiency and prudence. Prudence refers to the 'reasonable manager standard' under which the regulator determines if a reasonable manager, given the information that was or could have been available at the time, had made a decision in good faith. The regulator does not substitute its judgement for that of the manager. Yet the standard of prudence refers to reasonableness rather than market efficiency, and markets are obviously not always and everywhere efficient. Managers of unregulated firms sometimes make inefficient decisions, and the reasonableness standard, therefore, is probably not too different to the market standard. Nevertheless, a prudent regulator recognises the potential for the uneven quantity or quality of information to 'tip the scales of justice'.[20] The utility usually has much better information on opportunities for cost reduction or investments than the regulator (ie asymmetric information). Information asymmetry increases regulatory 'decision costs', such as the search for findings of fact as the basis for establishing rates, the acquisition of supportive evidence, or the procurement of counterevidence contesting the utility's claims.[21]

# V. Capture of Transboundary Regulatory Processes

These benefits are negated by regulatory captured. This section briefly recalls the generic risk of such capture, before turning to specific risks of capture such regulation faces in transboundary settings.

## A. Regulatory Capture

Under an economic theory of regulation, regulators maximise their utilities. All regulators, whether elected or appointed, campaign for positions or seek

---

[19] See J Church and R Ware, *Industrial Organization: A Strategic Approach* (Irwin McGraw-Hill, 2000).

[20] See J Beecher, 'The Prudent Regulator: Politics, Independence, Ethics, and the Public Interest' (2008) 29 *Energy Law Journal* 577.

[21] See A Fremeth and G Holburn, 'Information Asymmetries and Regulatory Decision Costs: An Analysis of U.S. Electric Utility Rate Changes 1980-2000' (2010) 28 *Journal of Law, Economics & Organization* 1.

political approval. In the presence of information asymmetries or transaction costs, interest groups in the regulatory process with low organisation costs can impose burdens on those with high organisation costs, and the result is inefficient. To the extent that the regulated industry continuously has lower organisation costs than consumer or other interest groups, there is an ongoing threat of regulatory capture.[22] Regulatory capture is manifested as 'regulatory actions that serve the ends of industry',[23] in essence, a private interest conquering the public interest.[24]

In a situation of capture, a private actor commandeers the regulatory process for its benefit at the expense of society as a whole. If the regulatory process lacks the sophistication to govern a misalignment between private and public interests, there is a motive for a private actor to allow or encourage the faulty formulation or untidy execution of legal instruments deemed to bring it disproportionate advantages. A central thesis in the empirical literature is that 'regulatory policy is largely purchased by those most interested and able to buy it', and indeed there are various channels of regulatory capture, such as cultural capture, influence through expertise and information, corrosive capture, or the capture of scholars in academia.[25] Regulatory capture amplifies the inclination for manipulation or lack of transparency in regulatory proceedings.[26] There is evidence that the settlement process during ratemaking proceedings is perverted into a spectacle in which the utility requests a large increase in revenue requirements or authorised returns, the regulatory staff balks at the high number, the utility and the regulatory staff negotiate to approximately half of it, and the PUC approves it. In such a situation, the utility obtains an increase in profits, the regulator claims to serve the public interest, but consumers suffer. In complex rate cases with voluminous testimony on revenue or return calculations, 'many investments can be deemed sufficient, prudent, and acceptable' reportedly because 'all aspects' are susceptible to manipulation.[27] If a PUC, without judicial oversight, can grant a wide range of utility requests, regulation is said to be 'the very definition of arbitrary and capricious'.[28]

---

[22] E Benvenisti and A Morag, 'Regulatory Capture and the Marginalised Majority. The Case for the Constitutional Protection of the Majority's Disposable Income', June 2019, *SSRN Electronic Journal*, DOI: 10.2139/ssrn.3409945.

[23] See J Kwak, 'Cultural Capture and the Financial Crisis' in D Carpenter and D Moss (eds), *Preventing Regulatory Capture: Special Interest Influence and How to Limit It* (Cambridge University Press, 2014) 79.

[24] See C Devaux, 'Towards a legal theory of capture' (2018) 24 *European Law Journal* 458.

[25] See D Carpenter and D Moss, 'Introduction' in Carpenter and Moss, *Preventing Regulatory Capture* (2004) 9, 10, and 22.

[26] See H Payne, 'Game Over: Regulatory Capture, Negotiation, and Utility Rate Cases in an Age of Disruption' (2017) 52 *University of San Francisco Law Review* 75.

[27] ibid 78.

[28] ibid 79.

## B. Regulatory Capture in a Transboundary Setting

In a transboundary setting, such as the EU, there is an additional twist in the problem of regulatory capture.[29] As will be discussed in more detail below, investments in interconnection capacity, notwithstanding an increase in net benefits overall, tend to bring about winners and losers.[30] Managing the threat of regulatory capture depends on how the size, ownership, and jurisdictional or spatial distribution of assets affects the cost of politically organising for the frustration of the public good.

To aid our reflections on these matters, we conduct a thought experiment involving a simple simulation of an electric power system with three nodes (see Appendix) feasibly representing three countries, 1, 2, and 3, subject to transboundary regulation. Imagine them interconnected as an equilateral triangle, with 1 situated in the north, 2 in the east, and 3 in the west. There is load and generation in each country, but two interconnections – the line connecting 1 and 2, and the line connecting 2 and 3 – are constrained (ie a 'low' transmission capacity scenario). Now, consider the prospects for investments in transmission, such that the constraints are fully relieved (ie a 'high' transmission capacity scenario). As expected, prices across countries 1, 2, and 3 transition from fragmentation to unification (see Figure 8.1). Under a low transmission capacity scenario, cheap electricity in 2 could not contest the expensive markets of 1 and 3, and the spread of prices across the three countries reveals the economic value of transmission capacity investments. But under a high transmission capacity scenario, there is competition across 1, 2, and 3, and the alignment of prices indicates that the three countries constitute a unified market.

Moreover, the transmission investments have increased economic welfare, defined as the sum of consumer surplus and producer surplus, in each country (see Figure 8.2). In other words, from the viewpoint of social welfare, the transboundary regulator can rightly claim that the countries are individually and collectively better off with the transmission investments. However, given the disparity of net benefits in each country (see Figure 8.3), there could be tension nationally or internationally. In 1 and 3 (where prices have decreased), consumers enjoy a gain in surplus arising from the enhanced access to cheap electricity, but generators suffer a loss in surplus. In 2 (where price has increased), consumers suffer, but generators gain due to an expansion of their deliveries. Now, if generators have a lower

---

[29] E Barrett, 'A case of: who will tell the emperor he has no clothes? – market liberalization, regulatory capture and the need for further improved electricity market unbundling through a fourth energy package' (2018) 9 *The Journal of World Energy Law & Business* 1.

[30] See S Spiecker, P Vogel and C Weber, 'Evaluating interconnector investments in the North European electricity system considering fluctuating wind power generation' (2013) 40 *Energy Economics* 114.

**Figure 8.1** Nodal prices

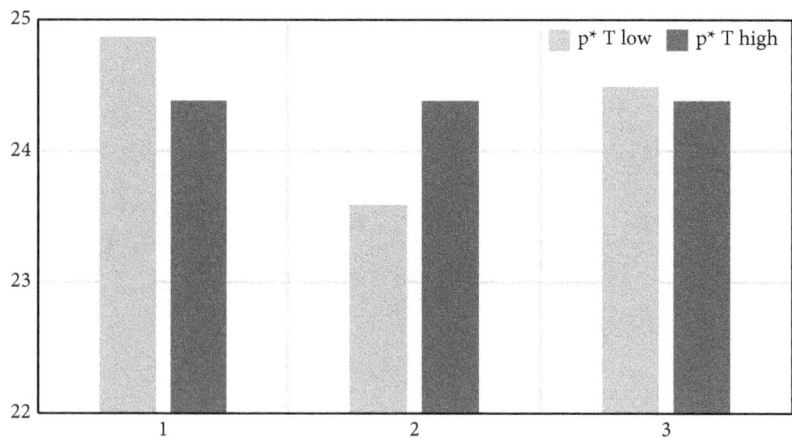

cost of politically organising than consumers, the support for the transmission investments could be different across jurisdictions. Generators in 1 and 3 have an incentive to capture their domestic regulator for the purpose of blocking the transmission investments (in conflict with the motivation of the transboundary regulator). Meanwhile, generators in 2 have an incentive to capture their domestic regulator for the purpose of promoting the transmission investments (consistent with the motivation of the transboundary regulator).

**Figure 8.2** Change in total welfare

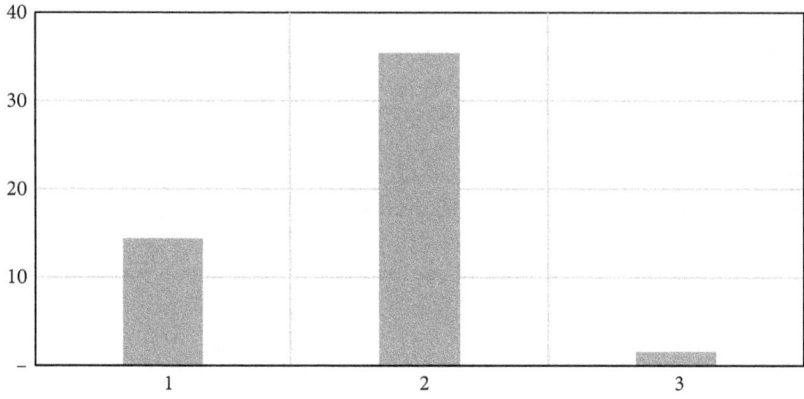

**Figure 8.3**  Change in consumer surplus and producer surplus

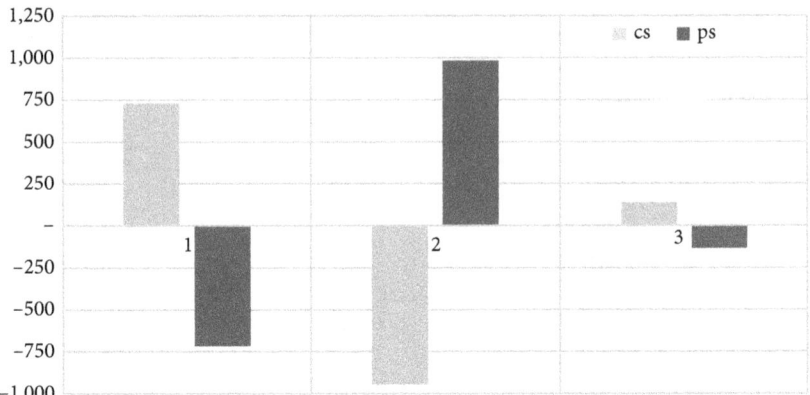

Ultimately, tough political decisions are necessary in the integration of electric power systems in Europe:

> Political buy-in from member states so that they will be willing to facilitate this level of integration requires them to have confidence in the integrated market to deliver the energy and security of supply their constituents desire, as they would if they were representing just a small part of a larger country, thus to break out of the self-sufficiency mind-set that most countries still retain.[31]

Fortunately, 'mechanisms are available to protect negatively affected parties at member state level, if national governments choose to employ them'.[32] The next step, logically, is to determine the details of such protection, including an improvement in the precision of loser compensation across specific EU Member States.

These distributional risks are compounded by the risk of cultural capture, pertaining to persuasion through 'a set of shared but not explicitly stated understandings about the world',[33] that may have especially strong social aspect in a transboundary setting. Under its spell, regulators tend to support positions advocated by those whom they perceive as part of their 'in-group' (identity); those whom they perceive as having higher social, economic or intellectual standing (status); or those in their social networks (relationships).[34] The higher the complexity or information requirements of an issue and the lower the regulatory capacity, the greater the tendency for cultural capture, and indeed one of the strategies for

---

[31] See Booz & Company, 'Benefits of an Integrated European Energy Market', *European Commission Directorate-General – Energy* (2013) 5.

[32] ibid.

[33] Kwak, 'Cultural Capture' (2014) 79.

[34] There is evidence of cultural capture involving government and the financial sector in OECD countries. Central bank governors with experience in the financial sector pursue stronger deregulation policies than those without. See the Wirsching working paper 'The Revolving Door for Political Elites: Policymakers' Professional Background and Financial Regulation'.

controlling cultural capture is to raise the scientific or evidentiary standards for decisions. There is evidence that regulators are more (less) disposed to authorise rate reductions (increases) if regulatory commissioners have long experience in office, there is a relatively large number of regulatory staff, or other regulatory agencies have made similar rate decisions or assessed operational penalties for the same utility.[35] An improvement in informational flows, as it were, reduces the evidentiary costs of regulators in securing a rate reduction or debating a request for a rate increase. Otherwise, deciding between competing explanations and the public interest, regulators are likely to rely on such social signals as identity, status, or relationships.[36]

# VI. Three Maxims for Mitigating Regulatory Capture Risks in Transboundary Energy Industries

Capture is a 'genuine threat' to regulation, and 'the crucial question is whether capture, where it exists, can be mitigated or prevented'.[37] What, then, to do about these specific risks? This section proposes three procedural maxims based on regulation as a communicative process. The first maxim (section A below) seeks to establish shared meaning of the collective interest among the parties to the process. The second maxim (section B below) proposes that each adopts the viewpoint of other parties, and the third (section C below) advances the tool of cost–benefit analysis in aid of that communication and, and, importantly, any compensation.

## A. Shared Meaning in the Regulatory Process

Our first maxim rests on the notion that efficient transboundary energy markets presuppose an effective transboundary regulatory process. Regulation, like a market, indeed becomes a price-discovery process, where price indicates scarcity. It substitutes for the mechanism of the market. In a market, buyers and sellers, enjoying the freedom to be creative, generate and spread value in the trading process, and accordingly establish a spontaneous order through property, contract and justice.[38] In the spontaneous order of a market process, the 'miracle' of the price system, in which an equilibrium price is eventually discovered between buyers and sellers having different valuations at the outset, reveals the scarcity of resources and directs them to their best use. For this to happen, it is vital for a market to have liquidity, the ability to buy or sell in a timely manner and without,

---

[35] Fremeth and Holburn, 'Information Asymmetries' (2010).
[36] Kwak (n 23).
[37] Carpenter and Moss (n 25) 5.
[38] See E Butler, *Classical Liberalism – A Primer*, The Institute of Economic Affairs, London (2015).

or with minimal, loss of value.[39] Liquidity is measured in terms of breadth (ie the range of valuations), depth (ie the transaction size needed to move the market), and immediacy (ie the time needed to execute a trade at a certain cost).

Similarly, the idea of price discovery is central to the regulatory process in multi-level jurisdictional settings. For example, in the US and Canada, the vigorous involvement by federal regulators of customers or their representatives in negotiations with utilities yields outcomes perceived by all parties as superior to what a formal regulatory process would have delivered.[40] The negotiations focus on the discovery and ultimately the satisfaction of customer wants at an acceptable price. In such a situation, the role of the regulator is to encourage conversations and, ideally, agreement, rather than to make decisions itself. As a result, the process of price discovery is facilitated, and the burden of regulation reduced. The regulatory process bears witness, as it were, to a naturally emerging arrangement in which the discovery of price occurs during a sincere dialogue.

Meaningful transboundary regulation is imbued with the normative pursuit of social welfare maximisation for all participating states and spatial or temporal equity for all participating national societies. The point, then, is to encourage a sense of shared meaning[41] amongst multiple jurisdictions in a regulatory process for transboundary energy industries. Regulation thus becomes a meaningful exchange amongst adversarial parties to the proceeding. There ought to be honest conversation, a real prospect for a proper prudence review of the various interests represented in the regulatory procedure. There ought to be a bona fide journey towards an understanding of each other's valuations, a shared meaning aligned with the collaborative use of words to reach an accord. There is a series of purposeful articulations; in essence, a persistent quest for contract, rather than mere form-filling.

The establishment of a shared meaning in search of accord implies, at least, a mutual appreciation for opposing perspectives, not just of consumers and generators but of consumers and generators from different countries. How, then, to put adversarial parties in 'each other's shoes'?

## B. Putting Adversarial Parties in 'Each Other's Shoes'

Our second maxim for mitigating the peril of regulatory capture in transboundary energy industries is the indifference of the parties, given their respective claims, if each was in its adversary's role. Here we draw inspiration from the justices of contract law. There are five principles of transactional justice:[42] the justice of the

---

[39] See Y Jiang and M Marcozzi, 'Asset liquidity and the Valuation of Derivative Securities' (2012) *Journal of Computational and Applied Mathematics* 4525.

[40] See S Littlechild, 'Regulation and Customer Engagement' (2012) 1 *Economics of Energy & Environmental Policy* 1.

[41] 'Pseudo-Contract and Shared Meaning Analysis' (2019) *Harvard Law Review* 132(4) 1135.

[42] T Rakoff, 'The Five Justices of Contract Law' (2016) *Wisconsin Law Review* 733–796.

equal exchange; the justice of the wager (ie symmetrical solutions to risk allocation); the justice of the term that 'fits' the parties or the situation; justice as the
deserved return; and justice as the advantage not taken. The third principle, the
justice of the term that 'fits', pertains to an appropriate distribution of responsibilities or contributions of the parties as a matter of fairness (rather than equality).
It enables an inference most consistent with the reasonable expectations of the
parties, what they must have meant or what the situation calls for, in the context of
their agreement (rather than a judicial imposition on an essentially private matter).
If transactional justice prevails, then reasonable and conscientious parties, acting
in self-interest, would accept the terms of a contract and be bound by it, even if
they did not know their roles.

A respect for the reasonable expectations of the parties, in fact, an appreciation for their intended messages or their contractual circumstances, aligns with
the nature of a shared meaning. The parties are exchanging meaningful communications in accordance with their particular milieu (rather than a judge's view)
in order to contract, and thus there is a consistency with the concerted application of words to establish a settlement, in short, a shared meaning. Moreover,
the indifference of a party to the prospect of being assigned its adversary's role
is indicative of whether or not an agreement is optimised to bring efficient and
equitable outcomes. For the parties to perceive that the justice of the term that 'fits'
is upheld, there ought to be minimal instances (ie bearable levels) of transactional
injustice, such as unconscionable disparities of value, lopsided gambles, unsuit-
able epilogues, opportunism or coercion. In principle, it is highly unlikely that all
occurrences of an economic bad are eliminated. For example, the optimal level of
pollution is not zero, but is the point at which the marginal social benefit of emission reductions is equal to their marginal abatement costs.[43] Similarly, additional
reductions in transactional injustice, up to its complete removal, are unlikely
worthwhile. A court 'should usually tolerate' contractual imperfections because it
cannot correct 'most imperfections in private transactions', in much the same way
that market imperfections are usually tolerated and business is allowed to carry
on unregulated. In other words, the regulator, a trusted broker-dealer prudently
managing the imperfections of an international regulatory framework, has to
demonstrate that a treaty, customary law or conciliation is approaching perfection,
as perfect as it can be, up to the point at which further decreases of transactional
injustice are not worthwhile.

Finally, the indifference test implied by the justice of the term that 'fits' is
consistent with the test for prudence under a 'reasonable manager standard'. If
a party is indifferent to being assigned its adversary's role, then the agreement
is likely optimal, the best available outcome given the constraints, signifying a
tolerable level of contractual imperfection or transactional injustice. Similarly,
for a reasonable manager, prudence is inferred from reasonableness, suggesting

---

[43] See W Viscusi, J Harrington and J Vernon, *Economics of Regulation and Antitrust* (MIT Press,
2005).

a tolerable level of inefficiency, but unlikely far from a market standard. If a party happens to pass, as it were, an indifference (a prudence) test, the regulator would have served the public interest, and it would be uneconomic to entirely eradicate all instances of transactional injustice (market imperfection). Thus, under meaningful regulation, it is judicious and practical to impute optimised provisions which reasonable parties would have accepted if they had engaged in the most efficient form of cooperation and in diligent price discovery, whilst comfortably in 'each other's shoes'.

## C. The Use of Cost–benefit Analysis

We now turn to our third maxim addressing the most pertinent problem of transboundary regulation: the creation of winners and losers that are not equally distributed. The diagnostic devices of Pareto and Kaldor–Hicks efficiency emphasise the availability of leftover surplus and, respectively, the reality or possibility of its redistribution. Second, in the interest of overall social welfare maximisation, such regulation may seek a shift from possible to actual compensation.

In principle, the vision of winners compensating losers under Kaldor–Hicks efficiency supports a decision to proceed with a policy or project whose benefits exceed costs. Indeed, regulation could bring net benefits in social welfare terms, but net costs in monetary terms. What matters is the practicality of moving from possible to actual compensation. Distributional implications of efficient policies should not be abstracted away.[44] For there is a broader consequence of such inequities for the very possibility of transboundary regulation. The presence of losers per se does not justify the dismissal of efficiency-enhancing policy, but utterly aggrieved losers could organise themselves politically to block the enactment of efficiency-enhancing policy. In other words, if not all losers are compensated, then the prospects for efficiency-enhancing policy depend on the number of particular losers to be compensated and the amount of compensation they require.[45] It is quite tempting to hide behind a cynical view that the regulator simply has to identify and compensate the specific subset of losers who are politically organised enough to ruin the chances for efficiency-enhancing policy. Yet a prudent regulator, as a trusted broker-dealer, cannot shirk the task of making value judgements inadvertently affecting spatial or temporal matters of equity. If losers are unavoidably created due to the imprecision in compensation, then other elements of the regulatory compact, across the multitude of mutual obligations, rights or benefits, may serve as additional levers setting the gears in motion for meaningful exchanges between regulated companies and their customers. Such an expansion

---

[44] See J Sallee, 'Pigou Creates Losers: On the Implausibility of Achieving Pareto Improvements from Efficiency-Enhancing Policies', Energy Institute at Haas Working Paper 302 (University of California, Berkeley, 2019).
[45] ibid.

in the set of 'choice variables' of the optimisation process may include a need for side payments, such as money or perhaps compromises on other issues, in order to ensure that states benefit enough to accept the regulation.

Notwithstanding the uncertainty of equity-reducing but efficiency-enhancing policy, cost–benefit analysis remains crucial to the control of capricious regulation. This indeed is at the heart of our third maxim: mitigating the peril of regulatory capture in transboundary energy industries through the use of cost–benefit analysis as a basis for compensation across jurisdictions. Quantitative cost–benefit analysis, focusing directly on the impact of regulation, is the 'best available method for assessing the effects of regulation on social welfare',[46] even though its outcome should not be a sole metric for such a controversial concept as social welfare. The results of cost–benefit analysis provide necessary information on whether or not the regulatory goal of increasing social welfare is achieved. If costs or benefits are not quantified or not shown to have a favourable ratio, some kind of explanation or justification (eg the technicalities of quantifying costs or benefits; the prevalence of standards pertaining to equity, dignity, or a fair distribution; or the presence of non-monetary costs or benefits) is compulsory. The absence of a cost–benefit analysis may increase the severity of information asymmetry. One of the major sources of information asymmetry between regulators and private actors is the imbalance in their access to, or their ability to digest, voluminous technical material.[47] Accordingly, mitigating the peril of regulatory capture in transboundary energy industries, demands non-arbitrary justification in the absence of a cost–benefit analysis. The capacity to provide informed explanations for missing or weak cost–benefit analysis hinges on the extent to which regulation is suitably optimised or justly fits, especially if adjudication on monetary or non-monetary side payments is imminent as a consequence of the imprecision in loser compensation.

Judicial review has to effectively manage the misuse of cost–benefit analysis or stipulate the provision of non-arbitrary justifications. The right to judicial protection and the corresponding effective judicial review are crucial to the control of regulatory capture.

## VII. The Need for Effective Regulation and the Vulnerability to Regulatory Capture in the Electric Power Industry in the EU

In defending against regulatory capture in transboundary context, how to contend with the nuances of the electric power industry operating across the EU? There

---

[46] See C Sunstein, 'Cost-Benefit Analysis and Arbitrariness Review' (2017) 41 *Harvard Environmental Law Review* 1, 9.

[47] One solution is to require the articulation of legislative or regulatory proceedings in general terms accessible to non-specialists.

are obviously many themes worthy of commentary, but we select three that have disruptive potential: the inequities of energy market integration; the limited availability of locational pricing; and the relationship between the signal for adding and the investment in transmission capacity. We now briefly comment on each of them.

First – and this is the often-overlooked theme with the largest disruptive potential – the process of European energy market integration, while overall welfare maximising for all Europeans, probably produces both winners and losers, especially in the short run. In principle, justifying the transmission investments to improve the economic efficiency of an electric power system requires the calculation of economic benefits, and there is a need to ascertain that benefits are likely to outweigh costs and that costs and benefits are fairly apportioned amongst parties. Yet the benefits of investments in a transmission line linking to a lower-price area tend to be negative not only for consumers there, but also for generators in the higher-price area. Consequently, on either side of a planned transmission line, there may be enough losers who, depending on their costs of politically organising and the fortitude of the regulator, could succeed in blocking the investment in transmission capacity.

Nevertheless, the rewards of electricity market integration in Europe are rich. A fully integrated electricity market, facilitating energy trading, achieving supply security across political boundaries, and increasing competition in generation, brings massive gains. The use of smart grids enabling demand response further cuts the need for additional transmission capacity. If policy supports commercial decisions to locate renewable generation capacity in the most conducive sites, further gains are available, and the spatial distribution of transmission capacity investments would change accordingly.

However, a jurisdictional practice of seemingly disregarding the transboundary role of interconnectors, a key measure of energy market integration, would be imprudent to the European Energy Union. Assessments of generation adequacy at a national (rather than a pan-European) level tend to ignore or underestimate the significant contribution of interconnectors.[48] Such a national approach to assessments of generation adequacy could lead to overcapacity at the expense of consumers. A pan-European approach to generation adequacy is estimated to bring annual benefits of EUR 3 billion.[49] If loser compensation remains imprecise or non-arbitrary justification is unavailable, a clear expectation of consumer harm should strengthen a regulatory policy against efforts to preserve such a status quo practice.

The second theme is that the limited availability of highly granular commercial signals in European electric power systems could threaten the efficiency of operation or expansion decisions. A commodity, in general, has attributes of

---

[48] See Agency for the Cooperation of Energy Regulators and the Council of European Energy Regulators, 'Annual Report on the Results of Monitoring the Internal Electricity and Gas Markets in 2017': Electricity Wholesale Markets Volume, 22 October 2018.
[49] ibid.

space and time, but space or time is typically ignored only because of the lack of data (ie there is a tendency to aggregate economic information across space or time).[50] The hope is that, under such an aggregation, little of economic interest is lost. Yet electricity, by nature, is a space–time commodity with hyper-spatial and -temporal attributes. In an electric power system, the equilibrium between supply and demand, in essence, the delivery of the appropriate quantity of electricity to customers, has to hold at all locations and times.[51] The economic value of electricity varies across space or time, and the difference in locational prices represents the economic value of transmission.[52] In the EU currently, there is limited implementation of spot pricing (ie typically zonal), there is limited participation by the demand-side, and demand is insensitive to price because retail rates are disconnected from short-term system conditions.[53] Indeed the major weaknesses of the transmission arrangements across Europe are rooted in the lack of efficient transmission access pricing due to the absence of locational pricing for electric power.[54] The lack of efficient pricing (ie locational price differences representing the optimum short-term prices for transmission access) leads to cross-subsidies amongst network users. Extensive cost socialisation practiced in the majority of power markets weakens the 'incentives for network user engagement'.[55] Indeed, if a sentiment of disengagement amongst stakeholders somehow takes hold, the flow of information or support crucial to the meaningful regulation of transmission assets could be constrained. Providentially, there are efforts in the EU to establish 'clear, stable and non-discriminatory regulatory rules to send consistent signals – both to investors in grids as well as to users of the infrastructure'.[56]

The jurisdictional response to recent incidents of transboundary price volatility points to the significance of granular commercial information. Price, as discussed above, is a signal guiding operation or expansion decisions, and price volatility, providing precious information on further gains from trade, could indicate persistent spatial or temporal mismatches between supply and demand. For example, an analysis of electric power system integration involving two adjacent countries, France and Germany, shows that wind generation reduces the level but increases the volatility of prices across borders, and that additional

---

[50] Mas-Colell Whinston and Green, *Microeconomic Theory* (1995).

[51] FERC, *Energy Primer* (2014).

[52] MIT, 'The Future of the Electric Grid' (2011).

[53] See O Ozdemir, F Munoz, J Ho and B Hobbs, Economic Analysis of Transmission with Demand Response and Quadratic Losses by Successive LP' (2014).

[54] G Strbac, M Pollitt, C Konstantinidis, I Konstantelos, R Moreno, D Newbery and R Green, 'Electricity Transmission Arrangements in Great Britain: Time for Change?' (2014) 73 *Energy Policy* 298.

[55] In the US, the early engagement with stakeholders and the general public, and the adequate satisfaction of the public interest, pre-empt organised opposition to transmission projects and increase the likelihood of completion, especially for multi-state projects. See J Eto, 'Building Electric Transmission Lines: A Review of Recent Transmission Projects, Energy Analysis and Environmental Impacts Division, Lawrence Berkeley National Laboratory' (2016).

[56] European Commission Expert Group, 'Towards a Sustainable and Integrated Europe' (2017) 6.

interconnection capacity decreases price volatility in both countries.[57] In other words, as a mechanism for coping with the intermittency of renewable energy generation, the opportunity to trade due to the extra transmission capacity across jurisdictions dampens transboundary price volatility. However, during some price spike occurrences in 2017, several EU Member States made unilateral decisions to put limits on electricity exports.[58] Such decisions are apparently disallowed under legislation except in emergencies, are 'usually inefficient', and highlight the importance of 'robust, coordinated and cost-effective' action on issues pertaining to adequacy.[59] Unless non-arbitrary justifications are compelling, such decisions on electricity export limitations in the EU could have hindered the capture of further gains from electricity trade across jurisdictions. After the dust of such decisions had settled, a question begging to be asked and answered is whether or not there were arrangements for winners to provide money or non-money side payments to losers.

Third and finally, we would like to comment that the reduction in locational price differences, naturally resulting from additional transmission capacity, may hinder the cost recovery of transmission investments. Under merchant investment, transmission capacity is added if there are significant locational price differences.[60] Yet the new transmission line will reduce or eliminate such price differences, and because transmission investments are lumpy, respond to reliability criteria, and have scale economies, reductions in price differences are substantial. The response to investment opportunities destroys the very signal for them. As locational price differences shrink, it is vital to establish suitable cost-allocation principles, such as proportionality to benefits, independent of transactions, or *ex ante* before the project is built, in order to sustain the incentive for transmission capacity investments. Of course, there are many other complicating factors, such as future environmental policies, generation additions or retirements, technological change, fuel costs, or the long lives of assets. It is especially difficult to assess the prospects for new lines relative to counterfactual situations requiring the hypothetical untangling of all subsequent investments or assumptions on what would have been built.

The persistence of price differentials across Europe, especially where they are largest, emphasises the need to maximise the amount of tradable cross-zonal capacity. In 2017, the spread of average absolute day-ahead prices was less than EUR 0.50/MWh on the borders between Estonia and Finland, Portugal and Spain, as well as Latvia and Lithuania, but exceeded EUR 10/MWh on various borders, including those between the German/Austrian/Luxembourg bidding zone and

---

[57] See S Annan-Phan and F Roques, 'Market Integration and Wind Generation: An Empirical Analysis of the Impact of Wind Generation on Cross-Border Power Prices' (2018) 39 *The Energy Journal* 19.

[58] See ACER and CEER, 'Annual Report' (2018).

[59] ibid.

[60] MIT (n 14).

five of its neighbouring countries, as well as all British borders.[61] During the same period, the Baltic and Central-West Europe (CWE) regions had the highest occurrences: 80 per cent and 41 per cent of hours, respectively, of full price convergence, due to the new interconnectors in the Baltic region and the continued implementation of flow-based market coupling in CWE.[62] There is a recommendation to establish an indicative threshold of EUR 2/MWh between relevant countries, regions, or bidding zones for the consideration of additional interconnectors in Europe.[63] In order to support a lasting motivation for transmission capacity investments across jurisdictions, meaningful regulation has to encourage open discourse prudently reviewing technical or commercial considerations related to such an indicative threshold, especially the possibility of fleeting cost recovery, in the search for a covenant amongst transboundary stakeholders, some of whom may have to be imprecisely compensated.

# VIII. The Clean Energy for All Europeans Legislative Package

The EU, in its self-perception, is a leader in the global climate action effort, with a commitment in reach to achieve a net zero carbon economy by mid-century.[64] The electric power sector, the largest source of greenhouse gas (GHG) emissions, has considerable scope to reduce them through the generation of renewable energy.[65] The 2015 EEU is the EU's strategic project to reduce the consumption of fossil fuels and hence GHG emissions within an integrated electricity market.[66] To this effect, the EEU aims to develop arrangements on the right regulation and their distributional implications to bring about such an integrated market. The EU expects its legislation on the energy system to produce efficient *and* equitable outcomes. 'While not everybody may benefit from the energy transition in the short term, it will, if carefully managed, ultimately benefit the entire EU economy, by creating new job opportunities, bringing savings on energy costs or improving

---

[61] See ACER and CEER (n 46).

[62] Of course, reaching full price convergence, as such, is not the goal.

[63] See European Commission Expert Group, 'Sustainable and Integrated Europe' (2017).

[64] Programme of the Finnish presidency of the Council: 'continue the work on defining the key elements for the EU's long-term climate strategy for 2050 in the European Council by the end of 2019 at the latest' (2019), available at https://eu2019.fi/en/priorities/climate-leadership.

[65] See N Fabra, F Matthes, D Newbery, M Colombier, M Mathieu and A Rüdinger, 'The Energy Transition in Europe: Initial Lessons from Germany, the UK and France' (Centre on Regulation in Europe, 2015).

[66] The strategy comprises five dimensions, for the period 2021 to 2030: Security, solidarity and trust; A fully integrated internal energy market; Energy efficiency; Climate action – decarbonising the economy; and Research, innovation and competitiveness. European Commission, 'A Framework Strategy for a Resilient Energy Union with a Forward-Looking Climate Change Policy' COM(2015) 80.

air quality.'[67] Still, as we have argued, in principle, if this policy reform is absent or careless, unmerited economic rent of favourably situated private interests tends to be preserved, and they have an indisputable motive to perpetuate the capture of regulation or legislation, where it exists, for their own benefit.

In May 2019, the EU legislature comprehensively reformed its legislative framework to facilitate the transition away from fossil fuels towards cleaner energy. The completion of this Clean Energy for all Europeans legislative package, marks a significant step towards the implementation of the EEU strategy. Based on Commission proposals published in November 2016, the package consists of eight new legislative acts.[68] Four of these are directly concerned with designing a genuinely integrated, Europe-wide electricity market, the software to complement the hardware of an interconnected grid: these are the electricity directive, electricity market regulation, the renewables directive, and the regulation on the Agency for the Cooperation of Energy Regulators (ACER). The common objective is set up a regulatory framework to design a market, allowing electricity moving freely following the price signal, to drive investment, and to integrate greater share of renewables.

The recast Electricity Directive[69] confirms the foundational liberalising rules on unbundling, third-party access, and independent, national regulation of transmission and distribution system operators. But the recast directive now enables active participation of consumers in the market by putting in place a strong framework for consumer protection. Member States will be responsible for ensuring that household customers and, if the state so wishes, small enterprises, have access to electricity of a certain quality at clearly comparable, transparent and competitive prices. The directive also phases out financial support to generation capacity emitting 550gr $CO_2$/kWh or more. The recast Electricity Regulation[70] provides the regulatory framework for transboundary electricity flows and trading. The recast RES Directive addresses generation. It sets the EU-wide target of a 34 per cent contribution of renewably produced energy in the final gross energy consumption. The Directive permits Member States to limit financial support to national renewable sources, but if a Member State decides to support producers

---

[67] See European Commission, 'Third Report on the State of the Energy Union (2017)' COM(2018) 688, 6 (emphasis added); 'Fourth report on the State of the Energy Union (2018)' COM(2019) 175.

[68] Directive (EU) 2018/844 of 30 May 2018 amending Directive 2010/31/EU on the energy performance of buildings and Directive 2012/27/EU on energy efficiency [Energy Performance in Buildings], OJ L 156/75; Directive (EU) 2018/2001 of the European Parliament and of the Council of 11 December 2018 on the promotion of the use of energy from renewable sources (recast) [Renewable Energy Directive], OJ L 328/82; Directive (EU) 2018/2002 of 11 December 2018 amending Directive 2012/27/ EU on energy efficiency, OJ L 158/125 [Energy Efficiency Directive]; Regulation (EU) 2018/1999 Governance of the Energy Union; Regulation (EU) 2019/942 of 5 June 2019 establishing a European Union Agency for the Cooperation of Energy Regulators (recast), [ACER Regulation], OJ L 158/22; Directive 2019/944 of 5 June 2019 on common rules for the internal market for electricity and amending Directive 2012/27/EU (recast), [Electricity Directive], OJ L 158/125.

[69] Replacing Electricity Directive 2009/72/EC of the Third Energy Package.

[70] Replacing Electricity Regulation EC/714/2009.

located in other Member States, then the Commission shall assist with the setting up of cooperation arrangements between the relevant Member States by providing information and analysis, including quantitative and qualitative data on the direct and indirect costs and benefits of cooperation. The Commission, here, becomes a functional regulator.

## IX. The Model of a Transboundary Regulator of the Clean Energy Package, ACER and the Maxims Guarding against Regulatory Capture

Because of the 2019 reform, ACER now has the potential to serve as a transboundary regulator. Or has it?

The clean energy package relies on a decentralised organisational architecture to oversee this integrated market. This architecture comprises the regulator of each Member State and the ACER. In each Member State there is to be an independent regulator that retains the exclusive competence to regulate domestic operations. At EU level, these cooperate through ACER.

Established already under the Third Energy Package of the then European Community,[71] ACER's functions were originally confined to coordination, advising and monitoring. As the new rules of the clean energy package envisage an integrated market, the lack of cross-border oversight becomes a potential problem, with the risk of diverging decisions and unnecessary delays by national regulators. Hence, the role of ACER in the energy market has been enhanced. Under the 2019 reform, ACER is a decentralised EU agency, but not endowed with the status of a regulatory agency with full decision-making powers. Decisions and recommendations are adopted by the director, but in most instances with the approval of the board of regulators that brings together representatives of the national authorities. In addition to coordinating the action of national energy regulators, the 2019 reform has granted ACER additional, but limited competences in those areas where fragmented national decisions of cross-border relevance are likely to lead to problems for the internal energy market. For example, ACER will guarantee regulatory oversight over the future regional entities (Regional Coordination Centres)[72] where Transmission System Operators (TSOs) will be able to decide on those issues where fragmented and uncoordinated national actions could negatively affect the market and consumers, and

---

[71] The Third Energy Package opens up the gas and electricity markets. The legislative package entered into force on 3 September 2009. The package provides for ownership unbundling, the separation of companies' generation and sale operations from their transmission networks, the establishment of a National regulatory authority for each Member State, and establishes the Agency for the Cooperation of Energy Regulators (ACER).

[72] Electricity Regulation, preambular para 8, Art 4(6) and Electricity Directive, Arts 59 and 62.

the review of bidding zones.[73] ACER will also be able to streamline regulatory procedures which are subject to direct approval by ACER instead of separate approvals by all national regulators.[74] National regulators, deciding within ACER on those issues through majority voting, will remain fully involved in the process. ACER also supervises the work of by the Organisation of (national) Energy Transmission System Operators Electricity (ENTSO-E) in drafting the technical codes that underpin the working of an interconnected electricity grid.[75] The work programme indicates the agency's priorities over the next three years under this reformed framework.[76]

ACER is functionally, if not organisationally, on the way to becoming a genuine transboundary regulator, able to pursue an independent assessment of the overall social welfare. Our three maxims pertain to this procedure within this regulatory architecture, on which the ACER Regulation provides is mostly mute. It is precisely how to deploy its additional competences for harmonising potentially fragmented national decisions with cross-border implications. As our simulations show, the motivations of generators and their domestic regulators, depending on their location or technological profile, may not perfectly align with those of a transboundary regulator. There is hardly any literature deliberately and dispassionately addressing this matter.

Indeed, ACER may have to engage with an overarching legal framework authorising the design or implementation of highly granular side payments for addressing inefficiency or inequity in transboundary energy markets in order to assist the search for a cooperative equilibrium. That, rather, is the remit of the general institutional decision-making level, executive or legislative. In the case of the EU, legislation could task the Commission to design and implement such a programme.

Probably one of the biggest challenges for ACER will arise under the first maxim. The promotion of shared meaning in the regulatory process demands substantive and procedural reforms not only in the operations of national regulators and ACER, but also in the relationships between them. Shared meaning would be established through the normative pursuit of social welfare maximisation throughout the regulatory architecture. The basis is the increasingly market-oriented approach of the clean energy package, from the cross-border trade of electric power, the rationalisation of subsidies, to the active participation of consumers, all of which in a binding manner seek to enhance the prospects for efficient and/or equitable outcomes. Yet shared meaning, as we also know, demands that ACER, in its deliberations, actively reinforces these precepts as a shared language. It cannot engage

---

[73] Regulation (EU) 2019/943 with Electricity Regulation, Art 5(7).
[74] Electricity Regulation, Art 6.
[75] Electricity Regulation, Art 5.
[76] ACER, 'Programming Document 2019–2021', Revised December 2018, available at www.acer. europa.eu/en/The_agency/Mission_and_Objectives/Documents/ACER%20Programming%20 Document%202019-2021-Revised%20December%202018.pdf.

in a mere box-ticking spectacle, or just hope that national regulators will naturally 'break out of the self-sufficiency mind-set'.

Our third maxim, the use of cost–benefit analysis as a basis for transboundary compensation, seems to be another major challenge, notwithstanding the general direction of an increasingly market-oriented approach under the clean energy package. As explained earlier, there are various nuances associated with operation or expansion decisions in the electric power sector, and some appear to be more amenable to cost–benefit analysis than others. If ACER is to contend successfully with the risk of regulatory capture, it has to simultaneously manage the propensity for information asymmetry and subject its decisions to judicial review. This will maintain the trust of the parties, all the national regulators, not only as collaborators in the quest for the truth, but also as the ultimate guardians of its legitimacy. Going beyond the circle of national regulators, already represented in ACER's decision-making, there should be flow of appropriate information and support from multiple stakeholders, especially private actors. Thus, under the Energy Union, the participation of private actors in regulatory proceedings neither harms the integrity of the regulatory regime, but fosters non-arbitrary justifications for policy. The ACER Regulation would permit the design of such a procedure.

Our second maxim, the indifference of the parties, given their respective claims, if each was in its adversary's role, asks of national energy regulators and ACER to be comfortable in 'each other's shoes'. As explained above, it is wise to impute optimised provisions which reasonable parties would accept under ideal conditions. A proposal to streamline regulatory procedures to allow direct approval by ACER (rather than separate approvals by all national regulators) provides a unique opportunity to lift, as it were, the 'veil of ignorance' possibly hindering parties from seeing the situation from each other's viewpoint. It would be sensible, then, for ACER to demonstrate to each of the parties, all the national regulators, that its approval is as perfect as it can be relative to each of their respective claims. In other words, ACER would procedurally be hosting a transparent debate in which a common language, the analytical tool for social welfare maximisation, is used by all the parties. If further decreases of transactional injustice are widely perceived to be not worthwhile, then the ACER approval is likely to be an optimised decision.

Judicial protection and its counterpart, judicial review, by the CJEU are essential to judicialisation of European regulation.[77] We suggest that judicial oversight requiring sound reasons for the limited use or non-use of cost–benefit analysis, as a procedural matter, serves as another piece of armour against the danger of regulatory capture in the electric power industry in the EU.

---

[77] Attention in the literature has been mostly focused on judicial constitutionalisation, rather than judicialisation of regulation; see M Rasmussen and D Martinsen, 'EU Constitutionalisation Revisited: Redressing a Central Assumption in European Studies' (2019) *European Law Journal* 1. But see V Roeben, 'Judicial Protection as the Meta-Norm of the EU Judicial Architecture' (2019) 11 *Hague Journal on the Rule of Law* 1.

# X. Conclusions

Regulation of transboundary energy industries is highly desirable, but the genuine threat of its capture could darken the horizon for efficient or equitable outcomes. The intellectual tradition of law and economics provides the diagnostic and prescriptive equipment to construct analytical barricades against the threat of regulatory capture. The Clean Energy for all Europeans package is not just an important step towards a genuine transboundary regulation of an EU-wide energy market that is social welfare maximising. As we demonstrate, long-term success will depend on the regulator addressing, through appropriate procedure, the inevitable distributional consequences of such regulation. As such, European energy becomes a laboratory for transboundary energy markets elsewhere that are an essential for a global energy transition.

# Appendix

We use the Cunningham et al model[78] as a starting point. Three utilities are configured to have a triangular connection demonstrating the physical characteristics of transmission lines and the flow of electricity along them. A central operator determines the market prices in a spatial equilibria involving a marginal cost function and a demand function in each of the three locations. In our low transmission

**Figure 8.4** Low transmission capacity scenario

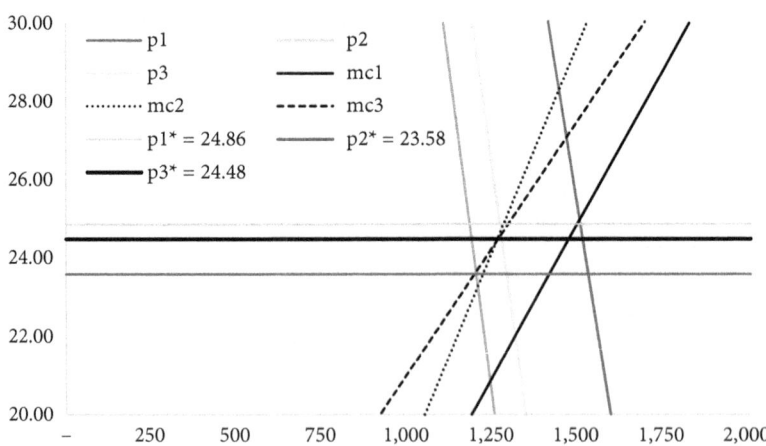

---

[78] See L Cunningham, R Baldick and M Baughman, 'An empirical study of applied game theory: transmission constrained Cournot behavior' (2002) 17 *IEEE Transactions on Power Systems* 166.

capacity scenario, the line connecting 1 and 2 and the line connecting 2 and 3 are constrained at 10MW, but the line connecting 1 and 3 has unlimited capacity (see Figure 8.4). In our high transmission capacity scenario, all the lines have unlimited capacity, a situation consistent with the baseline scenario of the Cunningham et al model (see Figure 8.5).

**Figure 8.5** High transmission capacity scenario

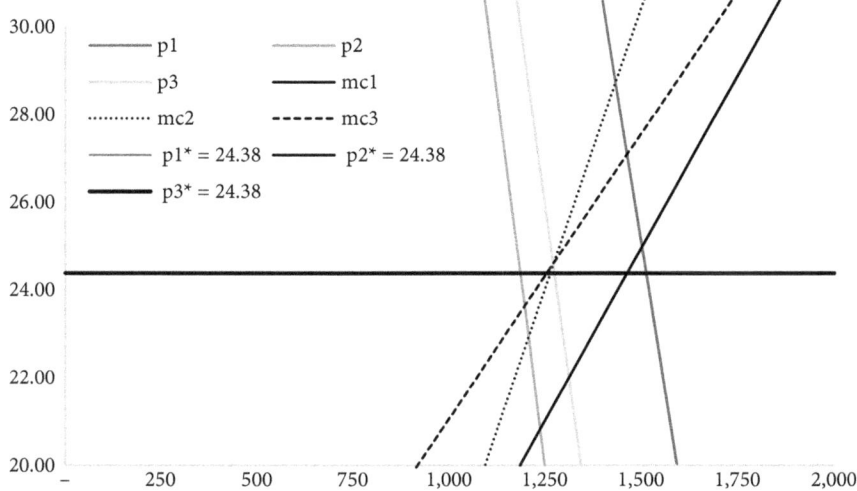

# 9

## Power Over Power:
## The Global Energy Interconnection
## and Potential Cyber-threats

JAKOB HAERTING

## I. Abstract

To solve the most pressing problems of our time it needs ambitious visions to solve them. One such vision becoming reality is China's Global Energy Interconnection (GEI). Its goal is to create a truly global electricity network. Its aim is to tackle climate change while facilitating the ongoing energy transition and providing security of energy supply. At the helm of the project is the Global Energy Interconnection Development and Cooperation Organization (GEIDCO). In this chapter I look at the institutional setup of the GEI and GEIDCO and compare them to the only other truly global network, the Internet. The comparison allows me to explore cyber-attack and cyber influence operation threats that the GEI and GEIDCO face. With a focus on the legal perspective I then provide recommendations on how to mitigate these threats. With the Internet and the energy supply constituting a part of critical national infrastructure and the Internet and the energy network becoming increasingly intertwined and inseparable, the matters addressed in this chapter are highly relevant for the successful realisation of the GEI and similar projects.

## II. Introduction

With the harbingers of global warming appearing across all continents and the upper limit of warming set by the Paris Agreement,[1] the energy transition from

---

[1] Paris Agreement, adopted 12 December 2015, entered into force 4 November 2016.

fossil energy sources to renewable ones is no longer predominantly a question of *if* and *when*, but rather *how*. The challenges faced by a fast transition required to meet the maximum 2°C and ideally 1.5°C global warming target, as set out in Article 2(1)(a) of the Paris Agreement, will have to be met with large scale energy infrastructure projects and the implementation and widespread use of smart grid technologies. The steadily improving efficiency, decreasing cost and competitiveness of renewable energy sources such as wind, water and solar mean that electricity will eventually come to be the primary form of energy in the twenty-first century,[2] ie an energy transition/transformation is taking place.[3] The flow of electricity across all continents will require a global electricity network which would make an immeasurable contribution to global energy supply and security. To this effect, one of the most comprehensive energy infrastructure projects and strategies is the Global Energy Interconnection (GEI) – a part of the Belt and Road Initiative (BRI) – proposed and spearheaded by China since 2015.[4] As crucial as such projects are for combatting climate change and reducing poverty, policy makers, scholars and investors have so far largely failed to examine the unique security risk cyber operations pose to initiatives like the GEI. The threat posed by such operations will only grow in importance as the global energy network and the global information network become further intertwined, making them increasingly inseparable and indistinguishable.

In this chapter I will analyse these risks from cyber operations and argue that it needs a concerted, unified and multilateral effort to minimise the risks the GEI faces. To do so I will first provide a brief view of the relevant features of the GEI. Second, I will distinguish between two types of malicious cyber operations. One is the deliberate disruption and/or destruction of energy infrastructure. The other is the deliberate manipulation of a target population or group that can in turn lead to serious problems for such a project in a particular area or state. By comparing the GEI and its controlling organisation the Global Energy Interconnection

---

[2] This change is based on predictions as well as changes necessary to meet the target of the Paris Agreement. British Petrol, 'BP Energy Outlook 2018' 26, available at www.bp.com/content/dam/bp/en/corporate/pdf/energy-economics/energy-outlook/bp-energy-outlook-2018.pdf; Shell, 'Shell Scenarios: Sky' (2018) 40–44, 49–51, available at www.shell.com/promos/business-customers-promos/download-latest-scenario-sky/_jcr_content.stream/1530643931055/eca19f7fc0d20adbe830d3b0b27bcc9ef72198f5/shell-scenario-sky.pdf; Global Commission on the Geopolitics of Energy Transformation, 'A New World: The Geopolitics of the Energy Transformation' (International Renewable Energy Agency, 2019) 15–19; International Energy Agency, 'World Energy Outlook 2018: Executive Summary' (2018) 2–3, available at https://webstore.iea.org/download/summary/190?fileName=English-WEO-2018-ES.pdf.

[3] A Goldthau, M Keim and K Westphal, 'The Geopolitics of Energy Transformation' SWP Comments (2018) 1–2, available at www.swp-berlin.org/fileadmin/contents/products/comments/2018C42_wep_EtAl.pdf; Global Commission on the Geopolitics of Energy Transformation (ibid) 14–18.

[4] Global Energy Interconnection Development and Cooperation Organization, 'The Forum on Energy Interconnection & "Belt and Road" Development in Arab States Was Held in Beijing' (2018), available at https://en.geidco.org/2018/0704/1225.shtml; A Litovsky, 'China Plans Super-Grid for Clean Power in Asia' *Financial Times*, 5 December 2017, available at www.ft.com/content/e808a542-d6c6-11e7-8c9a-d9c0a5c8d5c9.

Development and Cooperation Organization (GEIDCO) to the Internet and the Internet Corporation for Assigned Names and Numbers (ICANN) I will show how the GEI's institutional structure creates weak points that can be targeted by cyber influence operations. Ideally, this would also be a starting point for future research. Finally, I will provide a tentative solution to the unique risks created for the GEI by cyber operations.[5]

## III.  The GEI and GEIDCO – Origin, Mission, Structure

The initial impetus for the creation of the GEI was given by Chinese President Xi Jinping. In 2015 during a speech at the United Nations (UN) Sustainable Development Summit President Xi Jinping announced that 'China will propose discussion on establishing a global energy Internet to facilitate efforts to meet the global power demand with clean and green alternatives'.[6] Coincidentally – and interesting for the later analysis in this chapter – the first mention of the GEI used the term 'Internet' instead of 'Interconnection' to describe the reach and significance of the project.

In brief, the GEI is a project that seeks to create an energy network through the use of ultra-high voltage (UHV)[7] electricity technology.[8] This network will link states, regions and ultimately continents. This interconnection will connect areas rich in renewable energy sources, eg deserts in Asia, Africa and America ripe with solar energy and regions in the far North with an abundance of wind energy, with the global centers of consumption.[9] By doing so, the GEI will facilitate the ongoing energy transition and enable the reliable and global supply of clean energy.[10] To promote and implement the GEI, GEIDCO was founded in China in 2016.[11] Apart from planning and executing the GEI, GEICO pursues the ambitions goals set out in its Articles of Association.[12] On a broader scale, GEIDCO seeks to contribute

---

[5] In this chapter, the terms 'Internet' and 'cyberspace' will be used interchangeably.

[6] X Jinping, 'Towards Win-Win Partnership for Sustainable Development' (2015), available at www.fmprc.gov.cn/mfa_eng/wjdt_665385/zyjh_665391/t1306508.shtml.

[7] Transmitting electricity by using ultra high voltage – systems capable of transmitting at 800kV and more using direct current – allows for the transport of large quantities of electricity by reducing dissipative losses at distances of well above 1000km.

[8] Z Liu, *Global Energy Interconnection* (Elsevier, 2015) X.

[9] ibid 188–90.

[10] ibid 188.

[11] Global Energy Interconnection Development and Cooperation Organization, 'Global Energy Interconnection Development and Cooperation Organization Was Established in Beijing and Liu Zhenya Was Elected as the First President' (2016), available at https://en.geidco.org/2016/0330/1477.shtml.

[12] GEIDCO, 'Articles of Association' (2016), available at web.archive.org/web/20180224123517/www.geidco.org/html/qqnyhlwen/col2017080768/2017-09/23/20170923165703413703537_1.html.

to the global fight against climate change, pursue the energy related goals set out by the UN in the 2030 Agenda for Sustainable Development,[13] and 'serve the sustainable development of humanity'.[14] On a more technical level, GEIDCO intends to promote the creation of common technical standards, research, and policy-making to implement the GEI.[15] Being a project with such far-reaching effects, it is important to understand the structure of the organisation tasked with its creation.

According to Article 2 of its Articles of Association, 'GEIDCO is a non-governmental, non-profit international organization among willing firms, associations, institutions and individuals' and 'incorporated in accordance with the laws of the People's Republic of China' as an '"association legal person" (社团法人)'.[16] Moreover, according to Article 7 of GEIDCO's Articles of Association, the 'Initiating Member' and principal institution behind GEIDCO is the State Grid Corporation of China (SGCC).[17] The SGCC in turn is owned by the Chinese state, is the largest utility company in the world, and the second largest company in the world by annual revenue.[18] Although GEIDCO's current leadership is relatively diverse as it consists of three Chinese, one American, one Russian and one Japanese national, the Chinese Government likely retains a significant amount of influence and control over GEIDCO's activities.[19] As I will explore later on, this will be a likely obstacle for any GEIDCO-promoted GEI project since exercising significant control over such an ambitious project would put any country in a considerable position of power which could be a deal-breaker for others.

Though the project is far from complete, GEIDCO has taken as number of concrete steps to promote and implement the GEI. Since 2015 it has signed a host of agreements – both bilateral and multilateral in nature – which include, amongst others: cooperation agreements signed in 2017 between GEIDCO and the United Nations Department of Economic and Social Affairs, GEIDCO and United Nations Economic and Social Commission for Asia and the Pacific, GEIDCO and the African Union, GEIDCO and the League of Arab States, and GEICO and the Gulf Cooperation Council Interconnection Authority (GCCIA);[20]

---

[13] General Assembly, 'Transforming Our World: The 2030 Agenda for Sustainable Development', SDG 7 A/RES/70/1 (2015) 19.

[14] GEIDCO, 'Articles of Association' (2016) Art 4.

[15] ibid Art 8.

[16] GEIDCO (n 12).

[17] ibid.

[18] State Grid Corporation of China, 'Corporate Profile' (2019), available at www.sgcc.com.cn/html/sgcc_main_en/col2017112300/column_2017112300_1.shtml; MO Otieno, 'The Largest Companies in the World By Revenue' (2018), available at www.worldatlas.com/articles/the-largest-companies-in-the-world-by-revenue.html.

[19] GEIDCO, 'Leaders', available at https://en.geidco.org/overview/leadership.

[20] GEIDCO, 'GEIDCO Signs Five Agreements to Facilitate GEI in Asia, Africa and Belt and Road Nations' (2017), available at https://en.geidco.org/2017/0815/1347.shtml.

GEIDCO and Chile;[21] GEIDCO and Brazil;[22] an agreement on the promotion of the China–South Korea Grid Interconnection Project between GEIDCO, SGCC and Korea Electric Power Corporation;[23] as well as an agreement on the promotion of the Ethiopia–Gulf Region Interconnection Project between GEIDCO, GCCIA and Ethiopia.[24] Moreover, if one looks more broadly at the BRI, which includes the GEI, it becomes quickly apparent that many of its projects are of a bilateral nature or at best multilateral on a regional level.[25] Much like GEIDCO's structure, the nature of the GEI (BRI) agreements is likely to be a point of conflict that I will further examine below.

# IV.  Justification for Comparing the GEI to the Internet

For the purposes of this chapter I will in part compare the GEI to the Internet as well as GEIDCO to ICANN to better explain some of the challenges that the GEI and GEIDCO will certainly encounter. What justifies this comparison? First off, both the Internet and access to electricity are indispensable for our modern way of life, with the latter being a precondition for the former. Though electricity grids have existed prior to the birth of the Internet, the latter has developed into a truly global network. If the GEI is to be realised, it too would create a global network. The International Telecommunications Union's (ITU) most current data estimates that as of 2018 just over 50 per cent of the world population *uses* the Internet.[26] As for electricity, the World Bank estimates that currently just over 87 per cent of the world's population has *access* to it.[27]

Though the percentages seem to differ greatly, two things need to be noted. Internet use does not equal access. The ITU estimates that at roughly 81 per cent

[21] GEIDCO, 'Deepening Cooperation to Promote the Implementation of Global Energy Interconnection in Chile and South America' (2017), available at https://en.geidco.org/2017/1013/1308.shtml.

[22] GEIDCO, 'Deepen China-Brazil Cooperation and Promote Renewable Energy Development' (2017), available at https://en.geidco.org/2017/1013/1306.shtml.

[23] GEIDCO 'GEIDCO Signed Cooperation Agreement for China-South Korea Grid Interconnection Project with SGCC and KEPCO' (2017), available at https://en.geidco.org/2017/1218/1273.shtml.

[24] GEIDCO, 'GEIDCO, GCCIA, and MWIE Signed Cooperation Agreementfor Ethiopia-Gulf Region Interconnection Project' (2019), available at https://en.geidco.org/2019/0118/1192.shtml.

[25] For a website that tracks these projects see: L Hielscher and S Ibold, 'BRI Projects' (2019), available at www.beltroad-initiative.com/projects.

[26] International Telecommunications Union, 'Measuring the Information Society Report 2018', vol 1 (ITU Publications, 2018) 13, available at www.itu.int/en/ITU-D/Statistics/Documents/publications/misr2018/MISR-2018-Vol-1-E.pdf.

[27] The World Bank, 'Tracking SDG7: The Energy Progress Report 2019' (International Bank for Reconstruction and Development/The World Bank, 2019) 15; For a continuously updated source see: The World Bank, 'Access to Electricity (% of Population)' (2019), available at https://data.worldbank.org/indicator/EG.ELC.ACCS.ZS.

of people using the Internet, the developed world is fully saturated when it comes to Internet users as the very young usually do not tend to do so.[28] At the same time the developed countries enjoy near 100 per cent access to electricity.[29] Moreover, the percentage of global Internet users has grown significantly faster than the percentage of global population having access to electricity in the past decade, and ultimately access to the Internet is limited by access to electricity.[30] Furthermore, universal access to both is set as a goal in the UN 2030 Agenda for Sustainable Development, though interestingly enough, the UN wants to establish universal Internet access 10 years prior to universal electricity access.[31] Keeping continuous growth in mind, with the ongoing development and implementation of smart grid technology as well as the continuous growth of the Internet of Things, cyberspace and electricity networks will become increasingly inseparable if not indistinguishable. Especially for the GEI, smart grids form the backbone of the project and it is noted that:

> With a growing number and coverage of energy types, the energy system will move from simple energy development and supply toward developing multiple functions in terms of information, service, and interconnection. As a result, the integration of energy technology with information, material, and Internet technologies will also become an inevitable trend.[32]

Based on these points alone, it already seems feasible to compare the two to each other. However, there are further, equally weighty reasons for a comparison.

Both the Internet and the electricity gird and generation belong to what has been identified as critical infrastructure, and find themselves in every major country's security strategy. As such, protection of and control over this infrastructure is vital to a nation's security interests. While the Internet is part of critical infrastructure that allows unhindered communication and facilitates the conduct of business, it also enables cyber operations against other critical infrastructure. The latest US National Security Strategy states that 'Cyberattacks offer adversaries low-cost and deniable opportunities to seriously damage or disrupt critical infrastructure' and notes that the 'vulnerability of U.S. critical infrastructure to cyber [...] means that adversaries could disrupt', amongst others, 'the electric grid, and means of communication'.[33] In a similar vein, the UK recognises the same threats and concludes that interconnectivity of industrial control systems across all sectors has created an 'Industrial Internet of Things' that can now be interfered

---

[28] ITU, 'Measuring' (2018) 14.
[29] World Bank, 'Tracking SDG7' (2019).
[30] ITU (n 26) 13; World Bank (n 27).
[31] General Assembly, 'Transforming Our World' (2015) Goal 7.1, Goal 9.c.
[32] Liu, *Interconnection* (2015) 100.
[33] Donald J Trump, 'National Security Strategy of the United States of America' (2017) 12, available at www.whitehouse.gov/wp-content/uploads/2017/12/NSS-Final-12-18-2017-0905.pdf.

with through cyber-attacks, creating 'potentially disastrous consequences'.[34] The EU also recognises the need to shore up defences against cyber operations targeting critical infrastructure.[35] Russia likewise notes that threats for 'state and public security' originate from within the 'information sphere'.[36] Finally, China too states that it sees 'Critical information infrastructure' facing 'considerable vulnerability and potential risk' due to threats originating in cyberspace.[37] The fact that critical infrastructure, ie electricity generation and distribution, and the risks it faces because of cyber threats features so prominently in various security strategies, lends support to the idea to compare them.

Lastly, ICANN and GEIDCO are well suited for a comparison because both constitute an institution tasked with the technical organisation and promotion of a specific type of network.[38] Given ICANN's age it has already faced problems and criticism that I posit GEIDCO has yet to fully experience and thus can learn from. Since the basic structure and mission of GEIDCO was briefly described above, I will only look at ICANN here and compare where necessary. As per its Articles of Incorporation, ICANN is a 'nonprofit public benefit corporation' created in accordance with the California Nonprofit Public Benefit Corporation Law.[39] According to Article III of its Articles of Incorporation ICANN exists for the sole purpose of performing the IANA (Internet Assigned Numbers Authority) functions.[40] Initially ICANN administered the IANA functions under a stewardship contract with the US Department of Commerce National Telecommunications and Information Administration (NTIA).[41] The IANA functions include the administration of the domain name system, the allocation of Internet protocol addresses (IP4 and IP6), and standardisation of Internet protocols that ensure interoperability.[42] In essence, ICANN is and does for the Internet what GEIDCO is and intends to do for the GEI,

---

[34] HM Government, 'National Cyber Security Strategy 2016–2021' (2016) 22, available at www.gov.uk/government/uploads/system/uploads/attachment_data/file/567242/national_cyber_security_strategy_2016.pdf.

[35] European External Action Service, 'Shared Vision, Common Action: A Stronger Europe' (2016) 22, available at https://eeas.europa.eu/archives/docs/top_stories/pdf/eugs_review_web.pdf.

[36] V Putin, 'Russian National Security Strategy' (2015), available at www.ieee.es/Galerias/fichero/OtrasPublicaciones/Internacional/2016/Russian-National-Security-Strategy-31Dec2015.pdf.

[37] Chinese Ministry of Foreign Affairs, 'International Strategy of Cooperation on Cyberspace' (2017), available at http://news.xinhuanet.com/english/china/2017-03/01/c_136094371.htm.

[38] Neither ICANN nor GEIDCO control or will control the entire network that they are administering and or promoting. There is a wealth of organisations and parties that have a stake in development, control, operation, etc of both. With regard for cyberspace see for example: JS Nye, 'The Regime Complex for Managing Global Cyber Activities' (CIGI Publications, 2014) 1.

[39] Internet Corporation for Assigned Names and Numbers, 'Articles of Incorporation' (2016) Art II, available at https://pti.icann.org/articles-of-incorporation.

[40] ibid Art III.

[41] ICANN, 'Stewardship of IANA Functions Transitions to Global Internet Community as Contract with U.S. Government Ends' (2016), available at www.icann.org/news/announcement-2016-10-01-en.

[42] ICANN, 'The IANA Functions' (2015) 7, 12, 14, available at www.icann.org/en/system/files/files/iana-functions-15jun15-en.pdf.

and both share significant similarities in their institutional structure. Based on the above, I believe that valuable lessons for the GEI and GEIDCO can be learned by looking at the debates that have and are surrounding the Internet and ICANN, and possible points of weakness that could be exploited in a cyber influence operation can be addressed before they seriously impair realisation of the project.

# V.  Two Threats, One Origin

Two cyber enabled threats for projects like the GEI exist.[43] One is an attack in the conventional sense that targets the physical infrastructure of the GEI by means of a cyber-attack and destroys or temporarily disables it.[44] The other is a cyber influence operation – irrespective of whether it is over or covert – aimed at delaying or permanently preventing the realisation of parts of the GEI or one targeting the integrity of GEIDCO. The former is mostly a question of cyber security as well as the suitability of existing law to address such cyber-attacks, the latter question of the institutional setup often faced by large projects and organisations that is influenced by larger trends such as ongoing shifts in the global balance of power. I will examine both in turn.

## A.  Destructive Cyber Operations

The Internet has led to a phenomenon dubbed 'the great irony of the information age'.[45] In 2009 President Obama coined the term stating it is 'the great irony of our Information Age – the very technologies that empower us to create and to build also empower those who would disrupt and destroy'.[46] This leads to the realisation that those countries which benefited most from, and are consequently relying extensively on, cyberspace are also those that are now the most exposed to cyber threats.[47] While in most cases large leaks of sensitive data that are the results of hacks make the headlines, eg the breach of the US Office of Personnel Management which saw the theft of 22 million sets of data on US government employees,[48]

---

[43] I use the term 'cyber-enabled' to describe threats/risks that would not exists or be very unlikely to materialise if it was not for the Internet.

[44] For a detailed discussion of cyber-attacks see, for example: T Rid, *Cyber War Will Not Take Place* (Oxford University Press, 2013) 3; MN Schmitt (ed), *Tallinn Manual 2.0 on the International Law Applicable to Cyber Operations* (Cambridge University Press, 2017).

[45] M Carr, *US Power and the Internet in International Relations: The Irony of the Information Age* (Palgrave Macmillan, 2016).

[46] BH Obama, 'Remarks by the President on Securing Our Nation's Cyber Infrastructure' (2009), available at https://obamawhitehouse.archives.gov/the-press-office/remarks-president-securing-our-nations-cyber-infrastructure.

[47] Carr, *US Power and the Internet* (2016) 2, 37.

[48] M Adams, Why the OPM Hack Is Far Worse Than You Imagine, *Lawfare* (11 March 2016), available at www.lawfareblog.com/why-opm-hack-far-worse-you-imagine.

debilitating cyber-attacks on critical infrastructure – including energy systems – have occurred as well.[49]

In 2009 Stuxnet managed to penetrate an air-gapped system in Iran's Natanz nuclear facility and destroyed centrifuges used to enrich uranium.[50] Though the origin of Stuxnet was never officially confirmed, digital forensics point at the US and Israel as the developers of the operation.[51] In this case the cyber operation supported their concerted strategy of denying Iran nuclear weapons, thus preventing a change in the regional power balance if Iran was to acquire them. There have also been attacks on electricity systems. In 2015, during the ongoing conflict between Ukraine and Russia over Crimea and Ukraine's eastern oblasts, a large-scale blackout occurred. In the Ivano-Frankivsk region of Ukraine, some 225.000 Ukrainians suddenly lost electricity.[52] The cause for the blackout was a concerted cyber operation that targeted several power substations and disabled them for a period of several hours.[53] A number of different methods were used to conduct the attack with remote operation capabilities ultimately enabling the attackers to disable roughly 30 substations.[54] Though attribution was never officially confirmed, the likely origin of the attack was Russia.[55] In this event, as was the case with Stuxnet, a cyber operation was used during an international dispute to supplement other official state action. Though the culprit in both of these cases is likely to be a state actor, it is entirely possible to an individual or an organisation conducts to similar operation just for personal gain. In 2017 several UK hospitals – another component of critical infrastructure – were hit with a ransomware attack, encrypting their systems and demanding money to make them available again.[56] In the light of the above incidents targeting critical infrastructure, it appears entirely feasible that the GEI could be subject to a similarly disruptive cyber operation.

Once completed, the GEI will be one gigantic network utilising smart grid technologies.[57] The GEI even envisages 'the full-scale integration of power grids,

---

[49] For comprehensive overview over industrial security incidents caused by cyber-attacks up until 2015 see 'RISI Database' (2015), available at www.risidata.com/Database/event_date/desc.

[50] D Albright, P Brannan and C Walrond, 'Did Stuxnet Take Out 1,000 Centrifuges at the Natanz Enrichment Plant?' (Institute for Science and International Security, 2010), available at www.isis-online.org/isis-reports/detail/did-stuxnet-take-out-1000-centrifuges-at-the-natanz-enrichment-plant.

[51] DE Sanger, 'Obama Order Sped Up Wave of Cyberattacks Against Iran' *The New York Times*, 1 June 2012, available at www.nytimes.com/2012/06/01/world/middleeast/obama-ordered-wave-of-cyberattacks-against-iran.html.

[52] K Zetter, 'Everything We Know About Ukraine's Power Plant Hack' *Wired*, 20 January 2016, available at www.wired.com/2016/01/everything-we-know-about-ukraines-power-plant-hack; RM Lee, MJ Assante and T Conway, 'Analysis of the Cyber Attack on the Ukrainian Power Grid' (2016) iv, available at ics.sans.org/media/E-ISAC_SANS_Ukraine_DUC_5.pdf.

[53] Zetter (ibid).

[54] Lee, Assante and Conway, 'Analysis of the Cyber Attack' (2016) 13–14.

[55] P Polityuk, 'Ukraine Sees Russian Hand in Cyber Attacks on Power Grid, Reuters, 12 February 2016, available at www.reuters.com/article/us-ukraine-cybersecurity-idUSKCN0VL18E.

[56] S Anthony, Massive Ransomware Attack Hits UK Hospitals, Spanish Banks, *ars technica* (12 May 2017), available at https://arstechnica.com/information-technology/2017/05/nhs-ransomware-cyber-attack.

[57] Liu (n 8) ch 5.

information networks, and the Internet to bring information flows and electricity flows together'.[58] Such large systems necessarily have a lot of exposure, especially if fully implementing smart grid technologies, and are therefore an even bigger target for cyber operations. Furthermore, in the case of cyber-attacks the defender is at a disadvantage as all possible points of entry into the system need to be denied whereas the attacker need only find a singly vulnerability to compromise the system.[59] Moreover, with increasing complexity of a system comes increased cost for the defence.[60] A proposed solution to the problem – and also to reduce risk posed by large centralised structures in the event of an armed conflict – could be to rely on decentralisation in electricity generation and smaller electricity grids.[61] However, that would entirely defy the sole purpose of the GEI and is therefore no option here. Yet, whilst many states and politicians have often imagined doomsday scenarios, like that of a cyber-attack causing a nuclear meltdown, Thomas Rid rightly points out that so far such cyber operations are best known for their absence.[62] Whilst such cyber operations do have the potential to be extremely disruptive, there are a few factors other than increased cyber security that reduce the potency of the threat. One of these is that the law – on the national and international level – is finally catching up with malicious cyber operations.

Whilst the legal debate concerning such destructive cyber-attacks and the specific application of international law is still ongoing, a predominant opinion is increasingly taking shape. In 2013 the 'Group of Governmental Experts on Developments in the Field of Information and Telecommunications in the Context of International Security' concluded that international law applies to cyberspace.[63] This group included, amongst others, American, Russian and Chinese experts.[64] The implication is that the entire regime of international law applies to cyber operations, especially when conducted by a state actor. If a cyber operation was to target and destroy critical infrastructure, like those identified in the national security strategies above of which the GEI would certainly be a part, it could potentially amount to a use of force or even armed attack under Article 2(4) or 51 of the UN Charter respectively.[65]

---

[58] ibid 222.

[59] R Slayton, 'What Is the Cyber Offense-Defense Balance?' (2017) 41 *International Security* 72, 107–108.

[60] ibid 107.

[61] K Verclas, 'The Decentralization of the Electricity Grid – Mitigating Risk in the Energy Sector' (2012), available at www.aicgs.org/publication/the-decentralization-of-the-electricity-grid-mitigating-risk-in-the-energy-sector.

[62] Rid, *Cyber War* (2013) 3–4.

[63] UNGA, 'Group of Governmental Experts on Developments in the Field of Information and Telecommunications in the Context of International Security' (2013) A/63/98 8.

[64] ibid 5.

[65] Schmitt, *Tallinn Manual* (2017) 328–56; Office of General Counsel Department of Defense, *Department of Defense Law of War Manual* (Department of Defense, 2015) 998–1000.

To assess whether a cyber operation against for example the GEI constitutes a use of force or even armed attack one has to consider the effects of the cyber operation. If the effects could otherwise only be achieved by conventional military attack, ie kinetic attack, and 'kill persons or physically damage or destroy objects' it is highly likely that the cyber operation amounts to a use of force and if the damage is significant even an armed attack.[66] In case of the GEI the initial victim would be the state on whose sovereign territory the damaged or destroyed infrastructure – both cyber and electric – is located.[67] However, with networks such as the GEI it is entirely possible that secondary effects, eg power outages, also lead to deaths and destruction of property in a state that was not the initial target of the cyber operation. The severity of such an event combined with the fact that many states, as shown above, identify the power grid and supply as critical national infrastructure makes it even more likely that they will consider such a cyber operation to fall under Article 2 (4) or even 51 of the UN Charter even if it has only indirect effects.[68] This would carry with it serious consequences and several states have acknowledged this to be possibility under international law,[69] and NATO's Cooperative Cyber Defense Centre of Excellence has published the Tallinn Manuals that extensively discuss such scenarios from an international law perspective.[70]

In the event that the actor behind a cyber-attack targeting critical infrastructure is a private person or organisation, the criminal law of the affected country will usually be applicable and provide for remedies. Moreover, the Council of Europe's Convention on Cybercrime has led many states to include cybercrime in their criminal statutes.[71] The Convention on Cybercrime includes amongst other the obligation for all state parties to create criminal law provisions that punish the illegal access of and interference with computer systems,[72] both of which would be implicated in a destructive cyber operation against energy infrastructure, eg the GEI. Notable signatories to the Convention are the US, the UK, Germany, Israel and Japan and even though China and Russia are not parties to the Convention their respective criminal codes that punish the same acts.[73]

---

[66] Schmitt (n 44) 333; For a distinction between use of force and armed attack see *Nicaragua v United States of America* [1986] ICJ Rep 101.

[67] ibid 333–37; for one of the earliest works suggesting that cyber infrastructure is still merely physical infrastructure and therefore subject to the principle of sovereignty see JL Goldsmith, 'The Internet and the Abiding Significance of Territorial Sovereignty' (1998) 5 *Global Legal Studies Journal* 475, 476.

[68] ibid 333–56.

[69] See, for example: Office of General Counsel Department of Defense, *War Manual* (2015) 996–97, 1000; Australian Cyber Security Centre, 'Threat Report' (2015) 8; Ministry of Defense, 'Finland's Cyber Security Strategy' (2013) 33–34, available at www.defmin.fi/files/2378/Finland_s_Cyber_Security_Strategy.pdf.

[70] MN Schmitt (ed), *Tallinn Manual on the International Law Applicable to Cyber Warfare* (Cambridge University Press, 2013); Schmitt (n 44).

[71] Convention on Cybercrime, entered into force 1 July 2004, ETS No 185.

[72] ibid, Arts 2, 5.

[73] Convention on Cybercrime (n 71); Criminal Law of the People's Republic of China, Arts 285, 286; The Criminal Code of The Russian Federation No 63-Fz of June 13, 1996, Arts 272–274.

Lastly, and related to remedying the situation once an has attack occurred, is the fact that digital forensics have improved in the past few years and it becomes increasingly difficult to avoid attribution and maintain plausible deniability.[74] Whilst a destructive cyber operation remains a realistic threat to critical infrastructure,[75] including the GEI, I believe that cyber influence operations constitute a more significant one.

## B.  Cyber Influence Operations

Whilst a destructive cyber operation will likely strengthen a country's resolve to repair the damage and unite the population in the rejection of the aggressor, a successful cyber influence operation has the potential to divide or even completely shift public opinion and prevent or facilitate a certain event. This has the added benefit of creating a longer lasting effect as it is better suited for winning 'hearts and minds' of the target population.[76] Two examples can serve to illustrate the potential of such operations. The first is the 2016 US presidential election and the second is the Cambridge Analytica scandal.

During the 2016 US presidential election campaign, Russia actively interfered in the opinion-making process of the American population.[77] In doing so the Kremlin sought to divide the American population, promote Donald Trump's ideas and ultimately see their preferred candidate win.[78] Through social media, the Internet has enabled states to directly reach their competitor's populations.[79] By steering and shifting opinion it is likely that Russia managed to influence the outcome of the election without much risk of negative repercussions whilst creating a lasting effect. The second is the Cambridge Analytica scandal that again revealed the potency and possibilities of the cyber influence operations conducted

---

[74] For a more detailed discussion T Rid and B Buchanan, 'Attributing Cyber Attacks' (2015) 38 *Journal of Strategic Studies* 4.

[75] United Nations General Assembly, 'Report of the Group of Governmental Experts on Developments in the Field of Information and Telecommunications in the Context of International Security' (2015) A/70/174 6.

[76] EV Larson, RE Darilek, D Gibran, B Nichiporuk, A Richardson, LH Schwartz and CQ Thurston, 'Foundations of Effective Influence Operations: A Framework for Enhancing Army Capabilities' (RAND, 2009) 2.

[77] For a US intelligence assessment of the interference see: Director of National Intelligence, 'Background to "Assessing Russian Activities and Intentions in Recent US Elections": The Analytic Process and Cyber Incident Attribution' (2017).

[78] M Aaltola and M Mattiisen, 'Election Hacking in Democracies' 204 FIIA Briefing Paper 3; C Timberg and T Romm, 'New Report on Russian Disinformation, Prepared for the Senate, Shows the Operation's Scale and Sweep' *The Washington Post* (17 December 2018), available at www.washingtonpost.com/technology/2018/12/16/new-report-russian-disinformation-prepared-senate-shows-operations-scale-sweep.

[79] Aaltola and Mattiisen (ibid) 3, 7.

through social media.[80] Cambridge Analytica offered influence services to the extent of influencing elections by shifting public opinion.[81] It is certainly a possibility that a cyber influence operation will take place within the context of the GEI or BRI. It just remains to be seen whether such an operation will seek to create positive or negative opinions about the GEI. What, then, could be weaknesses that such an operation could target?

When looking at the most common criticism facing the Internet and ICANN, two points that are equally applicable to the GEI and GEIDCO can be identified. The first is that China is the driving force behind the GEI as well as the BRI, through which it takes part in strategic competition – with regard to the Internet it is/was the US[82] – the second relates to the biased structure of GEIDCO and relates to governance – ICANN faced similar criticism[83] – which ultimately ties back into the same debate. These will most likely be used in a cyber influence operation targeting the GEI or GEIDCO. However, the fact that China is the country that champions the GEI adds an interesting dynamic to the possibility of cyber influence operations, which I will examine below.

One of the causes for cyber influence operation targeting the GEI can be found in the ongoing transition in the global balance of power. This is one of the dominant trends identified in the international relations literature as power transition and often includes a perceived or real decline in American power as well as the emergence of another or several other centres of power, aka the rise of the rest, with China being a strong contender for a second pole of power.[84] Besides the military and economic dimension, this debate has also revolved around the role the US played in the creation of the Internet and the control thereof.[85] The US sees the Internet as a tool to combat authoritarian regimes, including China and Russia, and a way to promote its own ideals.[86] Evidence of this perception finds itself in a number of US policy documents and statements issued by the Obama and the

---

[80] R Meyer, 'The Cambridge Analytica Scandal, in Three Paragraphs' *The Atlantic* (20 March 2018), available at www.theatlantic.com/technology/archive/2018/03/the-cambridge-analytica-scandal-in-three-paragraphs/556046.

[81] Channel 4 News, 'Cambridge Analytica Uncovered: Secret Filming Reveals Election Tricks' (2018), available at www.youtube.com/watch?v=mpbeOCKZFfQ.

[82] See, for example, J Nocetti, 'Contest and conquest: Russia and global internet governance' (2015) 91 *International Affairs* 111, 122.

[83] T Maurer, 'Cyber Norm Emergence at the United Nations – An Analysis of the Activities at the UN Regarding Cyber-security' (Belfer Center for Science and International Affairs, 2011), 46; Carr (n 45) 117–48.

[84] M Mastanduno, 'Order and Change in World Politics: The Financial Crisis and the Breakdown of the US–China Grand Bargain' in GJ Ikenberry (ed), *Power, Order and Change in World Politics* (Cambridge University Press, 2014) 169; JS Nye Jr, *The Future of Power* (PublicAffairs, 2011) 153–204; CA Kupchan, *No One's World: The West, the Rising Rest, and the Coming Global Turn* (Oxford University Press, 2012) 74–85.

[85] See JS Nye Jr, 'Cyber Power' (Harvard Kennedy School, Belfer Center, 2010), available at belfercenter.ksg.harvard.edu/files/cyber-power.pdf.

[86] DJ Trump, 'National Cyber Strategy of the United States of America' (2018) 24–25, available at www.whitehouse.gov/wp-content/uploads/2018/09/National-Cyber-Strategy.pdf.

Trump administration.[87] This has often been criticised by China and Russia and led to a clash of ideas over how the Internet should be governed.[88]

Whilst the US and most of its allies advocate for a free and open Internet jointly administered by individuals, companies and governments through institutions like ICANN, Russia, siding firmly with China, has promoted a vision where governments retain ultimate decision-making power over the Internet by shifting control to intergovernmental institutions like the ITU.[89] With the GEI creating a network of proportions equal to that of the Internet and the two becoming increasingly intertwined, a similar divide and conflict could occur and cyber influence operations could function as an important catalyst. Whilst it has previously been possible to rally people to support or oppose a certain project, cyberspace has allowed for easier manipulation and has the potential to magnify the effects. A cyber influence operation, arguing that Chinese control over the GEI would put it in a considerable position of power,[90] could lead to concerns over China's actual motives for creating the GEI and thus lead to a rejection of related projects. Such worries, largely a result of how China has been approaching the realisation of BRI projects, have already been exhibited by smaller and less powerful countries that see the BRI – and GEI by extension – as an attempt to grow Chinese power and expand its sphere of influence.[91] Cyber influence operations in regions where China is planning or conducting GEI projects could seriously impede its ability to do so. By pointing to China's ambitions to grow its influence and cement its position as an emerging power or by pointing to Chinese control over GEIDCO, similar to how the US was criticised for controlling ICANN, a cyber influence operation could create enough popular opposition to force a (local) government or company to permanently halt any such projects with China. With the latest

---

[87] B Obama, 'International Strategy for Cyberspace' (2011) 23–24, available at obamawhitehouse. archives.gov/sites/default/files/rss_viewer/international_strategy_for_cyberspace.pdf;   C   Painter, 'International Cybersecurity Strategy: Deterring Foreign Threats and Building Cyber Norms' (2016), available at https://2009-2017.state.gov/s/cyberissues/releasesandremarks/257719.htm; Trump (ibid) 24–25.

[88] J Kerry, 'An Open and Secure Internet: We Must Have Both' (2015), available at https://2009-2017. state.gov/secretary/remarks/2015/05/242553.htm.

[89] R Radu and J-M Chenou, 'Global Internet Policy: A Fifteen-Year-Long Debate' in R Radu, J- Chenou and RH Radu (eds), *The Evolution of Global Internet Governance: Principles and Policies in the Making* (Springer, 2014) 4–15.

[90] This correlates with a realist view of international relations where technological advances and economic strength directly result in increased power. See Carr (n 45) 33–36. For the use of networks as a 'tool of power politics' see: K Raik, 'EU Foreign Policy in a Networked World: Webs against Power Politics' (FIIA Analysis, 2018) 7.

[91] M Majumdar, 'BRI: Implications for Southeast Asia' (2017), available at https://theasiadialogue. com/2017/09/15/bri-implications-for-southeast-asia; D Dhillon, 'Wary of a Debt Trap, Malaysia's Government Has Backed out of Three China-Funded Infrastructure Projects' *Business Insider India* (18 August 2018), available at www.businessinsider.in/wary-of-a-debt-trap-malaysias-government-has-backed-out-of-three-china-funded-infrastructure-projects/articleshow/65502165.cms; T Greer, 'One Belt, One Road, One Big Mistake' *Foreign Policy* (6 December 2018), available at https://foreign-policy.com/2018/12/06/bri-china-belt-road-initiative-blunder.

US National Security Strategy clearly identifying China as a competitor for the US,[92] it is likely that the Trump administration will also utilise influence operations to achieve more desirable outcomes. Suggestions to that effect have already been made[93] and even been proposed before Senate Armed Services Committee.[94] This time around, the target for the criticism is not the US, but China. However, China could have one important advantage.

The USA has usually perceived cyber-attacks against critical infrastructure as one of the main threats faced by a country that heavily relies on digital infrastructure.[95] China, on the other hand, has continuously emphasised that the power of information and ideas spread over the Internet constitutes an equally important threat and consequently heavily emphasised the principle of state sovereignty in cyberspace.[96] As a result, the Chinese Government has gone to great lengths to control the Internet in China. China has created capabilities to monitor and steer the discourse on the Chinese Internet.[97] Through that control China seeks to bring all citizens in line with the positions of the Chinese Communist Party and as a result create a harmonious society.[98] No other government on earth, with perhaps the exception of North Korea,[99] has created such an effective system to combat dissenting opinions, regardless of whether they are created out of independent thought our propagated by a cyber influence operation. The experience China has gained by censoring and controlling its own part of the Internet could translate to a comparative advantage when faced with a cyber influence operation. The US has in the past conducted such operations, eg against Iran,[100] and it has been suggested that such capabilities be also developed to target China and enable the free flow of information.[101] However, the target of a cyber influence operation against the GEI likely to be a country or region outside of China as the majority of projects will be realised there. It therefore remains to be seen how well China can apply its control capabilities outside the Chinese information space to curb such

---

[92] Trump, 'National Security Strategy' (2017) 2, 46.

[93] D Kliman and A Grace, 'Power Play: Addressing China's Belt and Road Strategy' (2018) 22–24, available at https://s3.amazonaws.com/files.cnas.org/documents/CNASReport-Power-Play-Addressing-Chinas-Belt-and-Road-Strategy.pdf.

[94] E Ratner, 'Blunting China's Illiberal Order: The Vital Role of Congress in U.S. Strategic Competition with China' (Center for New American Security 2019) 8–9.

[95] Trump (n 33) 12; Barack Obama, 'National Security Strategy' (2015) 3, 12–13, available at https://obamawhitehouse.archives.gov/sites/default/files/docs/2015_national_security_strategy_2.pdf.

[96] Chinese Ministry of Foreign Affairs, 'International Strategy' (2017). This becomes even more evident considering the contents of Document No 9 that has leaked outside of Chinese Communist Party circles. C Buckley, 'China Takes Aim at Western Ideas' *The New York Times* (19 August 2013), available at www.nytimes.com/2013/08/20/world/asia/chinas-new-leadership-takes-hard-line-in-secret-memo.html.

[97] For a thorough description of China's capabilities see: PeW Singer and ET Brooking, *LikeWar: The Weaponization of Social Media* (Houghton Mifflin Harcourt Publishing Company, 2018) 95–103.

[98] ibid 96.

[99] ibid 90.

[100] Nye, 'Cyber Power' (2010) 6–7.

[101] Ratner, 'Blunting China's Illiberal Order' (2019).

an operation. Alternatively, China could launch a cyber influence operation of its own to promote the GEI to a target population. Judging by Russia's success, it is potentially easier to target a country where free flow of information exists rather than a controlled authoritarian state.[102]

## VI.  Recommendations for the Realisation of the GEI

Having analysed the potential threats facing the GEI and GEIDCO from cyberspace, a few recommendations to avoid them can be made. Concerning the threat of destructive cyber operations, cyber security must be taken into consideration right from the beginning of the GEI. This means that all systems must be thoroughly tested for security cyber flaws, especially since smart grid technology will be used extensively and, in case of acts by non-state parties, the criminal laws of all states participating in the GEI must have provisions dealing with system intrusion and manipulation. One possibility for participating states to facilitate this would be to join the Convention on Cybercrime. However, both China and Russia, who would play an important role in the GEI, have so far refused to become a party to the Convention in Cybercrime for a variety of reasons.[103] As for destructive cyber operations carried out by states, international law as it is provides ample recourse, as briefly alluded to above.

Whilst all countries are burdened with the threat of destructive cyber operations, the threat posed by cyber influence operations to the GEI and GEIDCO could be mitigated. If China wants to see the GEI come to fruition – especially considering that such an infrastructure project becomes a necessity for all countries in light of climate change and the maximum 2°C global warming goal set by the Paris Agreement – two points are worth considering. First, the agreements concluded to further the GEI should be predominantly multilateral and not bilateral in nature. Secondly, GEIDCO, the organisation tasked with overseeing the implementation of the GEI should consider transitioning to a multi-stakeholder model of governance. Implementing these recommendations would reduce already existing concerns, increase trust[104] and limit future discussion of China using the GEI – and by extension the BRI – as a means to challenge the US and cement its role as a rising power. Enabling this would be the increased legitimacy the GEI would experience if based on a multilateral agreement instead of a variety

---

[102] Kupchan, for example, elaborates on how authoritarian states are better suited to withstand globalization, including the spread of or resistance against certain ideas and ideologies; Kupchan, *No One's World* (2012) 8.

[103] KE Eichensehr, 'The Cyber-Law of Nations' (2015) 103 *Georgetown Law. Journal* 317, 359.

[104] N Morris, 'Developing a Sustainable Legal System for the Belt and Road Initiative' in W Shan, K Nuotio and K Zhang (eds), *Normative Readings of the Belt and Rioad Initiative* (Springer, 2018) 48.

of bilateral or limited regional agreements, as is happening at the moment.[105] Moreover, to reduce or eliminate any concerns regarding the structure of and control over GEIDCO, China should consider handing over GEIDCO to a multi-stakeholder community comprised of individuals, corporations and states – much like the US did with ICANN to address similar concerns[106] – whilst clearly separating it from the SGCC and the Chinese Government. Following these two points would address the vulnerability they create for exploitation by cyber influence operation. Moreover, this would not only expedite the project but also encourage broader participation from Western governments and institutions. Adhering to these recommendations would allow China to fortify its image of a forerunner in fighting climate change and serve as a role model for other countries. Such a position in itself already conveys a significant amount of power, which can only be in China's interest. However, if nothing is done to address these concerns it is entirely possible that, and possibly catalysed by cyber influence operations targeting the identified vulnerabilities, the GEI sees protests like many other energy infrastructure projects have seen, eg the German project Südlink has seen significant protests and even been halted to some extent,[107] or the Keystone XL pipeline that has seen clear opposition and been implicated in legal proceedings.[108]

# VII. Conclusions

This chapter has shown how two types of cyber operations – destructive cyber operations and cyber influence operations – could impact the GEI, potentially a critical piece of transmission infrastructure for a Eurasian electricity market. Whilst any computerised system faces threats by destructive cyber operations, cyber influence operations could also pose a significant obstacle to the GEI. It remains to be seen if China's control over the GEI process and the mostly bilateral agreements are something that will lead to problems as the project sees realisation. Through a comparison with the Internet and one of its controlling institutions, ICANN, this chapter has shown that with the current institutional setup it is likely that the GEI and GEIDCO will face criticism. Moreover, the impact of such criticism could be

---

[105] For a discussion on increase legitimacy see eg: M Kahler, 'Multilateralism with Small and Large Numbers' (1992) 45 *International Organization* 681, 703.

[106] L Denardis, 'Internet Architecture as Proxy for State Power' (2015) *IP Justice Journal* 1, 7.

[107] Deutsche Presse Agentur, 'Stromtrasse: Bayerisches Kabinett bekräftigt Moratorium' (11 February 2014), available at www.nordbayern.de/region/stromtrasse-bayerisches-kabinett-bekraftigt-moratorium-1.3450582; Focus, 'Thüringen klagt gegen geplante Stromtrasse Suedlink' (15 January 2019), available at www.focus.de/finanzen/boerse/wirtschaftsticker/unternehmen-thueringen-klagt-gegen-geplante-stromtrasse-suedlink_id_10188545.html.

[108] L Friedman and C Davenport, 'Judge Blocks Disputed Keystone XL Pipeline in Setback for Trump' *New York Times* (9 November 2018), available at www.nytimes.com/2018/11/09/climate/judge-blocks-keystone-pipeline.html.

seriously exacerbated through cyber influence operations. At the same time, it has been shown what can be done to mitigate these points of criticism which might otherwise slow or even prevent the realisation of a crucial project needed to meet the goals of the Paris Agreement and facilitate the ongoing energy transition. The question that remains is whether China is willing to relinquish some power over power by opting for a combination of multi-stakeholderism and multilateralism to govern the GEI. If the concerns with regard to the GEI can be addressed right from the beginning, the chances that they have a serious impact on the realisation of the project, or later on once it is operational, can be minimised and the GEI can come to fruition.

## PART IV

# Attracting Investments and the Challenges of Multi-level Governance

# 10

# Implementing the Energy Transition in the Face of Investment Protection Standards

MARTIN JARRETT****

## I. Abstract

The Energy Charter Treaty ('ECT') is set for a seismic change. Over the coming years, the treaty parties will be locked in negotiations for its 'modernisation'. The theory is that investors with carbon-based energy investments can use this treaty to claim compensation from states for the damage that clean-energy policies will inflict on their investments, thereby making it an obstacle to the energy transition.

This chapter examines that theory. The examination primarily focuses on the two investment protection standards in the ECT that investors with carbon-based energy investments are likely to argue that clean-energy policies breach, namely 'expropriation' and 'fair and equitable treatment'.

In respect of the 'fair and equitable treatment', the conclusion is that implementing the energy transition will not necessarily breach this standard, assuming that the relevant policies do not conflict with prior commitments made to investors. But herein lies the facilitative potential of the ECT for the energy transition. Because states breach this standard when they act contrary to their commitments to investors, it can incentivise states to stay true to their policies for promoting clean-energy investments.

**** Senior Research Fellow, Max Planck Institute for Comparative Public Law and International Law. I thank the anonymous reviewer who offered several helpful comments on an earlier draft. Additionally, I was the beneficiary of some very fruitful conversations with Prof Chester Brown and Prof Stephan Schill regarding the expropriation standard, conversations which steered me away from some egregious errors. Finally, this contribution was written with the support of a generous research grant from the University of Mannheim, a grant which facilitated an invaluable research stay at the University of Sydney. The usual caveat applies: all errors are my own.

Expropriation is more problematic for states. Some clean-energy policies will breach it. To avoid paying compensation, states will need to plead the police powers defence. Given its current absence from the ECT, this defence needs to be added to it. As argued in the conclusion, a well-drafted police powers defence can fairly distribute the burdens of the energy transition between investors and states.

# II. Introduction

In the euphoric atmosphere prevailing after the conclusion of the Cold War, states proceeded with great urgency to conclude the Energy Charter Treaty (ECT).[1] From the perspective of investment,[2] it was to serve as the legal infrastructure for (Western) capitalism to be infused into the (Eastern) energy supply sectors. Since its conclusion some 25 years ago, it has seen some reversals, most particularly with the withdrawals of Italy[3] and Russia[4] and the attempted[5] interdiction on future

---

[1] J Doré, 'Negotiating the Energy Charter Treaty' in T Waelde (ed), *The Energy Charter Treaty: An East-West Gateway for Investment and Trade* (Kluwer, 1996) 137.

[2] On the trade front, the ECT was originally designed to secure energy supply from East to West, see E Gaillard and M McNeill, 'The Energy Charter Treaty' in K Yannaca-Small (ed), *Arbitration Under International Investment Agreements: A Guide to the Key Issues*, 2nd edn (Oxford University Press, 2018) para 2.01.

[3] The official line from the Italian Government is that it withdrew from the ECT to save costs, see I Kustova, 'A treaty à la carte? Some reflections on the modernization of the Energy Charter Process', (2016) 9 *Journal of World Energy Law & Business* 359. Although in light of the 11 claims that have been made against Italy in the past five years, one cannot help wonder whether this is a pretence masking another more substantial reason, namely that Italy is seeking to limit its liability under the ECT. In this context, however, it should be noted that the ECT contains a survival clause extending its application for 20 years to investments made in the time during which the relevant contracting state was a party to the treaty, see ECT, Art 47(3). See also C Baltag, 'What's New with the Energy Charter Treaty?', Kluwer Arbitration Blog (13 June 2015), available at http://arbitrationblog.kluwerarbitration.com/2015/06/13/whats-new-with-the-energy-charter-treaty.

[4] T Voon and A Mitchell, 'Ending International Investment Agreements: Russia's Withdrawal from Participation in the Energy Charter Treaty' (2017) 111 *American Journal of International Law Unbound* 466.

[5] At the time of writing, in all of the publicly known ECT investor-state arbitrations where the state raised the objection that the decision of the European Court of Justice in C-284/16 (the 'Achmea Decision') means arbitral tribunals for intra-EU investor-state arbitrations lack jurisdiction, no arbitral tribunal has accepted it; *see Hydro Energy 1 Sàrl and Hydroxana Sweden AB v Kingdom of Spain*, ICSID Case No ARB/15/42, Decision on Jurisdiction, Liability and Directions on Quantum (9 March 2020) [502]; *The PV Investors v Spain*, PCA Case No 2012-14, Final Award (28 February 2020) [549]; *Watkins Holdings Sàrl. and others v Kingdom of Spain*, ICSID Case No ARB/15/44, Award (21 January 2020) [226]; *RWE Innogy GmbH and RWE Innogy Aersa SAU v Kingdom of Spain*, ICSID Case No ARB/14/34, Decision on Jurisdiction, Liability, and Certain Issues of Quantum (30 December 2019) [373]; *BayWa r.e. Renewable Energy GmbH and BayWa r.e. Asset Holding GmbH v Spain*, ICSID Case No ARB/15/16, Decision on Jurisdiction, Liability, and Directions on Quantum (2 December

intra-EU investment arbitrations.[6] But with more than 50 states and international organisations contracted to it, the continual accession of new states, and the establishment of a functional dispute settlement mechanism for investor-state disputes, the ECT counts among the most successful treaties in international economic law.[7]

But in a gloomier atmosphere compared to that which prevailed at the time of its conception, considering the threat that climate change represents, the Energy Charter Conference in December 2018 signalled that the ECT needed to be 'modernised' and:[8]

> In the frame of the modernisation process, investment protection of the ECT should be further developed, as well as transit issues. We strongly commit to start discussions on the modernization [sic] of the ECT and will undertake every effort to reach a final conclusion on the most suitable policy options in a timely and proper manner, reflecting the new realities of the energy sector.

2019) [283]; *Stadtwerke München GmbH, RWE Innogy GmbH, and others v Kingdom of Spain*, ICSID Case No ARB/15/1, Award (2 December 2019) [146]; *OperaFund Eco-Invest SICAV PLC and Schwab Holding AG v Kingdom of Spain*, ICSID Case No ARB/15/36, Award (6 September 2019) [388]; *Belenergia SA v Italian Republic*, ICSID Case No ARB/15/40, Award (6 August 2019) [340]; *InfraRed Environmental Infrastructure GP Limited and others v Kingdom of Spain*, ICSID Case No ARB/14/12, Award (2 August 2019) [273]; *SolEs Badajoz GmbH v Kingdom of Spain*, ICSID Case No ARB/15/38, Award (31 July 2019) [252]; *Rockhopper Italia SpA, Rockhopper Mediterranean Ltd, and Rockhopper Exploration Plc v Italian Republic*, ICSID Case No ARB/17/14, Decision on the Intra-EU Jursdictional Objection (26 June 2019) [211]; *9REN Holding Sarl v Kingdom of Spain*, ICSID Case No ARB/15/15, Award (31 May 2019) [173]; *Photovoltaic Knopf Betriebs GMBH v Czech Republic*, PCA Case No 2014-21, Award (15 May 2019) [359]; *Eskosol SpA in liquidazione v Italian Republic*, ICSID Case No ARB/15/50, Decision on Termination Request and Intra-EU Objection (7 May 2019) [236]; *NextEra Energy Global Holdings BV and NextEra Energy Spain Holdings BV v Kingdom of Spain*, ICSID Case No ARB/14/11, Decision on Jurisdiction, Liability and Quantum Principles (12 March 2019) [357]; *Landesbank Baden-Württemberg and others v Kingdom of Spain*, ICSID Case No ARB/15/45, Decision on the 'Intra-EU' Jurisdictional Objection (25 February 2019) [202]; *Cube Infrastructure Fund SICAV and others v Kingdom of Spain*, ICSID Case No ARB/15/20, Decision on Jurisdiction, Liability and Partial Decision on Quantum (19 February 2019) [543]; *CEF Energia BV v Italian Republic*, SCC Case No 158/2015, Award (16 January 2019) [96]; *Greentech Energy Systems A/S et al v Italian Republic*, SCC Case No V 2015/095, Final Award (23 December 2018) [403].

[6] EU Member States, 'Declaration of the member states of 15 January 2019 on the legal consequences of the Achmea judgment and on investment protection' (17 January 2019) 1–2, available at https://ec.europa.eu/info/sites/info/files/business_economy_euro/banking_and_finance/documents/190117-bilateral-investment-treaties_en.pdf.

[7] K Hobér, 'Overview of Energy Charter Treaty Cases' in M Scherer (ed), *International Arbitration in the Energy Sector* (Oxford University Press, 2018) para 8.86.

[8] Energy Charter Conference, 'Bucharest Energy Charter Declaration' (27 November 2018), available at https://energycharter.org/fileadmin/DocumentsMedia/ECC/20181128-FINAL_Bucharest_Energy_Charter_Declaration.pdf. For a similar sentiment, see European Commission, 'Recommendation for a Council Decision authorising the entering into negotiations on the modernisation of the Energy Charter Treaty' (14 May 2019) COM(2019) 231.

This extract might be a typically weasel-worded diplomatic announcement, but the message is clear enough that, at 25 years of age, the ECT needs to mature and take on other responsibilities other than providing the legal infrastructure for facilitating investments. But what are those responsibilities? Assuming that the 'new reality' is the imminent and catastrophic environmental harm caused by climate change, the theory that this contribution proceeds on is that there must be an energy transition to tackle climate change, that transition will phase out the consumption of carbon-based energy, and this phasing-out means the devaluation or disappearance of existing carbon-based energy investments. Accepting that theory, the new responsibility for the ECT is to determine: where do these investment losses relating to this process of phasing-out fall most fairly, on investors or states? One view is that, in its current form, the ECT will operate to inevitably impose the costs on states.[9] The theory underpinning this view is that states' measures phasing out carbon-based energy investments will necessarily breach the investment protection standards of the ECT, noting that these standards create obligations for states vis-à-vis their treatment of carbon-based energy investments covered by the ECT. Breaches of those investment protection standards translate into compensation payments from states to investors, thereby placing the economic burden of the energy transition on states.

This chapter investigates this logic. In undertaking this investigation, the first task is to identify the pinch points; in other words, the investment protection standards that investors will use to claim compensation for their losses. That identification process reveals that two standards are the prime candidates: expropriation; and fair and equitable treatment. Each of these standards is analysed in turn, beginning with fair and equitable treatment. Rather than being an obstructionist force for the energy transition, it is argued that fair and equitable treatment can be a facilitator. As regards expropriation, the starting assumption is that state-mandated decommissioning of carbon-based energy production and distribution facilities will necessarily expropriate investments. The question then becomes whether these expropriations might be justified by the police powers defence. In answering that question, the first point of consideration is whether the ECT makes provision for the police powers defence. After concluding that Article 24 excludes its invocation to defend against a breach of the expropriation standard,

[9] See Y Saheb, 'Europe's Green Deal is under threat from Energy Charter Treaty' (Euractiv, 20 September 2019), available at www.euractiv.com/section/climate-environment/opinion/europes-green-deal-is-under-threat-from-energy-charter-treaty; D Keating, 'A Little-Known EU Investor Dispute Treaty Could Kill The Paris Climate Agreement' (Forbes, 5 September 2019), available at www.forbes.com/sites/davekeating/2019/09/05/a-little-known-eu-investor-dispute-treaty-could-kill-the-paris-climate-agreement; F Simon, 'Luxembourg leads EU push to climate-proof Energy Charter Treaty' (Euractiv, 4 September 2019), available at www.euractiv.com/section/energy/news/luxembourg-leads-eu-push-to-climate-proof-energy-charter-treaty; P Eberhardt, C Olivet and L Steinfort, 'One Treaty to Rule Them All' (The Transnational Institute, 12 June 2018) 77, available at www.tni.org/files/publication-downloads/one_treaty_to_ruled_them_all.pdf.

a treaty-based police powers defence is proposed. The final sections are dedicated to illustrating its application to (indirect) expropriatory measures implemented in pursuit of the energy transition.

# III. The Pinch Points: Expropriation and Fair and Equitable Treatment

The task of reviewing the ECT[10] with a view to identifying the complications that it will create for states implementing the energy transition might serve as the opening to discuss the problems that the opponents to the regime of international investment law have identified with it more generally,[11] but the current brief is narrower in scope. Only the substantive provisions of the ECT are under examination, of which there are arguably 10.[12] But for governmental actions taken in pursuit of the energy transition, most of these provisions should not raise any concerns.

## A. The Discrimination-based Rules

The discrimination-based rules, being arbitrary or discriminatory measures, most-favoured nation, and national treatment, can be summarily excluded from consideration. As regards the latter two rules, they can be analysed together because the process to determine whether they have been breached is the same:[13] the treatment of the relevant investor is measured against the treatment of investors from other states and local investors, respectively. If, in effecting the energy transition, states treat all investors equally without regard to their nationality, these two rules will not give rise to any complications.

The rule on arbitrary or discriminatory measures is seemingly more problematic, particularly where states favour investors in one sector of the economy, such as the renewable energy sector, over others, such as those operating in carbon-based

---

[10] Although other investment treaties might be used by investors to sue states for investment losses caused by the implementation of the energy transition, this contribution is limited to the ECT given, one, its special application to energy investments and, two, the frequency with which it is used by investors to launch claims against states, noting that it is currently the most frequently used among all investment treaties, see Hobér, 'Overview' (2018) (n 7) para 8.08.

[11] See generally Eberhardt, Olivet and Steinfort, 'One Treaty to Rule Them All' (2018) (n 9).

[12] The number of provisions creating discrete obligations for states with respect to investments varies according to the investment treaty in question, but the ECT contains arguably 10, with five in Art 10(1) ('favourable and transparent conditions', 'fair and equitable treatment', 'full protection and security', 'arbitrary and discriminatory measures', 'most favoured nation', and 'observance of undertakings'), one in Art 10(2) ('national treatment'), one in Art 10(12) ('effective means for asserting claims'), one in Art 13(1) ('expropriation'), and one in Art 14(1) ('free transfer').

[13] C McLachlan, L Shore and M Weiniger, *International Investment Arbitration: Substantive Principles*, 2nd edn (Oxford University Press, 2017) paras 7.267–7.269.

energy production and distribution. Although there is some authority to the effect that favouring one economic sector over another amounts to unlawful discrimination, the consensus view is that it does not.[14] One case illustrating this point is *BR Group v Argentina*. There, the investor contended that Argentina's preferential treatment for electricity distributors over gas distributors was discriminatory.[15] The arbitral tribunal summarily dismissed this contention.[16]

## B.  Free Transfer of Capital, Protection and Security, and Observance of Undertakings

Three other rules that can be eliminated from consideration are the rules on free transfer of capital, protection and security, and observance of undertakings. The elimination of the first of these rules requires no explanation. As the second rule generally activates[17] when states fail to offer sufficient police protection against the legally[18] and physically destructive conduct of third persons and state organs vis-à-vis the investor's investment,[19] this explains its exclusion.

As regards the applicability of the observance of undertakings standard, much depends on its interpretation. For this reason, it is worth setting out in full, as it appears in the ECT:[20]

> Each Contracting Party shall observe any obligations it has entered into with an Investor or an Investment of an Investor of any other Contracting Party.

Relying on the decision in *Khan Resources v Mongolia*, it has been opined that this provision extends its application not only to contractual obligations between investors and states, but also covers other obligations of a legal nature, such

---

[14] R Dolzer and C Schreuer, *Principles of International Investment Law*, 2nd edn (Oxford University Press, 2012) 204.

[15] *BG Group Plc v The Republic of Argentina*, ad hoc arbitration (UNCITRAL Rules), Final Award (24 December 2007) [347].

[16] ibid [357]–[360].

[17] Although Dolzer and Schreuer raise the possibility of the rule on protection and security being breached by regulatory instability, see Dolzer and Schreuer, *Principles* (2012) 204. Generally, however, regulatory instability is one circumstance that can be alleged to establish a breach of the fair and equitable treatment standard, see K Yannaca-Small, 'Fair and Equitable Treatment Standard: Recent Developments' in A Reinisch (ed), *Standards of Investment Protection* (Oxford University Press, 2008) 123.

[18] T Waelde, 'Energy Charter Treaty-based Investment Arbitration' (2004) 5 *Journal of World Investment & Trade* 390–91. Although states have in more recent investment treaties signalled that 'full protection and security' does not cover legally destructive conduct, see, for example, 2019 Belgium-Luxembourg Model Bilateral Investment Treaty (28 March 2019) Art 4(5), available at www.lachambre.be/flwb/pdf/54/1806/54K1806007.pdf. In light of this push to restrict the scope of the protection and security standard, an arbitral tribunal might be inclined to adopt a narrow interpretation. In any case, legal security generally refers to the ability of domestic courts to give effect to investor rights under domestic law, see G Cordero Moss, 'Full Protection and Security' in Reinisch (ibid) 144–46.

[19] McLachlan, Shore and Weiniger, *International Investment Arbitration* (2017) para 7.242.

[20] ECT, Art 10(1).

as those sometimes found in governmental permits and foreign investment legislation.[21] Other commentary on this provision, however, has not endorsed this broad interpretation.[22] Most tellingly, when the arbitral tribunal in *RREEF v Spain*, an ECT investment arbitration arising out of Spain's changes to its regulatory regime for solar parks, it reasoned:[23]

> On the one hand, the expression 'any obligations' calls for a broad interpretation but, on the other hand, the phrase 'it has entered into' seems to refer exclusively to bilateral relationships existing between the Respondent and the Claimants, to the exclusion of general rules; and the Spanish ('las obligaciones que haya contraído con los inversores') or French ('les obligations qu'elle a contractées vis-à-vis d'un investisseur') lead to the conclusion that *the last sentence of Article 10(1) ECT only applies to contractual obligations.*

Following this pronouncement, unless states enter into obligations of a contractual nature with investors to, for example, preserve the current regulatory regime favouring carbon-based energy production or distribution, the observance of undertakings standard in the ECT should not be problematic for states implementing the energy transition.

## C. Expropriation and Fair and Equitable Treatment

There is nothing inherent in the process of transiting to clean energy that necessarily gives rise to legal liability for states under any of the investment protection standards mentioned above. The same assertion cannot be made in respect of the two remaining investment protection standards: expropriation and fair and equitable treatment.[24] With respect to expropriation, it will invariably challenge states because the gist of this rule is a loss, or complete or substantial devaluation, of an investment[25] on account of state conduct. Considering that the energy transition will, in some cases, require the complete discontinuation of some carbon-based energy production and distribution activities, it is apparent how expropriation will be one of the foremost rules that states will have to navigate.

---

[21] Gaillard and McNeill, 'Energy Charter Treaty' (2018) para 2.39.

[22] D Mejía-Lemos, 'Article 10 – Promotion, Protection and Treatment of Investments' in R Leal-Arcas (ed), *Commentary on the Energy Charter Treaty* (Edward Elgar, 2018) para 10.44.

[23] *RREEF Infrastructure (GP) Limited and RREEF Pan-European Infrastructure Two Lux Sàrl v Kingdom of Spain*, ICSID Case No ARB/13/30, Decision on Responsibility and on the Principles of Quantum (30 November 2018) [284] (emphasis added).

[24] G Coop and I Seif, 'ECT and States' Right to Regulate' in Scherer, *International Arbitration* (2018) para 10.05 and Y Selivanova, 'Changes in Renewables Support Policy and Investment Protection under the Energy Charter Treaty: Analysis of Jurisprudence and Outlook for the Current Arbitration Cases' (2018) 33 *ICSID Review* 436–37.

[25] K Yannaca-Small, 'Indirect Expropriation and the Right to Regulate: Has the Line Been Drawn?' in Yannaca-Small, *Arbitration Under International Investment Agreements* (2018) para 22.07.

Navigating the rule on fair and equitable treatment will also challenge states. At the time of writing, many investment arbitrations had been initiated under the ECT by investors with investments in the renewable energy sector,[26] including 46 publicly known claims against Spain alone.[27] Looking at the 20 arbitral awards on liability in these investor–Spain arbitrations[28] that have become public,[29] it is apparent that investors are enjoying some success. In 17 of those 20 cases, the investors have prevailed using a breach of the fair and equitable treatment rule[30] as their cause of action.[31]

# IV. The Standard on the Fair and Equitable Treatment: Obstructor or Facilitator?

It would be wrong to look at this record of Spanish losses and conclude that the standard on fair and equitable treatment will inevitably obstruct the energy

---

[26] Hobér (n 7) para 8.15.

[27] For a list of all of these claims, see International Energy Charter, 'List of cases' (25 March 2020), available at https://www.energychartertreaty.org/fileadmin/DocumentsMedia/Statistics/Chart_ECT_cases_-_15_April_2020.pdf.

[28] Additional claims arising out of changes to clean energy regimes have also been made against Bulgaria, Czechia and Italy. As reviewing all of the ECT investor–state arbitrations coming out of regulatory changes to clean energy regimes is not the focus of this paper, the claims against Bulgaria, Czechia and Italy will not be considered in this chapter. Further, focussing on 'investor–Spain arbitrations' means that the various arbitral awards can be compared because they arise out of the same state measures.

[29] *Hydro Energy v Spain* (n 5); *PV v Spain* (n 5); *Watkins v Spain* (n 5); *RWE v Spain* (n 5); *Stadtwerke München v Spain* (n 5); *BayWa v Spain* (n 5); *OperaFund v Spain* (n 5); *SolEs v Spain* (n 5); *Infrared v Spain* (n 5); *Cube v Spain* (n 5); *9REN v Spain* (n 5); *NextEra v Spain* (n 5); *Greentech v Italy* (n 5); *Antin Infrastructure Services Luxembourg Sàrl and Antin Energia Termosolar BV v Kingdom of Spain*, ICSID Case No ARB/13/31, Award (15 June 2018); *Masdar Solar & Wind Cooperatief UA v Kingdom of Spain*, ICSID Case No ARB/14/1, Award (16 May 2018); *Novenergia II - Energy & Environment (SCA) (Grand Duchy of Luxembourg), SICAR v The Kingdom of Spain*, SCC Case No 2015/063, Final Award (15 February 2018); *RREEF v Spain* (n 23); *Eiser Infrastructure Limited and Energía Solar Luxembourg Sàrl v Kingdom of Spain*, ICSID Case No ARB/13/36, Final Award (4 May 2017); *Isolux Netherlands, BV v Kingdom of Spain*, SCC Case V2013/153, Final Award (17 July 2016); *Charanne and Construction Investments v Spain*, SCC Case No V 062/2012, Final Award (translation by Mena Chambers) (21 January 2016).

[30] Using a breach of the expropriation rule has not enjoyed as much success because of the hurdle of proving that the withdrawal of the subsidies to the investors has caused a complete or substantial devaluation of the investments, see Selivanova, 'Changes in Renewables Support Policy' (2018) 437.

[31] *Hydro Energy v Spain* (n 5) [770] (qualified finding of international responsibility as the arbitral tribunal needed more information on the extent of the investor's investment loss); *PV v Spain* (n 5) [909]; *Watkins v Spain* (n 5) (by majority) 606]; *RWE v Spain* (n 5) [600]; *BayWa v Spain* (n 5) [496]; *OperaFund v Spain* (n 5) (by majority) [746]; *SolEs v Spain* (n 5) [576]; *InfraRed v Spain* (n 5) [455]; *Cube v Spain* (n 5) [48]; *9REN v Spain* (n 5) [449]; *NextEra v Spain* (n 5) [37]; *Foresight Luxembourg Solar 1 SÁR1, et al v Kingdom of Spain*, SCC Case No 2015/150, Final Award and Partial Dissenting Opinion of Arbitrator Raül Vinuesa (14 November 2018) [562(b)]; *Antin v Spain* (n 29) [748(b)]; *Masdar v Spain* (n 29) [697(b)]; *Novenergia v Spain* (n 29) [860(b)]; *RREEF v Spain* (n 23) [600(3)]; *Eiser v Spain* (n 29) [486(b)].

transition. In fact, as argued below, the opposite is true: this standard can act as a facilitator of the energy transition.

As its name suggests, the standard on fair and equitable treatment assesses whether a state's conduct vis-à-vis investments is fair and equitable. Because state conduct can become unfair and inequitable in a number of different ways,[32] some facts are needed on how states can pursue the energy transition in order to determine whether this standard will necessarily obstruct this process. For this purpose, the assumption is that states have two options. The first is for states to prohibit the production or distribution of carbon-based energy. How a state actually goes about implementing this prohibition could bring it within the scope of the standard of fair and equitable treatment, but if it pursues prohibition in a transparent and non-discriminatory manner, there is nothing inherent about prohibition that will bring such conduct within the scope of this standard. The exception is when the state has made commitments to investors with carbon-based investments;[33] for example, representing to such investors that they will enjoy certain privileges, such as a government-backed tariff for their produce, over a period of time. If such a commitment is subsequently breached, this standard comes into play. This is known as 'frustration of legitimate expectations'.

A second option for states pursuing the energy transition is subsidising the construction of clean-energy infrastructure or the consumption of clean energy. Again, there is nothing about these measures that makes them inherently likely to breach the standard on fair and equitable treatment. If, however, a state makes commitments to maintain their subsidies for investors investing in clean-energy infrastructure and they subsequently withdraw their support, then international responsibility comes into view. This explains why Spain has been held in breach of the standard on fair and equitable treatment on so many occasions. In all of the ECT investor–Spain arbitrations, the investors claim that Spain created an incentive-based regime for investments in clean energy; that regime was subsequently changed by lowering the tariff paid for the electricity produced by the investors' clean-energy infrastructure; and, because this change contradicted an (alleged) commitment to keep the incentive-based regime in place for a certain period, the investors should receive compensation equalling their losses caused by this change.

If the standard on fair and equitable treatment, particularly the strain on legitimate expectations, can be invoked to hold states accountable for not properly performing their support role to private investors in the energy transition, it should be apparent that this an investment protection standard that does not necessarily hinder this process, but potentially helps it. But this potential is at risk.

---

[32] For a list of the various strains of the standard on fair and equitable treatment, see McLachlan, Shore and Weiniger (n 13) ch 7.

[33] At the time of writing, the Netherlands was facing a claim that it breached an investor's legitimate expectations because it dishonoured its commitments to coal investments; see D Charlotin, 'The Netherlands is put on notice of a treaty-based dispute' (*IAReporter*, 12 May 2020), available at https://www.iareporter.com/articles/netherlands-put-on-notice-of-a-treaty-based-dispute.

Given its open-textured nature, there are various debates on what the doctrinal content of the standard on fair and equitable treatment should be. These debates are examined below with a view to establishing what doctrinal content could best promote the energy transition.

## A. Realising the Potential of Legitimate Expectations as a Facilitator of the Energy Transition

To prove frustration of legitimate expectations, the investor must establish that the state made a commitment vis-à-vis its investment in its favour. Divisions have emerged about the formalities of this commitment.[34] One view is that a commitment must be a 'specific commitment'; in other words, for the investor to have the benefit of a commitment from a state, it must be personally communicated by the state to the investor. Under this view, if the state's legislation on regulating tariffs for solar parks contained words to the effect that a certain tariff would be paid to solar-park operators over a certain period of time, then the idea of specific commitment asks that the investor approach the state for a written confirmation that it should benefit from this regulatory regime. A minority of arbitral tribunals in the ECT investor–Spain arbitrations have adopted this view[35] and it is the one preferred by the European Commission for a modernised ECT.[36] A majority of arbitral tribunals for the same cases has adopted the idea of a 'general commitment';[37] in other words, if the document containing the commitment has the requisite degree of officialness and the investor fits into the class of persons to whom the commitment is addressed to, then a commitment will have been proven. Practically speaking, what the idea of general commitment means is that the investor does not need to seek confirmation of its status as a beneficiary.

The question is, out of specific commitment and general commitment, which is best suited for promoting the energy transition? The idea of general commitments has to be preferred. The first reason for this preference is that there is no apparent reason for the need to seek out confirmation, which is what the idea of specific commitment requires. If the commitment is contained in official governmental documents, then this should adequately indicate the seriousness of the state's representations. Additionally, seeking confirmation practically creates another bureaucratic step for investors to secure the benefit of the standard on fair

---

[34] *Masdar v Spain* (n 29) [490]. For further analysis, see Mejía-Lemos, 'Article 10' (2018) paras 10.34–10.36.

[35] *InfraRed v Spain* (n 5) [407]; *Isolux v Spain* (n 29) [772]; and *Charanne v Spain* (n 29) [490].

[36] European Commission, 'Energy Charter Treaty Modernisation: Draft EU Proposal' (2 March 2020) 4, available at www.politico.eu/wp-content/uploads/2020/03/Proposal_Treaty.pdf?utm_source= POLITICO.EU&utm_campaign=75bec6754f-EMAIL_CAMPAIGN_2020_03_25_06_46&utm_ medium=email&utm_term=0_10959edeb5-75bec6754f-189693589).

[37] *Watkins v Spain* (n 5) [526]; *OperaFund v Spain* (n 5) [485]; *SolEs v Spain* (n 5) [421]–[426]; *Cube v Spain* (n 5) [401]; *9REN v Spain* (n 5) [307]; *Novenergia v Spain* (n 29) [681]; *Foresight v Spain* (n 31) [387]–[388]; *RREEF v Spain* (n 23) [384]; and *Antin v Spain* (n 29) [538].

and equitable treatment. And this point leads to the second reason for discarding the idea of specific commitment: it unfairly disadvantages smaller investors. Compared to larger investors, smaller investors presumably do not have the same clout in the hallways of governmental departments and might lack the legal know-how to secure a specific commitment, which would be an acute problem particularly among startup companies. Further, if a smaller investor does have the know-how, it might find it more difficult to procure a specific commitment because it lacks the financial heft of a larger investor with a larger investment project; in other words, states have a greater incentive to give a specific commitment to larger investors because they bring more capital with them. If states choose to implement the energy transition by relying on private investment, equality demands that all investors receive the same beneficial treatment. The idea of general commitment is best designed to give effect to this principle.

The other debate concerns the issue what it means for an investor's expectation deriving from the state's commitment to be 'legitimate'. Again, there are two views. The first view might be called the 'objective meaning view'. As its name suggests, this view holds that an investor's expectation becomes legitimate if it accords with the objective meaning of the state's commitment. For example, if the state commits to paying a 'reasonable rate of return' to investors, then what the investors could have legitimately expected hinges on the objective meaning of 'reasonable rate of return'. The second view holds that there is more than the objective meaning of the commitment when determining legitimacy. Another aspect to consider is whether the state can be expected to actually perform the commitment. A minority of arbitral tribunals for the ECT investor–Spain arbitrations have adopted this view.[38] They have reasoned that as it was lawful under Spanish law to change the original regulatory regime applicable to investments in solar parks and Spain had previously changed a similar regulatory regime, there could be no legitimate expectation that investments in solar parks registered under the original regulatory regime would continue to receive the tariffs provided for under this regime for their operating lives,[39] which is what the investors claimed they legitimately expected.

The second view is doctrinally incorrect. Evidence concerning the question whether the state will actually perform its commitment is relevant to another legal concept, namely contributory fault.[40] As the arbitral tribunal held in *MTD v Chile*,[41] if an investor invests in the face of evidence that the state will breach an investment

---

[38] *Stadtwerke München v Spain* (n 5) [264]; *Charanne v Spain* (n 29) [505]; *Frontier Petroleum Services Ltd v Czech Republic*, PCA Case No 2008-09, Final Award (12 November 2010) [287].

[39] *Stadtwerke München v Spain* (n 5) [308], [277]–[278] and [281]; *Charanne v Spain* (n 29) [507]; and *Isolux v Spain* (n 29) [785] and [792].

[40] For the modern expression of this doctrine, see International Law Commission, *Responsibility of States for Internationally Wrongful Acts*, with commentaries, *Yearbook of the International Law Commission* (2001) vol II, Part Two, Art 39.

[41] *MTD Equity Sdn Bhd. and MTD Chile SA v Republic of Chile*, ICSID Case No ARB/01/7, Award (25 May 2004) [242]–[246].

protection standard and, in fact, does so breach, the state may seek to have its international responsibility reduced on account of this. If arbitral tribunals insist that evidence on the state's likelihood of performing its commitment is relevant to the question of the investor's legitimate expectations, then when this evidence is produced, it will mean no international responsibility for the state under the standard on fair and equitable treatment. The problem with this outcome is that it denies the reality that if a person makes a commitment, another person relies on it, and the first person does not perform the commitment, that non-performance is wrongful.[42] And because it is wrongful, it should attract international responsibility. The fact that there was evidence that the state would not actually perform does not justify nor does it excuse its non-performance. That logic does not mean that the investor's conduct of investing in the face of evidence that the state would dishonour its commitment is not worthy of condemnation. But this condemnation can be achieved under the umbrella of contributory fault, noting how this concept applies to divide up international responsibility.[43]

## B. Preserving Regulatory Flexibility for States

By preferring an approach insisting that evidence on the state's likelihood of performing the commitment is relevant to a pleading of contributory fault, this creates a robust conception of the standard on fair and equitable treatment. What justifies this robustness is that if states choose to take a support role in the energy transition, then international law needs to hold them accountable in that role. The objection against that conception is that states need flexibility when implementing the energy transition. Translated, what this objection means is that states must have the option of changing their position according to changing circumstances.

Yet even a robust conception of the standard on fair and equitable treatment offers states this flexibility. Merely dishonouring a commitment cannot amount to a frustration of legitimate expectations. Only a disproportionate change of position will suffice. Looking at the ECT investor–Spain arbitrations, arbitral tribunals have recognised that, in the midst of a sovereign debt crisis, the 'tariff deficit', which was the difference between what Spain paid clean-energy investors and what Spain collected when it sold the electricity on to consumers, was a legitimate target for reduction. But its efforts to address this deficit could not go too far.[44] Practically speaking, this concession grants states the option of scaling back on the extent of its commitments. Finally, there is the defence of necessity.[45] For exceptional

---

[42] Teerawat Wongaew, *Protection of Legitimate Expectations in Investment Treaty Arbitration* (Cambridge University Press, 2019) 9.

[43] For a theory on how to equitably divide responsibility when contributory fault is found, see Martin Jarrett, *Contributory Fault and Investor Misconduct in Investment Arbitration* (Cambridge University Press, 2019) 93–104.

[44] *Eiser v Spain* (n 29) [363].

[45] International Law Commission (2001) (n 40) Art 25.

circumstances, such as a severe economic crisis, this defence applies to suspend states' international obligations during the currency of the crisis.[46]

## V.  The Application of the Expropriation Standard to Measures Prohibiting Carbon-based Energy Production or Distribution

An alternative to the incentivisation of investments in the renewable energy sector is the prohibition of carbon-based energy production or distribution. Assuming that a state did not previously make commitments to investors with investments in these sectors regarding the maintenance of the current regulatory regimes, it will be able to take prohibition-measures without accruing liability under the standard on fair and equitable treatment. But by the same act, a state will expose itself to potential liability under the expropriation standard. Expropriation fundamentally differs from the standard on fair and equitable treatment because the former lacks a legal element examining the quality of the state's conduct, while the latter has such a component because it assesses whether the state's conduct was 'fair and equitable'. With the standard on expropriation, the quality of the state's conduct is not in question because the focus is solely on the consequence of the state's conduct.[47] That consequence is the loss or complete or substantial devaluation of an investment,[48] a consequence that will necessarily befall many investors with investments in carbon-based energy production or distribution in the future if states choose the option of prohibiting these activities.

## A.  The Police Powers Defence in International Investment Law

The potential saving grace for states is the police powers defence. Seemingly nowhere more applicable than in the context of the energy transition, the police powers defence justifies an indirect expropriation if the conduct constituting that expropriation proportionately and non-discriminately pursues some legitimate public policy.[49] Protection of the environment is the paradigm example of a

---

[46] For an example of a case where the defence of necessity was successfully pleaded, see *LG&E Energy Corp, LG&E Capital Corp, and LG&E International, Inc v Argentine Republic*, ICSID Case No ARB/02/1, Decision on Liability (3 October 2006) [266].

[47] B Wortley, *Expropriation in Public International Law* (Cambridge University Press, 1959) 19.

[48] JM Cox, *Expropriation in Investment Treaty Arbitration* (Oxford University Press, 2019) para 5.12.

[49] Adopting the narrow conception of the police powers defence as laid down in *Philip Morris Brands Sàrl, Philip Morris Products SA and Abal Hermanos SA v Oriental Republic of Uruguay*, ICSID Case No ARB/10/7, Award (8 July 2016) [305]. For overviews of the different conceptions, see further Y Radi, 'Regulatory Measures in International Investment Law: To Be or Not To be Compensated?' (2018) 33

legitimate public policy.[50] When it applies, it has the effect of completely excluding states' international responsibility for the indirect expropriation, meaning that no compensation is payable.

Over the past decade, the inclusion of the police powers defence in investment treaties has been standard, but for investment treaties concluded before this time, such inclusion is exceptional. The ECT is not one of these exceptional investment treaties, which gives rise to the question: as the police powers defence is not explicitly included in the ECT, can a police powers defence derived from customary international law be read into it?

# B.  The Police Powers Defence in the Energy Charter Treaty

That question makes two assumptions. First, it assumes that the police powers defence is part of customary international law. In light of the long line of authority in favour of its inclusion,[51] this assumption should not provoke any objection. Second, there is an assumption that customary international law is an applicable substantive law in investment arbitrations initiated under the ECT. Again, this is not controversial because Article 26(6) stipulates that arbitral tribunals should apply rules and principles of international law in investment arbitrations initiated under the ECT. On account of these two premises, the ECT implicitly makes provision for the police powers defence.

## i.  The Exclusion of the Police Powers Defence via Article 24

That conclusion, however, hits a snag in the form of Article 24 of the ECT:

ARTICLE 24

EXCEPTIONS

(1)  This Article shall not apply to Articles 12, 13 and 29.

(2)  The provisions of this Treaty other than

(a)   those referred to in paragraph (1); and
(b)   with respect to subparagraph (i), Part III of the Treaty

shall not preclude any Contracting Party from adopting or
enforcing any measure

      (i)   necessary to protect human, animal or plant life or health;

...

---

*ICSID Review* 78; and P Ranjan, 'Police Powers, Indirect Expropriation in International Investment Law, and Article 31(3)(c) of the VCLT: A Critique of Philip Morris v Uruguay' (2019) 9 *Asian Journal of International Law* 113.

[50] A Pellet, 'Police Power or the State's Right to Regulate' in M Kinnear, and others (eds), *Building International Investment Law – The First 50 Years of ICSID* (Kluwer, 2015) 448.

[51] *Saluka Investments BV v The Czech Republic*, PCA 2001-04, Partial Award (17 March 2006) [262].

For proper context, it should be noted that Article 13 contains the expropriation standard in the ECT. Thus, if the defence of Article 24(2)(b)(i) can be shown to have the same substance as the police powers defence, then Article 24(1) would exclude the application of the police powers defence to justify an indirect expropriation.

But the idea that the defence of Article 24(2)(b)(i) and the police powers defence are substantively the same is controversial.[52] First, it has been contended that Article 24(2)(b)(i) does not create a defence because:[53]

> [T]he wording of the exceptions clause 'nothing in this Agreement shall be construed to prevent a Party from adopting or enforcing measures necessary for ...' (or something equivalent) does not imply that the government does not have to pay compensation.

Yet if these words do not make that implication, then what do they mean? If they do not eliminate the liability created by a breach of the investment protection standards, which is the basic function of a defence, what is their legal operation? A contention to the effect that Article 24 aids the interpretation of investment protection standards does not change the assumption that its provisions contain a bevy of defences for states to plead. Assuming that it is only intended as an interpretative aid, it would operate to cut down the scope of circumstances in which the investment protection standards apply, which is ultimately what defences do. Moreover, the dominant view of the clause on which Article 24 is based, namely Article XX of the GATT,[54] holds that it operates as a defence.[55] Finally, the title of Article 24 is 'exceptions' – an oft-used synonym for defence. For these reasons, the provisions of Article 24 create defences that a state may invoke to eliminate its liability for breaching investment protection standards in the ECT, excluding those investment protection standards which are referenced in Article 24(1).

What is more important is whether the substantive content of Article 24(2)(b)(i) and the police powers defence can be paired. If they do pair, then the most important step towards concluding that Article 24(1) implicitly excludes the police powers defence from the ECT will have been made. With a view to establishing that step, the first point of note is that Article 24(2)(b)(i) and the police powers defence are both justification-based defences; in other words, they justify wrongful conduct because they recognise that some policies have priority over the policy underlying the rule that has been breached.[56] For both of them, those overriding

---

[52] But see B Legum and I Petculescu, 'GATT Article XX and international investment law' in R Enchandi and P Sauvé (eds), *Prospects in International Investment Law and Policy: World Trade Forum* (Cambridge University Press, 2013) 362.

[53] C Levesqué, 'The inclusion of GATT Article XX exceptions in IIAs: a potentially risky policy' in Enchandi and Sauvé (ibid) 368.

[54] C Grasso and G Alvarez, 'Article 24 Exceptions' in R Leal-Arcas (ed), *Commentary on the Energy Charter Treaty* (Edward Elgar, 2018) para 24.01.

[55] L-M Chauvel, 'The Influence of General Exceptions on the Interpretation of National Treatment in International Investment Law' (2017) 14 *Brazilian Journal of International Law* 144.

[56] See J Kurtz, *The WTO and International Investment Law: Converging Systems* (Cambridge University Press, 2016) 169.

policies are the same:[57] human health and the environment. The point of difference between them appears to be the legal element describing the quality of the state's conduct. To invoke Article 24(2)(b)(i), the state must prove that its conduct was *necessary* to achieve the identified human health objective or environmental objective, while the police powers defence requires that the state's conduct be *proportionate* to achieve one of the same objectives.

But there is an argument that 'necessary' in Article 24(2)(b)(i) and 'proportionate' in the police powers defence have the same meaning. In the jurisprudence of international trade law, it is well recognised that a necessary measure for the purposes of Article XX needs to be a proportionate one,[58] remembering that Article 24(2)(b)(i) is based on Article XX. This argument is admittedly not without its weaknesses. First, because the content of the police powers defence is not precisely defined,[59] it is difficult to confidently compare it to other legal concepts. Second, there is no guarantee that an arbitral tribunal in an ECT investment arbitration would use the jurisprudence on Article XX to interpret Article 24(2)(b)(i). While these weaknesses are acknowledged, they are not terminal blows to the original conclusion that 'necessary' in Article 24(2)(b)(i) and 'proportionate' in the police powers defence are the same or, at least, very similar.

Assuming that they are very similar, the next step is determining the scope of the exclusion in Article 24(1). The specific question to be answered asks: the words 'This Article shall not apply' in Article 24(1), do they only exclude the pleading of the defences listed in the provisions of Article 24 (the narrow interpretation) or both the defences of Article 24 *and* defences similar to them (the broad interpretation)? As with most questions of interpretation, arguments can be made both ways. If the words 'This Article' are given their ordinary meaning, then only the defences of Article 24 are covered by the exclusion. But looking to the context and purpose underlying Article 24(1), the argument for the broad interpretation is the more cogent one. The starting premise for this argument is that all of the defences of Article 24 are justificatory in nature; in other words, on account of a higher purpose, the state's breach of an investment protection standard should not give rise to international responsibility. This means that the general tenor of Article 24(1) is to stop states pleading justification-based defences to breaches of Article 13. The police powers defence is a justification-based defence. Accordingly, if the exclusion of Article 24(1) does not apply to the police

---

[57] But Legum and Petculescu opine that Art XX is broader than the police powers defence in this regard because the former covers both 'public health measures' and 'conversation measures', while the latter only covers public health measures, see Legum and Petculescu, 'GATT Article XX' (2013) 361–362.

[58] See P Mavroidis, *The General Agreement on Tariffs and Trade: A Commentary* (Oxford University Press, 2005) 190–192. But see generally D Regan, 'The meaning of "necessary" in GATT Article XX and GATS Article XIV: the myth of cost–benefit balancing' (2007) 6 *World Trade Review* 347.

[59] *Saluka v Czechia* (n 51) [263].

powers defence, the general tenor of this provision is undermined. This is a critical factor for preferring the broad interpretation. What can confirm this preference for the broad interpretation is a comparison to other treaty provisions found in other investment treaties that are the same as Article 24.[60] In those treaties, the state parties have specifically designated that the Article 24-like treaty provisions apply to the standard on expropriation.[61] The state parties to the ECT did not make the same specification. That exclusion should be respected.

## ii. The Irrelevance of Article 24 for the Application of the Police Powers Defence

Putting this analysis together, the conclusion is that the police powers defence cannot be invoked to defend a breach of Article 13. An argument standing in the way of that conclusion, however, is that Article 24 is generally irrelevant to the question of the application of the police powers defence. The first premise of that argument holds that the police powers defence is not a 'defence'[62] at all, but rather forms part of the definitional content of indirect expropriation. On this view, Article 24 is irrelevant as regards the question whether the police powers defence is recognised in the ECT because Article 24 is ultimately concerned with creating a number of discrete defences for other investment protection standards. Accepting that, the second premise provides that the jurisprudence on investment treaties has developed to a point where, even absent a treaty-based police powers defence, the legal elements of the police powers will be read into the definition of indirect expropriation.

The second premise of this argument is unobjectionable, but the first should not be accepted. Appeals to authority can be made both in favour[63] and against it.[64] But appeals to authority should not resolve this dilemma. What ultimately resolves it is recognising that legal elements, specifically those making up the police powers

---

[60] Since 1994, most Canadian investment treaties have included an article equivalent to Art 24; see A Newcombe, 'The use of general exceptions in IIAs: increasing legitimacy or uncertainty?' in A De Mestral and C Lévesque (eds), *Improving International Investment Agreements* (Routledge, 2013) 274.

[61] See, for example, Agreement Between the Government of Canada and the Government of the Republic of Benin for the Promotion and Reciprocal Protection of Investments (effective: 12 May 2014) Art 20.

[62] The equivalent expression in German law is 'Rechtfertigung'.

[63] See Y Fortier and S Drymer, 'Indirect Expropriation in the Law of International Investment: I Know It When I See It, or *Caveat Investor*' (2004) 19 *ICSID Review* 293. For an example of a case where the legal elements of the police powers defence were seemingly treated as falling within the definition of expropriation, see *Burlington Resources Inc v Republic of Ecuador*, ICSID Case No ARB/08/5, Decision on Liability (14 December 2012) [506].

[64] For example, in *Philip Morris v Uruguay* (n 49), the arbitral tribunal held that the application of the police powers defence would 'defeat a claim of expropriation', see [287] (emphasis added). See further Ranjan, 'Police Powers' (2019) (n 49) 108.

defence, can either form part of a rule creating international responsibility, namely the rule on expropriation, or a rule completely eliminating or partially reducing international responsibility, what is properly called a defence.[65] The decision where they are placed is a normative one. This means that treaty parties to an investment treaty might specifically designate that the legal elements should be placed in the rule on expropriation, but, in the absence of such a designation, the question is: where should they be placed? Two factors dictate that the legal elements of the police powers defence should create a separate rule. First, when an indirect expropriation is proven, the minimum harm that the rule on expropriation seeks to avoid, the loss or devaluation of investments, has already been reached, thereby implicitly giving rise to an obligation to the state to justify its conduct. In this context it should be noted that if the onus of proving the legal elements of a rule falls on the respondent, then the presumption is that it must be a defence.[66] Second, the state is better positioned to prove the legal elements of the police powers defence as much of the evidence to establish the legal element of proportionality should be readily within its reach.

# VI.  Designing a Police Powers Defence for the New Energy Charter Treaty

With the failure of this counterargument and in the absence of any arbitral jurisprudence to the contrary,[67] the original conclusion that Article 24(1) excludes the invocation of the police powers defence stands. This exclusion makes the inclusion of a police powers defence in the modernised ECT a necessity.[68] Drawing from other renditions of the police powers defences in treaties, the police powers defence for the ECT could look this:[69]

ARTICLE 13

EXPROPRIATION

...

(4) It is a defence to a breach of Article 13(1) by way of a measure or measures having effect equivalent to nationalization or expropriation (indirect expropriation) if such

---

[65] See J Goudkamp, *Tort Law Defences* (Hart, 2013) 71.

[66] Although in some scholarship on defences in international law, this presumption has been questioned, see F Paddeu, *Justification and Excuse in International Law: Concept and Theory of General Defence* (Cambridge University Press, 2018) 168.

[67] In their review of the cases concerning states' right to regulate under the ECT, Coop and Seif did not identify any cases where the police powers defence was applied; see Coop and Seif, 'ECT' (2018).

[68] A view subscribed to by various state parties to the ECT, see Energy Charter Secretariat, 'Policy Options for Modernisation of the ECT' (6 October 2019) 22–23, available at www.energycharter.org/fileadmin/DocumentsMedia/CCDECS/2019/CCDEC201908.pdf.

[69] For another version of a treaty-based police powers defence for the ECT, see European Commission, ECT Modernisation (2020) (n 36) 7.

measure or measures were non-discriminatory and proportionally directed towards a legitimate public welfare objective, such as public health, safety, and the environment.

In the application of this police powers defence, there are three legal concepts that will habitually come under examination: (i) indirect expropriation; (ii) proportionality; and (iii) non-discrimination. The jurisprudence that has been developed with respect to each is analysed below with a view to determining how the police powers defence would apply to investment disputes arising out of the energy transition.

## A. Measures for the Energy Transition as Indirect Expropriations

Every treaty-based police powers defence contains an embedded admissibility rule that the former can only be invoked in respect of indirect expropriations, that is, a state's conduct must amount to 'a measure or measures having effect equivalent to nationalization or expropriation'. This makes the distinction between direct expropriation and indirect expropriation critical,[70] which is why in investment treaties that include a police powers defence, most seek to illustrate the distinction, as the Argentina-Japan bilateral investment treaty does:[71]

Article 11

Expropriation and Compensation

(2) Paragraph 1 addresses two situations. The first is direct expropriation, in which an investment is nationalised or otherwise directly expropriated through formal transfer of title or outright seizure. The second is indirect expropriation, in which an action or a series of actions by a Contracting Party has an effect equivalent to direct expropriation without formal transfer of title or outright seizure.

This distinction conveys that direct expropriation occurs if ownership of an investment *transfers* from the investor to another person, typically the state. By contrast, indirect expropriations do not involve transfers of ownership. They occur if either the investor is completely or substantially *deprived* of its investment or its investment is completely or substantially *devalued*.[72] Accordingly, indirect expropriation divides between two rules: 'investment deprivation' and 'investment devaluation'. An example of investment deprivation can be seen in *Philip Morris v Australia*. There, the asset in question was intellectual property.[73]

---

[70] For an overview of the jurisprudential difficulties that have been accounted in distinguishing the different forms of expropriation, see McLachlan, Shore and Weiniger (n 13) paras 8.03–8.06.

[71] *Agreement between the Argentine Republic and Japan for the Promotion and Protection of Investment* (signed: 1 December 2018), Art 11(2).

[72] Coop and Seif (n 24) para 10.12.

[73] Although the investor's investment in Australia consisted of more than intellectual property rights, see *Philip Morris Asia Limited v The Commonwealth of Australia*, PCA Case No 2012-12, Notice of Arbitration (21 November 2011) [4.1]–[4.6].

As Australia generally prohibited the use of this intellectual property, neither the investor nor any other person could use it.[74] *Burlington v Ecuador* offers an example of the second form. In that case, the investor's investment activities were the production of crude oil. After Ecuador imposed a series of tax measures,[75] it unsuccessfully[76] argued that its investment (a shareholding in a local company) had been expropriated because it was near worthless.[77] What this jurisprudence means is that for states implementing energy transition via the prohibition of carbon-based energy production and distribution, such implementations should ordinarily be classified as indirect expropriations, thereby leaving open the door to plead the police powers defence.

## i. The Application of the Proportionality Test

The next hurdle that states will have to clear in any successful invocation of the police powers defence is the proportionality test. Even in those investment treaties where it is not mentioned, it is indisputable that proving proportionality is a requirement in the application of the police powers defence given that the recognition of that requirement in customary international law[78] and the rule of interpretation that treaty provisions must be interpreted with reference to customary international law.[79]

Depending on the source from which it is taken,[80] the test for proportionality comprises three or four components.[81] The first of these looks at the legitimacy of the objective that the state's conduct pursues, something that will not pose any problems if it is directed towards one of the objectives mentioned in the proposed police powers defence. Second, there must be a causal link between the state's

---

[74] *Philip Morris Asia Limited v The Commonwealth of Australia*, PCA Case No 2012-12, Award on Jurisdiction and Admissibility (15 December 2015) [7].

[75] For an overview of these tax measures, see *Burlington* (n 63) [29]–[36].

[76] ibid [457]. Two qualifiers have to be mentioned here, however. First, Arbitrator Orrego Vicuña issued a dissenting opinion on this point in which he concluded that a '99% tax level is simply not just an expropriation but a confiscation'; see *Burlington* (n 63) [27]. Second, the arbitral tribunal did eventually find that the investor's investment had been expropriated on account of other measures that Ecuador implemented; see ibid [535] and [537].

[77] *Burlington* (n 63) [110].

[78] See *Philip Morris v Uruguay* (n 49) [305].

[79] *Vienna Convention on the Law of Treaties*, (effective: 27 January 1980), Art 31(1)(c).

[80] The concept of proportionality finds its origins in German administrative law, where it consists of three components; see M Cohen-Eliya and I Porat, 'American balancing and German proportionality: The historical origins' (2010) 8 *International Journal of Constitutional Law* 274. Although German law combines the second and third components into one, see D Grimm, 'Proportionality in Canadian and German Constitutional Jurisprudence' (2007) 57 *University of Toronto Law Journal* 387, 389.

[81] For a comprehensive overview, see C Henckels, *Proportionality and Deference in Investor-State Arbitration: Balancing Investment Protection and Regulatory Autonomy* (Cambridge University Press, 2015) 24–26 and B Schlink, 'Proportionality (1)' in M Rosenfeld and A Sajó (eds), *The Oxford Handbook of Comparative Constitutional Law* (Oxford University Press, 2012) 722–24.

conduct and the identified objective, which was the contentious point in the application of the test for proportionality in *Philip Morris v Uruguay*.[82] The third component examines whether another course of action could have effected the identified objective in a manner less detrimental to the investor's ownership interest. The fourth component performs a balancing exercise where the benefit of the identified objective is weighed against the harm that the least detrimental method, as identified in the third step, would inflict. Only if the benefit outweighs the harm will the state's conduct be declared proportionate.[83]

Out of these four components, only the third component is likely to become contentious in an investment arbitration where the state indirectly expropriates an investment with a view to transiting to a low-carbon economy.[84] The reason for this is the macro-scale on which this component will need to be applied. The story of proportionality begins in German administrative law where it was originally developed to place legal limits around the discretion that the state's administrative functionaries, particularly the police,[85] enjoyed in carrying out their duties.[86] Accordingly, proportionality has been developed with respect to cases of a smaller scale. For present purposes, it needs to be applied to a situation where there could be many courses of action for achieving the same environmental benefit. Take the example of a state that voids an investor's ownership of a coal mine with a view to re-establishing the previous natural environment around the mine. Although this state action undoubtedly assists in tackling climate change, the investor might counter that banning dairy farming would effect the same outcome. Equally, if the state changes its policy and bans dairy farming, then farmers would argue that shutting down all coal mines is a better alternative.

The path out of this quagmire begins with defining what 'detriment' means for the purposes of this third component. Detriment might be ascribed one of two meanings. First, it could refer to the detriment that falls on the particular investor by virtue of the state's conduct. Yet if this definition is accepted, it would induce the type of argument that the detriment to this investor can be avoided if it is placed on another person. A second definition might revolve around the detriment that the state's action inflicts on society as a whole. Applying this definition, an investor might prove that a state's action was not suitable if the societal impact of its detriment was greater than the societal impact of placing the detriment elsewhere.

---

[82] *Philip Morris v Uruguay* (n 49) [306].

[83] It is somewhat preposterous to think that the relevant benefit and harm might be accurately weighed, but Robert Alexy has proposed a method for completing this process that is a reason-based approach which eliminates much of the arbitrary decision-making that the application of this component might induce; see Schlink, 'Proportionality (1)' (2012) (n 81) 724.

[84] Concurring with the more general trend regarding the frequent controversy surrounding the application of this component, see Henckels, *Proportionality and Deference* (2015) 25 and Grimm, 'Proportionality' (2017) (n 80) 389.

[85] For an overview, see Schlink (n 83) 294–95.

[86] Grimm (n 82) 384–85.

The rationale behind the preference for this conception of detriment is that tackling climate change benefits society as a whole, thereby meaning that the detriment should be calculated with reference to society as a whole.

## B. The Meaning of Discriminatory

But if this second definition is accepted, then the law ostensibly condones placing the cost of arresting climate change on others for the mere fact that they are the cheapest victims. For example, the state might identify dairy farming as the industry that has to suffer because its economic contribution dwarfs that of other carbon-emitting industries. Considering that they only make a partial contribution to climate change, dairy farmers would rightly feel aggrieved that they have to bear a disproportionate cost for reaching the desired environmental objective. This is where the requirement of discrimination might be invoked by the dairy farmers. In addition to measuring the proportionality of the state's action, the police powers defence incorporates a requirement that the same action must be non-discriminatory.[87] But as detailed in section III. A. above, the general view is that discrimination between investors according to which economic sector they operate in is not unlawful discrimination in international investment law. Given that this jurisprudence has been developed for the rule on arbitrary or discriminatory measures, it might be argued that discrimination assumes a different meaning in the police powers defence, but the presumption in favour of consistent interpretation shuts the door on this line of argument.[88]

# VII. Conclusions

This application of the police powers defence means that the costs of the energy transition will fall on investors with investments in carbon-based energy production and distribution. Considering that societies have also benefited from carbon-based energy in the past, this outcome seemingly does not achieve justice. In its current form, however, the police powers defence is a binary concept: if it applies, it completely eliminates liability, but if it does not, then the state assumes full liability. Yet, it might be postulated whether a third way could be developed, a way that more equitably balances the interests and duties of investors and states,

---

[87] Pellet, 'Police Power' (2015) (n 50) 49.

[88] Although in international trade law, the WTO Appellate Body in its report 'EC – Measures Affecting Asbestos and Asbestos-containing Products' indicated that discrimination bore two different meanings in the GATT, although the soundness of this approach has been questioned, see Mavroidis, *The General Agreement on Tariffs and Trade* (2005) (n 58) 185–86.

respectively, such as transforming the police powers defence from a complete defence into a partial defence which operates to reduce states' international responsibility. As with all partial defences, the challenge is to formulate an equation that fairly apportions international responsibility, without recourse to arbitrary decision-making that typically characterises this process. One alternative would be to limit states' international responsibility to the extent of the investors' inflation adjusted costs for the investment, but this option too closely mirrors the existing rule on lawful compensation requiring payment of compensation for expropriated investments.[89]

In the absence of any method to rationally divide liability in cases where the police powers defence applies, the conclusion is that the police powers defence should have a binary operation. There is no third way. But this is not unfair on investors with investments in production and distribution of carbon-based energy. In this context, it must be appreciated that investments are ultimately code for income-generation enterprises. That income comes from societal consumption of the investment produce and, in this position, it is society which will determine the success or failure of an investment. When an investment financially fails, it is for the simple reason that society rejects it. This rejection can never be questioned; in other words, consumers cannot be blamed for exercising their free choice in choosing not to purchase an investor's investment produce. Any such rejection will either be premised on society's lack of desire for the investment's products or society having the option of consuming an alternative product offering the same benefit. This is the situation with respect to the energy transition because society is sourcing the same benefit (energy) from a different product (renewable energy sources). But this rejection of carbon-based energy is not being directed by society on its own volition, but by states. Should that circumstance transform the situation from one where compensation is not owed, such as where a society rejects the investment because it prefers another similar product, to one where investor needs to be compensated?

The answer to this question must be in the negative, but there is more to this answer than the fact that the state has a good reason, namely a legitimate public objective, for directing society not to consume the investor's products. If there is such a reason, then society should first be accorded the respect to make the determination itself, whether to consume the investment's product or not. An exception to that rule, however, must be admitted if society cannot come to a determination as a result of a defect in its reasoning. For example, as tobacco products make their consumers addicted, states must assume the onus of directing, through their legislative capacities, those consumers with tobacco-control laws for their benefit.

---

[89] How this compensation is calculated depends on the nature of the investment, although investments that have not progressed to the income-generating phase are generally compensated on a costs basis; see B Sabahi, *Compensation and Restitution in Investor-State Arbitration: Principles and Practice* (Oxford University Press, 2011) 131–33.

Carbon-based energy consumption is not addictive, but various mental barriers stand in the way of consumers turning away from it to renewable energy. Most prominently, there is a misinformation campaign about climate change claiming that global temperatures are not rising, human activity is not causing rising temperatures, or the science is unsettled. Additionally, carbon-based energy consumption has perceived economic benefits that renewable energy does not, including carbon-based energy is cheaper or it supports local jobs. For these reasons, as is the case with consumers of tobacco products, consumers of carbon-based energy cannot reason their way to the conclusion that they must change their consumption habits. On account of that, a state-directed rejection of carbon-based energy consumption is justified, meaning that states should not be liable to pay compensation for investment losses in implementing the energy transition.

# 11

## The EU FDI Screening Regulation as an Example of the Proliferation of FDI Screening Processes Affecting the Energy Sector

LEONIE REINS AND DYLAN GERAETS

## I. Abstract

This chapter departs from the premise that energy is undergoing transformational change in the context of the transition to a low-carbon economy and the shale gas and oil revolution. One of the parameters of change that determine the trajectory of the transformation is investment in (renewable) energy infrastructure. Foreign direct investment (FDI) plays an increasingly important role in this transformation as it enables enterprises to grow and may provide a source for innovation that promotes energy efficiency. Simultaneously, however, governments of states seeking to attract FDI in the energy sector are adopting regulations establishing mechanisms that enable for the screening of such FDI. These screening processes are typically carried out to assess whether particular investment from particular sources may pose a threat to national security. Therefore, such screening mechanisms may apply to investments in the energy sector, as this sector is often covered under the heading of 'critical infrastructure' for which such screening is required or mandated. This contribution analyses the potential impact of the proliferation of these FDI screening mechanisms on the energy sector. It focuses on the EU's FDI Screening Regulation of March 2019.

# II. Introduction

On 5 March 2019, the Council of the European Union (the Council) adopted a regulation establishing a framework for the screening of FDIs into the EU.[1] Regulation (EU) 2019/452 of 19 March 2019 establishing a framework for the screening of FDIs into the EU ('FDI Screening Regulation') was officially published on 21 March 2019.[2] The new rules entered into force 20 days later and apply as of 11 October 2020, as per Article 17 of the Regulation.

FDI screening typically involves the screening of a planned foreign direct investment in order to determine whether the investment, or the investor, may pose a risk to the national security of the host state.[3] The concepts of national security or essential security interests are flexible, and their definitions have evolved, and will continue to evolve over time.[4] In 2016, the United Nations Conference on Trade and Development reported that, since 2006, at least eight developed, developing and transition economies had adopted legislation on FDI screening on grounds of national security: Canada, China, Finland, Germany, Italy, Korea, Poland and the Russian Federation.[5] Similarly, it was observed that several other states had amended their respective legislation to increase the sectors, guidelines or thresholds applicable to existing FDI screening mechanisms.[6]

Against this background, the adoption of the EU FDI Screening Regulation followed an extremely swift legislative process, which was initiated with a European Commission proposal presented on 13 September 2017. The relative speed with which the legislative process was concluded reflects the increased attention for FDI in certain strategic sectors of the economy as prevalent in several EU Member

---

[1] Regulation of the European Parliament and of the Council establishing a framework for the screening of foreign direct investments into the Union. Document 2017/0224 (COD), PE-CONS 72/18. The new rules will enter into force 20 days later and will apply 18 months later.

[2] Regulation (EU) 2019/452 of the European Parliament and of the Council of 19 March 2019 establishing a framework for the screening of foreign direct investments into the Union [herein after the FDI Screening Regulation], OJ LI 79/1.

[3] In a broader conception, FDI Screening may also be done in order to determine the economic need of a certain investment, but for the purpose of this contribution, FDI screening is defined as the screening of foreign direct investment in respect of national security concerns.

[4] WJ Moon, 'Essential Security Interests in International Investment Agreements' (2012) 15 *Journal of International Economic Law* 481, 500. Recently, a number of disputes in the World Trade Organization have seen the invocation of the national security exception under Article XXI of the General Agreement on Tariffs and Trade 1994 (GATT 1994) by Respondent Members. Notably, the Panel in a dispute between Russia and Ukraine on measures concerning traffic in transit determined that WTO panels have jurisdiction to review a Member's invocation of the national security exception. The national security exception has also been invoked by the United Arab Emirates, the Kingdom of Bahrain and the Kingdom of Saudi Arabia in three disputes initiated by Qatar (DS526, DS527 and DS528). The United States relies on Article XXI of the GATT in the disputes initiated against it in respect of the US Section 232 measures on steel and aluminium.

[5] UNCTAD, 'World Investment Report 2016 – Investor Nationality: Policy Challenges' 95, available at https://unctad.org/en/PublicationsLibrary/wir2016_en.pdf.

[6] ibid.

States. In this regard it is noteworthy that there have been calls for an EU-wide FDI screening mechanism, particularly with regard to China, since 2009.[7] As the German Federal Minister for Economic Affairs and Energy, Peter Altmaier, stated: 'The rapid agreement at EU level reflects the great significance attached to this legislative project by all parties'.[8]

The EU is, however, not the only jurisdiction in which regulators have become more responsive to concerns surrounding investments by third-country investors in companies that develop, commercialise and/or operate technologies and infra-structure that are deemed 'essential' or of a 'strategic interest' in terms of national security considerations. The World Investment Report 2018 compiled by the United Nations Conference on Trade and Development (UNCTAD) noted in this regard that:

> Recently, an increasing number of countries have taken a more critical stance towards foreign investment. New investment restrictions or regulations in 2017 mainly reflected concerns about national security and foreign ownership of land and natural resources. Some countries have heightened scrutiny of foreign takeovers, in particular of strategic assets and technology firms. Several countries are considering tightening investment screening procedures.[9]

As Lundqvist observes, the United States, Australia, and Canada have recently amended or proposed new legislation for the screening of FDI in certain key sectors of the economy.[10] In this regard the Committee on Foreign Investment in the United States (CFIUS) is an interagency committee authorised to review certain transactions involving foreign investment in the United States, in order to determine the effect of such transactions on the US's national security. The jurisdiction of CFIUS was expanded by means of the Foreign Investment Risk Review Modernization Act of 2018 (FIRRMA).[11] In Australia the Foreign Investment Review Board (FIRB) advises the treasurer and the Government on Australia's Foreign Investment Policy and the administration thereof, with the ultimate

---

[7] M Okano-Heijmans and F-P van der Putten, 'Europe needs to screen Chinese investment', 18 August 2009, East Asia Forum, available at www.eastasiaforum.org/2009/08/18/europe-needs-to-screen-chinese-investment.

[8] German Federal Ministry for Economic Affairs and Energy, 'Minister Altmaier: Need to protect sensitive sectors of industry against state-controlled strategic takeovers from abroad – agreement at European level marks important step', press release, 21 November 2018, available at www.bmwi.de/Redaktion/EN/Pressemitteilungen/2018/20181121-altmaier-muessen-sensible-industriebereiche-vor-staatlich-gelenkten-strategischen-uebernahmen-aus-de-ausland-schuetzen.html.

[9] UNCTAD, 'World Investment Report 2018 – Investment and New Industrial Policies – Key Messages and Overview' (2019), available at https://unctad.org/en/PublicationsLibrary/wir2018_overview_en.pdf.

[10] J Lundqvist, 'Screening Foreign Direct Investment in the European Union: Prospects for a "Multispeed" Framework' [2018] *European Union Law Working Papers* No 36, 2, available at www-cdn.law.stanford.edu/wp-content/uploads/2018/09/lundqvist_eulawwp36.pdf.

[11] US Treasury, 'Summary of the Foreign Investment Risk Review Modernization Act of 2018', available at www.treasury.gov/resource-center/international/Documents/Summary-of-FIRRMA.pdf.

decision-making responsibility residing with the treasurer. The role of the FIRB is to, inter alia, examine proposed investments in Australia that are subject to the Policy, the Foreign Acquisitions and Takeovers Act 1975.[12] There have been several changes to the treatment of wind and solar farms under the Foreign Acquisitions and Takeovers Regulation 2015, which apply as of 1 July 2017.[13] In Canada the screening of FDI is provided for under the Investment Canada Act that was adopted in 1985.[14] A national security review regime that is similar to CFIUS was created in 2009.[15] In 2015, amendments were made to the Investment Canada Act in respect of investments made by foreign investors that are considered to be state-owned enterprises (SOEs) by the Government of Canada. These changes were made in response to two proposed acquisitions of Canadian oil companies in 2012: (i) the takeover of Progress Energy Resources by Petronas; and (ii) the acquisition of Nexen by China National Oil Company (CNOOC).[16] Since the mechanisms in the US, Australia and Canada typically apply to all kinds of FDI, regardless of the particular sector in which the FDI is planned, they include the energy sector, as illustrated by the examples above.

Similarly, in Europe, several investments have contributed to increasing concerns on the part of citizens in Germany, particularly in regard of Chinese investments. These investments have included the 2016 takeover of the German robotics firm Kuka, by Chinese home appliance maker Midea. These concerns related, in particular, to the fact that the sale of a company active in the Industry 4.0 innovation sector would be paired to a loss of intellectual property and know-how.[17] However, there have equally been concerns relating to FDI in sectors other than automation, robotics and artificial intelligence. The 2016 investment by Beijing Enterprises in Germany's Energy from Waste equally raised concerns.[18] These concerns have resulted in the political call for action.

This chapter examines recent developments relating to the adoption and implementation of FDI screening mechanisms and the potential impact thereof on the energy sector. Section III introduces the recently adopted EU FDI Screening

---

[12] See http://firb.gov.au/about.

[13] See Guidance Note 50 of the FIRB, available at https://cdn.tspace.gov.au/uploads/sites/79/2017/06/50_GN_FIRB.pdf.

[14] Investment Canada Act (RSC, 1985, c 28 (1st Supp), available at https://laws-lois.justice.gc.ca/eng/acts/i-21.8/index.html.

[15] See Pt IV of the Investment Canada Act.

[16] S Globerman, 'An Economic Assessment of the Investment Canada Act', Fraser Institute, May 2015, 13, available at www.fraserinstitute.org/sites/default/files/an-economic-assessment-of-the-investment-canada-act.pdf. See also D Assaf, and R McGillis, 'Foreign Direct Investment and the National Interest. IRPP Study No 40' (Institute for Research on Public Policy, 2013).

[17] DW, 'Changes at German robotics firm Kuka raise questions over Chinese intentions', 26 November 2018, available at www.dw.com/en/changes-at-german-robotics-firm-kuka-raise-questions-over-chinese-intentions/a-46456133.

[18] Handelsblatt, 'EEW TAKEOVER – Chinese Interest in German Waste', 29 January 2016, available at www.handelsblatt.com/today/companies/eew-takeover-chinese-interest-in-german-waste/23535554.html?ticket=ST-107010-Qdmof63piXwug6dcYqMg-ap4.

Regulation and analyses its impact on the division of competences over FDI screening between the Union and its Member States. Section IV analyses its operation. Section V assesses application of the regulation to the energy sector. Section VI then discusses the potential impact of FDI screening on investments in the (renewable) energy sector in the EU. It concludes that the additional hurdles of screening may make attracting desirable foreign investment for the energy transition more complicated.

# III. The EU's FDI Screening Mechanism

## A. Origins of the FDI Screening Mechanism

The European Commission's proposal for an FDI Screening Regulation as presented in September 2017 came, at least in part, in response to concerns expressed by larger EU Member States such as Germany, Italy and France. In a joint letter dated February 2017, the ministers of economic affairs of these three countries expressed their concern to EU Commissioner Malmström in respect of the fact that '[i]n the last few years, non-EU investors have taken over more and more European companies with key technological competences for strategic reasons'.[19] In addition to this concern, the letter highlights the lack of reciprocity as 'European investors do not enjoy the same rights in the respective countries of origin as these non-EU investors in the investment-friendly European Union'.

The European Commission's proposal was amended in a few ways in subsequent rounds of negotiations between itself, the Council and the European Parliament. In particular, there have been discussions on the appropriate allocation of competences between the EU Member States and the EU, as well as on the appropriate legal basis for the EU FDI Screening Regulation.[20] On 20 November 2018, the 'trilogue' reached a political agreement on the text of the Regulation after which the European Parliament officially approved the text of the EU's FDI Screening Regulation on 14 February 2019. The Council approved the text of the Regulation on 5 March 2019, thereby laying down the new framework to screen FDI entering the EU.

---

[19] Joint Letter to Commissioner Malmström, sent by Germany, France and Italy. February 2017, available at www.bmwi.de/Redaktion/DE/Downloads/S-T/schreiben-de-fr-it-an-malmstroem.pdf?__blob=publicationFile&v=5.

[20] L Reins, 'The European Union's framework for FDI screening: Towards an ever more growing competence over energy policy?' (2019) 128 *Energy Policy* 665. See also S Schill, 'The European Union's Foreign Direct Investment Screening Paradox: Tightening Inward Investment Control to Further External Investment Liberalization, (2019) 46 *Legal Issues of Economic Integration* 105.

## B. Operation within the Divided Competence System of the European Union

The framework laid down by the FDI Screening Regulation does not replace the FDI screening mechanisms that may already exist in the EU Member States. It therefore does not establish a centralized EU-wide screening mechanism akin to, for example, CFIUS in the United States. In this regard, the Commission Staff Working Document that accompanied the Commission's initial proposal provides that an EU wide screening mechanism entirely operated at EU level

> could be very difficult to operate in practice due to possible differences of views amongst member states and also due to the fact that national security remains the sole responsibility of member states.[21]

So, whereas the FDI Screening Regulation provides a framework for FDI screening on grounds of security or public order, EU Member States are not obliged to adopt or implement an FDI screening mechanism. Similarly, the FDI Screening Regulation does not oblige them to screen particular FDI, even where a screening mechanism is in fact in place. EU Member States therefore retain the final decision-making power in terms of the actions to be taken in relation to FDI that is planned in their territory. Crucially, however, wherever an EU Member State implements or maintains an FDI screening mechanism or decides to screen particular FDI on grounds of security or public order, the mechanism and screening must be in conformity with the framework as provided by the EU FDI Screening Regulation.

The EU's FDI screening framework defines FDI as follows in Article 2(1):

> [A]n investment of any kind by a foreign investor aiming to establish or to maintain lasting and direct links between the foreign investor and the entrepreneur to whom or the undertaking to which the capital is made available in order to carry on an economic activity in a Member State, including investments which enable effective participation in the management or control of a company carrying out an economic activity.

The main type of FDI concerned by the Regulation are those made by 'a natural person of a third country or an undertaking of a third country, intending to make or having made a foreign direct investment'.[22] However, Article 3(6) of the Regulation also requires EU Member States that have a screening mechanism in place to 'maintain, amend or adopt measures necessary to identify and

---

[21] European Commission, 'Proposal for a Regulation of the European Parliament and of the Council establishing a framework for screening of foreign direct investment into the European Union', Commission Staff Working Document, SWD/2017/0297.

[22] Article 2(2) of the Regulation.

prevent circumvention of the screening mechanisms and screening decisions'. Circumvention would cover, according to Recital (10):

> [I]nvestments from within the Union by means of *artificial arrangements* that do not reflect *economic reality* and circumvent the screening mechanisms and screening decisions, *where the investor is ultimately owned or controlled by a natural person or an undertaking of a third country.* This is without prejudice to the freedom of establishment and the free movement of capital enshrined in the TFEU.[23]

Importantly, from an energy perspective, the European Parliament had sought to extend the coverage of the regulation by proposing the following amendment:

> [A]n investment of any kind, *irrespective of its volume or participation threshold* by a foreign investor *whether or not such investor is the ultimate investor,* aiming to establish or to maintain lasting direct *or indirect* links between the foreign investor and the entrepreneur to whom or the undertaking to which the capital is made available in order to carry on an economic activity in the territory of a Member State, *in its Exclusive Economic Zone declared pursuant to the United Nations Convention on the Law of the Sea (UNCLOS), or continental shelf,* including investments which enable effective participation in the management or *direct or indirect* control of a company carrying out an economic activity.[24]

Notably, the reference to the exclusive economic zones (EEZ) of the Member States also appeared in several other proposed amendments to the Regulation. Whilst this is not made explicit, the proposed amendments cannot be seen in isolation from the heavily debated Nord Stream 2 gas pipeline, which would provide an additional route for the transportation of natural gas between Russia and the EU. Indeed, in a policy paper by the European Commission's European Political Strategy Centre (EPSC), the following comments are made:

> There is also an investment dimension to the issue of Nord Stream 2. In September 2015, Gazprom made asset swaps with both BASF and OMV. Such agreements are not helpful to creating a level playing field for EU companies in Russia. So far, there have been no available EU reviews of foreign investments into critical sectors of the economy, including energy infrastructures, even though they are critical for European security. This is not specific to Russia and applies to all foreign actors increasingly active in EU energy markets, including the US, China, Azerbaijan, Turkey and others.[25]

Whereas ultimately the reference to the EEZ of EU Member States was not explicitly included in the FDI Screening Regulation, the Nord Stream 2 project appears to

---

[23] Emphasis added.

[24] European Parliament, Committee on International Trade (INTA), 'Report on the proposal for a regulation of the European Parliament and of the Council establishing a framework for screening of foreign direct investments into the European Union', COM(2017)0487 – C8-0309/2017 – 2017/0224(COD), 4 June 2018. Emphasis in the original.

[25] European Political Strategy Centre (2017), 'Nord Stream 2 – Divide et Impera Again? Avoiding a Zero-Sum Game', 12, available at https://ec.europa.eu/epsc/sites/epsc/files/epsc_-_nord_stream_-_divide_et_impera_again.pdf.

have been made subject to EU energy laws through the amendment of the Gas Directive.[26] In this regard, discussions have arisen as to whether EU law applies to the EEZ. In this regard, the Commission's proposal for the amendment of the Gas Directive provided that 'EU law in general applies in the territorial waters and the exclusive economic zone of EU member states'.[27] However, in response to the Proposal the Legal Service of the Council concluded on 1 March 2018 that:

> The Union does not have jurisdiction to apply energy law on unbundling, transparency, third-party access and regulated tariffs, which is unrelated to the economic exploitation of the EEZ, to pipelines crossing the EEZ of member states. The application of the Gas Directive to the EEZ would be contrary to Articles 56 and 58 of UNCLOS as interpreted by the Court of Justice.[28]

Turning back to the FDI Screening Regulation, it appears that the understanding that EU law applies to the exclusive economic zones of EU Member States has prevailed, and that therefore no explicit reference was included in the final text of the regulation.

# IV.  The Structure of FDI Screening

In essence, the FDI screening provided by the regulation is based on two pillars: (i) a common framework for screening FDI into the EU on grounds of security or public order; and (ii) a cooperation mechanism between the Member States, and between the Member States and the European Commission.

## A.  The Common Framework

The common framework provided by the Regulation is relatively limited and consists of two elements. First, in Article 4 of the Regulation, illustrative criteria are provided which may be considered by the Member States and the European Commission in determining whether FDI is likely to affect security or public order.[29] The concerns listed include energy-related critical infrastructure, critical

---

[26] Directive (EU) 2019/692 of the European Parliament and of the Council of 17 April 2019 amending Directive 2009/73/EC concerning common rules for the internal market in natural gas, OJ L 117/1. See in this regard K Talus, 'EU Gas Market Amendment – Despite of Compromise', Problems Remain, OGEL 2 (2019).

[27] European Commission, 'Proposal for a Directive of the European Parliament and of the Council amending Directive 2009/73/EC concerning common rules for the internal market in natural gas' COM(2017) 660, 2.

[28] Council of the European Union, 'Opinion of the Legal Service to the Energy Working Party', 1 March 2018, 2017/0294 (COD), para 21.

[29] Article 4(1) refers to: (a) critical infrastructure, whether physical or virtual, including *energy*, transport, water, health, communications, media, data processing or storage, aerospace, defence, electoral or financial infrastructure, and sensitive facilities, as well as land and real estate crucial for the use

technologies relating to, inter alia, energy storage and nuclear technologies, as well as the supply of critical inputs as including both energy itself as well as the raw materials necessary to generate energy or energy-generating infrastructure. Second, as part of the common framework, the Regulation lays down in Article 3 a number of minimum procedural requirements for the screening mechanisms that Member States may maintain or adopt. In particular, the rules and procedures should be transparent, non-discriminatory, and subject to timeframes. All aspects are important in order to ensure that FDI is not unduly restricted as a result of burdensome and non-transparent administrative requirements. In addition, the common framework requires Member States to ensure procedures for the handling of confidential information and to ensure that foreign investors have the 'possibility to seek recourse against screening decisions of the national authorities'.

Crucially, however, the Regulation does not harmonise the circumstances that would trigger the screening of a particular investment, nor the grounds for such screening. Similarly, it does not define whether investment screening should be *ex ante* or *ex post*, whether notifications of planned FDI is required, or what actions should be available under the screening mechanism. Therefore, whereas the mechanism lays down ground rules for FDI screening in the EU, significant differences between the screening regimes applicable in different EU Member States will continue to exist.

## B. The Cooperation Mechanism(s)

In addition to the common framework as described above, the EU FDI Screening Regulation provides for an elaborate cooperation mechanism between the EU Member States and the EU Member States and the European Commission.

Under Articles 6 and 7 of the Regulation, Member States other than the one in which an FDI is scheduled to take place may provide comments to the latter if they consider that the FDI is likely to affect their security or public order, if they have relevant information relating to this particular FDI, or whenever the Member State in which the FDI is scheduled to take place requests this. Moreover, under

---

of such infrastructure; (b) critical technologies and dual use items as defined in point 1 of Article 2 of Council Regulation (EC) No 428/2009 (15), including artificial intelligence, robotics, semiconductors, cybersecurity, aerospace, defence, *energy storage*, quantum and *nuclear technologies* as well as nano-technologies and biotechnologies; (c) *supply of critical inputs*, including *energy* or *raw materials*, as well as food security; (d) access to sensitive information, including personal data, or the ability to control such information; or (e) the freedom and pluralism of the media. In addition, Article 4(2) refers to: (a) whether the foreign investor is directly or indirectly controlled by the government, including state bodies or armed forces, of a third country, including through ownership structure or significant funding; (b) whether the foreign investor has already been involved in activities affecting security or public order in a Member State; or (c) whether there is a serious risk that the foreign investor engages in illegal or criminal activities.

the provisions of Articles 6–8 of the Regulation, there is an enhanced role for the European Commission. In particular, the European Commission may provide an opinion to the EU Member State in which an FDI is planned:

- if it considers that the FDI is likely to affect security or public order in more than one Member State;
- if it has relevant information relating to this FDI;
- following comments from other Member States;
- at the request of the Member State in which the FDI is planned; and
- (of particular relevance to the energy sector), in relation to 'projects or programs of Union interest' (PCIs).

In addition, as part of the cooperation mechanism, the provisions of the Regulation lay down detailed reporting and information exchange obligations. These obligations should allow for EU Member States as well as the Commission to issue the aforementioned comments and opinions. In this regard, the Regulation frames the ability of Member States and the Commission to comment on FDI planned in another Member State in procedural terms. However, this possibility exists regardless of whether: (i) the relevant FDI is being screened in the first place; and (ii) the Member State in which the FDI is taking place has a mechanism in place for screening FDI.

Importantly, however, even though the comments and opinions are not binding on the EU Member State in which the FDI is taking place, it must nonetheless:

(i) take 'utmost account' of a European Commission opinion relating to a PCI and justify any decision not to follow that opinion; but
(ii) give 'due consideration' to other member states' comments and the Commission's opinion in other cases.

In both instances, the EU Member States must have 'measures available under its national law, or in its broader policy-making', to give the required 'due consideration' or to take 'utmost account', in line with their duty of sincere cooperation under Article 4(3) TEU.

# V. Implementation and Practical Effects on the Energy Sector in the EU

The EU's FDI Screening Regulation will apply as of 11 October 2020 so as to leave sufficient time for the Member States to adapt any existing legislation that may already be in place. At the moment, 13 EU Member States and the UK operate FDI screening mechanisms and these mechanisms vary widely in their scope and design.[30] Thirteen of the existing FDI screening laws are applicable to the energy sector.[31] Whilst every mechanism has its own specificities – hence the need for the FDI Screening Regulation – certain common characteristics can be identified in terms of the organisation of, and powers conferred on, these screening mechanisms. Typically, the screening process starts with an assessment by the relevant authorities, triggered by a notification of the relevant investors, as to whether the contemplated investment is covered by the screening mechanism in question. Thereafter, the competent authority, which is usually the ministry of economic affairs, will start an in-depth investigation to assess the potential risks.[32]

As outlined above, the FDI Screening Regulation does neither require EU Member States to set up a screening mechanism, nor to screen specific FDI. Instead, it provides a framework for EU Member States that decide to implement a new, or maintain an existing, FDI screening mechanism. In doing so, the framework also provides for enhanced cooperation among EU Member States, as well as between the Member States and the European Commission. In particular and of specific relevance to the energy sector, the European Commission has obtained the right to intervene in case of FDI that would affect projects or programs of Union Interest (PCIs).

Of crucial importance for the energy sector is the fact that PCIs are defined in Article 8(3) of the Regulation as 'those projects and programmes which involve a substantial amount or a significant share of Union funding, or which are covered by Union law regarding critical infrastructure, critical technologies or critical inputs which are essential for security or public order'. In addition, a number of PCIs are explicitly listed in the Annex to the EU FDI Screening Regulation, including:

> 5. Trans-European Networks for Energy (TEN-E): Regulation (EU) No 347/2013 of the European Parliament and of the Council of 17 April 2013 on guidelines for trans-European energy infrastructure and repealing Decision No 1364/2006/EC and amending Regulations (EC) No 713/2009, (EC) No 714/2009 and (EC) No 715/2009 (OJ L 115, 25.4.2013, p. 39).

The aim of PCIs is to 'help the EU achieve its energy policy and climate objectives: affordable, secure and sustainable energy for all citizens, and the long-term

---

[30] European Parliament, 'EU to scrutinise foreign direct investment more closely, 14 February 2019. These member states are Austria, Denmark, Germany, Finland, France, Latvia, Lithuania, Hungary, Italy, the Netherlands, Poland, Portugal, Spain and the United Kingdom', available at www.europarl.europa. eu/news/en/press-room/20190207IPR25209/eu-to-scrutinise-foreign-direct-investment-more-closely.

[31] European Commission, 'Review of national rules for the protection of infrastructure relevant for security of supply – Final Report', February 2018, ISBN 978-92-79-70882-4, doi:10.2833/489902, 13, available at https://ec.europa.eu/energy/sites/ener/files/documents/final_report_on_study_on_national_rules_for_protection_of_infrastructure_relevant_for_security_of_supply.pdf.

[32] For a more detailed description, see European Commission, 'Review of national rules for the protection of infrastructure relevant for security of supply – Final Report', February 2018, ISBN 978-92-79-70882-4, doi:10.2833/489902, 14.

decarbonisation of the economy in accordance with the Paris Agreement.[33] The European Commission's third list of PCIs in the context of the TEN-E Regulation was published on 24 November 2017 and included no less than 173 projects. Among them were 106 electricity transmission and storage projects, four smart grid deployment projects, 53 gas related projects, six oil projects and four cross-border carbon dioxide networks ('$CO_2$ networks').[34] A project may be designated as a PCI if:[35]

- it has a significant impact on energy markets and market integration in at least two EU countries;
- it boosts competition on energy markets; and
- if it helps the EU's energy security by diversifying sources as well as by contributing to the EU's climate and energy goals by integrating renewables.

As per the European Commission's website, selected PCIs may benefit from:

- accelerated planning and permit granting;
- a single national authority for obtaining permits;
- improved regulatory conditions;
- lower administrative costs due to streamlined environmental assessment processes;
- increased public participation via consultations; and
- increased visibility to investors.

Considering the broad scope of the TEN-E Regulation and the fact that it includes a significant amount of energy-related infrastructure projects in the EU, the fact that it is explicitly covered by the EU's FDI Screening Regulation may have a significant impact on the foreign participation in projects that are designated as PCI.

# VI.  Potential Impact of FDI Screening on the (Renewable) Energy Sector

The importance of providing a stable and secure supply of affordable energy is a key objective of most governments. As a result, FDI in the energy sector is typically

---

[33] See 'Projects of Common Interest' (Energy – European Commission, 2019), available at https://ec.europa.eu/energy/en/topics/infrastructure/projects-common-interest.

[34] Commission Delegated Regulation (EU) 2018/540 of 23 November 2017 amending Regulation (EU) No 347/2013 of the European Parliament and of the Council as regards the Union list of projects of common interest and 'Energy Topics' (Energy – European Commission, 2019), available at https://ec.europa.eu/energy/en/topics/infrastructure/projects-common-interest.

[35] See Art 4 of Regulation (EU) No 347/2013 of the European Parliament and of the Council of 17 April 2013 on guidelines for trans-European energy infrastructure and repealing Decision No 1364/2006/EC and amending Regulations (EC) No 713/2009, (EC) No 714/2009 and (EC) No 715/2009.

regarded with a certain degree of suspicion. The varying degrees of openness to FDI in the energy sector are reflected in the large degree of variance in the national policies that govern the establishment of foreign investment in the energy sector.[36] Where FDI is permitted and partial or complete foreign ownership is allowed, countries will often adopt screening mechanisms. These mechanisms typically relate to national security or national economic benefits concerns.[37]

In historical terms, the sensitivity of FDI in the energy sector more generally has been articulated by Karl, who observed that:

> The balancing of public and private interests becomes relevant both with regard to the establishment of FDI and its subsequent treatment in the host country. As regards the entry phase, a decision needs to be taken whether to permit FDI in the energy sector, in what sub-sectors and under what conditions. This process may also imply choosing between alternative policy approaches. For instance, instead of imposing foreign ownership limits, host countries may wish to opt for less drastic approaches, such as a screening mechanism for inward FDI.[38]

As an example, it is notable that 9.7 per cent of Chinese investment in the UK between 2000 and 2016 was focused on the energy sector.[39] In this regard, the UK Government in the summer of 2016 delayed the approval of plans to build the Hinkley Point C nuclear energy facility due to concerns over Chinese ownership. The deal would be concluded between the UK's Department for Business, Energy & Industrial Strategy with NNB Generation Company (HPC) Limited (NNBG), itself owned for 66.5 per cent by Electricite de France (EDF), and for 33.5 per cent by China General Nuclear Power Group (CGN).[40] After the delay, the Secretary of State for Business, Energy & Industrial Strategy reported that:

> On the Hinkley project itself, the Government will now be able to prevent the sale of EDF's controlling stake prior to the completion of construction. This agreement will be confirmed in an exchange of letters between the Government and EDF. Existing legal powers, and the new legal framework, will mean that the Government is able to intervene in the sale of EDF's stake once Hinkley is operational. Furthermore, and even more importantly, we will reform the wider legal framework for future foreign investment in British critical infrastructure.[41]

Therefore, whilst this example relates to nuclear energy, rather than renewable energy generation infrastructure, it highlights the sensitivity of FDI in the energy

---

[36] J Karl, 'FDI in the Energy Sector: Recent Trends and Policy Issues' in E De Brandere and T Gazzini (eds), *Foreign Investment in the Energy Sector – Balancing Private and Public Interests* (Brill Nijhoff, International Investment Law Series, vol 2, 2014) 7–28, 15.

[37] ibid 16.

[38] ibid 22–23.

[39] J Percy, 'Chinese FDI in the EU's Top 4 Economies' (China Briefing News, 2019), available at www. china-briefing.com/news/chinese-fdi-eu-top-4-economies.

[40] 'UK decision to delay Hinkley Point plant catches China by surprise' *Financial Times*, 29 July 2016.

[41] UK Government, 'Oral statement to Parliament – Hinkley Point C – Secretary of State for Business, Energy & Industrial Strategy', Greg Clark, 15 September 2016, available at www.gov.uk/government/speeches/hinkley-point-c.

sector. Consequently, particular investments in specific energy-related infra-structure may have triggered calls for changes to the legal framework governing investments in critical infrastructure such as that relating to energy.

Recently, renewable energy (with the exclusion of hydro energy) has become the world's third largest industry for greenfield FDI attraction, with only the real estate and 'coal, oil and gas' sectors being bigger.[42] Particularly in the renewable energy sector, China has emerged as an important source of FDI, predominantly in the wind and solar sectors.[43] With Western Europe being the second largest destination region for renewable energy FDI between 2013 and 2018, the intro-duction of a broader EU-wide FDI Screening Regulation may have an impact on these investments.[44] However, it has also been pointed out that EU Member States' perceptions with regard to Chinese FDI in the energy sector may differ.[45] That FDI screening mechanisms adopted in the EU and the US have an impact on Chinese FDI in sectors other than the energy sector has already been reported.[46] However, whether and to what extent FDI screening mechanisms such as the EU FDI Screening Regulation will also impact investment in the energy sector is still an open question. In this regard, in 2018, Chinese investment in Eastern Europe may have dropped overall, but some growth was identified in, among others, renewable energy projects such as Unisun's solar farm in Hungary.[47]

In this regard, in January 2019 it was reported that the Chinese SOE China Three Gorges (CTG) had halted talks with the European Commission on the proposed takeover of the Portuguese energy company EDP-Energia de Portugal (EDP), which was estimated to be worth EUR 9 billion.[48] Among the reasons for CTG's loss of interest in the takeover was, according to anonymous sources, 'the prospect of tougher EU regulations on foreign investment'. EDP has, inter alia, subsidiar-ies in the field of renewable energy (wind farms and hydro plants) in Spain and is the fourth-largest wind operator globally. Although it would be speculative to attribute the collapse of the planned takeover to the EU FDI Screening Regulation, especially since a leadership change at CTG and higher European electricity tariffs were also quoted, it is evident that increased scrutiny over FDI in the EU played a

[42] S Shehadi, 'fDi Renewable Energy Investments of the Year 2019 – the winners', fDi Intelligence, 11 February 2019, available at www.fdiintelligence.com/Sectors/Alternative-Renewable-energy/fDi-Renewable-Energy-Investments-of-the-Year-2019-the-winners.

[43] X Tan, Y Zhao, C Polycarp and J Bai, 'China's Overseas Investments in the Wind and Solar Industries: Trends and Drivers', World Resources Institute Working Paper (2013) 18.

[44] Shehadi, fDi Renewable Energy Investments' (2019).

[45] RQ Turcsanyi, 'Central European Attitude towards Chinese energy investments: The cases of Poland, Slovakia, and the Czech Republic' (2017) 101 *Energy Policy* 711, 719.

[46] T Hanemann, M Huotari and A Kratz, 'Chinese FDI in Europe: 2018 Trends and Impact of New Screening Policies', March 2019, available at www.merics.org/sites/default/files/2019-03/190306_MERICS-Rhodium%20Group_COFDI-Update_2019.pdf.

[47] ibid. 11.

[48] 'China Three Gorges halts talks with EU regulators on EDP takeover: sources', Reuters, 25 January 2019, available at www.reuters.com/article/us-edp-m-a-china/china-three-gorges-halts-talks-with-eu-regulators-on-edp-takeover-sources-idUSKCN1PJ2CN.

role. Considering that one of EDP's objectives behind the planned investment was to set foot in the EU renewable energy market, this points at the existence of a clear impact of the EU FDI Screening Regulation on the energy sector.[49] At this section it is important to acknowledge that the EU's FDI Screening framework alone is not responsible for that impact. Riley has observed in this regard that 'hardly any EU regulatory mechanism [...] seek[s] to encourage investment in the energy sector' and that 'the EU and the Member States appear to be doing the reverse: they are adopting policies which undermine investment in the energy sector'.[50] However, against this background, it will be critical to ensure that the FDI screening framework provided does not impose an additional hurdle towards attracting FDI in, in particular, the renewable energy sector in the EU. Especially in times of increasing trade tensions, these additional hurdles may have a further dampening effect on investment flows between, for example, China and the EU.[51]

# VII. Conclusions

There is a clear global proliferation of FDI screening mechanisms that increasingly also cover investments in the energy sector. Concerns relating to foreign control over essential infrastructure have prompted governments to tighten existing screening mechanisms, or to set up frameworks for the establishment of new FDI screening mechanisms. The energy sector does not escape scrutiny under such mechanisms, which often explicitly identify energy-related infrastructure as 'essential infrastructure' that fall within the scope of projects that are subject to FDI screening on national security grounds.

This chapter has provided an overview of the recent developments in this regard and has highlighted that, in particular in Europe, the (potential) screening of FDI cannot be seen in isolation from the effects on the energy sector, in particular at a time when that sector is transforming from being fossil-oriented to placing emphasis on renewable energy. Whereas historical examples in Europe

---

[49] P le Corre (2018), 'China's Rise as a Geoeconomic Influencer; Four European Case Studies', Asia Focus #93, Institut de Relations Internationales et Stratégiques ('IRIS') 10, available at www.iris-france. org/wp-content/uploads/2018/11/Asia-Focus-93.pdf. The author interviewed an unidentified EDP insider who was quoted as saying 'The reason CTG invested in EDP [was] three-fold: first, the main Chinese player – State Grid was already targeting [Portugal's public power company]; second, we were in the same business and it made sense in our overseas markets; third, they wanted a foot in the EU renewable energy market,' said an EDP insider'. See also Hanemann et al, 'Chinese FDI in Europe' (2019) 15.

[50] A Riley, 'How the European Commission, European Court of Justice and member states are scaring away investors in the energy sector', 10 May 2018; A Riley, J V Mitchell and K Treadwell, 'EU Institutions and Member States are Scaring Away Investors in Energy' (Energy Post, 2019), available at https:// energypost.eu/how-the-european-commission-european-court-of-justice-and-member-states-are-scaring-away-investors-in-the-energy-sector.

[51] L Curran, P Lv and F Spigarelli, 'Chinese Investment in the EU renewable energy sector: Motives, synergies and policy implications' (2017) 101 *Energy Policy* 670, 679.

show that concerns relating to investment in the energy sector may have arisen predominantly in respect of nuclear technology, more recent examples show that with respect to foreign investment in renewable energy projects, national security concerns may equally play a role.

The EU's FDI regulation does not establish a CFIUS-style centralised EU-wide screening mechanism for FDI and it does not require EU Member States to implement an FDI screening mechanism. However, where such an FDI screening mechanism exists or is to be adopted by a Member State, it must meet certain basic screening requirements, such as judicial review of decisions, non-discrimination between different third countries and transparency. The Regulation applies to potential FDI in the energy sector, since Member States and the Commission, in determining whether such FDI is likely to affect public security or public order, may consider potential effects on, inter alia, critical infrastructure, including energy infrastructure, as well as critical technologies, including energy storage, as well as the supply of critical inputs, including energy.

With the establishment and enhancement of FDI screening mechanisms globally, investors that can play a critical role in the global energy transformation may face additional hurdles in respect of their planned investments. In this regard, it will be critical for policy-makers, legislators and screening authorities globally to ensure that the FDI screening mechanisms they have implemented do not impose an undue burden on investors. Whereas the aim of ensuring that foreign investment does not pose national security threats is entirely understandable, FDI screening mechanisms should be designed and applied in such a manner that they do not constitute unnecessary obstacles to investments that could play a vital role in the energy transition. In this regard the EU's FDI Screening Regulation appears to set adequate baseline standards in terms of transparency. It will be essential to monitor its implementation by the EU Member States in order to ensure that essential global investment flows are not unnecessarily hampered, especially in respect of investments in renewable energy.

# 12

## International Arbitration in the Renewable Field: Recent Developments in Spain

IÑIGO DEL GUAYO

## I. Abstract

Spain became a leader in the promotion of renewable energies from 1998 to 2012. The remarkable increase in the introduction of generation units producing with renewable energies (mainly solar and wind energies) was based on a generous feed-in-tariff system, together with a premium on top of the electricity price in the market. Those subsidies to renewable energies were paid by electricity consumers and they amounted to a big quantity, almost equal to the distribution costs. In the Spanish electricity system prices are collected by suppliers from consumers who, in turn, must pay the costs of the system (production, transport, distribution and other regulatory costs, such as the costs of promoting renewable energies). The system experienced a deficit, since prices paid by consumers were not enough to cover all costs. The deficit aggravated with the financial and economic crisis which started in 2008. The reaction of the Government was to progressively reduce the amount of subsidies to renewable energies. This led to legal disputes. Whereas investors did not succeed at national courts, a number of international arbitration cases have condemned Spain.

## II. Introduction

The 1997 Electricity Sector Act liberalised the Spanish electricity sector and laid down the grounds for the creation of a favourable legal framework for renewable energies. From 2004 onwards, Spain was a leader in the promotion of renewable energies, which was based on a generous system of feed-in-tariffs together with premiums awarded to electricity generated by means of renewable energies, mainly wind and solar.[1] Consumers paid those subsidies, which represented one-third of the total costs of electricity supply. The emergence of the financial and economic crisis in 2007 and the reduced energy consumption following said crisis led to a change in energy policy. From 2008 to 2014, the focus was put on the need to reduce electricity costs. Governmental action was directed by the progressive lowering of energy demand and the need to manage the increasing electricity economic deficit (ie the gap between income and costs within the electricity sector). The new policy tackled this problem by means of reducing the amount of remuneration of network activities (it is the government, which fixes the amount of remuneration that distribution and transport companies get annually) as well as the amount of subsidies renewable energies receive. This reduction of subsidies to renewable energies provoked many legal disputes at national and international levels, which are analysed in this chapter.

After a brief description of the importance of renewable energies in Spain (section III), the paper turns into the kind of support renewable energies had from 1998 to 2012 (section IV). In order to properly understand why and how the support to renewable energies started to decrease, section V is devoted to the so called 'electricity tariff deficit', as an introduction to section VI, where the progressive reduction of the support scheme, as from 2008, is analysed. In July 2013 a further change of the regulatory framework took place, as a prelude of the new Electricity Sector Act 2103 (December), which replaced the 1997 Electricity Sector Act. This is explained in section VII. The reduction of the amount of subsidies led to a number of legal disputes, at both national and international levels, addressed in section VIII. Within a European context, the problems experienced in Spain by investors in renewable energies pushed the introduction of a new provision in the new Renewables Directive about stable support mechanisms (section IX). A concluding evaluation of the legal disputes is contained in section X.

# III. Renewable Energy Sources

From 2004 to 2012 there was in Spain a remarkable increase of the use and production of renewable energies, by which Spain became a worldwide leader. The percentage of the share of renewable energies within the overall national energy production in 2018 was 38.5 per cent (hydroelectricity, wind, solar, geothermal, biogas, biomass, biofuels, marine waves and residues). Sources of electricity production in 2018 show the relevance of renewable energies: 13.1 per cent hydroelectricity, 19 per cent wind, 3 per cent photovoltaic, 1.7 per cent

---

[1] L Agosti and J Padilla, 'Promoción de las energías renovables: La experiencia de España' in B Mosdelle, J Padilla and R Schmalensee (eds), *Electricidad Verde* (Marcial Pons, 2010) 517.

solar thermal, and 1.7 per cent the rest of renewable sources.[2] Biofuels are another renewable source of energy, with strong relevance to transport.[3] The promotion of offshore wind energy is very slow, due to the fact that although there are important wind areas, the continental shelf of the Iberian Peninsula and that of the islands is very narrow and is not convenient for the location of wind farms. Some demonstration projects have been located by the Catalan and Canary Islands Governments. In accordance with the 2009 Renewable Directive of the European Union,[4] the Spanish Government approved the Action Plan for Renewable Energies 2011–20 (*Plan de Energías Renovables 2011–2020*).[5] The target for Spain was to have a share of 20 per cent of renewable energies in final energy consumption by 2020, and 10 per cent in transport. Due to the fact that in 2011 renewable energies contributed 11.6 per cent of the final primary energy demand (about half of the 2020 target), the target was put at risk by the decision of the Government to stop supporting new renewable installations in 2012.[6]

# IV. National Support to Renewable Energies

In implementing the 2009 RES Directive, Spain chose a system which combined priority dispatch and priority connection and access to the grid.[7] Additionally, electricity legislation included a subsidy scheme in the form of both a feed-in-tariff system and a premium.[8]

The Electricity Sector Act of 1997[9] marked a turning point in the promotion of renewable energies for electricity generation purposes. It dealt with the so-called 'special generating regime',[10] when carried out in installations where the installed capacity does not exceed 50 MW, including cogeneration (provided they involve high-energy performance) or renewable energies.

---

[2] See 'Las Energías Renovables En El Sistema Eléctrico Español 2018, Red Eléctrica De España', available at www.ree.es/es/datos/publicaciones/informe-de-energias-renovables/informe-2018.

[3] See I del Guayo, 'Biofuels: EU Law and Policy' in DN Zillman, C Redgwell, YO Omorogbe, and LK Barrera-Hernández (eds), *Beyond the Carbon Economy: Energy Law in Transition* (Oxford University Press, 2008) 265.

[4] Directive 2009/28/EC of the European Parliament and of the Council of 23 April 2009 on the promotion of the use of energy from renewable sources and amending and subsequently repealing Directives 2001/77/EC and 2003/30/EC (OJ L 140, 5.6.2009, p 16) [hereinafter 2009 Renewables or RES Directive].

[5] Available at www.idae.es/tecnologias/energias-renovables/plan-de-energias-renovables-2011-2020.

[6] I González Ríos, *Régimen Jurídico-Administrativo de las Energías Renovables y de la Eficiencia Energética* (Aranzadi, 2011).

[7] Art 26 of the 2013 ESA.

[8] LM Cazorla, 'El régimen tarifario de las energías renovables' in F Becker, LM Cazorla and J Martínez-Simancas (eds), *Tratado de Energías Renovables* (Aranzadi, 2010) 119.

[9] Act no 54, of the 27th November, 1997, of the Electricity Sector (BOE no 285 of the 28 November 1997).

[10] Arts 27–31 of the 1997 ESA as modified several times.

Producers under the special regime benefited from public subsidies, in two ways: a feed-in tariff; and a premium.[11] A particular feed-in tariff scheme was envisaged for producers subject to the special regime; remuneration was also guaranteed with an additional premium over and above the prices paid for electricity generated from ordinary sources. These subsidies were considered to be a diversification and security cost of the electricity system and financed by electricity consumers.

The Government managed to lay down a stable and attractive framework for companies investing in renewable energies by means of a Royal Decree passed in 2004,[12] which not only linked the premium to the average price of kWh in the pool, but also fixed high percentages for premiums. In the light of this Royal Decree and a set of other norms, much renewable generation was installed, particularly installations working with wind and solar photovoltaic.

# V. The Electricity Tariff Deficit (1998–2013)*****

In order to understand the reduction of subsidies in favour of renewable energies between 2010 and 2016, there is the need to explain what the electricity deficit is and how it was addressed by the 2013 Electricity Sector Act (2013 ESA[13]).

A key element addressed by the reform of the 2013 ESA was the accumulation between 2002 and 2012 of annual imbalances between revenues and costs of the electricity system and consequently the emergence of a structural deficit. The bad financial situation of the deficit could endanger the proper functioning of transport and distribution activities.

Although the Spanish electricity sector was liberalised in 1997, there are regulated tariffs paid by domestic and small commercial customers. In fixing tariffs, government has not been cost-oriented and kept electricity prices artificially low, the result being that there was a cumulative deficit as a result of the difference between regulated tariffs and the cost that should be paid by a customer in the liberalised market. In other words, electricity producers were forced to sell electricity at regulated prices which did not cover costs. The economic deficit was, therefore, the cumulative difference between what it costs companies to generate electricity and what they are allowed to charge for it. The deficit reached overwhelming levels. Among the costs of the electricity system not covered by

---

[11] Art 25 of the 1997 ESA.

[12] RD No 436 of 12 March 2004.

***** The bulk part of the text of this section is taken from I del Guayo, 'Energy Law in Spain' in M Roggenkamp, C Redgwell, A Ronne and I del Guayo, *Energy Law in Europe*, 3rd edn (Oxford University Press, 2016) 973.

[13] Act no 24, of the 26th December 2013, of the Electricity Sector (BOE no 310, of the 27th December 2017).

regulated prices were subsidies to renewable energies. Consequently, Spanish governments from 2008 onwards reduced subsidies to existing renewable installations and suppressed subsidies to new installations.

The deficit was caused by the tariff fixed by the Government, and paid by around 16 million small consumers, and which was not high enough to cover the actual costs of electricity generation and supply. This imbalance reached the point where the accumulated debt of the electricity system was EUR 26 billion. The structural deficit reached EUR 10 billion annually and not correcting this imbalance would have introduced a risk of bankruptcy in the electricity system.

From 2008 to 2013 electricity regulation was dominated by legislative and regulatory measures directed to address and mitigate the pernicious consequences of the increasing electricity economic deficit, accelerated as from July 2007, by a lowering of energy demand due to the economic crisis. In the Spanish electricity system prices are collected by suppliers who, in turn, must pay the costs of the system (production, transport, distribution and other regulatory costs, such as the costs of promoting renewable energies). The system experienced a deficit, since prices paid by consumers were not enough to cover all costs. The deficit aggravated with the financial and economic crisis which started in 2008, due to a lower demand which, in turn, lowered the total quantity collected to cover all costs. Several norms were passed by Parliament to tackle this thorny problem, and in December 2013 a whole new Electricity Act was passed by Parliament to replace the existing one passed in 1997. The debate was focused on which costs should be borne by the electricity tariff: electricity companies associated in UNESA (the association of electricity companies) were of the opinion that there were many policy costs borne by the tariff (such as the costs of promoting renewable energies) and the tariff was not high enough to cover all them. The options were either to increase the tariff up to unaffordable levels for most small consumers or to lower the number and/or quantity of costs to be included in the tariff.

In accordance with the 2013 Electricity Act, the deficit was to be covered by electricity companies, the renewable energies sector and by the state budget (one-third of the total amount, each). First, the Government reduced the remuneration of regulated electricity companies (transport and distribution). Second, there was a substantial reduction of the amount of subsidies in favour of the renewable sector. Third, some costs borne by the electricity tariff (such as the extra costs of supplying electricity to the extra-peninsular systems) were to be financed by the state budget.

# VI. The Progressive Reduction of the Support Scheme in the Period 2008–2013

Spanish electricity policy from 2008 to 2013 was dominated by legislative and regulatory measures directed towards fighting and mitigating the pernicious consequences of an increasing electricity deficit, accelerated as from the entry into force of Royal Decree No 661/2007 of 25 May (Royal Decree regulating the special system for the production of electricity). The Spanish economic crisis, encompassing a recession, a crisis in the financial system and its institutions, and, as a result, a drastic reduction of energy demand, aggravated the electricity deficit. Tariffs (or prices) paid by end consumers must be enough to cover all the costs of the electricity system, such as transport and distribution costs. Tariffs became insufficient to cover all costs. Subsidies for renewable energies were among the costs of the electricity system currently not covered by tariffs.

All those circumstances led the Government to pass a successive number of legislative measures directed, among other objectives, towards reducing the subsidies paid to existing installations generating electricity from renewable sources and suppressing subsidies to new installations. Main decisions adopted between 2010 and 2013 were the following:

(a)  Royal Decree-law[14] (hereafter RDL) No 14 of 23 December 2010 limited the number of hours produced by solar photovoltaic installations to be subsidized yearly; a Registry for the Allocation of Retribution was created, which meant that only renewable installations registered in said Registry will get subsidies, and the Government toughened the conditions to have access to the Registry.

(b)  RDL No 1 of 27 January 2012 suspended the procedures for the allocation of retribution, and suppressed economic incentives for new installations of electricity production from cogeneration, renewable energy sources (wind, solar, and other renewable technologies), and waste. In practice, under the scope of the special regime, this measure meant that the construction of new installations came to a stop. The measure did not affect existing projects pre-approved by the government, ie those installations already registered on the Registry for the Allocation of Retribution. The decision came as a surprise to the renewable energies sector.

(c)  Act No 15 of 27 December 2012 introduced a new tax on electricity generation, affecting also installations producing electricity with renewable energy sources.

(d)  Act No 17 of 27 December 2012 established a number of budget contributions directed to finance costs of the electricity system, linked to the promotion of renewable energy sources in a quantity equivalent to the yearly tax collection from Act No 15 of 27 December 2012, as well as 90 per cent of income collected as a result of the tender of emissions rights of greenhouse effect gases.

---

[14] RDLs are approved by the Government, but enjoy the same rank as a parliamentary act. According to Art 86 of the Spanish Constitution, the Government is allowed to promulgate an RDL only in cases of urgent and extraordinary necessity, subject to retrospective Parliamentary scrutiny. RDLs cannot affect the basic institutions of the state, the rights and freedoms of its citizens, the distribution of authority between the state and the autonomous communities, or the electoral law.

(e)  RDL No 29 of 28 December 2012 established that subsidies to facilities of the special generation regimen will not be applicable if, as a result of an inspection, there was evidence that the construction of a renewables installation provisionally registered within the Registry for the Allocation of Remuneration is not fully completed at the time of the expiration of the deadline to definitively register said installation within the Registry; for these purposes, it will be considered that the installation is fully complete if it has all the elements, equipment, and infrastructure needed for producing energy and feeding it into the electricity system, and the characteristics of which correspond to the approved implementation project; this measure was addressed to fight some fraud which had been identified; in summary, there was a stricter control on the rules applying to the construction of the installation and the moment at which the subsidy starts being paid.

(f)  Finally, RDL No 9 of 9 July 2013 introduced a new remuneration system for renewable energies, linked to investment and not to production; this new system was later included within the 2013 ESA, passed at the end of 2013.[15] The reform of July 2013 had a clear retroactive effect.

# VII.  The New Support Scheme of the 2013 Electricity Sector Act

A few months after the RDL No 9 of 9 July 2013, the 2013 ESA entered into force. It incorporated the reforms anticipated by RDL No 9 of 9 July 2013. The distinction between two systems of generation (ordinary and special) is terminated, and the 2013 ESA provides for a single legal framework for electricity generation. By unifying the pre-existing two systems, the 2013 ESA intended to make financial support to renewable installations an exceptional situation. The 2013 ESA states that, as an exception, the Government may establish a specific compensation arrangement to encourage production from renewable energy sources, cogeneration of high efficiency, and waste, if there is an obligation of energy objectives derived from policies or other standards of EU law or where its introduction involves a reduction of energy cost and external energy dependency.[16] The support, additional to the remuneration obtained from the sale of energy at market prices, will be composed of two terms: (a) term per unit of installed power, covering, as appropriate, the investment costs of a standard (or type) installation, of those costs which

---

[15] I del Guayo, 'Seguridad jurídica y cambios regulatorios (a propósito del Real Decreto-ley núm. 1/2012, de 27 de enero, de suspensión de los procedimientos de preasignación de retribución y de supresión de las primas para nuevas instalaciones de producción de energía eléctrica mediante fuentes de energía renovables)' (2012) 156 *Revista Española de Derecho Administrativo* 217.

[16] Art 14(7) of the 2013 ESA.

are not recovered from the sale of energy; and (b) a term linked to operation costs, covering, as appropriate, the difference between operating costs and revenues from participation in the market of production of such standard installation.

For the calculation of the specific remuneration, the following criteria shall be considered, for a standard installation, throughout their regulatory useful life, and in reference to the activity carried out by an efficient and well-managed company:

(a)   the standard income from the sale of the generated energy at market prices;
(b)   the standard operational costs; and
(c)   the standard value of the initial investment.

This means that under no circumstances shall costs or investments resulting from particular rules or administrative acts not applied throughout the Spanish territory be taken into account. This provision is intended to exclude from the calculation of the remuneration those costs which are the result of exigencies imposed upon generating companies by the autonomous communities. It is assumed that the companies operating in the territory of those autonomous communities will have to bear the extra cost. By means of this provision the central Government is indirectly fighting against those autonomous communities which, using their legitimate competences, are subjecting the generation of electricity (or its transport and/or distribution) to a particular territorial tax or to any other regulatory cost which does not exist in other autonomous communities. In the same way, when fixing the remuneration for renewable energies, the Government must only take into account those costs and investments directly linked to the activity of electricity production.

The fixed remuneration must not exceed the minimum level required to cover the costs of allowing the renewable installation to compete in the market with other generation technologies, while maintaining a reasonable return by reference to the standard installation, applicable in each case.

The 2013 ESA then goes into further detail and states the following: the reasonable profitability should be, before taxes, around the average yield (ie monetary return) within the last 10 years of the state bonds, to which an appropriate differential (to be determined by government) will be applied. Exceptionally, said remuneration may add an incentive to investment and execution within a given time, whenever the installation involves a significant reduction of costs in the non-peninsular territories (the Canary and Balearic Islands and Ceuta and Melilla in Africa; for these areas specific provisions may still be passed in favour of renewable installations).

By means of Royal Decree No 413 of 6 June 2014, and Ministerial Order No IET/1045 of 16 June 2014, the Spanish Government passed detailed rules developing the general framework for the promotion of renewables of the 2013 ESA. In particular, the remarkable long 2014 Ministerial Order fixes the standard costs of types of installations, and said standards are used by the Government to fix the amount each of the existing installations should get, once the actual costs of the installations are compared with the standard costs of the Ministerial Order.

These norms are a clear example of how the Spanish Government's current electricity policy is mainly directed to reducing supply costs borne by the regulated tariff, so that the paramount electricity deficit can be ended. That means, among other things, eliminating the cost of promoting the use of renewable energies. It seems clear that in the future Spain will be limiting aid to renewable energies to a minimum, it will extract said cost from the calculation of tariffs, and, when necessary, aid will be covered by the state budget.

## VIII.   National and International Legal Disputes Over the Modification of National Support

Constant changes of the regulatory framework for renewable energies and in particular of subsidies created a remarkable conflict atmosphere between investors and the Government. Under the 1998–2010 support framework, huge quantities were invested in photovoltaic plants, as well as in other renewable plants, not only by Spanish companies and individuals, but also by foreign investors. Since changes were included within Royal Decrees passed by the Government, incumbents appealed to the Supreme Court against those governmental norms passed to develop the above referred parliamentary Acts, as well as other new governmental norms related to subsidies for renewable energies. Applicants' main arguments were the retroactive character of the norms which had been prohibited by the Spanish Constitution, that they were violating the legal principle of protecting legitimate expectations, and that, in summary, they were in opposition to the constitutional principle of legal or juridical certainty. It was also argued that the decrease of subsidies was against the legal principle of reasonable remuneration contained in the 2013 ESA.

Around 40 decisions of the Spanish Supreme Court have constantly repeated that there is not a retroactive application of the new scheme (only a *lato sensu* retroactivity). The Supreme Court rejected the applicants' arguments: one of the last Decisions on the issue, which summarises the content of previous ones, is of 18 March 2015.[17] In particular, the Court refutes the retroactive character of the changes, since they are simple regulatory changes for future generation. It denies a violation of the legal provision of reasonable remuneration by the 1997 ESA, and finds no arguments to support the opinion that legitimate expectations are being frustrated, since it concerns a regulated sector, and companies only suffer the consequences of regulatory risks. There is not a violation neither of the legal provision of reasonable remuneration of the 1997 ESA, nor of the core principle of legal certainty. An underlying idea of all those decisions is that the Government's conducting of the issue is bad, leading to poor regulation, but bad regulation is not necessarily an illegal regulation (in the sense of a violation of the Rule of Law).

---

[17] ECLI: ES:TS:2015:965.

In addition, several complaints were submitted against the Kingdom of Spain in international arbitration institutions, since some foreign investors were of the opinion that by reducing subsidies to renewable energies, Spain had not fulfilled its international obligations (both bilateral investment agreements and the Energy Charter Treaty (ECT)). Under the ECT, investors are given the option to submit their disputes several international institutions.

There were two initial decisions issued by the Institute of Arbitration of the Stockholm Chamber of Commerce, favourable to the position of Spain. The first one was issued on 21 January 2016. In *Charanne BV and Construction Investments v Spain*,[18] the Institute of Arbitration of the Stockholm Chamber of Commerce found that the provisions of the ECT on the protection of investment have not been trespassed by Spain. This decision did only analyse the reforms which took place in 2010. Although remuneration has been seriously affected, there was no expropriation. Nor is there violation of the principle of regulatory stability. Applicants did not give evidence of legitimate expectations having been created. There is also no retroactivity.[19] With the Decision taken on *Isolux Infrastructure Netherlands, BV v Spain* of 16 July 2016,[20] the Institute also issued a favourable Decision towards Spain.

By contrast, by means of a third Decision of the Institute of Arbitration of the Stockholm Chamber of Commerce on 15 February 2018 (*Novenergia*[21]), Spain was found guilty of having violated Article 10(1) of the ECT.

A number of Decisions have been issued by the International Centre for the Settlement of Investment Disputes (ICSID), whereby Spain has lost several international arbitration proceedings over cuts to renewable energy subsidies. As opposed to the Stockholm decisions, which dealt with solar PV energy and changes made in 2010 and 2011, the ICSID case deals with thermal-solar and the radical changes of 2013.

The award of 4 May 2017 was in favour of the British company Eiser Infrastructure Limited and its subsidiary, Energia Solar Luxembourg (*Eiser Infrastructure Limited and Energia Solar Luxembourg SÀRL v Kingdom of Spain*). The ICSID considered the Spanish Government's actions to be a violation of Article 10 of the ECT, thus depriving the company of fair and equitable treatment.[22] Other cases already decided against Spain are the following ones: *Masdar Solar & Wind Cooperatief UA v Spain* of 16 July 2018,[23] and *Antin Infrastructure Services Luxembourg Sàrl and*

---

[18] SCC Case no 062/2012.

[19] See A De Luca, 'Lodo favorevole alla Spagna a conclusion del primo degli investiment arbitrations sorti da impianti fotovoltaici: un precedente rilevante?' (2016) *Diritto del Commercio Internazionale* 250; and I del Guayo, 'La Carta Internacional de la Energía en 2015 y las energías renovables. A propósito del Laudo de 21 de enero de 2016' (2016) 47 *Cuadernos de Energía* 50.

[20] SCC Case No 153/2013.

[21] SCC Case No 063/2015.

[22] ICSID Case No ARB/13/36.

[23] ICSID Case No ARB/14/1.

*Antin Energia Termosolar BV v Spain* of 15 June 2018.[24] The Stockholm Chamber of Commerce issued the *Foresight Luxembourg Solar 1 SÁR., et al v Spain* of 14 November 2018.[25] By these decisions, the Kingdom of Spain has been condemned to provide substantial compensation to the relevant companies which had invested in the field of renewable energies. There are dozens of further cases pending at the ICSID. On the one hand, several decisions have been taken against Spain by the ICSID. These are: *NextEra Energy Global Holdings BV and NextEra Energy Spain Holdings BV v Kingdom of Spain* of 31 May 2019;[26] *9Ren Holding SARL v Kingdom of Spian* of 31 May 2019;[27] *Cube Infrastructure Fund SICAV and others v Kingdom of Spain* of 15 July 2019;[28] *SolEs Badajoz GmbH v Kingdom of Spain* of 31 July 2019;[29] *InfraRed Environmental Infrastructure GP Limited and others v Kingdom of Spain* of 2 August 2019;[30] *BayWare Renewable Energy GmbH and BayWare Asset Holding GmbH v Spain* of 2 December 2019;[31] and *RREEF Infrastructure (GP) Limited and RREEF Pan-European Infrastructure Two Lux Sàrl v Kingdom of Spain ICSID* of 11 December 2019.[32] In one case, however, the ICSID has rejected the claimants' claims: *Stadtwerke München GmbH and others v Kingdom of Spain* of 2 December 2019.[33]

On 22 November 2019, the Spanish Government passed Royal Decree law no 17/2019.[34] Royal Decree laws have the rank of a Parliamentary Act, are adopted by the Government in cases of urgency and must be validated by Parliament afterwards. Among other provisions, Royal Decree law 17/2019 offers a deal to foreign companies, which have submitted a case against in Spain at international arbitration tribunals, based on the changes the Spanish Government has introduced into the support schemes in favour of renewable energies. The Royal Decree law guarantees to investors a stable remuneration of the investment made in renewable installations in Spain, whenever they desist of the arbitration proceedings. This was done in view of the continuous awards in favour of investors at international arbitration institutions, such as ICSID. The objective is to facilitate a non-contentious settlement of the disputes between Spain and foreign investors related to the lowering between 2007 and 2012 of the subsidies to support renewable energies. It is expected that an increasing number of companies, wishing to continue business in Spain, accept the Governmental offer. However, it is to be seen whether the Government succeeds in this endeavour.

---

[24] ICSID Case No ARB/13/31.
[25] SCC Case No 2015/150.
[26] ICSID Case No ARB/14/11.
[27] ICSID Case No ARB/15/15.
[28] ICSID Case No ARB/15/20.
[29] ICSID Case No ARB/15/38.
[30] ICSID Case No ARB/14/12.
[31] ICSID Case No ARB/15/16.
[32] ICSID Case No ARB/13/30.
[33] ICSID Case No ARB/15/1.
[34] Spanish Official Bulletin no 282, of 23 November 2019.

# IX.  Towards a Support Scheme Compatible with a Competitive Market Economy in a European Union Context

The case of renewable energies in the EU illustrates the interaction between technology and legal innovation. Actually, the content of the 2018 EU Renewables Directive[35] is rooted in the decrease of technological costs due to innovation. The decarbonisation of the energy systems opens to renewable energies the key role in the future energy mix. In the past 15 years the EU has become a worldwide leader in the field of renewable energies. Germany, Denmark and Spain have had remarkable importance in this trend. From the beginning, EU law on renewable energies assumed that the only way to promote the use of renewable energies was some kind of governmental support. This could have the form of feed-in-tariffs and/or premiums, which, in turn, were often recovered from prices paid by electricity customers. This created an atmosphere in which the promotion of renewable was nothing but an exemption (a huge one) of free market. Although these subsidies were similar to subsidies for more traditional energy sources and they might have been needed early in the development of renewables, the assumption that subsidies are necessary is no longer valid. On the contrary, it is clear now that support schemes or renewables must be aligned with competition among energy producers and suppliers.

When the process to create an internal market for electricity started in the EU, little consideration was made to renewable energies within EU law. They gained momentum when the first renewable energies Directive was passed in 2001[36] and reached its climax with the 2009 RES Directive.[37] This Directive became a good instrument to foster at EU level the use of renewable energies for electricity generation purposes. It addressed the problems this kind of energy was experiencing at that time. After some years of application, it became clear that several changes were needed in the text of the 2009 Directive. This explains why the European Commission drafted a new Directive, as a key component of the so-called 2016 Winter Package.

Several of the changes of the 2018 RES Directive are related to support schemes, either to guarantee that they are stable, or to impose upon Member States the obligation to choose a scheme that is compatible with a competitive

---

[35] Directive (EU) 2018/2001 of the European Parliament and of the Council of 11 December 2018 on the promotion of the use of energy from renewable sources, OJ L 328/82.

[36] Directive (EU) 2018/2001 of the European Parliament and of the Council of 11 December 2018 on the promotion of the use of energy from renewable sources, OJ L 382/82.

[37] Directive 2009/28/EC of the European Parliament and of the Council of 23 April 2009 on the promotion of the use of energy from renewable sources and amending and subsequently repealing Directives 2001/77/EC and 2003/30/EC, OJ L 140/16.

market economy. The rapid decrease of costs associated with renewable installations and the maturity of technology (solar and wind, mainly) operate towards the suppression of any governmental subsidy that gives renewable energies a privileged position. Amidst the governmental rhetoric of some governments that back the 2015 Paris Agreement but increase the use of, for example, national coal, some sort of support schemes in favour of renewable energies is not only acceptable but also desirable. The 2018 RES Directive tackles this problem with an express call to support schemes compatible with market-based law (Article 4). It also contains a new and explicit reference to the need for stable support frameworks whose change is subject to foreseeable procedures (Article 6). The directive indicates that legal innovation must continue to track technology innovation including changes in cost of technology, as well as market conditions that may allow innovations in the way government support schemes relate to the market.[38]

## X.   Conclusion: Conflicting Outcomes in Spanish Courts and International Arbitration Institutions

The Spanish Supreme Court has issued dozens of decisions by which it denies that the Spanish Government has violated the Rule of Law by lowering the support which electricity producers by means of renewable energies are to be paid. There is neither a violation of the principle of protection of legitimate expectations, nor a retroactive application of the lowered remuneration. The Court examines whether the lowering of the subsidies has violated the Electricity Act, which states that remuneration must comply with principle of 'sensible remuneration'. It finds that even though remuneration has been lowered it is still sensible. Some decisions of the Institute of Arbitration of the Stockholm Chamber of Commerce are of the same opinion. In the light of the ECT they also find that an expropriation has not taken place and that the protection of investment has not been violated. Those decisions of the Institute state that there are no reasons to think that the decisions of the Spanish Supreme Court are wrong, thus showing its willingness not to revoke what has been decided at national level.

Prior to liberalisation private companies operating a public service had the financial guarantee of the public contract signed with the relevant public administration, for the provision of a public service. That had a twofold meaning: on the other hand, if the responsible public power decided to change the conditions under which the contract is to be executed, then the private company had the right to be compensated, whenever said change had a negative impact on

---

[38] The content of this section is an update of my chapter, 'Support for Renewable Energies and the Creation of a Truly Competitive Electricity Market: The Case of the European Union' in D Zillman, L Godden, L Paddock, and M Roggenkamp, *Innovation in Energy Law and Technology: Dynamic Solutions for Energy Transitions* (Oxford University Press, 2018) 305.

the financial situation of the company; on the other hand, although the private company had to provide the service and at its own risk, there were certain extraordinary circumstances under which the public administration would also help with financial aid to the private contract; in ordinary contract law, those negative circumstances would have to be borne by the private company, too. After liberalisation, a number of services which were considered to be public service, enjoy no longer that character. The main consequence is that companies which operate in the relevant liberalised sector do not operate under a contractual formula. The former guarantee based on a contract between the private company and the public administration has been substituted by a guarantee contained in the liberalising act. Under this liberalised regime, private companies do not have the right to be compensated whenever the public administration changes the contract, since there is no contract in place. Compensation, if any, will be subject to the general conditions under which companies are to be compensated as a consequence of the change of existing regulation. In other words, the former *contractual risk* has been substituted by a *regulatory risk*. The problem lies in that the options to be compensated as a consequence of changes of regulation are much more limited than the options to be compensated as a consequence of a change of the contract.

Considering the radical changes introduced between 2010 and 2013 in the remuneration of renewable producers, there is the need to find a further explanation of the position of the Spanish Supreme Court. The series of decisions of the Court must be understood against the backdrop of the so called 'electricity tariff deficit'. The Spanish electricity system was close to collapse and the Government justified the lowering of the remuneration by the need to reduce or to put an end to the deficit. In is in this context that the decisions of the Court must be understood. Although it is not expressed with these exact words, the decisions are based on the following idea: in ordinary circumstances the Court would be ready to accept the arguments of the applicants and consequently to impose upon the Government the need to compensate them or even to bring things to where they were before the legal changes. However, taking into account the extraordinary circumstances of the electricity deficit, the Court is bound to accept that the Governmental decision to lower remuneration to renewable producers is not illegal. It is true that when there is a crisis (such as the crisis of the Spanish electricity system due to the deficit) then the ordinary law cannot be applied. There are some doubts as to whether this is the optimal way for courts to approach the problem. It is clear that Courts are not asked to evaluate governmental energy policies, but the decision to tackle the electricity deficit in a way which excludes any compensation should be in the hand of Parliaments. In any case, the situation created by the decisions of the Supreme Court on this issue should not be used as a pattern for future disputes in other areas, since they were issued in extraordinary circumstances.

The jurisprudence issued by the Spanish Supreme Court about the conflict on support to renewable energies brings into the debate an old challenge. There is the need for a better design of the relationship between the competences of the Regulator (in wide terms, including both the Government and the sectorial agency) and the Courts. The better the regulatory framework is designed, the less the judiciary will be asked to decide. It is obvious that it is for courts to have the final word about the respect to the Rule of Law, and that regulatory decisions must be subject to the scrutiny of Courts. It is also clear that in most cases, the problems about which the Spanish Supreme Court was asked to decide, involved a great deal of energy policy. If the regulatory procedures were well designed (which means that they create among incumbents a sense of confidence on the rationality and fairness of the regulatory decision), then the Supreme Court would not be asked to take a position on matters which do not belong to the realm of legality, but rather to the realm of energy policy and the discretion in the exercise of regulatory powers.

The decisions of the Spanish Supreme Court are in clear contrast with decisions of international arbitration institutions, in particular the ICSID. For the Spanish Supreme Court there is nothing illegal in the lowering of subsidies, and companies do not have the right to be compensated. They must bear the regulatory risk. On the contrary, the ISCD thinks that Article 10 of the ECT, under which each contracting party shall, in accordance with the provisions of this Treaty, encourage and create stable, equitable, favourable and transparent conditions for investors of other contracting parties to make investments in its area. Such conditions shall include a commitment to accord at all times to investments of investors of other contracting parties fair and equitable treatment. Since investors from third countries can submit their claims under the ECT to international arbitration institutions, but Spanish investors cannot, a clear discriminatory situation has emerged. This has been partially solved by the judgment of the European Court of Justice in *Achmea*.[39]

The need of a stable framework is of paramount relevance for the future of renewable energies in the EU. It surpasses the interest of Member States insofar the violation of the principles of stability and predictability of regulation endangers the accomplishment of the EU in the field of renewable energies. Consequently, stability of national support has an EU dimension. That is why Article 6(1) of the revised 2018 Renewable Directive states that without prejudice to adaptations necessary to comply with state aid rules, Member States shall ensure that the level of, and the conditions attached to, the support granted to renewable energy projects are not revised in a way that negatively impacts the rights conferred thereunder and the economics of supported projects.

---

[39] Judgment of 6 March 2018, Case C-284/16, EU:C:2018:158. See further DC Suciu, 'Renewable Energy Arbitration against Spain in the light of Court of Justice of the European Union Judgment in Achmea case' (2019) 37 *Revista Electrónica de Estudios Internacionales* 1.

# 13

## How should Shale
## Gas Extraction be Taxed?

PHILIP DANIEL, ALAN KRUPNICK, THORNTON MATHESON,
PETER MULLINS, IAN PARRY AND ARTUR SWISTAK*****

## I. Abstract

This chapter suggests that the environmental and commercial features of shale
gas extraction do not warrant a significantly different fiscal regime than recom-
mended for conventional gas. Fiscal policies may have a role in addressing some
environmental risks (eg greenhouse gases, scarce water, local air pollution) though
in some cases their net benefits may be modest. Simulation analyses suggest, moreover, that special fiscal regimes are generally less important than other factors in
determining shale gas investments (hence there appears little need for them), yet
they forego significant revenues.

## II. Introduction

The boom in 'unconventional' natural gas (shale gas extracted by fracking
processes) in the US has encouraged numerous countries to begin developing
their own reserves, though the contentiousness of fracking, including perceived
environmental risks in densely populated or protected areas, has led some others
to consider banning, or already ban, the activity.

An emerging literature discusses the transformational impacts of shale gas
on energy markets (causing, for example, reduced gas imports and displacement

***** © International Monetary Fund. Reprinted with permission. This chapter is based on IMF
Working Paper 17/254. The views expressed in this chapter belong solely to the authors. Nothing
contained in this chapter should be reported as representing IMF policy or the views of the IMF, its
Executive Board, member governments, or any other entity mentioned herein.

of coal generation in the US), and the associated environmental risks.[1] Little attention has been paid, however, to whether it also poses distinct new challenges for tax policy. Much thought has been given to this in context of conventional energy sources, both oil and gas and mining[2] – the question addressed here is whether different advice is needed for unconventional sources, taking the example of shale gas.

Specifically, this chapter attempts to answer two important questions:

- Do the environmental issues associated with shale gas extraction warrant corrective taxes in fiscal regimes for the upstream production activity, or are they better addressed through other instruments?

- Do the commercial and technical features of shale gas development suggest that the principles of fiscal regime design for conventional oil and gas development need to be modified?

As regards the first issue, the paper suggests that many of the upstream environmental risks (eg water contamination) are generally best dealt with through regulation, though ex post liability for individual firms (and possibly, for large risks, compensation from industry-level funds collected through production fees), can play an important role. Moreover, novel tax schemes for leakages of methane emissions – a highly potent greenhouse gas (GHG) – are feasible despite limited metering capabilities, while levying charges for the downstream carbon dioxide ($CO_2$) emissions from gas combustion on fuel supply is appealing on administrative grounds (either at the point of fuel extraction, processing, or distribution). At the same time, research on the nature and magnitude of environmental risks from shale gas is needed to guide policy design.

As regards the second issue, simulations of how existing fiscal regimes in different (US and non-US) jurisdictions suggest that special fiscal regimes and incentives granted for shale gas development have, at best, only slight effects on investment, despite resulting in significant foregone government revenues. For the most part, there is little evident need to consider specific incentives for shale gas development, compared with conventional gas, provided that the overall fiscal regime responds substantially to realised profit or rent.

---

[1] See, for example, C Hausman, R Kellogg, 'Welfare and Distributional Implications of Shale Gas', Working Paper 21,115, National Bureau of Economic Research, Cambridge MA (2015) for an introduction to the literature. Impacts on energy markets are discussed in P Brehm, 'Natural Gas Prices, Electric Generation Investment, and Greenhouse Gas Emissions', Working Paper, University of Michigan (2015). Technological aspects of fracking are discussed in T Fitzgerald, 'Frackonomics: Some Economics of Hydraulic Fracturing' (2013) 63 *Case Western Reserve Law Review* 1337. Literature on environmental impacts is discussed below.

[2] For example, P Daniel, C McPherson and M Keen, 'The Taxation of Petroleum and Minerals: Principles, Problems and Practice' (International Monetary Fund, 2010).

The rest of the chapter is organised as follows. Section III provides a quick over-view of shale gas development. Section IV discusses the environmental risks from shale gas and the potential roles for fiscal versus other mitigation instruments. Section V presents simulation results comparing fiscal regimes for conventional and unconventional gas in jurisdictions across North America and other coun-tries. The last section offers concluding remarks.

# III. Brief Overview of Shale Gas Industry

Shale gas exploitation targets gas deposits trapped in horizontal layers of organic-rich shale rock; by contrast, conventional gas reservoirs are formed by pockets of gas trapped in highly permeable reservoir rock by an overlying layer of imper-meable rock. Extraction of shale gas is thus more challenging and requires the application of three technologies: hydraulic fracturing (injection of pressurised water and chemicals to enhance gas recovery); seismic imaging (to understand the geology and where the pay zones are best); and horizontal drilling. These tech-nologies (invented for conventional gas and petroleum drilling) are generally used more intensively in shale exploitation, where the decline in well productivity is more rapid and a greater number of wells must be drilled to extract a given amount of gas. The capital intensity and operating costs of shale gas exploitation is thus generally higher than for conventional land-based drilling, as is water consump-tion and chemical use.

Large-scale shale gas production commenced in the US around 2000 with the development of the Texas Barnett shale deposit, or 'play'. Since then, production has ramped up from 300 billion of cubic feet (Bcf) to 18,5003 Bcf by 2017, total-ing about 40 per cent of US natural gas production, while proven reserves stand at 308,000 Bcf (Figure 13.1), or over a third of total US gas reserves.[3]

Canada (with production of 765 Bcf in 2013) is the only other country that has invested substantially in shale gas production. However, numerous countries (eg Argentina, Australia, China, Mexico, Poland) are exploring shale production, and technically recoverable reserves totaling roughly 7.3 million Bcf have been identified across the globe (Figure 13.2), equal to about one-third of total world gas resources.

---

[3] Hausman and Kellogg (n 1) estimate that US shale gas production increased economic welfare (leaving aside environmental impacts) by USD 48 billion per year between 2007 and 2013.

Besides reserve quantity and accessibility, the viability of shale gas in other countries depends on several factors, which all happened to be favourable in the US, including:

**Figure 13.1** Growth of the US shale gas industry

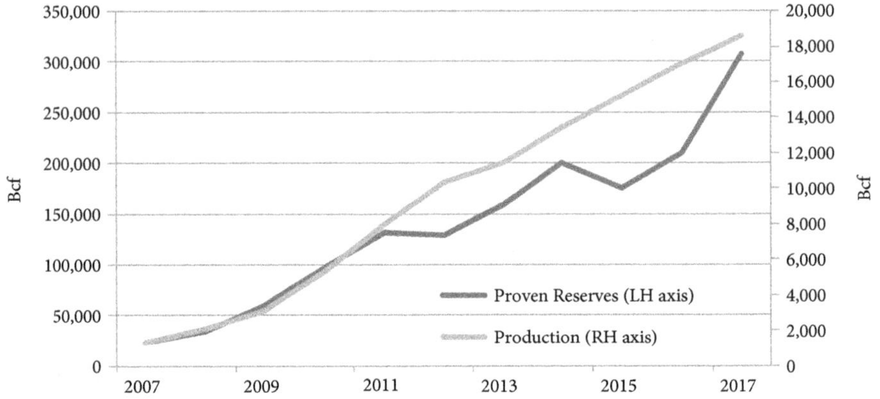

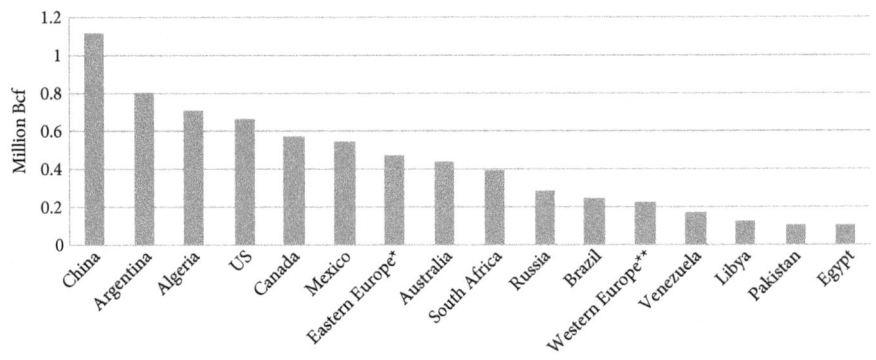

*Source*: www.eia.gov/dnav/ng/ng_enr_shalegas_dcu_NUS_a.htm.

**Figure 13.2** Top 10 countries' technically recoverable shale gas resources (2013)

*Source*: www.eia.gov/analysis/studies/worldshalegas.

*Notes*: *Bulgaria, Lithuania, Poland, Romania, and Ukraine. **Denmark, France, Germany, Netherlands, Norway, Spain, Sweden and UK.

- private ownership of subsurface mineral rights (in other countries these rights are state-owned or may be ill defined, creating legal challenges to rapid development);
- an abundance of independent gas companies with the requisite technical knowledge or the incentive to develop it;
- pre-existing gas pipeline infrastructure and capacity;
- fairly abundant water resources;

- low population density (and hence public opposition);
- deep capital markets; and
- (not least) high natural gas prices in the early 2000s.

To varying degrees, these factors tend to be less favourable in other countries and the price remains a wildcard, though for the foreseeable future prices seem unlikely to return to their previous peaks (see Box 13.1 below). In many cases, however, the unquantified nature of many of the risks has led authorities in some jurisdictions to ban fracking altogether – these restrictions apply, for example, at a national level in Bulgaria, France, Germany, South Africa and the UK, and at a subnational level in Australia, Ireland, Italy, Spain, Switzerland and the US (including New York, Vermont and cities and counties in California, Colorado, Texas and Ohio). These restrictions are a judgement not questioned in this chapter, nor are they a matter for fiscal policy (except to the extent any revenue loss can be estimated).

# IV. Environmental Risks and Policy Responses

## A. Risks

Differences in environmental impacts between conventional and shale gas are briefly introduced, followed by a closer look at the individual risks.[4]

### i. Differences with Conventional Gas

From an environmental perspective, there are many differences between a conventional (onshore) natural gas well drilled into reservoir rock and one drilled into shale rock, involving different pad footprint, water use, chemical use and pressure below ground.

Development of unconventional gas permits multiple wells on a single well pad. This could lead to a lower footprint per unit of gas extracted compared with conventional drilling (though many geological features would influence this comparison). However, the primary recipe for unconventional gas shale fracking involves the application of a mixture of water, sand and a variety of chemicals at high pressure – conventional drilling uses far less water and additives.

The greater concentration of wells on a pad, and the high pressures used for fracking, might create greater risks of groundwater contamination from casing and cementing failures and the return of some of the fracking fluid up the well

---

[4] For other overviews of environmental risks see Hausman and Kellogg (n 1); R Jackson, A Vengosh, JW Carey, RJ Davies, T Darrah, F O'Sullivan and G Petron, 'The Environmental Costs and Benefits of Fracking' (2014) 39 *Annual Review of Environment and Resources* 327.

creates additional concerns for liquid wastes handling, treatment and disposal. Pumping liquid wastes into deep disposal wells might also give rise to risks of seismic activity. And generating the high pressures required by the fracturing operation itself requires powerful diesel engines, which contribute to local air pollution. Furthermore, the much higher water demands also imply more infrastructure (pipelines, roads, water storage facilities) and greater potential for habitat disruption, community impacts, roadway wear and tear, and (due to both water withdrawals and spills) damages to land and waterways.

There appear to be no environmental risks posed by conventional gas-only wells that are not also posed by shale gas wells.

---

**Box 13.1 Trends in natural gas prices**

Gas prices have fallen from their peak of over USD 12 per thousand cubic feet (Mcf) in 2005 to current levels of around USD 2–3 per Mcf, which may be about as low as they will go (pre-2000 prices were around USD 2.50 per Mcf). Lower prices deter drilling of marginal wells, though the effect on (conventional and unconventional) gas and oil production is being offset (Figure 13.3) by cost-cutting and productivity gains. Future demand growth could come from many sectors and raise prices, though supply curve elasticities are uncertain (Hausman and Kellogg (n 1) [...] put them at between about 0.4 and 1.6).

Although natural gas prices have loosely followed oil prices in the past, as in the 2002–2008 upswing (Figure 13.3), prices are becoming increasingly decoupled (whereas oil prices are globally integrated, natural gas prices vary significantly across regional markets due to limited transportability). For example, after the sharp fall in energy prices at the onset of the Great Recession, oil prices quickly recouped much of their losses, whereas gas prices lingered well below their earlier peaks, and oil prices declined far more sharply than gas prices at the end of 2014.

US oil and gas prices are not strongly linked on the demand side, as the energy sources are not close substitutes – gas is used primarily for electricity generation and household fuel, while oil products are used primarily in transportation. However, there is some substitution on the production side: when gas prices collapsed in 2008 many US drillers switched production to oil, though the relatively steep slide in oil prices, if sustained, could reverse some of this effect. On the other hand, the price of liquids produced in gas extraction is tied to oil prices, so the latter's fall could lower the return on gas production from some wells.

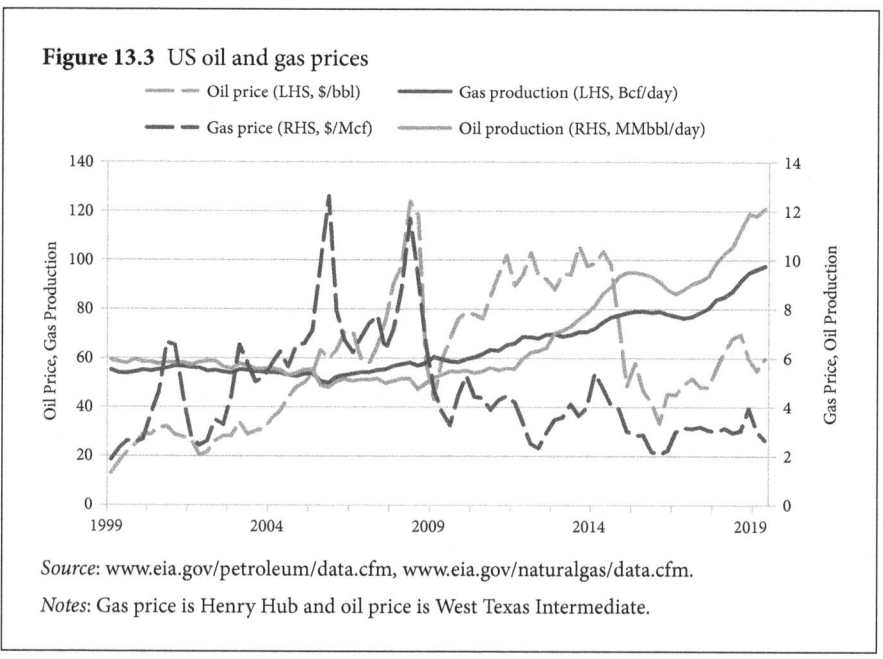

**Figure 13.3** US oil and gas prices

Oil price (LHS, $/bbl)     Gas production (LHS, Bcf/day)

Gas price (RHS, $/Mcf)     Oil production (RHS, MMbbl/day)

*Source*: www.eia.gov/petroleum/data.cfm, www.eia.gov/naturalgas/data.cfm.

*Notes*: Gas price is Henry Hub and oil price is West Texas Intermediate.

## ii. Water Quantity

Shale gas development requires large quantities of water[5] depending, for example, on maturity of the shale and formation thickness, and technologies used (eg horizontal versus vertical wells, and whether water is recycled). Per unit of energy content, shale gas uses a lot more water than conventional gas, similar amounts to coal (where water is used for coal cutting and dust suppression), and far less than enhanced oil recovery. And water consumption for shale gas is highly concentrated at a point in time (occurring over several days during fracking of the well), rather than spread out over the working life of the well. The opportunity costs of water use depend on usage *relative* to local water availability. For the US, for example, areas of high shale gas activity sometimes overlap areas of high water stress, depending on seasonality and whether withdrawals are from small or large water bodies. Although, for regions with chronic water scarcity, shale gas development presents obvious challenges to aquatic life and even water users, water demands for energy extraction are generally trivial compared with other demands, such as agriculture.

---

[5] Around 3–5 million gallons for development of a well, E Mielke, L Diaz Anadon and V Narayanamurti, 'Water Consumption of Energy Resource Extraction, Processing and Conversion', Discussion Paper 2010–15, Energy Technology Innovation Policy Discussion Paper Series (Belfer Center, Harvard University, 2010).

## iii. Water Quality

Liquid and solid wastes from the toxic fluids used in fracking or naturally occurring chemicals released by fracking can affect surface and groundwater quality.[6] The liquid wastes can contain fracking fluids and highly salted water, radioactive materials, heavy metals and volatile organics from the formation itself, called 'produced water'. Surface water quality can be affected by run-off, spills, and, when liquid wastes are treated and released, from waste stream discharges of treatment plants, though impacts are highly site-specific, depending on environmental conditions and the care taken to treat and dispose of liquid wastes. Groundwater quality can be affected through leakages due to faulty casing and cementing around the well bore, though this is a standard problem in oil and gas drilling. More contentious is whether fracking itself can pollute groundwater by methane or substances in produced and flowback water – evidence on this is mixed. Site-specific information on surface and ground water risks is needed, not least because public concerns over these risks have been a major impediment to shale gas development – current data gaps and uncertainties prevent a broad assessment of how often fracking harms water quality and how serious the effects are.

## iv. Climate Change

Downstream combustion of (conventional and unconventional) natural gas is responsible for 27 per cent of US fossil fuel $CO_2$ emissions[7] and these emissions should be priced at some point in the fossil fuel supply chain (see below). Shale gas development itself impacts climate change through two main mechanisms.

First is through altering downstream $CO_2$ emissions from fossil fuel combustion. Per unit of energy, combustion of natural gas (whether from shale or conventional) produces about 40 per cent less $CO_2$ emissions than coal,[8] so to the extent gas displaces coal it reduces $CO_2$, but the opposite applies to the extent it displaces (zero-carbon) nuclear and renewables – Newell and Raimi[9] and Brown et al[10] find the net effect (for the US) is a modest $CO_2$ reduction.

Second, however, leakage or venting of natural gas itself – mostly methane, which is about 25 times more potent in trapping heat than $CO_2$,[11] – can occur through the entire natural gas lifecycle (eg through faulty valves), including

---

[6] GA Burton, KJ Nadelhoer and K Presley, 'Environment/Ecology Technical Report', Graham Sustainability Institute Integrated Assessment Report Series (2013) 2.

[7] US Environmental Protection Agency, 'Inventory of U.S. Greenhouse Gas Emissions and Sinks 1990–2014' (2016) Table 3.5.

[8] 'Earthquake Swarm Continues in Central Oklahoma', available at: www.usgs.gov/newsroom/article.asp?ID=3710&from=rss#.UmluMhD6O9U.

[9] RG Newell and D Raimi, 'Implications of Shale Gas Development for Climate Change' (2014) 48 *Environmental Science and Technology* 13,036.

[10] S Brown, AJ Krupnick and MA Walls, 'Natural Gas: A Bridge to a Low-Carbon Future?', Policy Brief, (Resources for the Future, 2009).

[11] US EPA, Table ES 1.

drilling, production, processing, distribution and storage. These fugitive emissions have become a major concern and object of considerable research, though leakage rates are uncertain (a typical estimate is around 1.5 to 3.5 per cent) and vary across firms (eg due to technologies used) and sites.[12] Most recent literature[13] suggests that lifecycle GHGs are still significantly lower for natural gas –than for coal. Shale gas development therefore makes more sense from a climate change perspective if it can displace coal[14] and if the fugitive methane can, at least in part, be addressed. Federal, state and even voluntary industry initiatives in the US are all attempting to do just that.[15]

## v. Local Air Pollution

Combustion of diesel in engines used to pump fracking fluids and leaks of volatile organic compounds from storage and gas processing facilities contribute to local air pollution. A voluminous literature documents an association between ambient air pollution and mortality risks (eg from heart and lung diseases).[16] Although these health damages have not been quantified in the context of shale extraction, some ballpark sense might be inferred from damage estimates for diesel used in road vehicles shown (for selected shale-endowed countries) in Figure 13.4. For illustration, if the average population exposure per ton of emissions released in shale extraction (typically occurring in rural areas) is one-tenth of that for emissions from the average road vehicle, and (due to similar regulations) emission rates are comparable, pollution damages for the US might be around 3 cents per litre (12 cents per gallon) – a significant, though not dramatic cost.

Downstream combustion of natural gas also causes local air pollution, though the damages are typically modest relative to global warming damages because, unlike for coal, natural gas combustion does not produce direct fine particulate or sulfur dioxide emissions, and nitrogen oxide emission rates are smaller than those for coal.

---

[12] See, for example, AR Brandt, GA Heath, EA Kort, F O'Sullivan, G Petron, S Jordaan, P Tans, J Wilcox, AM Gopstein, D Arent, S Wofsy, NJ Brown, R Bradley, GD Stucky, D Eardley and R Harriss, 'Methane Leaks from North American Natural Gas Systems' (2014) 343 *Science* 733.

[13] DT Allen, VM Torres, J Thomas, DW Sullivan, M Harrison, A Hendler, SC Herndon, CE Kolb, MP Fraser, AD Hill, BK Lamb, J Miskimins, RF Sawyer, JH Seinfeld, 'Measurements of methane emissions at natural gas production sites in the United States' (2013) 110 *Proceedings of the National Academy of Sciences* 768.

[14] And (from a global perspective) the displaced coal is not exported elsewhere, though Newell and Raimi (n 9) suggest this effect is small.

[15] Under the 2016 'Three Amigos Agreement' the US, Canada, and Mexico agreed to cut methane emissions by 45% by 2025, though the current US Administration is halting work on methane regulations. US methane emissions from all sources were estimated at 731 million tons in $CO_2$ equivalent in 2014 (12% of total greenhouse gases) with about a quarter of the emissions coming from (conventional and unconventional) gas systems (US EPA, Table ES2). US Environmental Protection Agency, 2016, *Inventory of US Greenhouse Gas Emissions and Sinks 1990-2014*, Washington, DC.

[16] For example, WHO, 'Public Health, Environmental and Social Determinants of Health' (2014), available at: www.who.int/phe/health_topics/outdoorair/databases/en. Air pollution causes other damages (eg morbidity, impaired visibility, crop damage, building corrosion) but, even combined, these effects tend to be modest relative to mortality effects.

## vi. Ecological and Seismic Risks

Land conversions for shale gas infrastructure (wells, roads, pipelines, rights of way) potentially disrupt ecosystems (eg deer habitat), particularly in areas of high well density, though there has been little documentation of these effects.[17] Seismic impacts have also received media attention and have caused the shutdown of several deep-injection disposal wells in Arkansas and Ohio. The quake magnitudes from fracturing per se are small-to-trivial, though waste water disposal is nonetheless a contributing factor to earthquake risk – more evidence is needed on the probabilities of added wastes causing seismic events of different severities.[18] In short, the suitability of areas with endangered and highly valued (eg for recreational purposes) habitat, and where significant numbers of people are exposed to pre-existing seismic risks and lacking in viable means to dispose of liquid wastes, are probably not good candidates for shale gas development.

**Figure 13.4**  Estimated air pollution damages from on-road diesel vehicles (for year 2010 in USD)

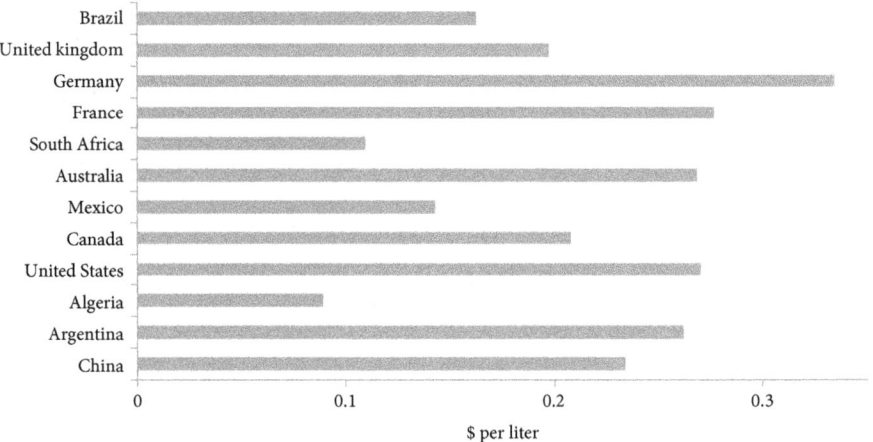

*Source*: Parry, D Heine, S Li, and E Lis, Getting Energy Prices Right: From Principle to Practice *(Washington, DC International Monetary Fund, 2014).*

*Note*: These figures represent an average (across urban and rural areas) of damages from diesel combustion in on-road vehicles (cars, trucks, buses) accounting for existing emissions controls. The comparable damages for emissions from diesel engines used in shale gas extraction are likely a lot lower, at least if emissions regulations are similar and field operations are located away from urban population centres.

---

[17] See, for example, C Mason, L Muehlenbachs and S Olmstead, 'The Economics of Shale Gas Development' (2015) *Annual Review of Resource Economics* 7.
[18] See, for example, US Environmental Protection Agency 2014 *Minimizing and Managing Potential Impacts of Injection-Induced Seismicity from Class II Disposal Wells: Practical Approaches.*

## vii. Community and Broader Impacts

Although local communities benefit economically from shale gas development, most likely they also bear the brunt of the environmental, health and broader impacts like noise, visual degradation, traffic congestion and accidents,[19] property value changes[20] and overloaded schools (though the latter impacts may arise with any industrial development). More general impacts include damages to agricultural productivity (eg from increased water scarcity or pollution), tourism (eg from habitat destruction), other industries (eg breweries) needing high-quality water inputs, and recreational activities (eg from habitat reduction, loss of hunted populations, loss of forested area available for hiking).

While these impacts are important in evaluating whether a given area is ripe for development, for policy there is a subtle distinction between 'direct' environmental impacts (which require corrective policies) and 'indirect' or 'pecuniary' effects (which should not). The former (eg health effects on exposed populations) are a cost on society, while the latter (eg reductions in housing values and hotel profits as residents and tourists relocate away from a despoiled region), largely reflect transfers among regions, firms or individuals, that approximately wash out in the aggregate. Pecuniary effects may, however, warrant compensation on equity (rather than efficiency) grounds.

## B. The Role of Fiscal Policy

This subsection discusses the possible use of fiscal policies to reduce the overall level of development, water use, air pollution and GHGs.

### i. Controlling Development

Suppose the primary policy objective is to prevent shale gas development in regions with especially large environmental risks. Consider Figure 13.5, where the market price for natural gas is fixed at $p^c$ and unit supply costs and environmental costs rise as reserves in progressively fragile areas are exploited. When environmental risks are ignored production is at the competitive level $X^c$. The efficient production level, however, is $X^*$, where supply and environmental costs equal $p^c$ and which

---

[19] For example, L Muelenbachs and A Krupnick, 'Shale gas development linked to traffic accidents in Pennsylvania' (Common Resources, 2013), available at: http://common-resources.org/2013/shale-gas-development-linked-totrafficaccidents-in-pennsylvania; the authors estimate that extra truck traffic results in nine extra road fatalities, and 12 extra (serious but non-fatal) injuries in Pennsylvania counties with shale gas development.

[20] These can be significant: for example, Muelenbachs and Krupnick (ibid) find that values for ground-water dependent properties fall by 16% as they become closer to shale wells, while values for properties with piped water access rise by 10%.

could be induced by a unit production tax of $t^x$, resulting in an economic welfare gain (savings in supply/environmental costs less forgone consumer benefits) shown by the shaded triangle. However, when there is uncertainty over the tax rate needed for adequate protection, a ban in fragile areas preventing production beyond $X^*$ may be more efficient. A ban alone leaves rents (the shaded rectangle in Figure 13.5) in the hands of producers and these rents could be captured through combining the ban with a production tax, though rent taxation could be integrated in the broader fiscal regime.

**Figure 13.5** Impacts of policies limiting shale gas production

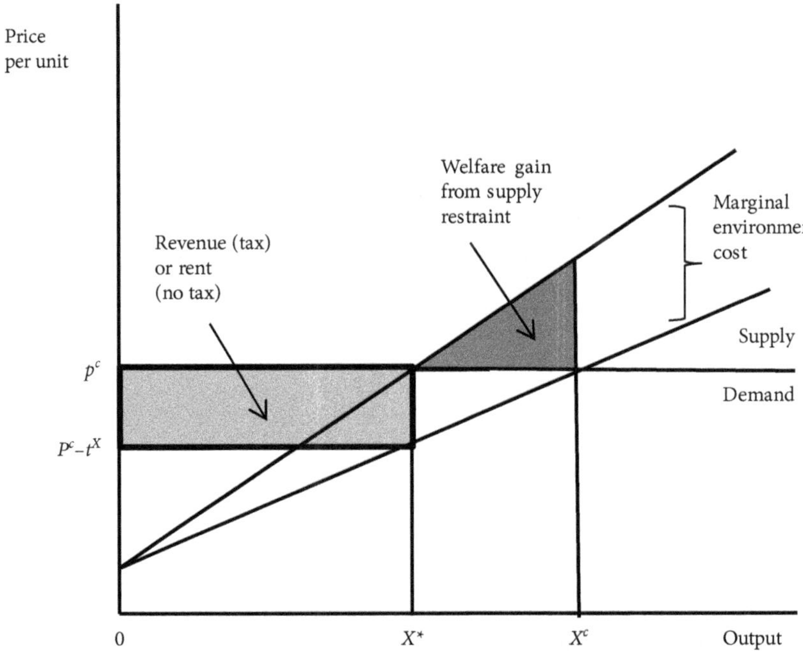

## ii. Pricing Water Use

Water (eg from rivers, lakes) for shale gas development is often controlled by regulation, but (even leaving aside fiscal benefits) a usage tax is potentially more efficient as it reflects (through tax payments) the opportunity cost of the water in firms' input costs, thereby promoting efficiency in the mix of developers' inputs and the extent of site development.

Prices would need to be set carefully depending, for example, on whether there is water stress. Consider Figure 13.6, where the local water supply curve is flat initially, but eventually becomes upward sloping and vertical as supply becomes exhausted. If total regional demand intersects the horizontal portion of the supply curve, then the efficient price is the unit supply cost $p^1$ and the economic welfare cost from failing to charge shale producers for water use would be the small shaded triangle (costs to water suppliers less benefits to shale gas producers from extra consumption $X^0 - X^1$). However, if the regional demand curve instead intersects the upward sloping or vertical part of the supply curve the efficient price is higher at $p^2$, reflecting the high opportunity cost from alternative water uses. Failing to charge shale producers for water use now results in much larger extra welfare costs shown by the sum of the shaded areas (associated with excess consumption of $X^0 - X^2$).

**Figure 13.6** Economic costs of mispricing water supply

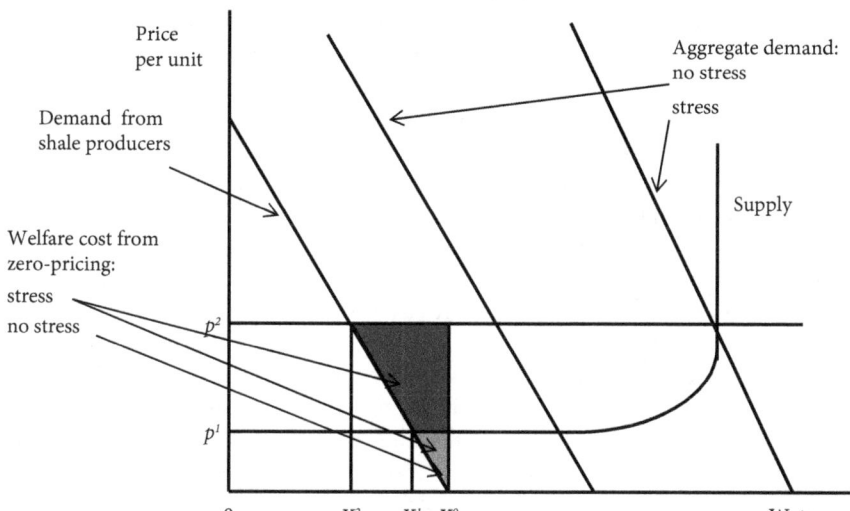

Again, however, the practical relevance of this argument is questionable given the typically small share of water resources used by shale gas developers.

## iii. Pricing Air Pollution

Fiscal instruments might have a role, alongside regulations, in mitigating air pollution emissions. Ideally emissions from diesel engines would be taxed directly, thereby promoting use of emissions control technologies or cleaner diesel that reduce emissions per unit of diesel use, as well as reductions in diesel use (through more fuel-efficient engines and use of other fuels). Taxing diesel rather than emissions may be the more practical option, but does not promote the first set of responses. The best practical approach may be to combine a fuel tax with an emission rate standard, thereby approximately mimicking the effect of the emissions tax. To the extent that emission rates from diesel engines are tightly controlled through existing regulation, shale gas development is located away from urban centers, and engines are already relatively fuel efficient, the environmental gains from higher fuel taxes may, however, be limited.

Taxes for downstream local air pollution could also be imposed on gas supply at the point of extraction or processing/distribution (with rebates for any downstream users adopting mitigation technologies) which could make sense, in principle, where taxing at the point of combustion is impractical from an administrative perspective. The net benefits of these taxes, however, may be limited because of the relatively small size of air pollution damages.

### iv.  *Taxing GHGs*

From an administrative perspective, charges for $CO_2$ emissions are generally best levied on fuel supply (in proportion to carbon content) as this covers all sources of emissions and minimises administrative burdens. In contrast, levying charges downstream at the point of combustion on large industrial emitters (as typically occurs under emissions trading systems) misses a significant portion of emissions (eg from small firms, vehicles and households) and administration is more complex (due to a greater number of taxpayers and the need to estimate emissions rather than infer them from already-observed fuel use and well-established emissions factors). Whether charges are best levied on gas extractors, processors, or distributors will depend on national circumstances, such as where taxes are already applied (and could be readily modified to include carbon charges) and the number of potential collection points at different stages in the fuel supply chain.

If methane leakage from wells, pipes, processors and storage sites could be monitored on a continuous basis, an emissions tax would be the ideal instrument. Monitoring technologies are advancing though currently provide only discrete measurements at a limited number of sites.[21] One possibility for the interim might be to tax fuel suppliers based on a default leakage rate but allow rebates to firms that are able to demonstrate lower leakage rates through mitigation and installing their own continuous emission monitoring systems.[22]

## C.  Alternatives to Taxes

This subsection discusses the potential role of regulations and liabilities.

### i.  *Regulation*

Regulatory approaches are attractive when the administration of environmental taxes is impractical and the Government is mainly targeting one specific,

---

[21] Top-down technologies include satellites, aircraft and drones while bottom up technologies include remote sensing (eg from vehicles).

[22] For both $CO_2$ and methane, ideally the tax levels would be set in line with countries' emissions mitigation pledges for the 2015 Paris Agreement.

observable behaviour. Regulations encompass numerous instruments (eg technology requirements, case-by-case permitting for sites) available to national and sub-national governments. Box 13.2 discusses the role regulations (usually at the state-level) have played in shale gas development in the US.

---

**Box 13.2 The regulation of shale gas development in the US**

Extractive industries in the US have traditionally been regulated primarily at the state level and this pattern has continued through the shale gas boom. States regulate the location and spacing of well sites, the methods of drilling, casing, fracking, plugging wells, the disposal of most oil and gas wastes, and site restoration. State common and public law governs the interpretation of lease provisions and disputes between surface and mineral owners and mineral lessees about payments and surface damage.

Federal authority is significant in some respects, however, including protection of air and surface water quality, endangered species and regulating in its capacity as a land-owner (many states with shale gas deposits include large areas of federally owned land). River basin commissions also issue relevant regulations to protect watersheds. And sometimes municipalities have a significant role: restricting the weight of equipment on roads; requiring operators to repair road damage; taxing oil and gas operations; and constraining well pad locations, drilling and fracking techniques, and waste disposal methods. Rapid expansion of shale gas has also created a dynamic regulatory environment which might help to explain the heterogeneity among state regulations of the same element (eg the required thickness of pit liners or distances between wells and water sources).

---

## *ii. Liability*

Litigation for shale drilling has increased rapidly since 2009[23] and has a key role both in penalising firms out of compliance with regulations and – which is discussed here – deterring one-off events like accidental leakage.[24] Firm-specific

---

[23] TE Kurth, MJ Mazzone, MS Mendoza and CS 'Kulander, American Law and Jurisprudence on Fracking – 2012' (Haynes and Boone, LLP, 2013).

[24] The focus here is on 'strict' liability, where firms are responsible for damages, regardless of whether they tried to avoid them. Under 'negligence' liability firms are only responsible if it is found that they did not exercise an accepted standard of care, but this can be difficult to prove.

penalties for ex post damages is potentially more efficient than upfront regulations or taxes when producers have better information than regulators about environmental risks and the costs of mitigating them (see Box 13.3), but there are three notable obstacles to efficient liability policy.

First, firms are not always held accountable for their environmental impacts through lawsuit. For one thing, where pollution damages affect a large number of parties, lawsuit formation will face standard collective action problems and also legal and institutional hurdles (eg class action qualifications). For another, it may be difficult to establish clear causality between a pollution source and its negative effects, especially those (eg an increase in disease or mortality) occurring with a lag – indeed, by the time the long-term effects of pollution become manifest, the shale gas producer may no longer exist. Ideally, the penalty would equal the ex post environmental damages divided by the probability of the lawsuit, though punitive penalties (in excess of actual damages) are rare.

Third is the existence of 'judgement-proof firms' declaring bankruptcy if liabilities exceed their net worth. In fact, businesses in hazardous industries may have some incentive to organise themselves to take advantage of this option by contracting out risky activities to small, undercapitalised firms.

There are nonetheless some possibilities for partly addressing these obstacles. The prospects for lawsuits might be enhanced by relaxing legal restrictions on class-action suits and requiring information disclosure by companies on environmental risks to enable third-party monitoring and reduce the cost of discovery for plaintiffs.[25] Operating licences can be conditional on minimum asset requirements, or liability insurance, and this is already a regular feature of many environmental protection laws. 'Vicarious liability', which may hold principals accountable for harms committed by their agents when the latter's resources are insufficient to cover liabilities, can discourage contracting out of risky activities to undercapitalised firms.[26]

A further possibility would be to require a supplementary industry-level insurance fund, collected through production levies on individual shale gas developers, to pay out compensation for large environmental damages that are impractical to recover from individual firms. The industry would have some incentive to self-regulate, by monitoring member firm's efforts to limit environmental risks, thereby containing the needed production fees. This arrangement would be analogous to the International Oil Pollution Compensation Funds,[27] which provide financial

---

[25] S Olmstead, N Richardson, 'Managing the Risks for Shale Gas Development Using Innovative Legal and Regulatory Approaches', Discussion paper (Resources for the Future, 2014).

[26] For example, the US Oil Pollution Act of 1990, enacted in the wake of the Exxon Valdez spill, increased the likelihood of vicarious liability for oil companies, thereby reversing the trend toward contracting out shipping services seen over the previous two decades (eg MR Brooks, 'Liner shipping regulation in North America: A Canadian perspective' (2002) 4 *International Journal of Maritime Economics* 281).

[27] IOPC Funds' Publications, available at www.iopcfunds.org/publications/iopc-funds-publications.

compensation for persistent pollution damage from oil from tankers, financed by contributions paid on the amount of oil received (by large consuming entities) in the relevant calendar year.[28]

Developing and some emerging countries may have additional constraints on their ability to internalise environmental risks through legal liability – judicial capacity may be constrained or subject to capture; civil society organisations that might monitor petroleum companies are likely underdeveloped; and governments themselves could be capacity constrained, preventing public lawsuits and effective regulatory oversight. These countries may need to rely more heavily on ex ante measures, particularly tax and/or insurance instruments that generate a revenue flow to help finance regulation, oversight, prosecution and/or remediation.

---

**Box 13.3 Private Information and the Relative Efficiency of Liability vs. Regulations/Taxes**

Consider Figure 13.7 where $MC^T$ denotes the true marginal cost of mitigating an environmental risk (eg limiting contamination leakage), $MB^T$ is the 'true' marginal environmental benefit in terms of reduced likelihood or scale of accidental damage, and $R^*$ is the efficient level of risk mitigation. Suppose the regulatory agency is imperfectly informed about either these costs or benefits. If, for example, the regulator incorrectly perceives marginal costs to be $MC^L$ (but knows environmental benefits) or incorrectly perceives marginal environmental benefits to be $MB^H$ (but knows mitigation costs), and sets a standard (or the equivalent tax) to maximise expected welfare, risk mitigation will be too high at $R^H$, resulting in a welfare loss, indicated by the lighter shaded triangle. Conversely, suppose the regulator incorrectly perceives marginal costs to be $MC^H$, or marginal benefits to be $MB^L$, and again sets the standard (or tax) to maximise expected welfare, risk mitigation will be too low at $R^L$, resulting in a welfare loss indicated by the darker shaded triangle. By contrast, mitigation will be efficient if producers are subject to strict liability for environmental damages *and* they correctly perceive mitigation costs and environmental risks (in which case the private marginal benefit from risk mitigation coincides with the true marginal benefit).

---

[28] See WK Viscusi and RJ Zeckhauser, 'Deterring and Compensating Oil-Spill Catastrophes: The Need for Strict and Two-Tier Liability' (2011) 64 *Vanderbilt Law Review* 1717 for further discussion on two-tier liability and compulsory insurance regimes to deal with extreme damage risks.

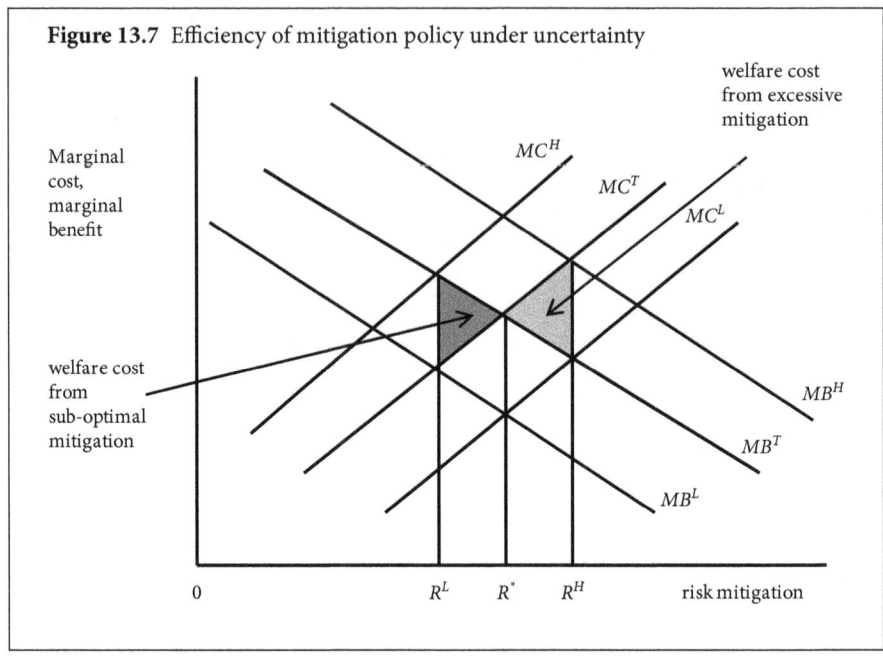

**Figure 13.7** Efficiency of mitigation policy under uncertainty

A second obstacle is that environmental damages may be difficult to quantify ex post – not least because the baseline level of environmental quality at different sites is frequently unavailable[29] – and some damages (eg to ecosystems) may extend beyond those suffered by victims of the lawsuit.

## D. Summary

Summing up this section, there are numerous and diverse environmental risks associated with shale gas development, but their severity is highly site-specific and there is scant quantitative evidence on the risks. Some combination of ex-ante (taxes, insurance and/or regulation) and ex-post (liability) controls seems most efficient response, given the diverse nature of the environmental risks and the varying strengths and weaknesses of different instruments in addressing each of them.[30] Table 13.1 provides a summary of appropriate instruments to address the identified risks.

[29] See, for example, JL Adgate, BD Goldstein and LM McKenzie, 'Potential Public Health Hazards, Exposures and Health Effects from Unconventional Natural Gas Development' (2014) 48 *Environmental Science and Technology* 307, 320; CW Moore, B Zielinska, G Petron and RB Jackson, 'Air Impacts of Increased Natural Gas Acquisition, Processing, and Use: A Critical Review' (2014) 48 *Environmental Science and Technology* 8,349; and MJ Small, PC Stern, E Bomberg, SM Christopherson, BD Goldstein, AL Israel, RB Jackson, A Krupnick, MS Mauter, J Nash and DW North, 'Risks and Risk Governance in Unconventional Shale Gas (2014) 48 *Environmental Science and Technology* 8,289.

[30] See, for example, S Shavell, 'A Model of the optimal use of Liability and Safety Regulation' (1984) 15 *RAND Journal of Economics* 271 for further discussion on instrument choice issues.

# V. Fiscal Regimes

Tax incentives for shale gas tax began in the US in the 1970s (Wang and Krupnick, 2013), and quickly spread. The same happened in other countries, especially in Europe, where vast shale resources have been identified. The usual rationale for these incentives is that without them development would not occur due to high costs, or would be very limited due to low returns on capital. Because fiscal systems in North America have traditionally been front-loaded (ie, relying on payment of taxes in early stages of a project, before capital cost is recovered through signature bonuses, royalties and/or severance taxes), these incentives may have been deemed necessary to overcome fiscal cost obstacles to development, but elsewhere, and with different fiscal systems, incentives may not have been needed. And even for the US, the case for tax incentives is debatable, given that many projects in the shale sector have remained viable (due to cost-cutting and, at least recently, declining costs of capital) despite the recent low commodity prices. Nonetheless, the impression has rapidly spread that shale gas 'needs' special incentives and a differentiated fiscal regime.

This section discusses whether the commercial and technical features of shale gas development suggest principles of fiscal regime design – namely that the specifics of the regime can vary with local factors, but there should be a balance among royalties, corporate income tax (CIT), and profit share (Box 13.4) – needs to be modified (eg in terms of favourable tax incentives) when applied to shale gas. A variety of fiscal regimes in different regions are tested to compare and contrast their implications for conventional and unconventional gas extraction. The focus of the discussion is on shale gas extraction which, by far, is the most common type of unconventional gas development.

**Table 13.1** Summary of instruments to address environmental risks of shale gas

| Risk | Fiscal | Regulation | Liability |
|---|---|---|---|
| **Overall development** | Possibly (though to capture rents) | Yes (especially if uncertainty over tax needed to deter drilling in fragile areas) | No |
| **Water use** | Yes (especially if local water stress, though charging larger water users is more urgent) | Used in practice (but pricing policies could be more efficient) | No |
| **Water pollution:** | | | |
|   **surface** | Limited practicality | Yes | Yes |
|   **underground** | Limited practicality | Yes | Yes |

*(continued)*

**Table 13.1** *(Continued)*

| Risk | Fiscal | Regulation | Liability |
|---|---|---|---|
| **Local air pollution** | Yes (for diesel fuel used in drilling/ pumping though environmental gains may be modest) | Yes (to encourage emissions control technologies) | No |
| **GHGs** | Yes (possibly for pricing carbon content and for methane leaks as metering technologies advance) | Yes (likely needed, in conjunction with taxes, to address methane releases) | No |
| **Ecological, seismic and other** | Limited practicality | Yes (eg regulations for well density and pipeline location for biodiversity, or wastewater disposal wells for seismic) | Limited (given diffuse impacts, though environmental agencies and civil society organisations could be defendants) |
| **Community and broader environmental** | Limited (congestion and road damage might be addressed through fiscal instruments) | Limited (as many impacts reflect pecuniary externalities) | Some applicability (but perhaps more for compensation than efficiency) |

---

**Box 13.4 Common advice on extractive industry fiscal regimes**

Previous advice (eg Daniel et al, 2010, n 2) suggests that fiscal regimes for raising revenues from extractive industries can vary with political, institutional and legal characteristics for particular jurisdictions. However, combining a royalty, an explicit rent tax, along with the standard CIT, with the economic substance of the instruments having similar properties (eg in terms of production sharing, risk service contracts, state participation, tax and royalty systems) has appeal in most cases. This regime ensures revenues are collected when production begins and that revenues increase with rents which, along with transparent rules and contracts, enhances the stability and credibility of the fiscal regime. Failure to address international tax issues (eg transfer pricing), however, can undermine revenue potential, and complex fiscal regimes and fragmented responsibilities among different government agencies can be major impediments to effective administration.

According to IMF[31] simulations, the potential government share in rents for mining is around 40–60 per cent and somewhat higher for petroleum at around 65–85 per cent (reflecting international practice and the potential for higher economic rents in petroleum projects), though actual rent shares may be lower due to revenue erosion possibilities like shifting profits to lower taxed jurisdictions.

## A. Fiscal Regimes

Fiscal regimes, where treatment differs between conventional and unconventional projects, are examined in a sample of 10 jurisdictions – six in North America (Alberta, North Dakota, Oklahoma, Pennsylvania, Saskatchewan and Texas) and four elsewhere (Algeria, China, Poland and the UK). Incentives for shale gas generally take the form of lower royalties and/or lower profit tax (commonly used in the US and outside of North America), or rates varying with well productivity or cost (commonly used in Canada) – the latter favouring unconventionals (due to the low productivity and high costs of wells).

North American regimes provide incentives for shale gas through a mix of direct and imbedded mechanisms (Appendix 13A, Table 13.3). Alberta, Oklahoma, North Dakota and Saskatchewan impose reduced royalty rates for horizontally drilled wells (which directly target shale hydrocarbon extraction), while Alberta and Saskatchewan also vary royalty rates with well productivity. Texas provides lower royalties for unconventionals through varying rates with well drilling and completion cost. Pennsylvania is the only jurisdiction that 'penalises' (through a special annual fee) unconventionals.[32]

The non-North American regimes (Appendix 13A, Table 13B) provide incentives for shale gas through a variety of measures including lower royalty rates in Algeria and Poland, lower profit tax rate in Algeria and special deductions for development costs under the additional profit tax in the UK. China provides for a direct price subsidy along with a waiver or reduction of certain mineral resource fees.

Many jurisdictions also offer incentives for gas (over oil), horizontal drilling, 'marginal' wells, 'deep' wells, and 'high-cost' operations. While there seems to be a view in countries that petroleum that is costlier to extract receives tax relief, the definition for the specific criteria that qualifies petroleum extraction for this relief

---

[31] 'Fiscal Regimes for Extractive Industries: Design and Implementation', International Monetary Fund, Washington, DC. Available at: www.imforg/external/np/pp/eng/2012/081512.pdf.

[32] Even within jurisdictions multiple regimes co-exist (for example, Kepes et al found 188 different fiscal systems within 10 Canadian Provinces and 25 US states), though these differences are beyond our scope; J Kepes, B Rodgers and P Van Meurs, 'Gas prices, other Factors Indicate Changes in North American/Shale Play Fiscal Systems' (2011) *Oil and Gas Journal* 56.

varies across jurisdictions. For example, North Dakota gives greater exemptions to wells that are 'horizontally drilled'[33] whereas Poland charges reduced rates below a defined level of permeability.[34] There is little consistency among criteria for these concessions, possibly because there is no common view of relative costs across the industry. The greater the reliance of the overall regime upon levies related to gross production or proceeds, the more likely there will be arguments for reducing the levies for higher cost operations in general, and for shale gas in particular.

We do note that various indirect tax incentives, including reduced tariffs and VAT for imports of equipment, are also offered to shale gas development in some jurisdictions.[35] Indirect taxes, however, are not part of our analysis.

## B. Modelling Strategy

The modelling approach is used to explore: (i) whether there is justification for fiscal regimes favouring shale gas extraction (in terms of whether the incentives impact investments for marginal projects); and (ii) potential revenues forgone from these incentives.

The analysis uses the Fiscal Analysis of Resource Industries (FARI) modelling tool,[36] which takes a discounted cash flow approach to individual projects and, through fiscal calculations, allocates the project's pre-tax net cash flows to the investor and government according to the fiscal regime. Analysis can then be done using standard indicators defined in Box 13.5, namely the average effective tax rate (AETR), breakeven price, and marginal effective tax rate (METR), and comparisons of alternative fiscal regimes.

The project-based approach allows for conventional and unconventional projects and regimes to be better compared than in singe well studies,[37] given that fiscal regimes often have income taxes ring-fenced at the project level, meaning that the revenue and costs from each well are consolidated into a single flow of revenues and deductions for company income tax payments.[38] Therefore, the

[33] Section 57-51 of North Dakota Tax Law and Regulations.
[34] Section 7a.6.1 of the Polish Act of March 2, 2012 on Certain Minerals Extraction Tax.
[35] L Tian, Z Wang, A Krupnick and X Liu, 'Stimulating Shale Gas Development in China. A Comparison with the US Experience', *Resources for the Future*, Discussion Paper 14–18, 2014.
[36] See O Luca and D Mesa Puyo, 'Fiscal Analysis of Resource Industries (FARI) Methodology' Technical Notes and Manuals 16/01 (International Monetary Fund, 2016).
[37] For example, J Kepes, B Rodgers and P Van Meurs, 'Gas prices, other Factors Indicate Changes in North American/Shale Play Fiscal Systems', *Oil and Gas Journal* 56–66, 2011.
[38] Ringfencing can also occur at the contract area, sector, or company level (eg Oklahoma has a reduced royalty rate applied to production from eligible wells in their first four years of production or until costs are recovered). For these cases, our analysis disaggregates projects into well production and costs by year and then applies the corresponding fiscal regime. Of the modelled jurisdictions, the UK has CIT and supplementary charge ringfencing around the upstream sector, Algeria has CIT and APT ringfencing around a contract area, and the US, Canada, China and Poland have no ringfencing provision, meaning that the CIT calculation considers all company activities generating income and deductions. The special hydrocarbon tax in Poland is, however, ringfenced at a sector level, ie only hydrocarbon operations of a given company enter the tax account and other streams of revenue (and cost) are ignored.

assumption of project-wide ringfencing is more realistic and very relevant for shale gas projects that incur large capital expenses throughout the life of the project. In reality, ring-fencing occurs at the project, contract area, sector or company level but the fiscal modeling used here assumes project level.[39] However, the modelling approach was altered to account for fiscal regimes that use individual well life and productivity to determine royalty rates, which is common in North America (see Box 13.6). This was done by disaggregating projects into individual well production and costs by year of well life and then applying this information to applicable regimes.[40]

---

**Box 13.5. Indicators used in fiscal regime analysis[a]**

*AETR.* The ratio of the net present value (NPV) of total government revenue to the pre-tax cash flows over the entire project life (exploration through decommissioning) received by the Government.

$$\text{AETR} = \frac{\text{NPV (government revenue)}}{\text{NPV (revenue} - \text{all project costs)}}$$

*Investor's post-tax IRR.* The discount rate at which the NPV of the investor's stream of post-tax cash flows is zero. In general, a project is perceived to be profitable if the IRR exceeds the investor's required rate of return (assumed below to be 10 per cent).

*METR.* The wedge driven by the tax system between the minimum after-tax return investors require and the pre-tax project return needed to realise it. It is calculated as the percentage difference between the pre- and post-tax IRR at the breakeven price. The METR reflects the burden placed by the fiscal regime on a project with marginal viability, thereby indicating the extent to which the regime affects investment decisions.

$$\text{METR} = \frac{\text{Pre tax IRR} - \text{Post tax IRR}}{\text{Pre tax IRR}}$$

---

[39] Of the modelled jurisdictions, the UK has CIT and supplementary charge ringfencing around the upstream sector, Algeria has CIT and APT ringfencing around a contract area, and the US, Canada, China and Poland have no ringfencing provision, meaning that the CIT calculation considers all company activities that generate income and deductions.

[40] For example, until 2015 Oklahoma had a reduced royalty rate for wells in their first four years of production or until costs are recovered. The reduced rate is applied to production from eligible wells; not the first four years of the entire project's production.

*Breakeven price.* The minimum constant real commodity price to yield a specific investor post-tax IRR. A breakeven price over the market price implies an unviable project.

[a] For a more detailed discussion of the above indicators see Luca and Puyo[41].

Four representative gas projects are created for conventional versus shale development and North America, using a generic US project, versus non-North America, using a generic European project. Contrasting North America and Europe is interesting as they have significantly different natural gas prices, petroleum geology and sector-wide systems (technical support, transportation systems, regulations). This approach does not recognise all the differences, which may be large among and within specific locations and even individual fields, but allows capturing the major ones to inform our analysis.

---

**Box 13.6. A closer look at shale incentives in Oklahoma**

More detailed analysis of the Oklahoma regime is given here to illustrate the intricacies of reduced royalty rates for shale and highlight mechanisms through which a regime can direct incentives at shale specific economics.

Oklahoma provides an interesting example of a regime that targets the differences in cost and production structures between shale and conventional gas. The state allows for a reduced royalty rate (1 per cent) for production stemming from horizontal drilling up until all well development costs are recovered or the well's production reaches four years.[a] Since shale, normally, has a much lower estimated ultimate recovery (EUR), and thus production value per well than that of onshore gas, the incentive applies to a greater percentage of a shale gas well's total production. However, due to the well cost recovery limit, low-cost wells, which are less likely to be marginal and need an incentive, will not receive a full exemption.

Figure 13.8 shows the effective royalty rate on natural gas production and its progressive and targeted nature. Due to the mechanisms just described, the rate for an unconventional regime rate increases with price when it is imposed on a shale gas project. However, for a conventional gas project, the unconventional regime performs nearly identically to the rate under the conventional regime.

---

[41] O Luca and D Mesa Puyo, 'Fiscal Analysis of Resource Industries (FARI) Methodology', *Technical Notes and Manuals* 16/01, International Monetary Fund, Washington, DC, 2016.

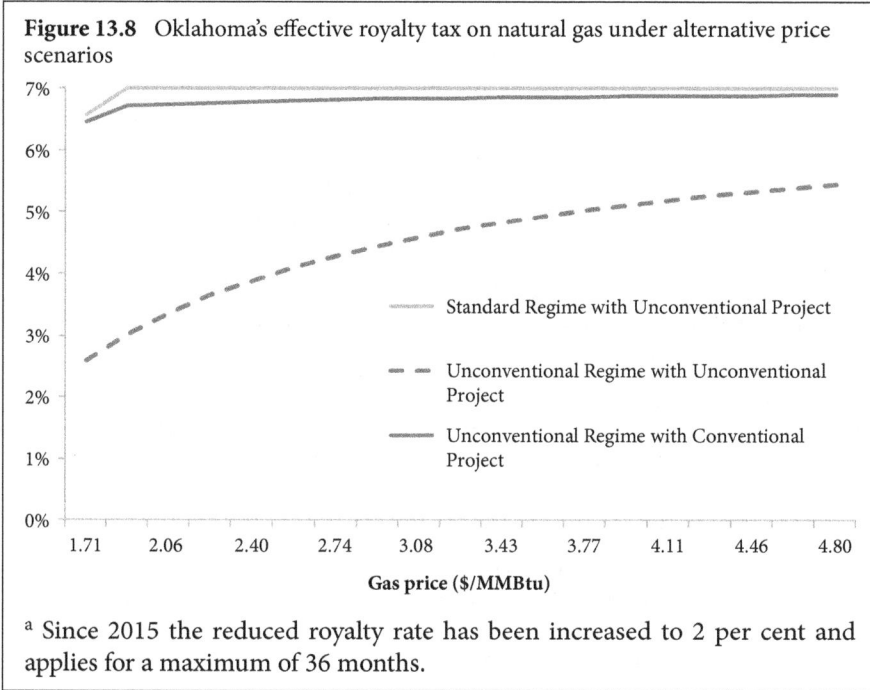

**Figure 13.8** Oklahoma's effective royalty tax on natural gas under alternative price scenarios

Legend:
- Standard Regime with Unconventional Project
- Unconventional Regime with Unconventional Project
- Unconventional Regime with Conventional Project

X-axis: Gas price ($/MMBtu)

[a] Since 2015 the reduced royalty rate has been increased to 2 per cent and applies for a maximum of 36 months.

Table 2 summarises parameters assumptions for the four projects,[42] at the project and well level, with the general differences and similarities between each type of extraction and region summarised in Box 13.7. Appendix 13B provides further details on the modelling approach.

---

**Box 13.7 Major differences: shale vs conventional gas and US vs Europe**

Shale versus conventional:

- *Exploration cost.* Success factors for shale are lower in Europe (70 per cent compared with 95 per cent for conventional gas) and exploration costs are 50 per cent higher. However, due to more favourable factors for the US exploration costs for shale are 50 per cent lower than for conventional gas and success rates are the same.

- *Well schedule and production profile.* Wells for conventional gas are mostly drilled as initial development, while those for shale gas are

---

[42] Parameters are based on IHS data, IMF's TA experience in petroleum project evaluation, and judgement.

drilled throughout the project life – the latter have a much steeper decline and shorter production life (15 years compared with 40 for conventional gas).

- *Production per well.* Production is much higher for conventional gas – 26.5 million barrels of oil equivalent (MMBOE) compared with less than 1 MMBOE for shale – therefore far more wells are drilled for shale gas (eg 403 in Europe per project compared with 8 for conventional).
- *Well drilling and completion cost.* Despite horizontal drilling and fracking, drilling and completion costs per well are lower for shale than conventional gas.
- *Operating expenditure.* About 60 per cent higher per unit of gas recovered for shale due to the cost of chemicals, higher water usage, environmental protection, higher energy consumption, cost of land access and general and administrative costs, including higher social and community relations costs.
- *Decommissioning.* Progressive ('clean as you go') for shale and lumped at the end of project life for conventional gas, however relative to well and non-drilling development costs decommissioning costs are taken to be the same for shale and conventional gas in the USs and somewhat higher for the former in Europe.

US versus Europe:

- *Well drilling cost.* Higher cost of drilling and well completion in Europe, partly also on account of a higher number of dry wells drilled (lower success factor).
- *Geology.* Less favourable for Europe, reflected in lower gas flow rates (2.5 Bcf per well compared with 3.5 Bcf for the US).
- *Operating expenditure.* Higher for non-US; in Europe operating expenditures are moderately higher for shale, mostly on account of higher energy and chemical costs.

*Natural gas price.* Lower for US (around USD 3/MMBtu) than Europe (USD 5–10/MBtu).

**Table 13.2** Parameters for simulated projects

| Parameters | Unit | North America | | Europe | |
|---|---|---|---|---|---|
| | | **Shale** | **Conventional** | **Shale** | **Conventional** |
| **Project Level** | | | | | |
| Project life | Years | 44 | 40 | 44 | 40 |
| Production | Years | 37 | 32 | 37 | 32 |
| Gas production | Tcf | 1.0 | 1.0 | 1.0 | 1.0 |
| Oil production | MMBbl | 50 | 50 | 50 | 50 |
| Total production[a] | MMBOE | 222 | 222 | 222 | 222 |
| Wells drilled | Wells | 286 | 8 | 403 | 8 |
| Success Rate | % | 95 | 95 | 70 | 95 |
| Gas price | $/MMBtu | 2.86 | 2.86 | 4.79 | 4.79 |
| Oil price | $/Bbl | 50.0 | 50.0 | 60.0 | 60.0 |
| Exploration | $bn | 0.1 | 0.2 | 0.1 | 0.2 |
| Capex | $bn | 1.5 | 0.2 | 3.4 | 0.3 |
| Opex | $bn | 1.0 | 0.6 | 1.5 | 1.3 |
| Total cost | $bn | 2.7 | 1.0 | 5.1 | 1.8 |
| Unit exploration | $/BOE | 0.6 | 0.7 | 0.6 | 0.9 |
| Unit capex | $/BOE | 6.9 | 1.0 | 15.5 | 1.3 |
| Unit opex | $/BOE | 4.5 | 2.8 | 6.7 | 6.0 |
| Total unit cost | $/BOE | 11.9 | 4.5 | 22.8 | 8.2 |
| Pre-tax cash flow | $bn | 2.8 | 4.4 | 2.9 | 6.1 |
| Pre-tax IRR | % | 25.2 | 27.3 | 22.9 | 28.8 |
| **Well Level** | | | | | |
| Well Life | Years | 15 | 40 | 15 | 40 |
| Gas production | Bcf | 3.5 | 119.1 | 2.5 | 119.1 |
| Oil production | MMBbl | 0.2 | 6.0 | 0.1 | 6.0 |
| Total production[a] | MMBOE | 0.8 | 26.5 | 0.6 | 26.5 |
| Production Decline | na | rapid[b] | slow | rapid[b] | slow |
| Gas revenue | $mm | 10.3 | 440.7 | 12.2 | 738.0 |
| Oil revenue | $mm | 8.7 | 375.4 | 7.4 | 450.5 |
| Drilling/Completion costs | $mm | 5.0 | 6.0 | 8.0 | 14.1 |

*(continued)*

**Table 13.2** *(Continued)*

| Parameters | Unit | North America | | Europe | |
|---|---|---|---|---|---|
| | | Shale | Conventional | Shale | Conventional |
| Facilities | $mm | 0.2 | 21.4 | 0.1 | 21.4 |
| Opex | $mm | 3.5 | 78.2 | 3.7 | 167.2 |
| Total cost | $mm | 8.8 | 107.9 | 11.8 | 205.2 |
| Unit capex | $/BOE | 6.6 | 1.0 | 14.7 | 1.3 |
| Unit opex | $/BOE | 4.5 | 3.0 | 6.7 | 6.3 |
| Total unit cost | $/BOE | 11.1 | 4.0 | 21.4 | 7.7 |
| Pre-tax cash flow | $mm | 10.2 | 695.3 | 7.4 | 953.2 |

*Note:* [a] Assumes 5.8 Mcf per barrels of oil equivalent (BOE). [b] Assumes 73 per cent of production occurs in first three years.

## C.  Results

Figure 13.9 shows the METRs and breakeven gas prices, and Figure 13.10 the AETRs, for all modelled regimes when applied to the stylised shale and conventional gas projects in the respective jurisdictions. There are several noteworthy points.

For the North American shale gas project, from Figure 13.9 the actual fiscal regime for shale might appear to provide at best modest extra incentive for development compared with applying the fiscal regime for conventional gas. For example, breakeven prices in Oklahoma are USD 2.42 and USD 2.51 per MMBtu, and METRs are 49 and 52 per cent, under the shale and conventional tax regimes respectively, and there is almost no difference between the fiscal regimes for shale and conventional gas in both Texas and North Dakota. Incentives for shale gas are somewhat more pronounced in the Canadian regimes – for example, the favourable regime for shale gas in Alberta reduces the breakeven price from USD 1.99 to USD 1.91 compared with the conventional regime. A look at the Figure 13.8 however, suggests that fiscal incentives have little effect on marginal investments under alternative gas price scenarios. The AETRs are upwards of 80 per cent in half of the jurisdictions – projects are deemed to be marginal if AETRs exceed 90 per cent – or put another way the breakeven prices in Figure 13.9 are not that different from the assumed gas price (USD 2.86/MMBtu). The Canadian shale gas regimes lower the government take by a few percentage points compared to (not so harsh) conventional fiscal regimes whereas the US shale gas regimes offer little relief, even though the overall level of taxation is much higher.

As regards the conventional US gas project breakeven prices, METRs and AETRs are essentially the same under the fiscal regimes for shale and conventional gas, underscoring that the favourable tax provisions are specific to the unique features of shale gas extraction and would do nothing to help conventional gas. The one exception is Alberta, where petroleum by-products are subject to a lower royalty than by-products from conventional gas extraction, though at current gas prices these provisions would have minimal effect on incentives, given larger differences between actual and breakeven prices (compared with shale gas) and lower AETRs (typically in the range of 55 to 65 per cent).

Fiscal regimes in Europe would provide stronger incentives for shale gas, for example, reducing the METR for the shale project in the UK from 28 to 8 per cent (relative to the conventional fiscal regime), in Algeria from 59 to 42 per cent, and in China from 59 to 36 per cent. In the case of Algeria and China, however, the breakeven prices are close the assumed gas price for Europe (USD 4.79 per MMBtu), suggesting incentives may not be sufficient to overcome currently unfavourable economics (put another way, the AETRs is only slightly below 100 per cent in Figure 13.8). Although revenue differences between the fiscal regimes for shale and conventional gas are substantial – the AETRs for the UK, for example, are 30 and 62 per cent respectively – marginal projects might not be developed without a favourable regime (in which case no revenues are raised).

As regards the conventional European gas project, unlike in the North American case, there are significant differences between treatment under the fiscal regimes for shale and conventional gas, most notably in China where the METRs are 49 and 21 per cent respectively (incentives here take the form of lower royalty rates or subsidies which are not specific to the characteristics of shale extraction). In Poland, both METR and AETR are almost identical under the two analysed fiscal regimes, implying that little incentive provided by the shale gas regime for economically viable projects. 50 per cent reduction in already modest royalty rate (1.5 vs 3.0 per cent) accounts only for a small fraction of the total government take and does not influence incentives to undertake a project.

Differences in AETRs achieved under different regimes point to a substantial fiscal cost of incentivising shale gas production, at least in non-American regimes. Revenue forgone due to applying a special shale gas regime rather than the one used for a conventional production is the largest in the UK – USD 145 million or 26 per cent of pre-tax cash flow (in discounted terms) from the analysed project is lost. The size of the fiscal subsidy in countries outside North America – at USD 33 million or 6 per cent of pre-tax cash flow – is the smallest in Poland. Amongst Canadian regimes Alberta's tax expenditure – at USD 55 million or 13 per cent of pre-tax cash flow – is double of that of Saskatchewan.

**Figure 13.9** Marginal effective tax rate (METRs) and Breakeven Gas Prices

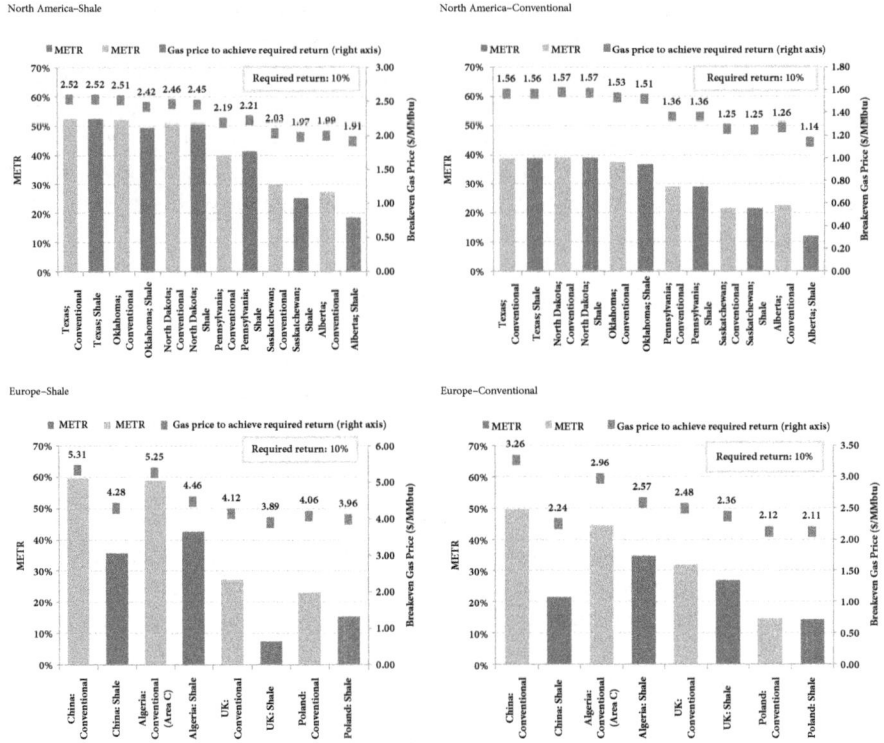

*Note*: The horizontal axis depicts conventional/non-conventional projects in different basins/fields.

**Figure 13.10** Average effective tax rates[43]

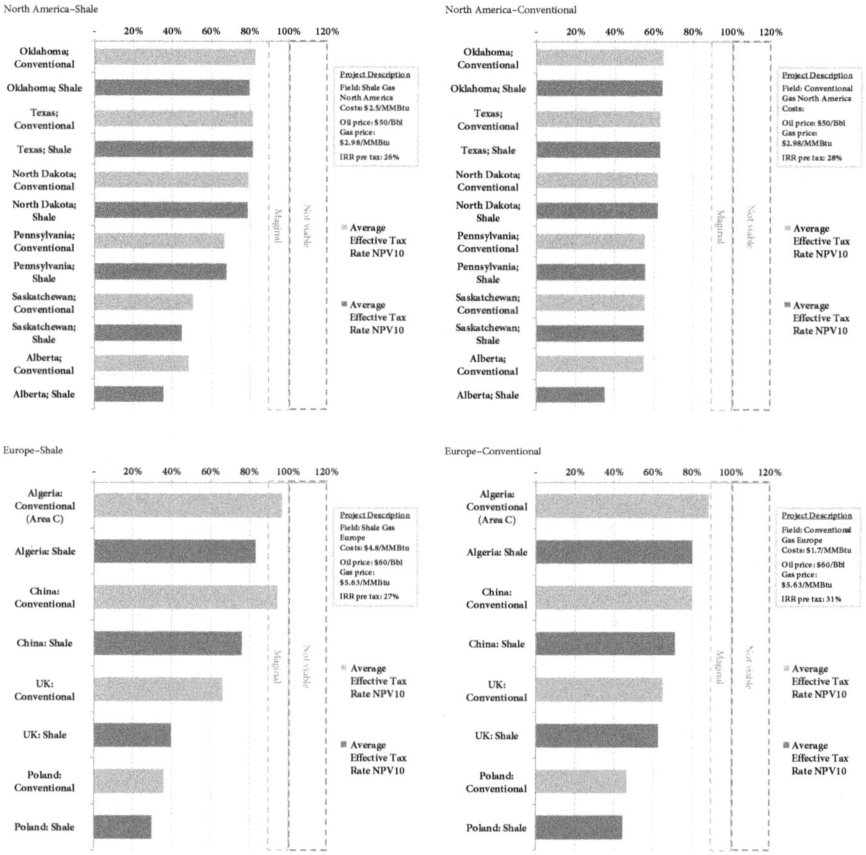

*Note*: The horizontal axis depicts Average effective tax rates (AETR) and vertical axis depicts conventional/non-conventional projects in different basins/fields.

[43] The discounted AETR is excluded from this graph as it does not provide meaningful results due to the slightly negative pre-tax net cash flow, which it the denominator in AETR.

# VI.  Conclusions

Although shale gas development poses a broader range of environmental risks than conventional gas, the implications for efficient fiscal regimes for extractives seem limited. For several risks (eg pricing water inputs, diesel fuel for pumping engines, greenhouse gas emissions) fiscal policies may have a role, though in some cases the net benefits from special tax provisions may be limited.

The modelling results in this paper suggest that special fiscal regimes and incentives granted for shale gas development in some jurisdictions have, at most, only a slight impact on likely decisions to invest, whereas they may result in substantial cost to the Government (tax expenditures). Other circumstances, such as private ownership of resource rights and availability of an extensive gathering and distribution infrastructure for gas, have probably played a much bigger role in promoting the rapid development of shale resources in the US.

For the most part, there is little evident need to consider specific incentives for shale gas development, compared with conventional gas, provided that the overall fiscal regime responds substantially to realised profit or rent. The principal exception comes where authorities seek to promote shale gas development in a jurisdiction that relies heavily on gross royalties or on initial or continuing flat fees or bonuses.

In short, the case for providing relative fiscal incentives to unconventional over conventional natural gas is not especially compelling.

# Appendix 13A

## Details of Fiscal Systems in the Sample Jurisdictions

Table 13.3 North American regimes

| | North Dakota – Conv. | North Dakota – Unconv. | Oklahoma – Conv. | Oklahoma – Unconv. | Pennsylvania – Conv. | Pennsylvania – Unconv. | Texas – Conv. | Texas – Unconv. | Alberta – Conv. | Alberta – Unconv. | Saskatchewan – Conv. | Saskatchewan – Unconv. |
|---|---|---|---|---|---|---|---|---|---|---|---|---|
| Primary royalty gas | 16% | 16% | 18.75% | 18.75% | 12.5% | 12.5% | 20% | 20% | 5%–36%[b]; limited reduced rate | 5%–36%[b]; further limited reduced rate | 0%–40%[b]; limited reduced rate | 0%–40%[b]; limited reduced rate |
| Primary royalty oil | 16% | 16% | 18.75% | 18.75% | 12.5% | 12.5% | 20% | 20% | 0%–40%; limited reduced rate | 0%–5% | 0%–40%[b]; limited reduced rate | 0%–40%[b]; limited reduced rate |
| Additional royalty gas | US$ 0.0833/Mcf | US$ 0.0833/Mcf | 1%–7%[a] | 1%–7%[a]; limited reduced rate | No | $5k–$60k per well | 0%–7.5%; varies with cost of well | 0%–7.5%; varies with cost of well | No | No | No | No |
| Additional royalty oil | 2%–6.5%[a] + 5% w/ limited exemption | 2%–6.5%[a] + 5% w/ increased exemption | 1%–7%[a] | 1%–7%[a]; limited reduced rate | No | No | 4.6% | 4.6% | No | No | No | No |
| CIT – rate (%) | Federal: 35% State: 5% | Federal: 35% State: 5% | Federal: 35% State: 6% | Federal: 35% State: 6% | Federal: 35% State: 9.9% | Federal: 35% State: 9.9% | Federal: 35% State: 1% | Federal: 35% State: 1% | Federal: 15% State: 10% | Federal: 15% State: 10% | Federal: 15% State: 12% | Federal: 15% State: 12% |
| Depreciation (exploration) | 7 years SL | 7 years SL | 7 years SL | 7 years SL | 7 years SL | 7 years SL | 7 years SL | 7 years SL | Immediate | Immediate | Immediate | Immediate |

*(continued)*

**Table 13.3 (*Continued*)**

| | North Dakota – Conv. | North Dakota – Unconv. | Oklahoma – Conv. | Oklahoma – Unconv. | Pennsylvania – Conv. | Pennsylvania – Unconv. | Texas – Conv. | Texas – Unconv. | Alberta – Conv. | Alberta – Uncov. | Saskatchewan – Conv. | Saskatchewan – Unconv. |
|---|---|---|---|---|---|---|---|---|---|---|---|---|
| Depreciation (capex) | IDC: 5 years SL Non-IDC: 200% accelerated w/7 year SL | IDC: 5 years SL Non-IDC: 200% accelerated w/7 year SL | IDC: 5 years SL Non-IDC: 200% accelerated w/7 year SL | IDC: 5 years SL Non-IDC: 200% accelerated w/7 year SL | IDC: 5 years SL Non-IDC: 200% accelerated w/7 year SL | IDC: 5 years SL Non-IDC: 200% accelerated w/ 7 year SL | IDC: 5 years SL Non-IDC: 200% accelerated w/7 year SL | IDC: 5 years SL Non-IDC: 200% accelerated w/7 year SL | 25%–30% DB | 25%–30% DB | 25%–30% DB | 25%–30% DB |
| LCF | 20 years | 20 years | 20 years | 20 years | 20 years | 20 years | 20 years | 20 years | Indefinite | Indefinite | Indefinite | Indefinite |

*Source:* IMF FARI Database, EY 2016, countries' tax legislation.

*Notes:* SL: Straight line (depreciation); IDC: intangible drilling costs; LCF: loss carryforward; [a] rate varies with commodity price; [b] rate varies with commodity price and well productivity.

**Table 13.4** Non-North American regimes

| | Algeria – Conv. | Algeria – Unconv. | China – Conv. | China – Unconv. | Poland – Conv. | Poland – Unconv. | United Kingdom – Conv. | United Kingdom – Unconv. |
|---|---|---|---|---|---|---|---|---|
| Royalty gas (%) | 12.5%–23%[a] | 5% | 11% | 11% | 3% | 1.5% | 0% | 0% |
| Royalty oil | 12.5%–23%[a] | 5% | 11% | 11% | 6% | 3% | 0% | 0% |
| Cost recovery limit | NA | NA | 60% oil; 70% gas | 60% oil; 70% gas | NA | NA | NA | NA |
| Production sharing method | NA | NA | Annual production | Annual production | NA | NA | NA | NA |
| Min government share | NA | NA | 5% | 5% | NA | NA | NA | NA |
| Max government share | NA | NA | 55% | 55% | NA | NA | NA | NA |
| CIT – rate | 20%–70%[b] | 10%–40%[b] | 25% | 25% | 19% | 19% | 30% | 30% |
| Depreciation (exploration) | Immediate | Immediate | 3 years SL | 3 years SL | Immediate | Immediate | Immediate | Immediate |
| Depreciation (capex) | 8 years | 8 years | Pre-production: 8 years SL Other: 10 years SL | Pre-production: 8 years SL Other: 10 years SL | 5 years SL | 5 years SL | Immediate | Immediate |
| Additional deductions | 13% development costs | 20% development costs | 0% | 0% | 0% | 0% | 10% uplift on LCF for 10 years | 10% uplift on LCF for 10 years |

*(continued)*

**Table 13.4** *(Continued)*

| | Algeria – Conv. | Algeria – Unconv. | China – Conv. | China – Unconv. | Poland – Conv. | Poland – Unconv. | United Kingdom – Conv. | United Kingdom – Unconv. |
|---|---|---|---|---|---|---|---|---|
| LCF | 5 years | 5 years | 5 years once production begins | 5 years once production begins | 5 years; unused is creditable against royalty | 5 years; unused is creditable against royalty | Indefinite | Indefinite |
| Additional Profit Tax rate | 15%–30%[b] 51% carried until | 15%–80%[b] 51% carried until | 0%–40%; varies with oil price 51% carried until | 0%–40%; varies with oil price 51% carried until | 0%–25%; varies with R-factor | 0%–25%; varies with R-factor | 20%; limited uplift on capex | 20%; uplift on capex |
| State participation | development w/repayment | development w/repayment | development w/o repayment | development w/o repayment | 0% | 0% | 0% | 0% |
| Other | | | | Subsidy of CNY 0.4/cubic meter | | | | |

*Source:* IMF FARI Database; EY 2016, countries' tax legislation.

*Notes:* LCF: loss carryforward; CNY: Chinese Yuan; [a] rate varies with production; [b] rate varies with profitability ratio.

# Appendix 13B

# Further Details on Representative
# Projects for Fiscal Regime Analysis

Production aims to maintain a plateau (though this may not necessarily be true for shale gas in the US). For Canadian regimes, where fiscal parameters depend on depth, reservoirs are taken to be at 3000 metres.[44] Associated liquids, so called 'wet gas' (eg ethane, butane) are included in shale production.[45]

Several other assumptions deserve mention. Tax regimes are taken to apply throughout the project life with taxes paid by one entity, the 'investor', and this entity receives all cash flows before paying taxes and interest.[46] 70 per cent of development expenses are financed through debt, while the rest of project costs are paid from investor equity, reflecting an assumption that investors are not able to borrow to fund exploration and prefer to avoid excessive leverage (capitalisation in line with prevailing debt-to-equity tax ratios). Inflation and interest rates are assumed to be constant throughout the project and, based on long-term forecasts published in the April 2016 World Economic Outlook, petroleum prices are in constant 2016 real dollars, meaning they annually adjust for inflation.[47]

---

[44] Additional simulations for Saskatchewan indicate that a well depth of 2,000 metres, rather than 1,500 metres, causes the pre-tax IRR to decrease by 0.4% due to the rise in costs. However, since a relatively large portion of oil becomes eligible for a lower royalty rate at the greater depth for the unconventional regime, the investor's post-tax return increases while the effective royalty rate sharply falls under the 2,000 metres scenario. A less significant impact is seen for the conventional regime due to the lower portion of petroleum eligible for the lower royalty rate.

[45] There is some substitutability between oil and gas flows which becomes important when gas prices decline sharply relative to those for oil. This feature is ignored in the analysis and a fixed ratio of oen barrel of oil for every 20 Mcf of natural gas is assumed.

[46] An exception is when there is state participation, meaning that the national oil company (NOC) has an equity stake in the project. Specifically, in the case of state participation within the Algerian and Chinese regimes, the NOC has its share of exploration costs 'carried', or paid for, by the investor and thereafter covers its share of costs, including the repayment of carried costs, with cash.

[47] Prices are USD 2.86/MMBtu and USD 48.00/bbl for North American gas and oil, respectively, and USD 4.79/MMBtu and USD 51.01/bbl for non-US gas and oil, respectively.

# 14

## Trinidad and Tobago's Oil and Gas Sector in a Changing World (2010–2019)

KEVIN RAMNARINE

## I. Abstract

Since 2010, Trinidad and Tobago has experienced shortfalls in the supply of natural gas to its industrial customers at the Point Lisas Industrial Estate and at the Atlantic Liquified Natural Gas (LNG) multi-train facility. This chapter examines the structure of the Trinidad and Tobago natural gas sector, the fiscal regime that governs its energy value chain and the root causes of the shortage in natural gas supply that emerged in 2010 and persists to the present day. These shortages are the result of internal factors such as periods of underinvestment from 2008 to 2010 and external factors such as the decision by BP to conduct planned maintenance in Trinidad and Tobago in response to the April 2010 Macondo oil spill. It describes the link between a strategic policy intervention by the Government of Trinidad and Tobago and the results it can have on production levels. Moreover, it demonstrates that problems of declining production are often due to above-ground conditions which include factors such as misaligned and inadequate fiscal regimes and an uncompetitive investment climate. The chapter examines the efficacy of the fiscal policies implemented by the Government of Trinidad and Tobago to stimulate investments in exploration and development drilling. These fiscal policies included a system of accelerated capital allowances to permit companies to recover their capital expenditure at a faster rate thus making the economics of upstream projects more attractive.

## II. Introduction

This chapter is a first-hand account of the challenges of the natural gas industry of Trinidad and Tobago since 2010 from the view of a former Minister of Energy of Trinidad and Tobago, who served in that office from June 2011 to September 2015.

Trinidad and Tobago has a very significant level of natural gas production that underpins its economy. In the first quarter of 2019, Trinidad and Tobago's natural gas production averaged 3.8 billion cubic feet (bcfd) per day.[1] By way of comparison, in 2018, Argentina's production was 3.8 bcfd. In 2018, Brazil's natural gas production was 2.4 bcfd. This makes Trinidad and Tobago one of the largest producers of natural gas in Latin America and the Caribbean, and the only exporter of LNG in that region.[2]

In 1999 Trinidad and Tobago's first LNG train was operationalised. By 2005 there were three more trains in operation. The major players in this LNG industry are currently BP plc, Shell (formerly BG Group) and the National Gas Company (NGC). The LNG industry created a significant demand for natural gas in Trinidad and Tobago, with the collective contractual demand of all four Trains being 2,212 million cubic feet per day (mmcfd). The four trains, however, had a 'name plate capacity' that was higher than their combined contractual demand. This was about 2500 mmcfd.[3]

In addition to LNG, Trinidad and Tobago has 11 ammonia plants, seven methanol plants, five gas-fired power generation plants, one steel plant and other small natural gas consumers. In the year 2015, all these plants accounted for a contracted demand of about 3,881 mmcfd. There was, however, a 'max gas demand' scenario of 4,268 mmcfd when name plate capacity was factored in. This means that the country has a large natural gas demand profile relative to its natural gas reserve base.[4]

In 2000, the Dallas-based Ryder Scott consultants started regular audits of Trinidad and Tobago's non-associated natural gas reserves. In that year the country's proven reserves stood at 19.67 trillion cubic feet of natural gas. By 2017, this number had fallen to 10.51 trillion cubic feet.[5]

The fall in proven reserves is due to the acceleration of demand, which was a feature of the demand created by four LNG trains and insufficient natural gas related exploration drilling in the first decade of the twenty-first century. As a consequence, curtailments in the supply of natural gas started to be noticed in late 2010. It could also be argued that the LNG industry aided the economics of upstream investments in Trinidad and Tobago.

There is also evidence that BPTT (a subsidiary of BP plc) started to reduce capital investment in Trinidad and Tobago in the period 2009 to 2011 as a result of an

---

[1] Ministry of Energy and Energy Industries, 'Ministry of Energy and Energy Industries Consolidated Energy Bulletin January 2019 to May 2019' (2019).

[2] BP, 'BP Working Towards Lower Carbon Future For T&T', BP News (Trinidad and Tobago) (2019), available at www.bp.com/en_tt/trinidad-and-tobago/home/news/press-releases/bp-keeps-advancing-its-trinidad-and-tobago-business.html.

[3] C Williams, 'Trinidad And Tobago Natural Gas Master Plan' (Poten and Partners, 2015), available at www.ogj.com/refining-processing/gas-processing/article/17229035/trinidad-and-tobagos-new-master-gas-plan-routes-lng-through-ngc.

[4] ibid.

[5] A Javeed, 'Natural Gas: What Are the Options?' Trinidad Express (2019), available at www.trinidadexpress.com/business/local/natural-gas-what-are-the-options/article_a71c42b2-84d2-11e9-997c-0fdf0d330d44.html.

oversupply in natural gas in the market. Between 2010 and 2014, BPTT also embarked on a maintenance programme of upstream assets in Trinidad and Tobago that disrupted supply. The cumulative effect of these and other factors led to the curtailments in natural gas supply in Trinidad and Tobago over the last eight to nine years.[6]

The challenge was therefore to get the international oil companies (IOCs) operating in Trinidad and Tobago to increase investments in exploration drilling and developmental drilling to levels that would reverse the downward trajectory of natural gas production. From a policy position a commitment was given in 2011 of no increased taxation. This provided a degree of certainty to investors. In the period 2011 to 2014 a number of amendments were made to the income tax law and the petroleum taxes laws of Trinidad and Tobago all aimed at making the investment environment more competitive. Comparisons to other oil and gas jurisdictions indicated that Trinidad and Tobago was not competitive as a destination for upstream related capital expenditure.

One major policy intervention was the introduction of 'accelerated capital allowances' which allowed companies to recover their exploration and developmental related capital expenditures at a faster rate thus improving the net present value and internal rate of return of investments.

These accelerated allowances were received favourably by the IOCs operating in Trinidad and Tobago, and led to the almost immediate sanction by BPTT of the Juniper project in August 2014. At a budget of USD 2.1 billion, this was the largest ever single investment by an IOC in the upstream of Trinidad and Tobago.[7] Other interventions by the Ministry of Energy and Energy Affairs (MEEA) such as the extension of the term for the Block 2C production sharing contract with BHP led to new investments such as the Angostura Phase 3 project. In 2017, BPTT also sanctioned the Angelin development project. The capital allowances for exploration led BP to resume exploration drilling after a hiatus of 11 years. This led to two discoveries, the Savannah and Macadamia.[8]

This chapter explains the link between a strategic policy intervention and the results it can have on production levels. It demonstrates that many times the problems countries face with declining production have less to do with subsurface conditions and more to do with aboveground conditions, which include factors such as misaligned and inadequate fiscal regimes and an uncompetitive investment climate.

# III. Trinidad and Tobago's Natural Gas Sector 2010–2019

In 2018, Trinidad and Tobago produced 3629 mmcfd or 3.63 bcfd of natural gas (Ministry of Energy and Energy Industries 2018). This makes Trinidad and Tobago one of the largest producers of natural gas in the Caribbean and Latin American

---

[6] BP, 'Sustaining A Competitive Gas Industry in Trinidad And Tobago' (Glasgow, 2014).
[7] ibid.
[8] A Ramdass, 'Good Gas News' Trinidad Express Newspaper (2017).

region. Most of Trinidad and Tobago's natural gas (56.9%) is converted into LNG in four LNG trains and exported. The remainder is used for the production of methanol (14.5%), ammonia (16.3%), steel (1.3%), and for power generation (7.2%). The remaining 3.9% is used in refining and in light manufacturing.[9]

In 2010, Trinidad and Tobago's natural gas production averaged 4.3 bcfd.[10] This was the country's peak natural gas production. In the first quarter of 2019, Trinidad and Tobago's natural gas production averaged 3.8 bcfd. In 2018 Argentina's production averaged 3.8 bcfd and was rising due to increased shale gas production at the Vaca Muerta shale plant. By comparison, in 2018 the UK produced 3.9 bcfd.[11] Table 14.1 is a history of Trinidad and Tobago's natural gas production from 2009 to 2018.

**Table 14.1** Trinidad and Tobago's natural gas production 2009 to 2018

| Year | Natural gas production (mmcfd) |
|------|-------------------------------|
| 2009 | 4219 |
| 2010 | 4330 (peak gas) |
| 2011 | 4169 |
| 2012 | 4122 |
| 2013 | 4145 |
| 2014 | 4071 |
| 2015 | 3835 |
| 2016 | 3330 |
| 2017 | 3356 |
| 2018 | 3629 |

*Source*: Ministry of Energy and Energy Industries, Consolidated Energy Bulletins, 2009 to 2018.

From late 2010 and continuing to the present day, Trinidad and Tobago has experienced shortages in natural gas supply which has impacted its position as an exporter of LNG, ammonia and methanol. This shortage has manifested itself in LNG, ammonia and methanol plants not receiving their daily contracted quantities (DCQs) of natural gas. As a consequence, since 2016 there has been the closure

---

[9] Ministry of Energy and Energy Industries, 'Ministry of Energy and Energy Industries Consolidated Energy Bulletin 2018' (2018).

[10] Ministry of Energy and Energy Industries, 'Ministry of Energy and Energy Industries Consolidated Energy Bulletin 2010' (2010).

[11] BP, 'BP Working Towards Lower Carbon Future For T&T', BP News (Trinidad and Tobago) (2019), available at www.bp.com/en_tt/trinidad-and-tobago/home/news/press-releases/bp-keeps-advancing-its-trinidad-and-tobago-business.html.

of the Mittal Steel complex,[12] two methanol plants owned by Methanol Holdings Trinidad Limited,[13] and the closure of one of the four LNG trains (Train 1) is expected in 2020.[14] These closures are due mainly to declining natural gas production and higher natural gas prices.

## A.  Industry Structure

The Trinidad and Tobago upstream sector is dominated by four IOCs, namely BPTT (a subsidiary of BP plc), Shell, EOG Resources and BHP. These four companies account for 98 per cent of Trinidad and Tobago's natural gas production. The majority of this production comes from offshore natural gas fields located off the south-east coast of Trinidad and off the north coast of Trinidad in a region called the North Coast Marine area (NCMA).

BPTT is the largest producer in Trinidad and Tobago. In 2018 it accounted for 54 per cent of natural gas production. BP plc through its subsidiaries has shareholdings in all four LNG trains and the Atlas Methanol plant located at the Point Lisas Industrial Estate.[15]

The other major player in Trinidad and Tobago is Shell, which has the majority position in LNG Trains 2, 3 and 4 and a minority position in Train 1. Shell is the second largest gas producer in Trinidad and Tobago. From 2013 to the present, Shell has been acquiring natural gas infrastructure and natural gas producing acreage in Trinidad and Tobago with the aim of creating an integrated natural gas business and securing a dominant position in the Atlantic basin LNG trade.

The mid-stream sector of the Trinidad and Tobago energy sector consists of the National Gas Company (NGC), which is 100 per cent owned by the Government of Trinidad and Tobago, Phoenix Park Gas Processors Limited (PPGPL) and Atlantic (formerly Atlantic LNG). The NGC has a monopoly for the marketing of natural gas into the domestic market. With the exception of the four Atlantic LNG trains and the Atlas Methanol plant all companies buy their natural gas from the NGC. While this is not codified in law it is accepted government policy. The NGC buys most of its natural gas from BPTT, Shell, EOG Resources and BHP. In most cases the price the NGC pays for the natural gas it buys is indexed to the price of ammonia and methanol. The price at which the NGC sells natural gas to its customers is also determined using indexation to international ammonia and methanol prices.

---

[12] CNC3 News, 'ArcelorMittal Closed', 11 March 2016, available at www.cnc3.co.tt/news/arcelormittal-closed.

[13] 'What MHTL Plant Closures Mean For T&T Energy?', available at https://energynow.tt/blog/what-mhtl-plant-closures-mean-for-tt-energy.

[14] 'BPTT Announces 'Disappointing' Challenges In Train 1 Gas Supply' (2019), available at www.looptt.com/content/bptt-announces-disappointing-challenges-train-1-gas-supply.

[15] Ministry of Energy and Energy Industries, 'Bulletin 2018' (2018).

PPGPL's core business is the processing of natural gas liquids (NGLs). PPGPL processes the NGC's natural gas stream by stripping out NGLs, which it then fractionates into component products. It also purchases the NGLs from Atlantic Trains 1, 2 and 3, which it then fractionates and markets. PPGPL also processes the NGLs from Atlantic Train 4 and is paid a processing fee for this service.

Atlantic consists of four LNG trains with a capacity of over 15 million tonnes per annum (mtpa). The four trains were constructed between 1996 and 2005. They have different ownership and commercial structures. The major shareholders in all four Trains are BP and Shell. Train 1 has a merchant structure, Trains 2 and 3 have a quasi-tolling structure and Train 4 is a strict tolling plant. LNG is sold to offtakers in the case of Trains 1, 2 and 3. In the case of Train 4, gas supply and offtake mirrors the fractions of shareholdings for the train.

The downstream sector consists of seven methanol plants, 11 ammonia plants, one urea plant and one steel plant. The major players in the downstream sector are MHTL, Methanex, Nutrien, Tringen and Yara. All electricity in Trinidad and Tobago is generated using natural gas. The power sector consists of five power plants with an installed capacity of 2,097 MW. However, Trinidad and Tobago's peak demand (2018 figure) was about 1,300.[16] The surplus capacity is largely due to the cancellation of an aluminium smelter project in 2010 and the closure of the Mittal steel complex in 2016.

The Government of Trinidad and Tobago regulates the natural gas sector through the Ministry of Energy and Energy Industries (MEEI). Government's participation in the natural gas value chain is dominant in the midstream where it has 100 per cent ownership of the NGC. The NGC in turn has a majority ownership position in PPGPL and a minority positions in LNG Train 1 (10 per cent) and LNG Train 4 (11.1 per cent). Contract sanctity is paramount in Trinidad and Tobago. Trinidad and Tobago's judiciary is independent, and its highest appellate court is the Privy Council in London.

## B.  Natural Gas Curtailments

Trinidad and Tobago's natural gas industry has experienced curtailments in natural gas supply since late 2010. There are several factors that contributed to this situation. One is maintenance works on several of BPTT's upstream assets. Others relate to fiscal and commercial issues and finally there is the failure of the BG T&T Starfish development programme in 2015. As it relates to maintenance, on 20 April 2010, BP lost control of the Macondo Well in the Gulf of Mexico. The result was the death of 11 workers, one of the largest oil spills ever recorded, billions of dollars in losses and reputational damage for BP and its subcontractors.

---

[16] Cabinet Appointed Committee on Power Sector of Trinidad and Tobago, 'Report of the Cabinet Appointed Technical Team' (2015).

In reaction to this event, BP decided to conduct maintenance on a number of its natural gas producing platforms and hubs in Trinidad and Tobago. This programme of maintenance started in late 2010 and extended to 2014. It impacted BPTT's deliverability of natural gas to the NGC and the four LNG trains. Trinidad and Tobago's downstream and midstream natural gas industry, which had hitherto enjoyed consistent and reliable supplies of natural gas, was now faced with curtailments from the NGC.

This natural gas shortage was due to a combination of factors. First, a prolonged period of maintenance among upstream natural gas producers (led by BPTT) which caused shortages from late 2010 to early 2014. This programme of maintenance was mainly a reaction by BPTT to the April 2010 Macondo oil spill incident in the Gulf of Mexico.[17]

Secondly, a decline in upstream investment from 2009 to 2011.[18] During this period, the country's major natural gas producers reduced levels of investment in Trinidad and Tobago's upstream for reasons related to the global financial crisis and issues related to the uncompetitive nature of the fiscal regime. These factors are not necessarily related, but both served to dampen the IOC's appetite for investment in Trinidad and Tobago in the same time window. The former led to lower prices for LNG and hence lower netback prices at the wellhead in Trinidad and Tobago. The latter is related to a threat by the Government to introduce supplemental petroleum tax (SPT) on natural gas production. SPT has only ever been applied to crude oil and condensate production.

Third, a period of natural gas oversupply in 2009 and 2010. From 2007 to 2008, the NGC signed three gas supply contracts with BG T&T (now Shell), BHP and EOG Resources for 550 mmcfd of natural gas. This new natural gas supply was contracted to supply new customers such as the Alutrint aluminium smelter project and the proposed Essar steel plant. These plants never materialised, and the NGC was left with supply for which there was insufficient demand. As a result, the NGC was faced with a major 'take or pay' problem. Around this time, the NGC advised BP (in 2010) that it would require a reduced natural gas supply.[19] The cumulative effect of the issues listed above were further explained by Mr Frank Look Kin, the former President of the NGC and advisor to the Minister of Energy and Energy Industries. On 9 May 2016, while appearing before a Joint Select Committee of the Trinidad and Tobago Parliament on State Enterprises, he described the reasons for the shortage as follows:

> A lot of this occurred as a result of what happened probably starting around 2008/2009. In that particular period of time, the NGC had acquired new gas sources, but then what had happened, they acquired gas supplies from three gas producers – BG, EOG

---

[17] Central Bank of Trinidad and Tobago, 'Monetary Policy Report, Port Of Spain' (2011).

[18] BP, 'Sustaining a Competitive Gas Industry in Trinidad and Tobago. Presentation to the Ministry of Energy' (2014).

[19] F Look Kin, 'National Gas Company Presentation to the Joint Select Committee Of The Parliament Of Trinidad And Tobago On State Enterprises' (Parliament of Trinidad and Tobago, 2016).

and also BHP Billiton – but the projects that were under consideration to use some of that gas, those projects failed to materialized. Those projects include the steel plant, in addition to a petrochemical facility and the aluminium smelter. So, there was a loss of demand at that particular point in time. So going into 2009 or thereabouts, what we had in Trinidad was a situation whereby there was a lot of extra excess gas capacity, and because the companies recognized we had excess gas capacity, they really started to cut back on the capital investment in terms of producing additional gas. So, we were in a dilemma. We were in a case of oversupply as compared to demand and, therefore, companies sought to kind of protect themselves in a sense because they do not want to get in a situation whereby NGC cannot buy their gas. But what happened right after that was the fact that there was this Macondo event in the Gulf of Mexico and the Macondo event, when it occurred, many companies basically started to consider new standards for operating in offshore, and those new standards require upgrades of their existing platform facilities, and so what you had happening right after that in 2010 to about 2013, companies shut their platforms down temporarily to do repairs, to do maintenance to upgrade the standards. So, what you had happening in Trinidad was a case of whereby you had platforms coming down, a decrease in production, combined with the fact that because most of the gas in Trinidad is produced with what is called solution gas drive reservoirs or depletion drive reservoirs, those deplete sometime in the order of about 15 per cent per year.[20]

A fourth reason was the failure of the first attempt by BG T&T (now Shell) to develop the Starfish field in early 2015. The initial Starfish project was expected to produce 225 mmcfd of natural gas from three development wells in the Starfish field. Although 'first gas' was realised in late 2014, for reasons related to failed well completions, these three wells had to be shut in. The failure had a significant impact on BG T&T's ability to deliver natural gas and was a major reason for their precipitous decline in its production post-2014. One of the consequences of this failure was the non-renewal of one of BG T&T's gas supply contracts with the NGC. This contract, called the Base Gas Sales Agreement, expired on 31 December 2015 and was not renewed.

Fifth and finally, there is also an argument that Trinidad and Tobago's decision to build a fourth LNG train committed the country to an unsustainable level of natural gas demand, which is one of the factors that contributed to a shortage emerging in late 2010. Train 4 has a capacity of 743 mmcfd, which is about 19 per cent of the total natural gas production using the 2019 year to date average production of 3.8 billion cubic feet per day.

## C.  Impact of Natural Gas Curtailments

All the consumers of natural gas in Trinidad and Tobago need approximately 4100 mmcfd of natural gas per day to satisfy their contractual demand for natural gas. Some plants such as the LNG trains can consume more than their daily

---

[20] F Look-Kin, 'Statement To The Joint Select Committee Of The Trinidad And Tobago Parliament On State Enterprises' (Hansard Department of the Trinidad and Tobago Parliament, 2016).

contracted quantities. This means their name plate capacity exceeds their daily contracted quantity of natural gas. The consequence of curtailments from late 2010 to the present has been the closure of the Mittal Steel plant, the closure of two methanol plants and the pending closure of Atlantic Train 1.

## IV. The Fiscal Regime and Petroleum Taxation

The Government of Trinidad and Tobago collects both tax revenue and non-tax revenue from the energy sector. The main taxes associated with upstream oil and gas production include:

- supplemental petroleum tax (SPT);
- petroleum profits tax (PPT); and
- unemployment levy (UL)

Revenues are also collected from:

- corporation taxes from petrochemical companies and LNG trains;
- ministers' share of profit petroleum from various production sharing contracts;
- royalties;
- petroleum levy;
- petroleum impost;
- business levy;
- green fund levy;
- withholding tax on dividends; and
- other smaller payments.

## V. Policy Intervention via Fiscal Incentives of 2013/2014

From 2011 to 2015, the Government of Trinidad and Tobago, represented by the Cabinet of Trinidad and Tobago, the Ministry of Finance and the Economy and the Ministry of Energy and Energy Affairs, recognised that the problem of insufficient natural gas supply was as a result of a lack of investment in exploration and developmental drilling. In the budget speech of 9 September 2013, the Minister of Finance and the Economy of Trinidad and Tobago, Senator Larry Howai introduced incentives called 'accelerated capital allowances'. It is worth quoting from that speech:

> Capital Allowances Capital allowance reliefs provide a mechanism that de-risks and allows for earlier recovery of investments. I propose that capital allowances for the upstream energy sector be simplified and accelerated as follows:

For Exploration the existing initial and annual allowances be replaced by a new allowance of 100 percent of exploration costs to be written off in the year the expenditure is incurred. This incentive will be applicable over the period 2014 to 2017, and from 2018, an allowance of 50 percent in the first year of the expenditure, an allowance of 30 percent in the second year of the expenditure and an allowance of 20 percent in the third year will be applicable.

For development in place of the existing initial and annual allowances, I propose to grant an allowance of 50 percent in the first year of the expenditure, an allowance of 30 percent in the second year of the expenditure and an allowance of 20 percent in the third year. This will be applicable to both plant and machinery (tangible) and the drilling of wells (intangible) expenses.

For Workovers and Qualifying Sidetracks I propose to allow 100 percent of the total costs of workovers and qualifying side-tracks in the year incurred. This will have an impact of attracting investment in already producing and idle wells.

For Gas Compression Facilities, I propose that with respect to the mid-stream natural gas sector, where deliverability is a key concern, the wear and tear allowance for compression facilities be increased from 25.0 percent to 33.3 percent under the relevant legislation.[21]

In April 2014, the Government of Trinidad and Tobago introduced and passed into law these aforementioned incentives including the accelerated capital allowances for exploration and developmental drilling with the intention of stimulating investment. It should be noted that capital allowances have long been a feature of the Trinidad and Tobago fiscal regime: they were introduced in 1992 to stimulate investment exploration.

The accelerated capital allowances were part of a wider package of fiscal incentives that had been introduced since 2011 with the aim of right-siding oil and natural gas production. These accelerated capital allowances were welcomed by the oil and gas industry. The accelerated capital allowances have, however, been greatly misunderstood. They have been blamed for the decline in government revenue from oil and gas from 2015 to 2016. According to the 2017 Review of the Economy, in 2015, the Trinidad and Tobago Government collected revenues of TT$ 57.3 billion. In 2016 this fell to TT$ 45.0 billion, or a 21.5 per cent decline.[22]

Prior to 2013/2014, public commentators such as the Energy Chamber of Trinidad and Tobago had spoken publicly for many years about the declining competitiveness of the oil and gas industry on account of its underlying fiscal regime. In its commentary on the 2012/2013 budget, accounting firm PWC opined that 'Our regime is not sufficiently competitive and requires the introduction of additional capital and investment allowances to encourage exploration'.[23]

---

[21] L Howai, Budget of the Government of Trinidad And Tobago (Hansard Report of the Parliament of Trinidad and Tobago, 2013).

[22] Ministry of Finance of Trinidad and Tobago, 'Review of the Economy 2017' (2017).

[23] PWC Budget Memorandum, 'Commentary, Port of Spain' (2013).

In the period 2011 to 2015, several fiscal incentives were offered to resuscitate both developmental drilling and exploration drilling. The effect of these incentives was a significant turnaround in drilling as reflected in rig days. In 2010 there were 1,132 rig days. By 2015, that number had more than doubled to 2,765 (Ministry of Energy and Energy Industries 2010 to 2016).[24] This is direct evidence of the impact of properly structured fiscal incentives.

During the same period, the Ministry of Energy and Energy Affairs was able to attract investment into the Trinidad and Tobago deepwater with the signing of nine production- sharing contracts with BHP, BP, BG (later Shell) and Repsol. In Trinidad and Tobago, deepwater is defined as waters deeper than 1000m. This definition often varies by country. Attracting investment in deepwater exploration was achieved by offering more attractive terms compared to what was offered in the 2005/2006 bid round, which was a disappointment that resulted in no deepwater acreage being contracted.

The results of all these efforts manifested itself in the BP Juniper project and the BP Angelin project. The Juniper project was sanctioned in August 2014 and the first gas was realised in August 2017. Juniper's planned production is 590 mmcfd. The incentivisation of the upstream also led to the Savannah and Macadamia discoveries in the first half of 2017 and the Trinidad Regional Onshore Compression (TROC) project, which started operations in 2017. Figure 14.1 shows the impact of Juniper on BPTT's production.

**Figure 14.1** BPTT's natural gas production: January 2017–February 2019

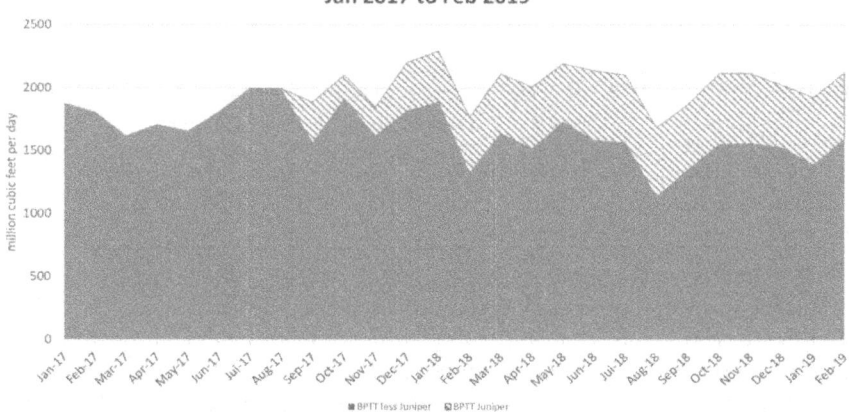

*Source*: Ministry of Energy and Energy Industries, Consolidated Bulletins 2017 to 2019 and BPTT reports.

---

[24] Ministry of Energy and Energy Industries, 'Consolidated Bulletins' (2015).

Other projects such as the 2015/2016 BHP Angostura Phase 3 project and the 2016/2017 EOG Resources Sercan project have also helped with the level of natural gas curtailment. As a result, in 2018, Trinidad and Tobago's natural gas output showed an increase after five years of decline. Of critical importance too is the 2011–2013 3D Ocean Bottom Cable (OBC)' Seismic survey which was conducted by BP and which is directly responsible for the progression and sanction of the Angelin project and the Macadamia exploration success in 2017. While all these projects will help, they will not eliminate the problem of the natural gas supply curtailments. Sustaining a contracted demand of around 4.1 bcfd in the medium term will continue to challenge the NGC and Trinidad and Tobago's natural gas producers. Even if production were to recover to levels that satisfy contractual demand, it is debatable how long this could be sustained.

# VI. Oil Price and Other Commodity Price Declines (2015–2016)

The Trinidad and Tobago economy experienced a major revenue shock in the period 2015–2016.[25] Government revenue from energy fell from $TT 21 billion in 2015 to $TT 8.7 billion in 2016, a decline of 58.5 per cent. A major reason for this significant decline in energy revenue was the fall in the prices of all commodities that Trinidad and Tobago exports. For the fiscal year 2015, WTI oil prices averaged USD 56.5 per barrel and in fiscal 2016 it averaged USD 41.3 per barrel. The pattern of price decline for natural gas, ammonia and methanol prices is set out in Table 14.2.

**Table 14.2** Change in prices of commodities

| Year | WTI oil price (USD per barrel) | Henry Hub natural gas (USD per mmbtu) | Ammonia (USD per tonne) | Methanol (USD per tonne) |
|---|---|---|---|---|
| 2015 | 56.5 | 3.04 | 458 | 403 |
| 2016 | 41.3 | 2.29 | 280 | 270 |
| Percentage change | −26.9% | −24.7% | −38.9% | −33.0% |

*Sources*: United States Energy Intelligence Agency, his Markit and Fertecon.

There is not a linear relationship between price, profits and taxation. This is especially so for the SPT. When prices of oil are below USD 50 per barrel, SPT is reduced to 0 per cent. This explains why for fiscal 2016 SPT collections fell sharply. The 2016 EITI reports show that SPT moved from USD 4.7 billion to USD 134.5 million from 2015 to 2016. The price sensitivity of SPT therefore contributes to the vulnerability of Trinidad and Tobago's energy revenue to price fluctuations.[26]

---

[25] Extractive Industries Transparency Initiative, 'Trinidad And Tobago EITI Report 2016' (2016).
[26] Extractives Industries Transparency Initiative (2016).

## VII. Accelerated Capital Allowances

Although the Trinidad and Tobago national budget of September 2013 mentioned government policy intervention on capital allowances, it was not codified into law until April 2014 via the Finance Act of 2014. The Government introduced accelerated capital allowances with the aim of stimulating the 'critically needed' exploration and developmental drilling activity.

The significance of this measure was underscored by the BPTT President Norman Christie. In an interview, former President of BPTT, Norman Christie confirmed that BPTT's investments in projects like Juniper and Trinidad Regional Onshore Compression (TROC) would not have happened had it not been for these incentives (Wilson 2018).[27]

According to Norman Christie,

> The truth is without the incentives that were provided the investments would not have been made. That being said, at the time of the investment, there was an expectation that prices were going to be a lot higher than they ended up being. So, in a way, the country benefitted because the allowances could not be used by the companies.[28]

Juniper and to a lesser extent TROC were at the heart of the turnaround in natural gas production in 2018 in Trinidad and Tobago. This is the core driver of the economic growth Trinidad and Tobago anticipated in 2018 and its effect flows into 2019. These trends are illustrated in Figure 14.2 below

**Figure 14.2** Natural gas production: January 2014–February 2019

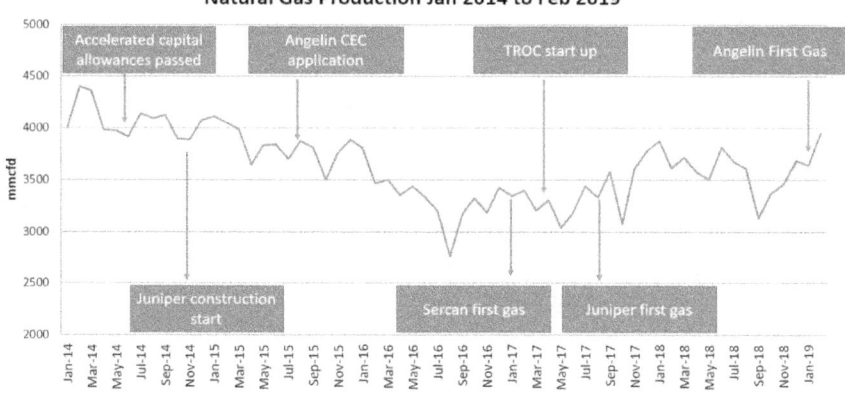

*Source*: Ministry of Energy and Energy Industries, Consolidated Bulletins 2014 to 2019.

---

[27] A Wilson, 'Interview with Norman Christie', Business Express (2018).
[28] ibid.

The accelerated capital allowances also stimulated the drilling of the Savannah and Macadamia exploration wells in early 2017, which discovered two trillion cubic feet of natural gas. This gas is expected to be in production between 2022 and 2024. These were BP's first exploration wells since the failed Ibis Deep well in 2007.

It should be noted that the system of capital allowances has always been a normal part of the Trinidad and Tobago taxation system, not only including the petroleum sector. Over the years, successive governments have used the capital allowance regime as a means by which to incentivise various sectors as a means of encouraging economic activity. For example, those companies that fall under the Income Tax (In Aid of Industry) Act enjoy an 'Initial Allowance' of 90 per cent of the expenditure incurred in the purchase of plant and machinery for use in the business, ie 90 per cent of the cost can be claimed as an 'initial' capital allowance in the year of purchase.

Companies operating in the upstream sector have always had the ability to claim capital allowances equivalent to 100 per cent of capital expenditure against their income. The amendment in 2014 did not increase the overall quantum of the claim to be made, but rather accelerated the period over which the expenditure incurred could be recovered by way of capital allowances.

In the regime prior to 2014, allowances for companies were as follows:

**For tangible costs**

Initial allowance:          20%

Annual allowance:          20% on the residue after the Initial Allowance each year

**For intangible costs**

Initial allowance:          10%

Annual allowance:          20% on a reducing balance basis

In the 2014 amendment, this was changed to allow for 100 per cent of exploration capital expenditure to be claimed in the financial year in which the expenditure is incurred, and for developmental drilling it was sequenced over three years as 50 per cent, 30 per cent and 20 per cent.

The accelerated capital allowances had no impact on government revenue from two perspectives:

The companies operating in the upstream *always* had the ability to claim 100 per cent of capital expenditure by way of capital allowances. The accelerated allowances of 2014 only allowed them to do this faster. This enhanced the economics of the investments by giving a higher net present value and thus made investment more attractive/acceptable to the investor company. For exploration-related capex the accelerated version of the capital allowance was time bound and expired on 31 December 2017.

Given that the upstream companies were in a loss-making position for 2015 and 2016, there was in fact, no taxable income against which these allowances could be applied. The accelerated capital allowance provision was, therefore of no immediate benefit to the upstream companies.

Since 31 December 2017, the system of capital allowances for exploration has reverted to what obtained prior to 2014, and consequently, companies can still recover their exploration capex, but at a slower rate.

## VIII. Carry Forward Losses

The main reason for the fall in GORTT's energy-related revenue was the collapse in oil and natural gas prices and the resulting operating losses. It caused SPT to almost vanish and negatively impacted both PPT and UL. Because of those sharply falling prices, oil and gas companies operating in Trinidad and Tobago recorded losses in 2015 and 2016. Table 14.3 shows the performance of BP plc and Shell at the level of the parent companies in 2014 and 2015. The year 2015 was the worst year for BP plc in terms of financial performance.

**Table 14.3** Impact of falling prices on BP and Shell

| Year | BP plc (billions of USD) | Shell (billions of USD) |
|------|--------------------------|-------------------------|
| 2014 | 4.003                    | 19.041                  |
| 2015 | −6.400                   | 3.842                   |
| 2016 | 0.172                    | 3.533                   |

*Source*: Morgan Stanley Research, 2018.

One hundred per cent of the large capital investments (Juniper, TROC, Macadamia and Savannah) of recent years will be claimed for, as has always been the case. But they could not have impacted government tax revenue in 2015/2016 because they did not affect the taxable profit computation as there was no profit. The allowances would have increased the tax losses realised in those years, and these losses will be available for carry forward and offset against the taxable income of future years, in accordance with section 16 of the Income Tax Act Chapter 75:01, as has always been the case. This is consistent with the general treatment of trading losses under the existing Trinidad and Tobago tax regime.

## IX. Conclusions

The reasons for the short fall in natural gas supply that Trinidad and Tobago experienced from late 2010 to the present are multi-dimensional, but all relate to fiscal conditions and commercial decisions. The decline in government-related energy revenues from 2015–2016 was pronounced, but were related to the collapse in oil prices in that period. Oil prices peaked in mid-2014 and started falling thereafter.

This had an impact on natural gas prices, ammonia and methanol prices. This would have impacted energy revenue negatively. The major component of the decline in energy revenue was the reduction in Supplemental Petroleum Tax by 97 per cent from 2015 to 2016. Supplemental Petroleum Tax is price-sensitive and is reduced to 0 per cent when oil prices are under USD 50 per barrel.

Falling prices caused IOC's operating in Trinidad and Tobago to record losses in 2015 and 2016. These losses were available for carry forward provisions as provided for in the Income Tax Act of Trinidad and Tobago. The losses were used to offset against profits of preceding years. The financial accounts for the subsidiaries of BP plc and Shell operating in Trinidad and Tobago are not publicly available. However, accounts for both BP plc and Shell are publicly available. These accounts indicate that both IOC's experienced a significant fall after tax profits in 2015–2016 because of low oil prices.

In terms of output, natural gas production fell from 4.3 bcfd in 2010 to 3.3 bcfd in 2016 or 23.2 per cent over that six-year period. This is a fall of some 1.0 bcfd. About half of that decline happened between 2015 and 2016. In that one-year period, production fell from 3.8 bcfd to 3.3 bcfd or 13.1 per cent. This decline impacted the reputation of Trinidad and Tobago as a producer of LNG, methanol and ammonia. It also impacted government revenue from the energy sector in that period.

The accelerated capital allowances that were passed into law in 2014 by way of the Finance Bill of 2014 had the desired effect of stimulating exploration and developmental drilling. Evidence of this is captured by the Ministry of Energy and Energy Affairs in its record of 'rig days', which is a proxy for drilling activity. In 2010, Trinidad and Tobago recorded 1,132 rig days.[29] By 2015 that figure had increased to 2765 rig days or a 244 per cent increase.[30]

The accelerated capital allowances introduced in 2014 also had the effect of stimulating BPTT to return to exploration drilling. In early 2017 they drilled two exploration wells Savannah and Macadamia, which discovered a collective two trillion cubic feet of natural gas. The former discovery has been sanctioned as the Matapal project and the latter discovery is nearing sanction as the Cypre project. Both projects will add to BPTT's natural gas production in the early part of the 2020s.[31]

It remains to conclude that host states governments retain effective tools to strategically attract investments in a global energy market in transition.

---

[29] Ministry of Energy and Energy Affairs, 'Consolidated Energy Bulletin' (2010).
[30] Ministry of Energy and Energy Affairs, 'Consolidated Energy Bulletin' (2015).
[31] BP, 'BP keeps advancing its Trinidad and Tobago business' (2019).

# The Concept of Global Energy Transition and its Agenda

PETER D CAMERON, XIAOYI MU AND VOLKER ROEBEN

## I. Introduction

This book has attempted to provide insights into the notion of *global energy transition*. As a shorthand expression for a global shift from dependence on a high-carbon base for growth, we have avoided a prescriptive or 'legalistic' approach. Instead, the diversity of approaches and, indeed, many national, or sub-national starting points for any transition has informed our examination of this long-term change, and the role of law in shaping it. At a high level, it springs from a conscious choice to achieve the twin goals of moving beyond a carbon-intensive economy in such a way as to deliver access to energy for all by the end of the century. Implementation requires not only some coordination of strategic direction, but also a new approach to global energy law.[1]

The book has used three hypotheses to analyse this process of legal change. First, the prospects of future worldwide energy supply and demand – based on demographic growth and a shift to the East – create a demand for strategic redirection of the energy system. Second, meeting this demand for strategic redirection means enhancing governance of the energy value cycle based on a dedicated legal regime. Third, this rules-based governance has certain priority dimensions of action.

Part I has sketched the fundamentals of global energy when faced with the prospect of a transition on a unique scale such as this one promises to be: what we can learn about the drivers of change in the global energy system (chapter one), and the challenges for states endowed with fossil fuel resources which have placed so much emphasis on their development as part of their national plans for growth (chapter two). The complex of features they present underlines the need – but not the inevitability – of strategic redirection of the energy system, a system that has always strenuously resisted any kind of centralised direction.

---

[1] The underlying assumption of this analysis is, of course, that a thin concept of functionalism accurately serves to describe global (energy) law (William Twining, *General Jurisprudence* (2009)).

Part II has examined the second hypothesis that such strategic direction should ideally be grounded in some kind of rules-based, multilateral governance of the energy-value cycle. It has found that this would entail the development of some overarching, ordering principles (chapter three); the design of a concept of the international law of energy with which other segments of international law become aligned (chapter four); and the continuous development of the Paris Agreement by the parties to serve as a mechanism for dynamic governance and rule-making on the extent and pace of global energy transition (chapter five). This framework for rules-based governance could then utilise several models of modern energy-market regulation (chapter six).

Parts III and IV of this volume have examined two dimensions of *international* action, based on the third hypothesis that the strategy and this rules-based governance are for priority actions. Part III has focused on the first dimension to link domestic and then regional energy markets in order to better integrate renewables, improve supply and drive down costs. It addresses key scenarios of such linkages and the governance challenges they pose and instruments they may require. Among these are transnational contracts on transboundary projects subject to competition (chapter seven), regulation of transboundary markets (chapter eight), and the regulation and organisational architecture for large-scale transboundary infrastructure (chapter nine).

Part IV has explored the second dimension of international action to foster international investment by supporting the *right* generation capacity and innovation (in relation to an energy transition). That, so the part demonstrates, involves multi-level governance. There is a search for prioritisation within international investment law (chapter ten). There are new challenges for the admission of desirable foreign direct investment, which is now being screened in many jurisdictions from the standpoint of national security (chapter eleven). There is also the conflict between the international law protecting investments in renewables and the interest of states to exit supportive policies (chapter twelve). However, as chapter thirteen demonstrates for natural gas, as a bridge fuel, the speed of the transition comes down to the aggregate investment and resource allocation decisions of individual states, and most importantly in the developing word.

On the basis of this analysis, we can now offer a synthetic view of energy law in the transition era. This is a period of moving to a novel general order for energy, embodying foundational norms that evolve through successive iterations, remain in effect only for discrete periods of time, and do not necessarily apply equally to all groups of actors. Such norms do not have any deontological quality, they are not binding, but they provide orientation. There are historic iterations of such general orders for energy, which we label global energy 1.0 and global energy 2.0.

Global energy 1.0 has been marked by such foundational norms. It has been dominated by security of supply from the perspective of both producers and consumers, separated national energy markets, and the legal principle of sovereignty over energy resources and the energy mix that allocates energy law to the national level.

In global energy 2.0, security of supply would be complemented by sustainable and affordable energy for all, carbon-neutral energy generation, linked national energy markets, and internationalisation of energy law, in the sense of a zoning up to international and regional levels. Foundational norms may apply to one set of actors while exempting others in general, but for global energy 2.0 to be a success, the foundational norms would have to be accepted by and applicable to all states. At a lower level of abstraction, the decision-making matrix on concrete policies to implement these norms becomes a trilemma of security of supply, sustainability and affordability, while in energy 1.0 it used to be a dilemma of security of supply versus affordability.

Global energy 2.0 may become dominant by the end of century. The current phase then indeed is one of transition between these different ways of ordering global energy. In such transitions, foundational norms belonging to different iterations will sometimes coexist. Indeed, concepts of national energy sovereignty are currently being reinvigorated, and a robust approach to national energy security that was a norm of global energy 1.0 is making a reappearance. As with all transitions, this one is contingent; its completion is not guaranteed.

The main feature of global energy 2.0 is integration of an ethos with patterns of inter-state relations, a set of institutions, a legal regime and an economic system which can be perceived as being all of a piece. The remainder of these conclusions will spell out five implications.

## II. The International Community of States as Collective Decision-maker on Energy Transition

Consensus on the norms of global energy 2.0 is necessarily being formed at the international level, because the ultimate reference is climate change, a truly global societal challenge. This is also where the key decisions would be taken. A concept to capture this consensus-building and decision-making is the international community of states. In this community, states have preferences that are aligned, rather than being antagonistic and power-orientated interests. They share some values that facilitate their cooperation. The term then refers to the collectivity of states formulating and acting on a common priority. Such a priority is the transition to a sustainable energy system, encapsulated in the SDGs 7 and 13 against which all states may be held accountable. This priority has been concretised, in binding international law, through the Paris Agreement's objective of limiting a global temperature rise to well below 2°C. Such an international community of states assumes responsibility for the design and implementation of a transition strategy, and that responsibility lies towards humanity. Success in the decarbonisation of the global energy economy in turn will be empirical confirmation of the existence of an international community for this sector of international affairs.

This causes a shift in the demand for multilateral governance of the energy sector. Governance is the process of institutionalised collective decision-making. This governance is centred on the UN, with the High-Level Forum for implementation of the SDGs and the meetings of the parties to the UNFCCC and the Paris Agreement for decision-making on the parties' climate and collective energy policies. The governance architecture comprises organisations of limited membership, such as IEF, IEA, IRENA, the Energy Charter, OPEC and others, whose activities are being reoriented. The role these organisations is certainly to provide mechanisms but also maintain a political consensus and to develop a moral-ethical consensus, grounded in the epistemological-scientific consensus institutionalised in the IPCC.

# III. The Integrated Legal Regime of Energy

Global energy 2.0 creates the basis for seeing the legal regime that supports and implements its norms. This integrated legal regime comprises international law, regional and domestic law.

The meta-norm of a climate change driven energy transition gives rise to a dedicated body of *international law of energy*, a thick value-bound concept, moving on from the plurality of the traditional international law *on* energy, a much thinner concept. This international law of energy reorientates extant international law to advance the norms. This reorientation is affecting all segments of international law, from the international law of climate action, world trade, the sea, water courses and transboundary infrastructure, to cross-border investments. A function of international law then becomes to make the deals stick that states strike on the collective transition to global energy 2.0. Only binding international law provides states with the certainty that investment in transition will be matched by those of other states. Breaches of (this) international law entail costs, legal, reputational and otherwise, and these costs have a preventive effect that induce rule-compliant behaviour. That means new international law is needed, and that this international law should be made binding over longer periods of time. Extending bindingness beyond national electoral cycles is a matter of innovative rules that limit the right of a state party to withdraw from key treaties such as the Paris Agreement through elongated notice periods. The paradox is that international law has to deliver on this challenge at a time where the trend seems to be for states to break away from international commitments.

International investment law illustrates this challenge. A key subject matter of the traditional international law on energy, it ensures international law-based stability for transboundary investments in energy generation. This stability serves security of supply, including supply of energy generated from renewables. A norm of sustainable energy would support this, while permitting host states to exit any support policy where it no longer serves social welfare. International investment law is reorienting itself here in order for states not to break away from it. More critically, increasingly undesirable investments for instance in coal-generation are undertaken by states or state-owned enterprises in other states. In such a scenario, international investment law may have to grant host states larger regulatory discretion in ending these.

This international law of energy is supplemented by further law on lower tiers of the global legal order, regional, domestic and transnational. The European Energy Union encapsulates such *regional* law-making on a continent-wide energy market, extending to third non-Member States, such as members of the Energy Community and potentially other states that accept foundational principles of EU energy law. The EEU could provide models for regional, rules-based cooperation elsewhere, for instance in Africa through regional organisations including the East African Community (EAC), the Economic Community of West African Countries (ECOWAS), and the Southern African Development Community (SADC). The international law of energy also directs *domestic* law-development of all states, both developed and developing. Each has specific circumstances that it is best placed to evaluate when charting its course and embarking on legal reform for an energy transition. Finally, *transnational* law that is contract-based becomes a law resource where infrastructure and large-scale private investment and capital projects are transboundary and undertaken by transnational actors.

This reorientation also extends to the *principles* of energy law. Principles concretise the norms of global energy 2.0. The principles of (common but differentiated) responsibility of states and complementary solidarity between states are foundational. Further principles as identified by Heffron et al develop these at a medium level of abstraction. In the next step, the operational principles of environmental law ought to be imported into the legal regime of energy. Following the late Professor Neil MacCormick, a principle can be conceived of as of unlimited substantive application. The norms of global energy 2.0 seek to make energy sustainable and that provides the rationale for bringing to bear the environmental principles. These have a strong legal status in positive international law, and they are operational. The environmental principles such as the precautionary principle or the polluter-pays principle then would apply also to decision-making on energy. They may help solve conceptual challenges of global energy, for instance on extending responsibility to the uses third parties will make of traded fossil energy sources.

The norms underpin with the same ethos energy law on all its tiers, and concretising principles fix the same objectives. Energy law, arising from international, regional and domestic sources, becomes an integrated regime. These comprised legal orders remain independent but interact and develop in a loop-like fashion. International law provides the impetus for regional and domestic law, but these then in turn drive forward the international standard. Within this integrated regime legal innovations disseminate easily. For instance, the science of probabilistically attributing events to actors in the energy system has consequences for the key concept of causation that cuts across all three tiers.

# IV. Instruments: Regulation, Competition, Contract and Treaty

These norms, this governance and this legal regime coalesce around certain instruments: international regulation, competition, contract and treaty. These instruments lie at the heart of the design of an energy system that delivers secure, sustainable and affordable supply for all. Regulation may be understood, broadly, as legal directives in the public interest. International regulation is essential for transboundary markets to work and to realise the benefits of trade and investment at scale. Regulated transboundary energy markets mitigate the volatility of renewable energy and allocate scarce resources through the price signal. Transboundary markets rely on transboundary infrastructure, which may require international regulation as well as novel regulatory agencies. International regulation creates a mechanism for common technical and legal language, a regulatory docket, and then trust between the states concerned. As Crossley demonstrates in this volume, the regulatory model is indeed flexible and adaptable to meet these tasks. International regulation is being pioneered under the European Energy Union. This finding entails a research agenda to improve the effectiveness and acceptability of international regulation: regulation as a price discovery process, regulatory capture, policy exit, the condition for linking markets across boundaries and its conditions, and the distributive effects that need to be identified clearly throughout the regulated space, both between consumers and producers and between the participating states, and then addressed through appropriate instruments.

However, regulation as an expansive concept has a scope of application beyond transboundary energy markets. It also permits states, based on a multilateral or bilateral treaty, to make better use of all transboundary energy resources and infrastructure. Such treaty-based regulation can be optimised. An optimal treaty allows the determination of efficient and equitable flows of electricity or related natural resources across borders. There may of course be a distortion in operation or expansion decisions, resulting in suboptimal outcomes for parties on either side of the border. The challenge for a transboundary regulator is to mitigate the potential damage to the aggregate social welfare of all parties.

This challenge leads to a plea for interdisciplinarity to ensure efficient and equitable international energy regulation. As Macatangay and Roeben demonstrate in chapter eight (and in their earlier works), devices of law and economics provide powerful analytic insights *and* assist in designing strategies for maximising global social welfare and mitigating the risks of inefficiency or inequity arising from suboptimal legislation or regulation affecting transboundary energy industries. A transboundary regulatory framework ideally provides for both the intensification of rivalry in competitive segments in which price-setting is accomplished through international markets, and the continuation of economic regulation in natural monopoly segments in which price-setting or firm behaviour is controlled through prudential review. It is, however, likely to result in winners and losers across space or time. As a result, the goals of energy producers or consumers may not perfectly align with those of transboundary legislative or regulatory initiatives, such as inter-jurisdictional investments in electric power transmission lines or oil or gas pipelines. This potentially opens the need for highly granular side payments as a form of compensation, either monetary or non-monetary, in pursuit of a cross-border cooperative equilibrium. Inter-jurisdictional legislative or administrative decisions on such compensation would be subject to judicial oversight by national or supra-national courts. This oversight ought to require the procedural means of cost–benefit analysis and provision of sound reasons for any limited use of such analysis. The corresponding research agenda features the formulation of first principles for managing regulatory suboptimality, as well as continuous assessment of their explanatory and predictive powers vis-a-vis transboundary regulation of energy markets in the EU or elsewhere.

This leads on to querying the legitimacy of this evolving international regulation of energy supporting global energy 2.0. Can one be content to rely on the consent of states as the traditional source of legitimation or is a broader social acceptance not required? Global energy 2.0 transcends states. It addresses the conduct of private actors who play an outsized role in the energy sector – IOCs and NOCs, utilities, the providers of finance and infrastructure – also that workforce whose skills risk becoming obsolete but more broadly 'all', that is (vulnerable or off-grid) consumers and 'prosumers'. Their involvement in the international regulatory process will reduce information asymmetries and secure better outcomes. The norm of ensuring access for all to clean and affordable energy thus has disruptive potential for the received concepts of legitimacy of international law.

# V.  Economics of Energy Transition

Energy transition is driven by policies and laws towards the norms we have associated with global energy 2.0, and the strength of the signal they send to economic actors is that transition is likely to be both global and irreversible. The economic system absorbs this signal through its processes centred on pareto-optimality, efficiency and price, and it will ultimately determine the speed of the transition. With supportive government policies, renewable energy technologies are fast-maturing and growing in market share. The levelised costs of energy for solar and wind power generation are falling, and electric vehicles are becoming cost-competitive with internal combustion engines particularly for short to mid-distance driving. Green hydrogen will assist in hard-to-decarbonise sectors. Yet, significant technological breakthroughs are needed before renewables can completely, if ever, replace fossil fuels in the energy mix. A rebalancing in the medium to long term is much more likely.

During this period of transition, there are many areas requiring further research from an economic perspective. For example, with the increasing penetration of renewables in the electricity market, what is the additional system cost to ensure a reliable electricity supply, and what is the implication for social welfare? How can the existing infrastructure be adapted for the expansion of alternative fuels such as electric vehicles and hydrogen? What new business models can be developed to accommodate the inconvenience of electric vehicles in terms of driving-range and charging? The emergence of 'prosumers' and the expansion of distributed energy could change the structure of the electricity industry, which could be a productive area of research into industrial organisation and competitive policies. The wider application of big data and digitalisation could make real-time pricing a reality even in the retail electricity sector. This will almost certainly lead to a more elastic demand curve from consumers, which could help better understand consumer behaviour and have implications for energy-efficiency measures.

This is of course not an exhaustive list. The most critical factor, however, may turn out to be consumer preferences shifting to low-carbon options, as renewable energy generation increasingly becomes ubiquitous and achieves grid-parity. A producer of fossil fuels, therefore, is potentially subject to commercial pressures from both the supply and demand sides of the market. It would have to contend with a reduction in its market share or economic rent if it is a low-cost producer. It would have to consider the orderly reconfiguration of its economy, or may decide to hold out against the global trends in supply or demand and not implement the structural adjustments necessary for its survival. The course of action also depends on what other states are doing (chapter 2). The challenge for economic research is to demonstrate that the lack of flexibility could threaten the aggregate social welfare of all parties, and that a low valuation for fossil fuels is consistent with the natural cycle of commodity valuations in economic history.

# VI.  An Agenda for Action

From conceptual clarity on energy transition as strategic governance and regulation of the global energy value chain, we can advance to formulating an agenda for action and law-making. That agenda could comprise the following list.

Climate action is energy action, and vice versa. The extant organisational architecture under the UNFCCC needs to focus on the development of long-term climate and energy strategies by all states that prioritise an energy mix based on life-cycle analyses of carbon emissions, with the need to reduce coal first. The roll-out of national climate change legislation constructed on a common template serves to ensure their effectuation and enforcement at domestic level. Ambitious government targets and direct regulation induces private actors, both the world's major oil and gas businesses and energy-intensive industries, to align themselves with them. The management of globally connected trading schemes under Article 6 of the Paris Agreement, but also under specialised UN organisations, and effective international exchanges of best practice through all parts of the architecture are further priorities to ensure a cost-effective transition. They need to stimulate research, innovation and technology-transfer.

Supporting energy transition in resource-rich, developing countries in the Global South and particularly Africa should be high on the agenda. These countries are not climate-change deniers and will be disproportionately affected by climate change. At the same time, they need to develop. Action on energy transition there would focus on the value-cycle of energy including through the decarbonisation of oil and gas extraction and transportation, greater efficiency and revenue generation, dissemination of best regional practices, and good governance while being respectful of the sovereign right to determine what constitutes sustainable development. Intensified multilateral development cooperation should prioritise investment in sustainable energy.

Worldwide, the design and regulation of regional energy electricity markets will unlock the potential of renewables in the move towards to electrification of the global economy. Hydrogen has the potential to address storage and transport problems. These markets can then be connected globally, considering the European Energy Union or parts of it as a model.

# INDEX

Lightning Source UK Ltd.
Milton Keynes UK
UKHW021123130821
388772UK00003B/184